STRIVE FOR A 5 ★

Preparing for the
AP⁺ World History Exam

Barbara Brun-Ozuna
Paschal High School, Fort Worth, Texas

Ryba L. Epstein
Rich East High School, Park Forest, Illinois

James Sabathne
Hononegah High School, Rockton, Illinois

Lisa Tran
California State University, Fullerton

Patrick Whelan
Saint Stephen's Episcopal School, Bradenton, Florida

WAYS OF THE WORLD:
A GLOBAL HISTORY WITH SOURCES
Second Edition

Robert W. Strayer

Bedford/St. Martin's   Boston ◆ New York

5 6   17 16 15

For information, write: Bedford/St. Martin's, 75 Arlington Street, Boston, MA 02116 (617-399-4000)

ISBN 978-1-4576-2801-6

Brief Contents

Contents

Preface for Teachers

Strive for a 5: Preparing for the AP World History Exam is a student prep guide, designed to provide your students with a thorough review of the course material while practicing AP test-taking skills that will help them on the AP World History Exam.

Designed to pair seamlessly with *Ways of the World: A Global History with Sources*, Second Edition, by Robert W. Strayer, *Strive for a 5* applies a strong AP-specific framework to the text's narrative and offers extended attention to the College Board exam format and test-taking strategies. Either assigned as a core component of your test preparation coursework or recommended to students as an independently navigable review and practice tool, *Strive for a 5* is designed to familiarize students with the exam format, thematically organize and review key concepts, and provide level-appropriate practice exams. For students who are striving for a 5, there is no better preparation guide.

Features of this Prep Guide

The **Strategies for the AP Exam** section serves as an introduction to the College Board's AP World History Exam and includes a breakdown of the scoring system, an overview of the different question forms, and essay-writing instructions.

Part overviews follow the textbook's structure and group course material into six chronological periods; these six parts closely correspond with the historical periodization of the AP World History Exam. Within each part, **thematic chapter reviews** organize and summarize the major developments of each era using the five themes in world history and the key concepts relevant to that time period. Using this format allows students to review information in the categories that are often used in AP World History Exam questions, especially the essay questions.

AP-style practice exams conclude each of the six parts. Each practice exam includes multiple-choice questions, a document-based question, a continuity and change-over-time essay question, and a comparative essay question. The practice exams can be assigned as a meaningful assessment at the end of each major unit, or students can independently measure their progress and areas in need of further review with level-appropriate practice tests. Each practice exam comes with guided model answers linked to *Ways of the World*. Thus, students will become increasingly comfortable with the AP style while completing a comprehensive review of the textbook material.

About the Authors

Barbara Brun-Ozuna is a teacher and academic coordinator with nineteen years of experience. As an AP World History consultant, Barbara has developed and implemented five-day summer institutes and has led one-day teacher workshops. As an AP World History table leader, she has trained new AP readers and helped develop the operational rubric for the AP World History Exam's change-over-time essay. She teaches at Paschal High School in Fort Worth, Texas, where she has developed and implemented three district-wide Advanced Placement courses.

Ryba Epstein is an AP World History workshop consultant, trainer, and AP World History table and question leader. As a member of the AP World History Development Committee, she created a syllabus for the AP World History Teacher's Guide, a pacing guide for the new AP World History course, and several other professional development resources. She has also taught Advanced Placement courses in European history and English literature. Ryba currently teaches at Rich East High School in Park Forest, Illinois.

James Sabathne teaches AP World History and AP U.S. History at Hononegah High School in Rockton, Illinois. He serves on the College Board AP United States History Curriculum Development and Assessment Committee. He has presented at the AP Annual Conference, scored essays at district-wide table readings, authored AP exam questions, and coordinated a district-wide implementation of DBQ essay formative assessments. As a reader and table leader, he has trained new readers and scored AP exams.

Lisa Tran is an associate professor at California State University-Fullerton, where she teaches courses on world history, modern China, and women's history. She received a fellowship from the American Council of Learned Societies in 2012 and a Franklin Research Grant from the American Philosophical Society in 2010. Her articles have appeared in numerous American journals, as well as French and Chinese publications. Her recent research focuses on the adoption of young girls as prospective brides in early twentieth-century China. She has conducted research in China, Taiwan, and Hong Kong, and is currently developing courses on discourses of Orientalism and the Chinese diaspora.

Patrick Whelan has scored AP World and European History examinations since 1998 and currently serves as a College Board institute and workshop consultant for AP World History. He teaches AP World History, AP U.S. History, AP European History, and AP Art History at Saint Stephen's Episcopal School in Bradenton, Florida, where he serves as head of the Social Studies department.

SECTION 1
Strategies for the AP Exam

Preparing for the AP World History Exam

By the time you open this book to help prepare you for the AP World History Exam, you are likely already immersed in the study of world history. Your AP World History course can be a deep and rewarding experience, demanding a high level of understanding and analysis as you read your textbook and consider other materials included in your course. If you work hard, you will find that this experience will hold great value beyond the AP course or the AP exam; you will have the intellectual tools to wrestle with complex ideas, to see connections between the past and the present, to write thoughtfully, and to know how to justify your thoughts as you prepare for college and adult life.

This book is designed to ease your way into a high score on the AP World History Exam. Many students feel overwhelmed by the amount of material that the exam covers—after all, ten thousand years of human history is nothing to scoff at! Do not be daunted—you can master this vast amount of knowledge and walk into the exam confident that you have the knowledge and skills not only to do well, but to strive for a 5!

What's in This Book?

While this study guide is designed to accompany Robert W. Strayer's *Ways of the World: A Global History*, Second Edition, it can be used with almost any world history text. The guide follows the organization of the Strayer text, but it is divided into the six world history periods and follows a thematic narrative, making it an easy addition to any test review regimen. Dividing the content of this guide into these six chronological periods helps structure the learning of the main themes of the course and puts the details of events and ideas into an overall context.

Each part provides an overview of the main developments of that period, followed by a succinct summary of each chapter of *Ways of the World*. Each chapter is summarized using the five themes of world history: interaction between humans and the environment; development and interaction of cultures; state-building, expansion, and conflict; creation, expansion, and interaction of economic systems; and development and transformation of social structures. After each period and the set of chapters that comprise that period is a practice exam in AP format and style—with multiple-choice questions, a document-based question essay (or DBQ), a continuity and change-over-time-essay, and a comparative essay.

The official AP World History Exam will, of course, cover the whole timeframe of the AP World History course, from about 8000 B.C.E. to the present. Each of the practice exams covers only the material you're likely to have covered through that period. By taking a practice test after each of one of the six chronological periods instead of at the end of the course, you will get valuable practice in the AP Exam format as you go and thus get meaningful and immediate feedback on your mastery of course content. If you can do well on these practice tests, we are confident you will do well on the AP Exam in May.

There are two good ways to use the practice tests. One is to review for the AP Exam. As you review each of the six chronological periods, test yourself, and then read the answers and rationales in the corresponding answer key section. Second, if you acquire this book before review begins, you should take the tests as you complete the relevant unit in your AP course, score them yourself, and evaluate your weaknesses and strengths.

But do not just get your score and leave it at that. Take the time to look over each question carefully and read the explanations for the correct answers. Make a list of what you got wrong. Are there topics in which you were particularly weak as indicated by a high proportion of wrong answers? Are there certain types of questions that you often got wrong? Did you struggle with your essays? Once you have a better sense of what you need to work on, you can prepare better for the actual AP Exam. Do not be shy about asking your teacher, too; he or she is likely to be able to make recommendations about where to focus your energies.

Registering for the Exam

Most likely your school will be taking care of this for you, but if not, make sure that you register in time, sometime during the month of February. If you are homeschooled, you need to contact AP Services at the College Board by March 1 to find out the name of an AP coordinator near you; you will have two weeks to make contact and locate a school near you where you can take the examination. If you qualify for extra time or are a student with a disability, make sure that all your paperwork is in order and that the AP coordinator at your school is aware of your special needs. The coordinator will have to submit an SSD form by mid-February if documentation is needed or early March if it is not. Check the AP Web site early for exact dates.

If your family is struggling to pay the examination fee of $89 ($145 if outside the U.S.), it can be reduced by the College Board through your school, so look into this early. Not only does the College Board provide a subsidy, but many states also help underwrite the cost of exams for low-income students. Qualification information is available on the College Board Web site (http://apcentral.collegeboard.com) in February, through your school's AP coordinator, or via your state's department of education Web site. There is also a useful downloadable Bulletin for AP Students and Parents at the site. If you have questions, e-mail apexams@info.collegeboard.org or call AP Services at 609-771-7300 or 888-225-5427.

Familiarizing Yourself with the Exam

If your teacher has not given you AP Exam questions or old AP Exams as practice, you should look closely at the six practice tests in this book. You can also go to the AP Web site (http://apcentral.collegeboard.com) and review the many past exams that have been posted there.

The AP World History Exam is three hours and five minutes long. It consists of two parts that count equally in determining your final score. The first part of the exam is the multiple-choice section, which is fifty-five minutes long. It contains seventy multiple-choice questions with four answer options for each question. The second part of the exam is the free-response section, which consists of three essays. You will have ten minutes of mandatory reading time at the beginning of the second part of the exam to read each essay question. You will then have two hours of total writing time to complete the three essays.

In the AP World History Exam, each of the three essays comprising the free-response section follow a set format. The first type of essay is the document-based question (DBQ). The DBQ includes a brief paragraph of historical background before the documents. It must be answered only on the basis of the provided documents, usually between six and ten documents total. You are expected to write the DBQ essay in forty minutes. The other two essays are a continuity and change-over-time essay and a comparative essay. Unlike the other two AP history courses (AP U.S. History and AP European History), you will not be able to choose among several essay questions; you must complete all three. You'll have five minutes of planning time and thirty-five minutes of writing time for each of these two essays.

Setting Up a Review Schedule

Your teacher will almost certainly organize review sessions or review in class, but often that is insufficient to feel really ready for the exam. You might want to reread the textbook to prepare, but for most students, that's impossible because of time constraints. Thus, a study guide like this one is an excellent way to prepare, as it crystallizes the information in the textbook and allows you to hear a fresh voice.

You should schedule three weeks of review time in order to prepare for the exam, but in most cases, your teacher will still be trying to teach the rest of the course in April. For this reason, you will have to begin reviewing while you are still learning new material. What is the best way to do this?

Ideally, take the three weeks leading up to the exam and read one chapter of the study guide a night, which, if you remain focused, should be about a half-hour's work. Since there are twenty-three chapters, this works out to a little over three weeks of review. If this plan doesn't work for you, try to set up a schedule before the end of April in which you complete two or three chapters a night. On the exam, time periods 3 to 6 each comprise 20 percent of the multiple-choice questions, while periods 1 and 2 combined make up the remaining 20 percent, so you can't afford to neglect any part of the year's curriculum during your preparation.

The time before the AP Exams is often very hectic for students. If you are on an athletic team, you may have playoffs or championship games, and the workload in all your classes may be getting intense as the year is coming to its conclusion. You do not want to let your other responsibilities get in the way of earning a 5 on the exam, so an absolute key to success is time management. While this is always useful, it is crucial in the period before AP Exams. Otherwise, you will not prepare much and have to rely on your innate abilities and your memory. In most cases, such "preparation" will not bring you to a score higher than 3. If you want the 5, you will need to spend the week or two before the AP Exam preparing for the test instead of socializing or focusing on your other activities. Is it worth it? Absolutely! In almost every college, a score of 5, and in some places a 4, will bring you three or more credits. Even if you do not receive college credit, you might be placed directly into advanced-level history courses. Since you are very likely taking this exam as a sophomore, garnering a good score is something you can include on your college applications. It will help set you apart as a good college candidate.

The AP Exam is physically grueling—an hour's worth of multiple-choice questions and two hours of writing. If you are not used to writing by hand, be sure to practice in the weeks before the exam, otherwise your hand might cramp up or get tired. Be sure to eat well, stay away from junk food, and get enough sleep the night before the exam so that your body will be an ally and not a detriment to you. Be sure to have a good and healthy breakfast before the exam so your energies will not flag in the last hour. Do not drink too many liquids; you don't want to lose valuable exam time making frequent bathroom visits. Take a snack in with you to the exam for the break if that's allowed, wear comfortable clothes and shoes, and bring a sweater or jacket in case the room is cold. You do not want anything to interfere with your ability to concentrate on the exam. Most importantly, bring a watch! You will not be able to use your cell phone to help you with timing. You need a good, reliable timepiece that will accurately tell you how much time is left. Do not assume there will be a clock in the room.

Your examination proctor will certainly remind you of this, but in any case, leave all cell phones and other electronic devices outside the examination room. If you are involved in a breach of security, your examination will likely be canceled, and there could be other consequences at your school. It's simply not worth it to take such a chance.

How the Exams Are Scored

It helps to know how the exams are scored so that you can understand how to earn the highest score. The multiple-choice question answers are scored electronically, but the essays are read by people. Your score on the multiple-choice section counts for half of your exam score.

In June, over 1,000 readers — university professors and high school teachers of AP World History — meet for a week in a central location to read and score the three essays. Readers are organized into groups of eight at a table, chaired by a table leader who is responsible for quality control.

For each free-response question (the DBQ, the continuity and change-over-time essay, and the comparative essay), a question leader meets with a small group before the reading begins to create a specific operational rubric for each essay question based on the generic rubric you will see later in this book. The question leader trains the table leaders, who then train the readers; the table leaders check that scores given by readers are accurate and that the rubric is being applied competently and fairly. Everything possible is done to ensure that the scoring rubrics and their application by readers are fair and consistent. After the reading, the raw scores are evaluated by statisticians at Educational Testing Services in Princeton, New Jersey, and with the chief faculty consultant (always a university professor), the cutoffs for the 5, 4, 3, 2, and 1 final scores are set, often after having looked at what college students scored on the essays and the multiple-choice questions. This helps ensure that scores accurately reflect what a college freshman can do.

The exams are scored in June, and the scores are sent out in July. You can call for your score after July 1 if you cannot wait to get it in the mail. For a fee, you can get your score by phone.

You should not need this, but just in case: if the exam proves to be a disaster — which it certainly should not — you can cancel the score in writing by mail or fax to AP Services by June 15, before you get your score. You can also have AP Services withhold a score from being sent to a college.

Taking the AP World History Exam

If you are well prepared, you will be successful on the AP Exam; however, there are key test-taking skills that will all but guarantee that you get the score that your level of mastery should bring you.

The single most common problem is not reading the question carefully or ignoring parts of a question. For the essays, read the question carefully, think about what the question is asking, and answer every part. Students sometimes answer the question they know or the one they wish had been asked, rather than the one that has been asked; this is particularly true on the essays but can be true on multiple-choice questions, too. Do not rush and assume you understand the question before you read it carefully.

Types of Multiple-Choice Questions

There are eight types of multiple-choice questions that appear on the AP Exam.

1. Causation

   Causation questions will ask you to look at the relationship between causes—either short term or long term—and effects.

   Example:

   1. Which of the following was the most immediate cause of the success of the Chinese Communist Revolution in 1949?
      (A) The survival of the Chinese Communist leadership during the Long March
      (B) The outbreak of the Cold War
      (C) The escape of the Nationalist government to Taiwan
      (D) The weakening of the Chinese Nationalist government during the war against Japan

   Answer: D

2. Chronological Reasoning

   Chronological reasoning questions will test your understanding of changes and continuities within or between time periods.

   Example:

   1. Which of the following was an important continuity in Eurasian history from 1000 C.E. to 1500 C.E.?
      (A) Hindu political dominance of the Indian subcontinent and Southeast Asia

(B) The importance of the Silk Roads in cultural exchanges across Eurasia
(C) The Abbasid Caliphate as the dominant power in Southwest Asia
(D) The military superiority of Western Europe over other regions of Eurasia

Answer: B

3. Comparison

Comparison questions ask you to compare related historical developments and processes across geography, chronology, or different societies, or within one society.

Example:

1. Which of the following is the basis for nearly all boundaries of today's sub-Saharan African states?
   (A) Postcolonial conquests of one African state by another
   (B) Fragmentations of countries after they achieved independence from Europe
   (C) Decisions by European powers during the process of colonization
   (D) Precolonial linguistic groupings

Answer: C

4. Contextualization

Contextualization questions test your ability to recognize how historical phenomena or processes connect to broader regional, national, or global processes. Most frequently, these questions are based on a stimulus.

Example:

> Never believe, as I have never believed, that the British are going to fail. I do not consider them to be a nation of cowards. I know that before they accept defeat every soul in Britain will be sacrificed.
>
> They may be defeated and they may leave you just as they left the people of Burma, Malaya and other places, with the idea of recapturing lost ground when they can. That may be their military strategy. But supposing they leave us, what happens to us? In that case Japan will come here.
>
> The coming in of Japan will mean the end of China and perhaps Russia, too. In these matters, Pandit Jawaharlal Nehru is my guru. I do not want to be the instrument of Russia's defeat, nor China's. If that happened I would hate myself.
>
> *Mohandas K. Gandhi, speech to the All-India Congress, August 7, 1942*

1. Gandhi's speech is best understood in which of the following contexts?
   (A) Calls for violent resistance to British rule in India
   (B) Disputes within the Indian independence movement over whether to support the British war effort
   (C) Divisions within the Indian independence movement between Hindus and Muslims
   (D) British offers of autonomy to India in return for help in the war against Japan

Answer: B

5. Historical Argumentation

Historical argumentation questions require you to identify the answer choice that best supports a conclusion or assertion from a historical argument.

Example:

1. Which of the following best supports the conclusion that Africans played a key role in acquiring slaves for the transatlantic slave trade between 1500 and 1800?

   (A) Europeans seldom ventured into the interior of Africa in this period.
   (B) Most slaves acquired in this period were intended for labor on plantations in the Americas.
   (C) Large-scale slavery was uncommon in sub-Saharan Africa before 1500.
   (D) Most African slaves were purchased with goods produced in Europe.

Answer: A

6. Historical Interpretation

Historical interpretation questions ask you to critique various historical interpretations of a specific event. Usually, a primary and/or a secondary source is provided as the stimulus for the question.

Example:

1. The fourteenth-century Arab historian Ibn Khaldun described pastoral peoples in the following way: "It is their nature to plunder whatever other people possess." Which of the following evidence would counter the view of pastoral societies expressed by Ibn Khaldun?

   (A) The Xiongnu Empire extorted tribute payments from Han dynasty China.
   (B) Nomadic Bedouin Arabs regularly raided nearby agrarian societies.
   (C) Mongol rulers offered merchants 10 percent or more above their asking price.
   (D) The Seljuk Turks spread Islam throughout the Middle East by military conquest.

Answer: C

7. Periodization

Periodization questions require you to pick the best model of periodization for the question. Usually, the stem will argue that one date is better than another date at emphasizing a particular phenomenon.

Example:

1. Historians who maintain that the approximate date 500 C.E. is the best choice for the transition between two major periods in world history and historians who maintain that the approximate date 600 C.E. is a better choice for that transition are most likely to disagree on the relative importance they assign to which of the following?

   (A) The emergence of the classical Maya civilization
   (B) The role of technological change in world history periodization
   (C) The decline of polytheism in the Mediterranean and the Middle East after the fifth century C.E.
   (D) The fall of the Western Roman Empire

Answer: D

8. Use of Evidence

In this question, students are expected to analyze one type of historical evidence: audience, purpose, point of view, format, or argument.

Example:

> Although many people might think it crazy, the development model of the global economy has a marked relation to gender. . . . Women in every household are suffering every day as a result of impoverished economies, and those who are exposed to the effects of foreign debt are women. . . . The adoption of austerity measures mean a curtailment of the state's commitment to social services. . . . Women keep the smallest portion of the meager family income. . . . As a result malnutrition among women is increasing at an alarming rate.
>
> *Gladys Acosta, Peruvian feminist*

1. In the excerpt above, Acosta's main purpose is to point out that
   (A) women in developing countries have tended to be largely responsible for financial decisions made by their families
   (B) malnutrition results from increases in the prices of basic goods
   (C) foreign debt and consequent austerity measures have had disproportionately negative consequences for women in developing countries
   (D) because women keep the smallest portion of the family income, they are least affected by foreign debt

Answer: C

Strategies for the Multiple-Choice Section

1. Pace yourself. You are expected to answer the questions in just under a minute per question, so do not spend a long time on any one question. If you are struggling to select the correct answer, leave it and return to it at the end of the allotted time. On the other hand, do not rush. Get to know how long a minute is. Time yourself often so you know the rhythm of the exam.

2. Make sure that you fill in your answers accurately and in a timely fashion. If you skip a question, be sure that you skip an answer on the answer sheet. Periodically check that you are filling in the circles on the correct line. You do not want to find at the end of the exam that you have filled in the wrong circles for your answers, as you may not have time to correct the errors. If you like working questions in your test booklet and THEN bubbling in the answers, make sure you leave plenty of time to do so. Once time is called, you will not be able to fill in the bubbles. Anything in your multiple-choice test booklet will not be scored.

3. About guessing: until 2011, there was a penalty of one-quarter of a point off for each wrong answer, but this has been eliminated for AP Exams in all subjects. As there is no longer a guessing penalty, answer every question, even with a wild guess. You have nothing to lose and a 25 percent chance of getting the answer right.

4. Some questions will be straightforward and easy, so don't assume that they are trying to trick you. The seventy questions will vary in difficulty; a number of them are easy and will be answered correctly by the vast majority of students. Similarly, there will be a few multiple-choice questions that are really tough, and only a small percentage of students will get them right.

5. In order to earn a 3 or higher, you need to answer about half the multiple-choice questions correctly. The higher you score on the multiple-choice section, the greater the likelihood of a high score on the exam. Remember, the multiple-choice section counts for half of your final score.

6. Read each question and its answer choices carefully and be sure to notice if the question is an "except" question. Use the process of elimination as you read the choices (you can write on the exam booklet), crossing out the choices you know for sure are wrong. General rules of thumb: absolute answers—"all of the above" or "none of the above"—are usually wrong. Remember, the correct answer for a multiple-choice question should be the best answer of the four options. Typically, one potential answer will be clearly and definitively wrong, two might be correct or partially true, while the remaining one is the most accurate or complete answer to the question.

Strategies for the Free-Response Section

As noted above, you will prepare and write three essays in two hours and ten minutes. You will have ten minutes of mandatory reading and preparation time, which students generally use for the document-based question. It is also a good idea to use this time to review the two free-response questions you will have to answer. Your reading time allows you to make notes in your exam booklet, but does not allow you to begin writing your essays in the response booklets.

The scoring scale for each essay is 0 to 9. Zero is a real score and is reserved for essays that make some sort of attempt to answer the question, perhaps just by restating it, but get almost nothing right in the process. Skipping an essay question entirely will not even earn a 0. In order to get a 5 on the exam, you will need to get a 7, 8, or 9 on the DBQ and at least a 5 or 6 on each of the other two essays.

The free-response essays are scored using a core scoring method. The first seven points are awarded for the completion of specific tasks; these points are considered the basic core points. If you earn all seven core points, you have the opportunity to receive one or two additional points based on the quality of your essay. These additional points are assigned in a more holistic manner, while the seven core points are assigned for very specific items in the essay.

Each essay requires a thesis statement. A thesis statement can often seem intimidating or difficult to write, so be sure you understand what it is and what it is not. Too often an essay that reveals substantial knowledge on the part of the student fails to get a high score because it lacks a clear thesis. Without one, an essay reads more like a report. A thesis statement is a short, one- or two-sentence articulation of what the essay will argue—the points you will try to prove in the essay. It is not a description or a re-wording of the question. A good thesis statement is often strengthened by a thesis paragraph that lays out some of the key points of the arguments to be made in the essay. While it is acceptable for a thesis statement to be found in the conclusion, you do not want the essay readers to have to search for it, so start out the essay with a strong thesis statement.

Document-Based Question Essay

The DBQ in each of the three AP history examinations is different, so if you have already taken AP European History or AP U.S. History, you have to retrain for the AP World History DBQ. The AP World History DBQ expects you to answer the question with all the documents presented to you, but no outside knowledge is required or expected in your answer. However, you are expected to come up with one additional document that would help you answer the question.

Sometimes the world history DBQ is on a topic about which you may know a lot, but quite often it deals with relatively obscure issues. Don't worry at all if you know nothing at all about the subject; you need not bring in any outside knowledge. Everything you need to write an excellent DBQ essay can be found in the documents themselves.

Core Scoring

The basic premise of core scoring is that there are specific and identifiable skills that can be articulated as demonstrations of competence in DBQ essay writing. One of these skills can earn you one or two points, while the rest will earn you one. If you earn all seven points, you can then earn up to two additional points, giving you a score of 8 or 9. However, if you miss a core point, the maximum score you can get on the DBQ is 6, regardless of the quality of your essay. The core points for the document-based question are listed below. Learn them and internalize each point so you know how to best approach answering the document-based question.

The 7 core points are:

1. The thesis statement is explicit and addresses all parts of the question (1 point).
2. The answer uses all documents and demonstrates the basic meaning of all or all but one of the documents. What does it mean to use a document? It means referring to the document by reference to its content. Simply quoting from the document does not demonstrate understanding (1 point).
3. The answer supports the thesis with appropriate evidence from all or all but one the documents (2 points); OR the answer supports the thesis with appropriate evidence from all but two documents (1 point). In order for evidence to count, it must link to the question that was asked.
4. The answer analyzes the documents by using point-of-view analysis (see below) for at least two documents (1 point).
5. The answer analyzes the documents by explicitly organizing them into two or more appropriate groups. A group is a minimum of two documents. How do you group them? You group them by determining what the prompt is asking and deciding how documents might be combined to address the prompt (1 point).
6. The answer identifies and explains the need for one type of appropriate additional document or source (1 point).

Point-of-View (POV) Analysis

One of the most common reasons why students fail to earn a 7 on the DBQ is because they do not properly analyze the documents using point-of-view analysis. For this reason, POV analysis is an important skill to learn and practice in advance of the exam.

Point-of-view analysis is different from point of view. The point of view of a document is the opinion expressed by the author; in other words, his or her viewpoint. Point-of-view analysis evaluates the degree to which the views expressed in the document reflect or contradict the likely views of similar authors. Every document in the DBQ will include the name of the author, the title of the work or document, the type of document, a date for the document, and some additional information about the author. Your task is to connect something within the document with something in the identification. The information given about the author and about the document will offer many opportunities for POV analysis. In order to analyze point of view effectively, you must determine how WHO the person is would affect WHY he or she would describe events in the way he or she does.

What is the point of asking students to do point-of-view analysis? Historians do research by finding and examining documents, and in each case, they have to evaluate the reliability of documents or how much the documents represent the views of various subgroups in society. Teachers of history want to know that students have learned to think like historians. A document is not the whole historical truth; it is a particular document written at a particular time by a particular person or persons for a particular purpose in a particular manner.

For many examples of point-of-view analysis, look at the explanations for the DBQs in the answer keys for each of the six practice tests in this guide.

Additional Document

The additional document request described in core point six goes hand in hand with the point-of-view analysis. This requirement is often referred to as the missing voice, since part of the task is to identify whose voice or point of view the DBQ does not contain.

Other DBQ Essay-Writing Tips

1. Pay attention to the wording of the question. It's crucial that you focus your essay according to the prompts. Pay particular attention if the question asks you to analyze change over time. Even if the question doesn't but the documents are from various periods, try to include a few sentences about changes over time. It's a sign of a sophisticated history student.

2. Do not repeat the historical background. Each DBQ begins with a question, followed by a paragraph called historical background, which is designed to give you key information you need to understand and analyze the documents. Do not repeat the historical background. You may use or refer to it, of course, but do not waste your time repeating it. The readers already know it well.

3. There are no intentionally misleading or trick documents; every document must be used. Think of this like a jigsaw puzzle: every document has a place in the narrative you are creating.

4. Do not simply paraphrase or summarize a document. While this counts for document usage, it doesn't show even a minimum level of analysis. Always try to have something to say about the documents you use.

Additional Points beyond the Core

Ideally, your DBQ essay should have a thesis statement, use all of the documents, discuss them individually, make few errors of interpretation, divide the documents into two or three groups, give a point-of-view analysis on at least two of the documents, and identify the need for an additional document or source. As you read the documents for the first time, mark up your examination booklet, making notes as to possible groupings and point-of-view analyses, and begin to formulate your thesis. If you do all this, you are likely to earn at least a 7 on the DBQ essay.

But you shouldn't just aim for a score of 7. If you want an AP Exam score of 5, then you must go far beyond the core. You can do this by composing a stronger and more comprehensive thesis, making more point-of-view analyses (try for four or five) or bringing in relevant outside information to enrich your analysis. If you do this, you will earn a high score of 8 or 9. As mentioned before, you need not bring in one iota of outside information to earn a 9, but if you have some accurate and relevant knowledge, by all means include it; it can only strengthen your essay.

Be sure to examine the DBQs, the essays, and the scoring guidelines available to you on the College Board Web site for students, www.collegeboard.com/testing.

Continuity and Change-Over-Time Essay

The continuity and change-over-time essay follows the same core scoring system as the document-based question but has somewhat different elements to the basic core. The core point system is:

- ✦ The thesis statement is explicit and addresses all parts of the question (1 point).
- ✦ The answer addresses all parts of the question, typically both continuity and change (2 points); OR the answer addresses part of the question, typically either continuity or change (1 point).
- ✦ The thesis is supported with appropriate evidence (2 points); OR the thesis is partially supported with evidence (1 point).
- ✦ The answer uses relevant world historical context of a global process to explain continuity and change (1 point).
- ✦ The answer analyzes the reasons for the continuity and change (1 point).
- ✦ Like the document-based question, you can earn a total of seven basic core points for the continuity and change-over-time essay, along with a possible two additional points for excellence.

Comparative Essay

The comparative essay examines both similarities and differences between two different regions. Its core point system is:

- ✦ The thesis statement is explicit and addresses all parts of the question (1 point).
- ✦ The answer addresses all parts of the question, typically both similarities and differences (2 points); OR the answer addresses part of the question, typically either similarities or differences (1 point).
- ✦ The thesis is supported with appropriate evidence (2 points); OR the thesis is partially supported with evidence (1 point).
- ✦ The answer makes at least one clear, direct comparison between regions (1 point).
- ✦ The answer analyzes the reasons for similarities and differences (1 point).

Strategies for the Continuity and Change-Over-Time and Comparative Essays

The answers for these two types of essays should reflect your knowledge and understanding in addition to your skills.

To write a good essay:

1. Formulate a clear thesis statement. Take a position on the question and express it in the thesis statement. Make sure you are addressing the prompt, not just what you know about the topic!
2. Answer all parts of the question. It may be that you know more about one part of the question than another, but be sure to discuss all parts, even if you devote more time and space to addressing specific parts.
3. In the comparative question, remember to draw both similarities and differences, even if you stress one more than the other. Similarly, in the continuity and change-

over-time question, you need to make sure you include both continuities AND changes, even if you stress one more than the other.

4. Develop well thought-out paragraphs that continually tie back to the prompt. The easiest way to do this is to have a "changes" paragraph and a "continuities" paragraph if you are working on the continuity and change-over-time essay, or a "similarities" paragraph and a "differences" paragraph if you are writing the comparative essay.
5. Be well organized. Although essays are not scored on their writing per se, it is typical that a good essay is a well-organized one.
6. Avoid making major errors. Small mistakes on dates or people's names are not taken all that seriously, and even an essay that earns a 9 doesn't have to be perfect, but many, many small errors—and certainly major errors leading to erroneous conclusions—will affect your score negatively.
7. Watch your time. You have two hours to write all three essays.

Calculating Your Score on a Practice Exam

The following is based on the *2011–2012 AP World History Professional Development Guide*, as well as the new College Board revised guidelines for the 2002 and 2007 exams.

Scoring the Multiple-Choice Section

Remember that the two parts of the exam—Section I: multiple-choice, and Section II: free-response essays—are equally weighted at 50 percent each in determining your final score. Each of the three essays—the DBQ, the continuity and change-over-time question, and the comparative question—has equal weight, or 33.3 percent of the other 50 percent of the exam.

Use the following formula to calculate your raw score on the multiple-choice section of the exam:

$$\underline{\hspace{3cm}} \times 0.8571 = \underline{\hspace{3cm}}$$

| **Number correct** | **Weighted Section I score** |
| (out of 70) | (do not round) |

The highest possible score for the multiple-choice section is seventy correct answers, for a score of 60.

Scoring the Document-Based Question Essay

1. Do you have a thesis that derives from the documents and clearly addresses the prompt?
2. Have you used all the documents?
3. Have you supported your thesis with appropriate evidence from the documents? (Remember to award yourself two points if you used all or all but one of the documents for your evidence. Give yourself one point if you used all but two.)
4. Have you analyzed point of view in at least two documents?
5. Have you grouped the documents in two to three ways? (A good rule of thumb is to create three groups for DBQs with more than seven documents.)
6. Have you identified and explained the need for one type of appropriate additional document or source?

Give yourself one point for each affirmative answer. If you have earned the seven core points, evaluate how much better than the minimum you have done and give yourself an additional one or two points. If you missed a core point, go back over the DBQ to see what you could have done differently.

Part A Score: _____ **(out of 9)**

Scoring the Continuity and Change-Over-Time Essay

The essays are scored on a scale of 0 to 9, with 0 being a real score. Here is the generic scoring rubric for the continuity and change-over-time essay.

1. Do you have a thesis that includes the date ranges, addresses at least one change and one continuity, and specifically addresses the prompt?
2. Did you address both continuities and changes? If so, you can give yourself two points. If your essay is only about changes OR only about continuities, you can only award yourself one point.
3. Did you give substantial evidence for the continuities and changes you described? If you gave evidence for both, give yourself two points. If you did so only for one aspect—changes or continuities—you only get one point. Remember that you must always link everything you write about back to the prompt.
4. Did you include the historical context in which these continuities and changes occurred? Did you link something going on elsewhere to what was going on in the area? Or did you tie what you described to what was going on elsewhere in the world? If you were able to link external events to internal events, give yourself one additional point.
5. Did you analyze a specific change or continuity? The best way to do this is to explain why a continuity or change occurred. If you did so, give yourself one point.

If you have earned the seven core points, evaluate how much better than the minimum you have done and give yourself an additional one or two points. If you missed a core point, go back over the question and your answer to see what you could have done differently.

Part B Score: _____ **(out of 9)**

Scoring the Comparative Essay

This essay is also scored on a 0 to 9 scale. Below is the generic comparison contrast rubric.

1. Did you write a thesis that addresses the prompt and specifies both similarities and differences?
2. Did you specifically address both similarities and differences between and among all areas and topics referenced in the prompt? If yes, give yourself two points. If you only partially addressed the prompt—gave only similarities, for example—give yourself one point.
3. Did you substantiate your thesis? In other words, did you give specific evidence for both the comparative and contrastive arguments? If yes, give yourself two points. If your evidence was limited or only supported comparisons or contrasts, give yourself one point.
4. Did you write at least one direct comparison? If yes, give yourself one point.
5. Did you analyze the reason for a similarity or difference identified in a direct comparison? You cannot do this if you did not give yourself a direct comparison point in item four above. Remember analysis answers **why**. If you did, give yourself one point.

If you have earned the seven core points, evaluate how much better than the minimum you have done and give yourself an additional one or two points. If you missed a core point, go back over the continuity and change-over-time essay to see what you could have done differently.

Part C Score: _____ (out of 9)

Use the following formula to calculate your raw score on the free-response section of the exam:

Question 1 _____ × 2.2222 = _____
           (out of 9)   (do not round)

Question 2 _____ × 2.2222 = _____
           (out of 9)   (do not round)

Question 3 _____ × 2.2222 = _____
           (out of 9)   (do not round)

Your Composite Score

_____ + _____ = _____
   Section I Score   Section II Score   Composite Score
                                    (round to the nearest whole)

Once you have calculated your composite score, see where it falls in the Composite Score Range below. Remember that your composite score is only an estimate of your performance on the AP Exam.

Composite Score Range AP Grade

Composite Score Range	AP Grade
77–120	5
64–76	4
48–63	3
34–47	2
0–33	1

In May 2012, more than 200,000 students took the AP World History Exam; 6.85 percent earned 5s and 15.65 percent earned 4s, meaning that about a fifth of the total students earned either a 4 or 5. Almost another third of students (30.44 percent) scored a 3. In total, just over half of the students who took the exam scored a 3 or higher. If you prepare well for the examination, you can reasonably expect to earn a 3, 4, or 5.

How to Interpret Your Practice Test Results

1. First, look at the multiple-choice score. It is a fair indicator of what your overall score will be. How many out of seventy did you get right?
2. According to College Board statistics, most students who got a score of 5 on the examination answered 84 percent, or about fifty-nine, of the multiple-choice questions correctly. Those students earning a 4 on the exam answered approximately 73 percent, or fifty-one, of the multiple-choice questions correctly. Students who earned a 3 on the exam answered, on average, 62 percent of the questions correctly.

This translates into answering about forty-three of the seventy questions correctly. These numbers demonstrate very clearly that if you want a 3, you must work to get at least half of the multiple-choice questions right; if you want a 4, you need to aim for two-thirds right; if you want a 5, you're aiming to get just under 90 percent right.

3. Check to see if you got too many wrong answers for the goal you have set for yourself. Examine the ones you got wrong to see if you got them wrong because you did not know the answer or because you guessed poorly. Look at those questions closely to see what you might have missed that would have helped you make a better choice.

4. Examine your essay scores. What strengths and weaknesses do you find? If you did not do as well as you would have liked, try to focus on whatever problems you had in writing the essays. Was it your thesis statement, use of evidence, errors, or lack of organization? Once you identify your difficulties, you can focus your attention on addressing them.

5. Set a realistic goal for yourself and realize that each point you earn on the essay is worth 2.59 points on the multiple-choice portion. Thus, it pays to write well. The more you can strive to become a well-rounded student, the more likely it is that you will be able to earn a 5 on the AP Exam.

6. Make it happen!

SECTION 2
A Review of AP World History

Technological and Environmental Transformations, to c. 600 B.C.E.

PART ONE
First Things First: Beginnings in History, to 500 B.C.E.

AP World History Key Concepts

1.1: **Big Geography and the Peopling of the Earth**

1.2: **The Neolithic Revolution and Early Agricultural Societies**

1.3: **The Development and Interactions of Early Agricultural, Pastoral, and Urban Societies**

The Big Picture: Turning Points in Early World History

The first unit for both the AP World History course and this textbook covers the largest span of time of the six units. Four major turning points in human history occurred during this period; the first three are covered in Chapter 1 and the last in Chapter 2.

- ✦ **The Emergence of Humankind:** According to scientists, about 5 to 6 million years ago, several species of bipedal primates emerged in eastern and southern Africa. Eventually, this line led to *Homo sapiens*—modern humans—with large brains, the ability to use language and communicate abstract ideas, and the ability to create tools.

- ✦ **The Globalization of Humankind:** Around 100,000 years ago during the Paleolithic era (Old Stone Age), humans began to migrate out of Africa, armed with stone tools, the ability to use fire, and the ability to use language to work together in small groups of hunter-gatherers. People adapted to a variety of environments, from bitter cold tundras to burning hot deserts to grasslands and forests. Gradually, changes took place in the "tool kits" of human groups, helping them adapt to changing environmental circumstances. In addition, they developed art, religion, rituals, and stories (see Map 1.1, p. 4 and pp.16–17).

✦ **The Revolution of Farming and Herding:** By about 11,000 years ago, in separate regions in the Middle East, Asia, Africa, and the Americas, humans developed farming and animal husbandry; this development is often called the First Agricultural Revolution. This development has been called the single most important event in human history and has led to the growth of civilization as we know it today. The increased reliability of food sources also led to a population growth. The type of agriculture—or whether farming developed or not—depended on the climate and available plants and animals in a region. Some regions, typically dry grasslands, were more conducive to herding or pastoralism, while others provided enough food resources so that people continued as hunters, fishers, or foragers. The types of crop varied from region to region, such as potatoes in the Andes, grains in Eurasia, or corn (maize) in Mesoamerica. The Americas had relatively few domesticable animals—and no draft animals—compared to Afro-Eurasia, where goats, sheep, pigs, cattle, and later horses and camels were available (see Mapping Part One, pp. 8–9). The first farming villages were small, with people growing their own food and living without elaborate political or religious systems. Pastoral groups also remained small.

✦ **The Turning Point of Civilization:** As farming provided a more reliable source of food, populations grew, and some settlements developed into civilizations. The earliest civilizations developed in seven separate areas between 3500 B.C.E. and 500 B.C.E. These First Civilizations gave rise to empires, cultural and religious traditions, new technologies, more hierarchical social and gender roles, and large-scale warfare.

First Peoples; First Farmers: Most of History in a Single Chapter, to 4000 B.C.E.

AP World History Key Concepts

1.1: Big Geography and the Peopling of the Earth

I. Archeological evidence indicates that during the Paleolithic era, hunting-foraging bands of humans gradually migrated from their origin in East Africa to Eurasia, Australia, and the Americas, adapting their technology and cultures to new climate regions.

Ironically, the longest span of time for human history is covered in the AP period that has the least weight on the test. It is important to realize that this huge period is seen through a "panoramic" lens—big picture and not much fine detail. Modern humans first evolved in Africa about 200,000 to 250,000 years ago. Using more refined tools, they gradually moved from collecting edibles and scavenging dead animals to hunting, fishing, and gathering a wider range of foods. The population slowly grew, leading to the first really big idea in human history: migration. Humans migrated from Africa to almost every part of the globe, adapting to a wide range of environments from frozen tundra to grasslands, from forests to desert regions. How did this happen? It happened because humans were able to create new technology and because they were able to communicate and cooperate between members of family groups. You'll need to know the routes and time periods of these migrations to different regions in Eurasia, Australia, the Americas, and the Pacific Islands, as well as some of the archeological evidence and controversies about who migrated where and when. See Map 1.1 on pp. 16–17 of *Ways of the World* for likely migration routes and dates. Finally, you should be aware of some of the ways that humans adapted to new environments in Eurasia, Australia, the Americas, and the Pacific Islands using new tools, such as bone needles to make layered clothing, spears and spear throwers, woven nets and baskets, and pottery, to name just a few.

1.2: The Neolithic Revolution and Early Agricultural Societies

I. Beginning about 10,000 years ago, the Neolithic Revolution led to the development of new and more complex economic and social systems.

II. Agriculture and pastoralism began to transform human societies.

During the Neolithic era, which began approximately 10,000–12,000 years ago, most people continued living as hunters or fishers and gatherers while populations rose, especially in areas with abundant resources. In some areas, humans began to settle down—at least for part of the year—in small villages based on horticulture while they also continued hunting or fishing. At various times in different regions, settled agriculture emerged based on the available domesticable plants and animals. This deliberate cultivation of particular plants and animals is termed the Neolithic Revolution or Agricultural Revolution. Other regions less suited to agriculture—such as savannas and steppes—encouraged the development of pastoralism, in which people relied on the milk, meat, and blood of domesticated animals that they raised. The earliest known sites for settled agriculture were in the Fertile Crescent (see Map 1.4, p. 31). See also Map 1.3, "The Global Spread of Agriculture and Pastoralism" (pp. 28–29), for the sites where different plants and animals were first domesticated. Humans were now changing the environment, not just adapting to it. These new ways of exploiting the environment led to the development of new cultural, social, economic, and to a lesser extent, political patterns in both village life and pastoral communities.

Theme 1: Interaction Between Humans and the Environment

Paleolithic humans adapted to different environments, while Neolithic humans modified their environments to greater and greater extents. Early humans were food collectors and scavengers. They developed tools such as hand axes and the use of fire and began to hunt and fish as well as collect foods such as berries, nuts, insects, and grains. As humans migrated out of Africa to other regions, they encountered many new environments—harsh tundra, forests, deserts, or large bodies of water—that required the creation of new tools. This migration was helped by the Ice Age, which lowered sea levels and created land bridges or narrower straits connecting regions such as the Americas, Indonesia, or Australia with Afro-Eurasia. New technologies such as layered clothing sewn with bone needles, spear throwers or bows, flaked stone tools, nets, and weaving allowed humans to enter into Ice Age Eurasia. Other species of human, such as Neanderthals in Europe or *Homo floresiensis* in Indonesia, became extinct soon after modern humans arrived. We don't know whether these other species died from being marginalized by the more technologically advanced *Homo sapiens* or whether disease or conflict killed them.

By the time of the Neolithic Revolution, humans had become proficient roving hunters and gatherers in many different environments, with about 70 percent of their food coming from gathering (often performed by women) and 30 percent from hunting (often undertaken by men). Perhaps as a response to environmental changes at the end of the last Ice Age, people began new methods of exploiting the environment, leading to the domestication of plants and animals and the rise of settled village life and pastoralism. This Agricultural Revolution created fundamental changes in the role of humans on the planet: they had become the shapers of their environment.

As people moved to agricultural life, they worked longer and harder for a more limited diet than that of their hunter-gatherer ancestors. The needs of agriculture led to drastic environmental change as a few domesticated crops replaced the variety of plants that had existed before. Both plants and animals were selectively bred to create desired results. Other environmental impacts included deforestation to grow food crops, terracing hillsides, digging irrigation canals, and soil depletion from overuse. In addition, new diseases passed from domesticated animals to humans.

Theme 2: Development and Interaction of Cultures

Our knowledge of Paleolithic and Neolithic human culture is based almost exclusively on physical objects studied by archeologists. Archeological sites for early humans are scattered and often discovered by chance. Even when we find artifacts, we do not know with certainty what they mean because the people who made them are not alive to tell us nor can anthropologists observe them actually using their artifacts. Scholars therefore study the few remaining stone-age cultures (in places like the Amazon basin or Australia and New Guinea) to try to draw analogies between the life and artifacts of people today and those of our ancient ancestors. Planned burials with grave objects such as beads, ochre pigments, and flowers imply a belief system. Female statuettes unearthed throughout Eurasia (sometimes called the stone-age Venus) may be connected to the diffusion of religious ideas centered on female fertility and certainly show communication networks operating over large areas. Diffusion of artifacts such as the Clovis points in the Americas also point to a widespread network of communication. Dramatic cave paintings often depicting animals that were hunted or herded have been found in both Eurasia (Lascaux in Western Europe and Bhimbetka in India) and Africa (Sahara and San rock art). In contemporary Australian stone-age cultures, the persistence of rock paintings and ceremonies associated with the Dreamtime provide a unique glimpse into what earlier Neolithic cultures may have been like.

During the Neolithic era, we begin to see the first monumental architecture, such as the complex at Göbekli Tepe in modern Turkey. Megaliths such as Göbekli Tepe and the more famous Stonehenge in England have been interpreted as religious centers or calendars to mark the solstices and equinoxes. Some archeologists argue that the need to feed the large number of people building and using such sites may have been one of the factors that encouraged a permanent horticultural lifestyle. The people living in early settlements in the Fertile Crescent, such as Ain Ghazal, created enigmatic statues, which may have represented deities, heroes, or leaders. Late in the Neolithic era, temples (with priests and priestesses), tombs, and their associated art developed in cities.

Theme 3: State-Building, Expansion, and Conflict

This theme is not well developed in this time period. Hunting and gathering bands tended to be small, relatively egalitarian, and mobile. Large-scale conflicts did not seem to arise: why fight and lose some of your precious kinsmen if there was other territory to move to? Leadership roles seem to have been fluid and related to a specific need. True state building did not begin before there were permanently settled agricultural villages competing for land and resources. By the end of this period, more powerful leaders emerged. In agricultural areas such as Mesopotamia, secular and religious power was inherited and reinforced through the personal charisma of leaders, their ritual roles, their ability to redistribute wealth through gift giving, and their roles as battle leaders. Pastoral societies also developed first as relatively egalitarian kinship groups and moved toward clan or tribal leaders with greater wealth or power.

Theme 4: Creation, Expansion, and Interaction of Economic Systems

Early humans were generalists, with each person creating the tools needed for exploiting the local environment for survival needs. However, very early in human history, items were exchanged or traded outside their place of origin: stone, flint, or special woods for tool making, decorative items (shells, feathers, pigments), new tools such as bone needles or Clovis points, and cultural artifacts such as carved figurines (see Theme 2).

The Agricultural Revolution sparked a rapid increase in the quantity and types of tools and weapons. Agriculturalists developed new technologies such as sickles, plows, kilns and potter's wheels, looms, sun-dried mud bricks, chisels, boats (including sails by Mesopotamians), and tools related to domestication of animals. Pastoralists invented saddles, bridles, harnesses, and new types of bows. Trade and communication systems expanded between villages, and between villages and the hinterlands that possessed resources that were not available locally. Often, pastoral groups transmitted goods and innovations across large areas between early civilizations and across ecological zones between pastoral and settled peoples. In the growing cities, wealth accumulated in the hands of leaders and priests. Priests, in addition to their religious roles, often controlled the exchange and creation of goods, organized large projects such as irrigation canals and monumental architecture, allotted fields, and controlled agricultural and artisanal labor.

Theme 5: Development and Transformation of Social Structures

While most hunter-gatherer bands seem to have had gender-specific tasks (women more often were the gatherers, men the hunters), there seems to have been relative equality between the sexes. Little difference in material wealth or social power is evident. All people contributed to the collection of food needed for survival and all shared the same skills set.

However, the development of agriculture and pastoralism gradually changed that egalitarian social structure. Wealth in the form of arable land or herds of animals became more unevenly distributed. Society therefore became more stratified, and labor became more specialized. Early horticultural villages seem to have remained relatively more balanced in gender and social roles. Men continued to hunt, while women continued to provide many of the major agricultural innovations and much of the labor, using digging sticks and hoes to work their fields, creating looms to weave fibers from plants or animals, creating pottery to store food, and so on. Evidence for the continued strong role of women is found in the dominance of female images in art, in matrilineal descent (tracing descent through the mother's family), and matrilocal marriage patterns (men left their birth families to live with their wives). As more animals were domesticated and the use of animal-drawn plows spread, men took over the heavier agricultural labor and began to dominate.

Village-based lineage societies tended to reduce the equalities of earlier societies: elders controlled the labor forces and sought to control women's reproductive lives to ensure growth of the (now often patrilineal) lineage or kinship group. The growth of warfare led to the collection of captives who were placed in forced labor roles. Intensification of agricultural production and increased conflict seem to have led to the development of larger cities and chiefdoms, intensifying social stratification and the dominance of men over women.

Pastoral societies tended to retain more of the relative gender equality of earlier Paleolithic cultures, as evidenced by the burial goods of some women who seem to have held high status as warriors or healers and shamans.

CHAPTER TWO

First Civilizations: Cities, States, and Unequal Societies, 3500 B.C.E.–500 B.C.E.

AP World History Key Concepts

1.3 The Development and Interactions of Early Agricultural, Pastoral, and Urban Societies

I. Core and foundational civilizations developed in a variety of geographical and environmental settings where agriculture flourished.

II. The first states emerged within core civilizations.

III. Culture played a significant role in unifying states through laws, language, literature, religion, myths, and monumental art.

The First Civilizations arose independently in the several millennia after 3500 B.C.E. You must be able to identify the locations of these civilizations (see Map 2.1, "First Civilizations," pp. 64–65) and understand the characteristics they shared as well as their unique characteristics.

- Sumer in ancient Mesopotamia
- Egypt along the Nile River in northeastern Africa
- The civilization of Norte Chico (and later the Chavín) in the coastal region of the Andes in present-day Peru
- The Indus Valley civilization in present-day Pakistan
- The Shang dynasty located in northern China
- The Oxus in what is today northern Afghanistan and Southern Turkmenistan
- The Olmecs of modern-day southern Mexico

Theme 1: Interaction Between Humans and the Environment

The First Civilizations arose in areas that had previously developed village agriculture, which was discussed in Chapter 1. All of these First Civilizations saw population increases due to intensified agricultural techniques that were adapted to their specific environments, ranging from lowland rain forest for the Olmecs, to desert oases for the

Oxus, to desert punctuated by rivers for the Norte Chico people, to the river valleys of the Nile, Huang He, Tigris and Euphrates, and Indus. All of the First Civilizations were based on water management. Some, such as the Xia dynasty in China (a precursor to the Shang), dug canals to control devastating flooding. Others employed terraced fields, irrigation, and swamp drainage in their farming. The Egyptians used the regular flooding of the Nile Valley, which yearly brought rich mud that replenished fields and provided agricultural bounty. Larger populations meant increased demand for food. Overuse of fields, especially where slash-and-burn agriculture was being practiced (Olmecs) led to soil depletion. Intensive irrigation could lead to the fields becoming too saline, as in the Indus Valley. Deforestation—whether to clear land for agriculture or to harvest wood for fuel or construction—led to erosion. Periods of drought brought further stress. Whatever the cause, environmental degradation often led to lower crop yields and sometimes even to the abandonment of cities.

Theme 2: Development and Interaction of Cultures

First Civilizations shared common cultural characteristics: more elaborate belief systems often rooted in fertility deities and supporting social and gender inequalities, writing and record-keeping systems, monumental art and architecture, and the explosion of the arts and literature. Distinctive writing systems emerged in most, but not all, of the early civilizations; the Oxus and the Andean regions, for example, did not develop true literacy. Writing served a number of functions, from celebrating the accomplishments of a society's leaders to recording transactions and taxes. Writing also gave birth to written laws such as the Code of Hammurabi (see Document 2.2, p. 95) and to literature (see Snapshot: Writing in Ancient Civilizations, p. 79). Monumental architecture (such as ziggurats and pyramids, tombs, temples, and palaces) and art (Olmec heads, Egyptian statues, etc.) reinforced the glory and power of the rulers and the gods.

Theme 3: State-Building, Expansion, and Conflict

Archaeologists and historians have long debated the origins of the state. It is clear that agriculture was a necessary precondition, but it was not the only factor in the rise of the state. One theory is that the growing density of population and the relative scarcity of fertile land for farming meant that highly organized states had an advantage in the competition for resources. This competition usually led to warfare. Most of these civilizations followed a similar pattern of state building: coercion tactics to force people to obey authority and military might to expand control into new areas. The system of kingship (often divine kingship) also bound people to their leaders and priests. The Xia began the enduring concept of the Mandate of Heaven, linking the ruler as "the Son of Heaven" to the gods. The Egyptian pharaoh also ruled as a descendant of the gods, as most likely did the Olmec rulers. Some civilizations, such as in the Indus Valley, seemed to have a high level of coordination and planning (streets were laid out on a grid, uniform measurements, sewers, and "zoning") without signs of a king or other central ruler, leading to speculation that they may have been governed by a council of some sort.

Theme 4: Creation, Expansion, and Interaction of Economic Systems

The economy of the early civilizations was based on agriculture, and control of the land was the major source of wealth. However, many skilled artisans created artifacts, textiles, pottery, weapons, and tools both for use within their own civilizations and for trade by merchants or gift exchanges between rulers. A number of early civilizations engaged in long-distance trade to obtain goods or materials (usually luxury items) that were not available locally. Many Indus Valley traders lived in Mesopotamia to facilitate trade between the two civilizations. Mesopotamia also had trade routes connecting it to Egypt and Central Asia. The Egyptians had similarly extensive trade routes, including to Nubia and the interior of Africa, the Red and Mediterranean Seas, as well as to their near neighbors in Mesopotamia. Trade often moved through middlemen, such as pastoral peoples, or through a series of merchant-traders working in a particular region. The Oxus civilization served as a hub in a trans-Eurasian trading network by conducting trade with China, India, Mesopotamia, and pastoral nomads of the steppes. The First Civilizations in the Americas, like the Olmecs and the Norte Chico people, developed in isolation from each other but did engage in more localized trade within their cultural region. The only item exchanged (indirectly) between the two regions was maize, which originated in Mesoamerica.

Theme 5: Development and Transformation of Social Structures

Many of the First Civilizations witnessed an "erosion of equality" as these societies developed hierarchies of class and gender. Upper-class people with greater wealth were able to avoid physical labor and occupied the highest political, military, and religious positions within their societies. The majority of people were free commoners, but most of the early civilizations also developed systems of slavery, which varied greatly from place to place. This kind of slavery differed greatly from the slavery that developed in the Americas after the seventeenth century. Slavery in the First Civilizations was not perpetual in that the children of slaves could become free and was also not associated with race. The cities of Norte Chico show less signs of economic specialization than the other First Civilizations, and the enigmatic ruins of the Indus Valley show little evidence of social hierarchy.

The most significant social division within human societies was based on gender. Patriarchy has been the most pervasive gender system in human history, in which men were regarded as superior to women, men had legal and property rights denied to women, and men were far more active in governing. Women's roles were increasingly confined to the home and defined by their relationship to a male (father, husband, or son). There is much speculation about why patriarchy developed with civilization. One approach suggests that the intensification of agriculture and the shift to plow-based agriculture, which required the greater strength more often found in men, led to a decline in the status of women. The increase of warfare and combat may have also contributed to patriarchy; increased warfare led to the glorification of the warrior as well as an increase in the number of women who were captured as slaves. Finally, the development of private property may have helped shape early patriarchy; men wanted to ensure that only their own children inherited their land or wealth, and to do so, they attempted to control women's reproductive freedom.

PRACTICE EXAM 1

WORLD HISTORY
SECTION I

Note: This exam uses the chronological designations B.C.E. (before the common era) and C.E. (common era). These labels correspond to B.C. (before Christ) and A.D. (anno Domini), which are used in some world history textbooks.

TIME — 25 Minutes
30 Questions

Directions: Each of the questions or incomplete statements below is followed by four suggested answers or completions. Select the one that is best in each case.

1. All of the following provide evidence to support the interpretation that Paleolithic peoples came up with innovative ways to adapt to their environment EXCEPT
   (A) spear throwers in southern France and northern Spain
   (B) partially underground dwellings in Central Europe
   (C) canoes in New Guinea in the South Pacific
   (D) sickles in the Fertile Crescent in the Middle East

2. The social organization of early pastoral and agricultural societies was based on
   (A) kinship relations
   (B) tribute relations
   (C) divine right
   (D) social contract

3. Which of the following was a technological innovation that occurred during the Age of Agriculture?
   (A) Magnetic compass
   (B) Pottery making
   (C) Mechanization
   (D) Use of stone tools

4. All of the following represent archeological evidence from Africa that supports the theory that humans originated on that continent EXCEPT
   (A) stone blades and points fastened to shafts
   (B) sickles, mortars, pestles, and storage pits
   (C) body ornaments, beads, and ochre
   (D) grindstones and tools made from bone

GO ON TO THE NEXT PAGE.

5. The Agricultural Revolution affected the environment in all of the following ways EXCEPT

(A) soil erosion
(B) deforestation
(C) new plant varieties
(D) global warming

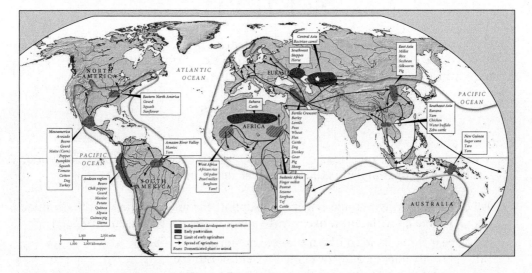

Questions 6–9 are based on Map 1.3.

6. Which of the following interpretations is supported by the information shown in Map 1.3?

(A) Agriculture developed independently in different parts of the world.
(B) Agriculture emerged at the same time in the Americas and Afro-Eurasia.
(C) Agriculture spread from the Mediterranean to the Americas.
(D) Agriculture was the human response to climactic changes.

7. What accounts for the absence of pastoral societies in the Americas?

(A) The lack of technological skill
(B) The practice of intensive agriculture
(C) The selective cultivation of cereal grains and beans
(D) The small number of animals that could be domesticated

8. The areas to first make the transition to agriculture (as shown in Map 1.3) represent the birthplace of all of the following foundational civilizations EXCEPT

(A) Mesopotamia
(B) Shang
(C) Egypt
(D) Olmec

9. What does Map 1.3 suggest was the basis of the economy in Central Asia, the Sahara, and the Southwest Steppes?

(A) Intensive agriculture
(B) Animal husbandry
(C) Metallurgy
(D) Textiles

GO ON TO THE NEXT PAGE.

10. Some historians attribute the birth of civilizations to the need to organize large-scale irrigation projects. Which of the following evidence challenges this interpretation?

   (A) Archeological findings that date complex water control systems to long after the establishment of states

   (B) Cave paintings that show bulls, horses, and other animals with hand impressions and abstract designs

   (C) Periodic flooding of river valleys in agricultural regions that supported the First Civilizations

   (D) Soil erosion and deforestation as a result of intensive agriculture in the First Civilizations

11. Differences in all of the following can be interpreted as evidence of the unequal and hierarchical societies of the First Civilizations EXCEPT

   (A) clothing

   (B) housing

   (C) burial practices

   (D) paper currency

12. All of the following represent the earliest forms of writing that emerged independently in the First Civilizations EXCEPT

   (A) cuneiform

   (B) hieroglyphs

   (C) alphabets

   (D) quipu

13. "To be gendered as masculine or feminine defines the roles and behavior considered appropriate for men and women in every human community."

   Robert Strayer, world historian, 2012

   Which of the following is an example of how roles were gendered in the First Civilizations?

   (A) The requirement that respectable women be veiled and the punishment of female slaves and prostitutes who veiled themselves

   (B) The portrayal of the Egyptian queen Hatshepsut dressed in male clothing and wearing a false beard

   (C) The view that the injured party in rape cases was the woman's father or husband and not the violated woman

   (D) The relegation of male deities to the home and hearth and the dominance of goddesses in the public arena

14. Which of the following reflects the influence of patriarchy on legal codes in the First Civilizations?

   (A) The legal definition of adultery as a criminal offense for women only

   (B) The legal avenues that allowed children of slaves to become free people

   (C) The penalty of a small fine for striking someone of equal rank

   (D) The meting out of punishments based on class differences

GO ON TO THE NEXT PAGE.

15. All of the following reflect a similar relationship between religion and politics in the First Civilizations EXCEPT

    (A) Hammurabi's linking of his law code to Marduk, the chief god of Babylon
    (B) Chinese emperors' claim to rule by the Mandate of Heaven in the Western Zhou
    (C) Urukagina's justification of reforms in the name of the patron god of Lagash
    (D) Roger Williams's argument for the separation of civil and religious authority

16. Beginning with the First Civilizations, cities assumed all of the following roles EXCEPT

    (A) administrative capitals
    (B) marketplaces
    (C) agricultural production
    (D) cultural centers

17. Scholars seeking to reconstruct the connections within the Afro-Eurasian ancient world have followed the spread of which innovation from Anatolia to China?

    (A) The horse-drawn chariot
    (B) Movable type printing
    (C) The magnetic compass
    (D) The lateen sail

18. Which of the following reflects a pattern of expressing political authority through monumental architecture in the First Civilizations?

    (A) Olmec statues of heads
    (B) Christian cathedrals
    (C) Islamic mosques
    (D) Chinese canals

19. Long-distance trade occurred between which of the following First Civilizations?

    (A) Mesopotamia and the Indus Valley
    (B) Mesopotamia and Mesoamerica
    (C) Egypt and South America
    (D) Mesoamerica and the Middle East

20. In his book *Black Athena*, historian Martin Bernal argues that ancient Greek culture was influenced by Egyptian culture. Which of the following offers evidence to support Bernal's interpretation?

    (A) The Phoenician adaptation of Sumerian cuneiform
    (B) The practice of divine kingship in Sudan and Egypt
    (C) Similarities between Mesopotamian and Greek architecture
    (D) Similarities between Egyptian and Minoan art

21. Which of the following reflects the Mesopotamian concept of kingship?

    (A) "When the gods created Gilgamesh, they gave him a perfect body."
    (B) ". . . the house whose people sit in darkness; dust is their food and clay their meat."
    (C) "Men are born and remain free and equal in rights."
    (D) ". . . the Emperor loves his subjects as his very own."

GO ON TO THE NEXT PAGE.

22. Which of the following shows how the Code of Hammurabi reinforced existing social hierarchies?

    (A) "If any one take a male or female slave of the court, or a male or female slave of a freed man, outside the city gates, he shall be put to death."
    (B) "If a man put out the eye of another man, his eye shall be put out."
    (C) "If any one strike the body of a man higher in rank than he, he shall receive sixty blows with an ox-whip in public."
    (D) "If any one is committing a robbery and is caught, then he shall be put to death."

23. What does the Negative Confession in the *Book of the Dead* reveal about changes in Egyptian religious beliefs during the New Kingdom period of ancient Egyptian history?

    (A) Idolatry was abandoned as people began to worship one supreme god.
    (B) The path to eternal life was now accessible to all who lived a moral life.
    (C) Dutiful performance of one's duties could now guarantee rebirth in a higher class.
    (D) Views of the afterlife now centered on the alternative worlds of heaven and hell.

24. The discovery in Mesopotamia of seals from the Indus Valley, such as the one shown in Visual Source 2.1, suggests that the seals were used in

    (A) warfare
    (B) diplomacy
    (C) marriages
    (D) commerce

25. All of the following are foreign influences that contributed to Egypt's empire-building efforts during the age of the First Civilizations EXCEPT

    (A) hieroglyphic writing
    (B) horse-drawn chariots
    (C) improved methods of spinning and weaving
    (D) cultivation of olive and pomegranate trees

26. In what respect did the Indus Valley civilization depart from the First Civilizations in the Middle East?

    (A) The absence of specialization of labor
    (B) The minimal impact on the environment
    (C) The lack of evidence of a centralized state
    (D) The ban on long-distance trade

GO ON TO THE NEXT PAGE.

27. The Andean civilization known as Norte Chico shared which feature with other First Civilizations?
    (A) Grain-based agriculture
    (B) Monumental architecture
    (C) Long-distance trade
    (D) Defensive walls

28. What did the First Civilizations of Norte Chico in the Andean region, Olmec in Mesoamerica, Oxus in Central Asia, and the early dynasties in China share in common?
    (A) They independently developed agriculture.
    (B) They retained the nomadic way of life.
    (C) They built large empires that encompassed much of the surrounding areas.
    (D) They established patterns that persisted in subsequent civilizations in the region.

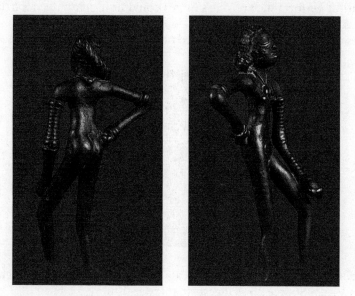

29. Visual Source 2.3 is a statue of a female nude cast in bronze from the Indus Valley that dates to around 2500 B.C.E. Which of the following inferences can be made about the Indus Valley civilization?
    (A) It had knowledge of bronze metallurgy.
    (B) Most slaves were female entertainers.
    (C) Physical fitness was emphasized for girls.
    (D) Patriarchy limited women's lives.

30. Before 500 B.C.E., Mesopotamia experienced periods of political unity under the foreign rule of which of the following groups?
    (A) Greeks
    (B) Assyrians
    (C) Romans
    (D) Mongols

STOP

END OF SECTION I

WORLD HISTORY
SECTION II

Part A
(Suggested writing time—40 minutes)
Percent of Section II score—33 1/3

Directions: The following question is based on the accompanying Documents 1–7. (The documents have been edited for the purpose of this exercise.)

This question is designed to test your ability to work with and understand historical documents.

Write an essay that:

+ Has a relevant thesis and supports that thesis with evidence from the documents.
+ Uses all of the documents.
+ Analyzes the documents by grouping them in as many appropriate ways as possible. Does not simply summarize the documents individually.
+ Takes into account the sources of the documents and analyzes the authors' points of view.
+ Identifies and explains the need for at least one additional type of document.

You may refer to relevant historical information not mentioned in the documents.

1. Using the following documents, analyze the similarities and differences in the civilizations of Mesopotamia and Egypt in the period from 2700 B.C.E. to 1000 B.C.E. Identify an additional type of document and explain how it would help your analysis of these civilizations.

Document 1

Source: Mesopotamian epic poem the *Epic of Gilgamesh*, c. 2600 B.C.E.

[Enkidu tells Gilgamesh about the afterlife.]
He turned his stare toward me, and he led me away to the palace of Irkalla, the Queen of Darkness, to the house from which none who enters ever returns, down the road from which there is no coming back. "There is the house whose people sit in darkness; dust is their food and clay their meat. They are clothed like birds with wings for covering, they see no light, they sit in darkness."

[Instructions from Enlil, the chief Sumerian god, to Gilgamesh]
Enlil of the mountain, the father of the gods, had decreed the destiny of Gilgamesh. So Gilgamesh dreamed and Enkidu said, "The meaning of the dream is this. The father of the gods has given you kingship, such is your destiny; everlasting life is not your destiny. Because of this do not be sad at heart, do not be grieved or oppressed. He has given you power to bind and to loose, to be the darkness and the light of mankind. . . . But do not abuse this power, deal justly with your servants in the palace, deal justly before Shamash."

Document 2

Source: Sumerian poet describing Agade, the Akkadian capital, during its period of rule over Mesopotamia, c. 2200 B.C.E.

In those days the dwellings of Agade were filled with gold,
its bright-shining houses were filled with silver,
into its granaries were brought copper, tin, slabs of
lapis lazuli [a blue gemstone], its silos bulged at the sides. . . .
its quay where the boats docked were all bustle. . . .

Document 3

Source: Mesopotamian poet, after the destruction of the city of Ur and the desecration of the city's temple, c. 2000 B.C.E.

After your city had been destroyed, how now can you exist!
After your house had been destroyed, how has your heart led you on!
Your city has become a strange city. . . .
Your house has become a house of tears.

GO ON TO THE NEXT PAGE.

Document 4

Source: *The Law Code of Hammurabi*, Mesopotamia, c. 1800 B.C.E.

15. If any one take a male or female slave of the court, or a male or female slave of a freed man, outside the city gates, he shall be put to death. . . .

17. If any one find runaway male or female slaves in the open country and bring them to their masters, the master of the slaves shall pay him two shekels of silver. . . .

253. If any one agree with another to tend his field, give him seed, entrust a yoke of oxen to him, and bind him to cultivate the field, if he steal the corn or plants, and take them for himself, his hands shall be hewn off. . . .

Document 5

Source: Egyptian school text copied by students training for positions as government administrators. Commonly titled "Be a Scribe," c. 1850 B.C.E.

Apply yourself to [this] noble profession. . . . You will find it useful. . . . You will be advanced by your superiors. You will be sent on a mission. . . . Love writing, shun dancing; then you become a worthy official. . . .

The merchants travel downstream and upstream. They are as busy as can be, carrying goods from one town to another. They supply him who has wants. But the tax collectors carry off the gold, that most precious of metals. . . .

Let me also expound to you the situation of the peasant, that other tough occupation. . . . By day he cuts his farming tools; by night he twists rope. Even his midday hour he spends on farm labor. . . .

If you have any sense, be a scribe. If you have learned about the peasant, you will not be able to be one. . . . Look, I instruct you to . . . make you become one whom the king trusts; to make you gain entrance to treasury and granary. To make you receive the shipload at the gate of the granary. To make you issue the offerings on feast days. You are dressed in fine clothes; you own horses. Your boat is on the river; you are supplied with attendants. You stride about inspecting. A mansion is built in your town. You have a powerful office, given you by the king. Male and female slaves are about you. Those who are in the fields grasp your hand, on plots that you have made. . . . Put the writings in your heart, and you will be protected from all kinds of toil. You will become a worthy official.

GO ON TO THE NEXT PAGE.

Document 6

> Source: A hymn to the pharaoh, c. 1850 B.C.E.
>
> He [the pharaoh] has come unto us . . . and has given peace to the two
>   Riverbanks
> and has made Egypt to live; he hath banished its suffering;
> he has caused the throat of the subjects to breathe
> and has trodden down foreign countries
> he has delivered them that were robbed he has come unto us, that we may
>   [nurture up?] our children and bury our aged ones.

Document 7

> Source: A hymn to the pharaoh on the afterlife, c. 1500 B.C.E.
>
> You shall come in and go out, your heart rejoicing, in the favor of the Lord of the Gods, [with] a good burial after a venerable old age, when age has come, you will assume your place in the coffin, and join the earth on the high ground of the west.
>
> You shall change into a living *Ba* [soul] and surely have the power to obtain bread and water and air. You shall take shape as a heron or swallow, as a falcon or a bittern, whichever pleases you.
>
> You shall cross in the ferryboat and shall not turn back. You shall sail on the waters of the flood, and your life shall start afresh. Your *Ba* shall not depart from your corpse and your *Ba* shall become divine with the blessed dead. The perfect *Ba's* shall speak to you, and you shall be an equal amongst them in receiving what is given on earth. You shall have power over water, inhale air, and be surfeited with the desires of your heart. Your eyes shall be given so you can see, and your ears so you can hear, your mouth speaking, and your feet walking. Your arms and your shoulders shall move for you, your flesh shall be firm, your muscles shall be easy and you shall exult in all your limbs. You shall examine your body and find it whole and sound, no ill whatever adhering to you. Your own true heart shall be with you, and you shall have your former heart.

END OF PART A

WORLD HISTORY
SECTION II

Part B
(Suggested planning and writing time — 40 minutes)
Percent of Section II score — 33 1/3

Directions: You are to answer the following question. You should spend 5 minutes organizing or outlining your essay.

Write an essay that:

+ Has a relevant thesis and supports that thesis with appropriate historical evidence.
+ Addresses all parts of the question.
+ Uses world historical context to show continuities and changes over time.
+ Analyzes the process of continuity and change over time.

2. Analyze the continuities and changes that occurred as humans transitioned from hunting/foraging to early agricultural societies starting 10,000 years ago.

WORLD HISTORY
SECTION II

Part C
(Suggested planning and writing time—40 minutes)
Percent of Section II score—33 1/3

Directions: You are to answer the following question. You should spend 5 minutes organizing or outlining your essay.

Write an essay that:

- ✦ Has a relevant thesis and supports that thesis with appropriate historical evidence.
- ✦ Addresses all parts of the question.
- ✦ Makes direct, relevant comparisons.
- ✦ Analyzes relevant reasons for similarities and differences.

3. Compare the cultural developments of TWO of the following early river valley civilizations.

- ✦ Shang in the Yellow or Huang He Valley
- ✦ Mesopotamia in the Tigris and Euphrates River Valleys
- ✦ Harappa in the Indus River Valley

STOP

END OF EXAM

Answer Key for Practice Exam 1

Answers for Section I:
Multiple-Choice Questions

1. D	9. B	17. A	25. A
2. A	10. A	18. A	26. C
3. B	11. D	19. A	27. B
4. B	12. C	20. D	28. D
5. D	13. B	21. A	29. A
6. A	14. A	22. C	30. B
7. D	15. D	23. B	
8. C	16. C	24. D	

Rationales:

1. Answer: D

    Explanation: Sickles were not developed until the eve of the Neolithic Revolution. The colder temperatures brought by the Ice Age led people in Central Europe, Ukraine, and Russia to create partially underground dwellings using the bones and tusks of mammoths. In the warmer climates of France and Spain, people changed their hunting techniques, as shown in the development of spear throwers to catch reindeer and horses. In the South Pacific, canoes were invented to enable people to travel the seas.

    Page Reference: pp. 14, 19

KEY CONCEPT	THEME	SKILL
1.1.I.B	1: Interaction Between Humans and the Environment.	Interpretation Evidence

2. Answer: A

    Explanation: The basic organizational unit in both pastoral and agricultural societies was the family. Kinship relations bound people together. In pastoral societies, they were referred to as clans or tribes. In agricultural societies, they were referred to as lineages.

    Page Reference: pp. 39, 41

KEY CONCEPT	THEME	SKILL
1.2.II.D	5: Development and Transformation of Social Structures.	Comparison

3. Answer: B

    Explanation: Mechanization did not occur during the Age of Agriculture. Stone tools were used before the Age of Agriculture, while the magnetic compass was not developed until much later. The spread of agriculture was accompanied by revolutionary breakthroughs in textile and pottery production. People also began to work with metals like gold, copper, bronze, and iron, marking a transition from the "stone age" to the age of metals.

Page Reference: p. 38

KEY CONCEPT	THEME	SKILL
1.2.II.C	1: Interaction Between Humans and the Environment.	Periodization

4. Answer: B

Explanation: Sickles, mortars, pestles, and storage pits emerged with the transition to agriculture, which occurred in the Neolithic era. The remains of tools made from stone and bone indicate human innovation in adapting to the environment. In addition, body ornaments, beads, and pigments such as ochre provide evidence of uniquely human activities.

Page Reference: pp. 13–14

KEY CONCEPT	THEME	SKILL
1.1.I.C	1: Interaction Between Humans and the Environment.	Evidence Interpretation

5. Answer: D

Explanation: Global warming is a modern phenomenon. As land came under cultivation, the quality of the soil declined and forests were cleared. New plant varieties emerged as a result of farming as the genetic makeup of certain plants was altered through human selection.

Page Reference: p. 37

KEY CONCEPT	THEME	SKILL
1.2.I.E	1: Interaction Between Humans and the Environment. 4: Creation, Expansion, and Interaction of Economic Systems.	Causation

6. Answer: A

Explanation: The map shows that the areas in green denote the independent development of agriculture. Since there are no dates provided in the map, no conclusions can be made about the simultaneous development of agriculture. The arrows showing the spread of agriculture do not indicate any interaction between the Americas and Afro-Eurasia. There is no information about climactic changes in the map.

Page Reference: pp. 27–29

KEY CONCEPT	THEME	SKILL
1.2.I.A	1: Interaction Between Humans and the Environment. 4: Creation, Expansion, and Interaction of Economic Systems.	Interpretation

7. Answer: D

    Explanation: The lack of large animals that could be domesticated impeded the development of pastoral societies in the Americas. The economy of pastoral societies was dependent on animal husbandry in which the products of animals were used for food.

    Page Reference: pp. 5–6, 39–40

KEY CONCEPT	THEME	SKILL
1.2.I.B	4: Creation, Expansion, and Interaction of Economic Systems.	Causation Comparison

8. Answer: C

    Explanation: Although Egypt was a foundational civilization, it was not a point of origin for the development of agriculture. The map shows that agriculture spread to the Nile River valley from the Fertile Crescent, where Mesopotamia emerged. The Shang emerged in the Yellow River valley in China. The Olmecs emerged in Mesoamerica.

    Page Reference: pp. 28–29, 62–68

KEY CONCEPT	THEME	SKILL
1.3.I	4: Creation, Expansion, and Interaction of Economic Systems.	Interpretation Contextualization Synthesis

9. Answer: B

    Explanation: The map shows that the domestication of animals occurred in those areas but not the domestication of plants. Thus, agriculture was not the basis of the economy. Camels, horses, and cattle provided the main sources of food (milk, meat, blood) for the societies that emerged in those regions.

    Page Reference: pp. 28–29, 39–40

KEY CONCEPT	THEME	SKILL
1.2.I.B 1.2.I.C	1: Interaction Between Humans and the Environment. 4: Creation, Expansion, and Interaction of Economic Systems.	Interpretation

10. Answer: A

    Explanation: Archeologists date the construction of large-scale irrigation systems to many years after the emergence of the first states and civilizations. This challenges the theory that the need to organize the labor necessary for large-scale irrigation projects led to the emergence of the first states.

    Page Reference: pp. 68–69

KEY CONCEPT	THEME	SKILL
1.2.I.D	1: Interaction Between Humans and the Environment. 3: State-Building, Expansion, and Conflict.	Argumentation Causation

11. Answer: D

Explanation: Paper currency had not yet been developed. Differences in clothing, housing, and burial practices distinguished the elite from the commoner. This was evident in First Civilizations like China and Mesopotamia.

Page Reference: p. 71

KEY CONCEPT	THEME	SKILL
1.2.II.D 1.3.III.G	5: Development and Transformation of Social Structures.	Evidence

12. Answer: C

Explanation: None of the earliest writing systems was based on alphabets. Cuneiform emerged in Sumer. Hieroglyphs were used in Egypt. Quipu was used in the Andes.

Page Reference: p. 79

KEY CONCEPT	THEME	SKILL
1.3.III.C	2: Development and Interaction of Cultures.	Comparison

13. Answer: B

Explanation: Although women in ancient Egypt enjoyed more freedoms than their counterparts in other First Civilizations, it was still a patriarchal society. Some women did hold political power, whether as regents for their sons or as queens in their own right. Yet this was not the norm, as political power was associated with masculinity. The portrayal of Hatshepsut as male reflects the association of royal power with masculine identity.

Page Reference: pp. 73, 75

KEY CONCEPT	THEME	SKILL
1.3.III.G	5: Development and Transformation of Social Structures.	Interpretation

14. Answer: A

Explanation: In Mesopotamia and China, for instance, only women were punished for adultery. A married man's extramarital sexual relations were tolerated, unless he engaged in illicit sex with another man's wife. In such cases, he was punished for abetting a married woman in committing her crime of adultery. The man was not punished for his own infidelity to his wife.

Page Reference: p. 74

KEY CONCEPT	THEME	SKILL
1.3.III.D 1.3.III.G	5: Development and Transformation of Social Structures.	Causation Comparison

15.   Answer: D

Explanation: Roger Williams's arguments for the separation of civil and religious authority became the basis for secularism; he also wrote in the sixteenth century, long after the First Civilizations. All the other choices reflect the religious basis for political authority in the First Civilizations.

Page Reference: p. 77

KEY CONCEPT	THEME	SKILL
1.3.II.A	3: State-Building, Expansion, and Conflict.	Comparison

16.   Answer: C

Explanation: As cities emerged, agricultural activity was relegated to the countryside. Cities became urban centers that hosted political, cultural, and commercial activities.

Page Reference: pp. 70–71

KEY CONCEPT	THEME	SKILL
2.2.III.A	3: State-Building, Expansion, and Conflict.	Continuity and Change

17.   Answer: A

Explanation: The spread of chariot technology in the ancient world enables scholars to map the connections within the ancient world in Afro-Eurasia. From its point of origin in southern Russia, the horse-drawn chariot passed to the Hittites in Anatolia by 1595 B.C.E., spread to Egypt and Mesopotamia, and reached China by 1200 B.C.E.

Page Reference: pp. 87–88

KEY CONCEPT	THEME	SKILL
1.3.III.F 1.3.II.D	4: Creation, Expansion, and Interaction of Economic Systems.	Evidence

18.   Answer: A

Explanation: Both Christianity and Islam did not emerge until long after the First Civilizations. The Olmec heads are an example of expressing political authority through monumental architecture in a First Civilization. Egyptian pyramids and Mesopotamian ziggurats are also examples of this monumental architecture. The states in all these civilizations sponsored construction projects to erect monumental architecture expressing the grandeur of their political power.

Page Reference: pp. 72, 78, 80

KEY CONCEPT	THEME	SKILL
1.3.III.A	3: State-Building, Expansion, and Conflict.	Comparison

19. Answer: A

Explanation: Before Columbus's voyage across the Atlantic, the people in the Americas and Afro-Eurasia had no contact with one another. Long-distance trade has been documented between Mesopotamia and the Indus Valley. Egypt also engaged in trade with Nubia and the civilizations of the Middle East.

Page Reference: pp. 85–87

KEY CONCEPT	THEME	SKILL
1.3.III.F	4: Creation, Expansion, and Interaction of Economic Systems.	Contextualization

20. Answer: D

Explanation: The Minoan civilization emerged on the island of Crete around 2500 B.C.E. and is identified with ancient Greece. The Egyptian influence on Minoan art suggests that Greek culture was also shaped by the civilizations of North Africa.

Page Reference: p. 87

KEY CONCEPT	THEME	SKILL
1.3.III.F	2: Development and Interaction of Cultures.	Argumentation Interpretation Evidence

21. Answer: A

Explanation: In Mesopotamia, as in most of the First Civilizations, kingship was associated with the gods. Gilgamesh was the legendary king of the Sumerian city of Uruk. He was believed to be semi-divine. The quote states that Gilgamesh was a creation of the gods.

Page Reference: pp. 77, 92–93

KEY CONCEPT	THEME	SKILL
1.3.II.A	2: Development and Interaction of Cultures. 3: State-Building, Expansion, and Conflict.	Interpretation

22. Answer: C

Explanation: The Code of Hammurabi stipulated different punishments for the same offense. An offense committed against someone who held a higher rank was punished more severely than the same offense committed against someone of a lower rank. The quote specifies that this penalty applies to an offense against "a man higher in rank than he," which highlights the class differences between the offender and the victim.

Page Reference: pp. 71–72, 95–97

KEY CONCEPT	THEME	SKILL
1.3.III.D	3: State-Building, Expansion, and Conflict. 5: Development and Transformation of Social Structures.	Interpretation

23. Answer: B

Explanation: In contrast to earlier periods in ancient Egypt, the New Kingdom was an era in which it was widely believed that access to eternal life was open to all who followed a moral life and not just the pharaohs. The Negative Confession identifies the qualities of a moral person: honesty, fairness, modesty, and concern for others.

Page Reference: pp. 98–99

KEY CONCEPT	THEME	SKILL
1.3.III.H	2: Development and Interaction of Cultures.	Continuity and Change

24. Answer: D

Explanation: The archeological record shows that most seals were affixed to goods. Scholars have inferred from this that the owners were merchants. The discovery of Indus Valley seals in Mesopotamia provides physical evidence of trade relations between these two First Civilizations.

Page Reference: pp. 85–56, 103–04

KEY CONCEPT	THEME	SKILL
1.3.III.F	4: Creation, Expansion, and Interaction of Economic Systems.	Interpretation Contextualization

25. Answer: A

Explanation: Hieroglyphic writing was indigenous to Egypt. The horse-drawn chariot came from the Hittites. Improved techniques in textile production as well as the spread of new crops like olives and pomegranates came from neighboring regions.

Page Reference: pp. 87–88

KEY CONCEPT	THEME	SKILL
1.3.II.B 1.2.II.C	3: State-Building, Expansion, and Conflict.	Causation

26. Answer: C

Explanation: The archeological record shows a highly complex society. However, there is no evidence to suggest that a centralized state or political hierarchy dominated the civilization. The evidence conventionally interpreted as signs of a centralized state (palaces, temples, elaborate graves) are missing.

Page Reference: p. 66

KEY CONCEPT	THEME	SKILL
1.2.II.B	4: Creation, Expansion, and Interaction of Economic Systems.	Comparison

27. Answer: B

Explanation: Archeologists have found large earthen platform mounds that suggest that Norte Chico was a civilization. They have also discovered large structures that seem to have served a public ceremonial purpose and stone buildings housing apartments.

Page Reference: p. 63

KEY CONCEPT	THEME	SKILL
1.3.III.A	2: Development and Interaction of Cultures.	Comparison

28. Answer: D

Explanation: Norte Chico cultural patterns can be identified in numerous civilizations that developed in the Andean region: Chavín, Moche, Wari, Tiwanaku, and Inca. Olmec influence is apparent in the Mesoamerican civilizations of the Maya and Teotihuacán. Oxus cultural patterns can be identified in later civilizations in Iran, India, and the eastern Mediterranean. The Xia, Shang, and Zhou dynasties established cultural and political patterns that would shape all subsequent Chinese dynasties.

Page Reference: pp. 66–68

KEY CONCEPT	THEME	SKILL
1.3.I	2: Development and Interaction of Cultures.	Comparison Continuity and Change

29. Answer: A

Explanation: The statue was cast in bronze using a "lost wax" method. This indicates that the Indus Valley had knowledge of bronze metallurgy.

Page Reference: p. 107

KEY CONCEPT	THEME	SKILL
1.2.II.C	2: Development and Interaction of Cultures.	Interpretation Evidence

30. Answer: B

Explanation: The Mongols, Greeks, and Romans did not build their empires before 500 B.C.E. However, the Assyrians ruled Mesopotamia from 900–612 B.C.E.

Page Reference: p. 83

KEY CONCEPT	THEME	SKILL
1.3.II.C	3: State-Building, Expansion, and Conflict.	Continuity and Change

Answer Guide for Section II:
Part A

General Guidelines for Answering a Document-Based Question (DBQ):

1. Pre-Write. Create a brief outline before you start writing.
2. Write your DBQ in a multiple-paragraph structure. In your first paragraph, write an introduction that clearly states your thesis.
3. Present your arguments in body paragraphs. Body paragraphs should integrate groupings of documents, demonstrate understanding of documents, support the thesis using documents as evidence, analyze point of view, and possibly include additional relevant historical content. Present your arguments in body paragraphs that focus on a grouping of documents and that put forth a single argument centered on answering the prompt.
4. In your final paragraph, write a conclusion that includes a reworded restatement of your thesis.

AP World History DBQ essays are scored using a core scoring method with a maximum score of nine. In the basic core, you may earn the following seven points:

✦ one point for a thesis
✦ one point for addressing and understanding the documents
✦ up to two points for using the documents as evidence to answer the prompt
✦ one point for grouping the documents
✦ one point for analyzing Point of View (POV)
✦ one point for identifying and explaining the need for an additional document

If you earn ALL seven basic core points, you have the chance to earn up to two additional points in what is called expanded core. Expanded core points may be granted for the following features:

✦ an excellent, sophisticated, and comprehensive thesis
✦ insightful document analysis
✦ analyzing POV in all or most documents
✦ including extra document groupings or additional documents
✦ incorporating relevant historical content not found in the documents

Below is a detailed description of what you will need to do in your answer to earn each basic core point for this essay.

Thesis (1 point): To earn a point in this category, you must write a thesis that responds to the entire prompt and outlines the specific arguments you will make based on a correct usage of the documents. You will need to mention the arguments you plan on making in your answer, and you will need to avoid generalizations that do not reflect reasonable interpretations of the documents. Thesis statements will only earn a point if they appear in the first or last paragraph of the essay. Common errors in thesis writing include merely rewriting the prompt or presenting an answer to only some parts of the prompt, so make sure you address the entire prompt and briefly present the specific arguments that you will use in your answer based on the documents.

> **Prompt:** Using the following documents, analyze the similarities and differences in the civilizations of Mesopotamia and Egypt in the period from 2700 B.C.E. to 1000 B.C.E. Identify an additional type of document and explain how it would help your analysis of these civilizations.

Examples:

Example Thesis: "In the period from 2700 B.C.E. to 1000 B.C.E., the civilizations of Mesopotamia and Egypt shared many similarities. Both had kingship, farming economies, technologies in metallurgy and grain storage, and systems of hierarchy that included slavery. Although quite similar, they showed differences as well, including their views of the afterlife and the fact that Mesopotamia experienced conquest while the documents showed Egypt as a conqueror."

✦ This thesis earns the point by identifying the specific arguments based on the documents that will be used to answer the prompt. It presents BOTH similarities and differences, so it answers the entire prompt. Thesis statements can be longer than a single sentence. A multi-sentence thesis should, however, be presented in contiguous sentences.

Unacceptable Example One: "There were similarities and differences in the civilizations of Mesopotamia and Egypt."

✦ This thesis does little other than state the obvious given the prompt.

Unacceptable Example Two: "Egypt and Mesopotamia were similar in how they both had kingship and used agriculture to support a settled civilization."

✦ This thesis improves upon the first example by including some specific similarities, but it would NOT earn a thesis point because it does not answer the entire prompt.

Addressing and Understanding Documents (1 point): To earn this point, you must address ALL of the documents and demonstrate understanding of "all but one." This means that throughout your answer, you must show understanding of at least six of the seven documents.

Using Documents as Evidence (2 points): To earn two points, you must correctly incorporate at least six documents (although seven would be better) into arguments that answer the prompt. You will earn only one point if you use five of the seven documents in your arguments. If you use four or fewer documents in your essay, you will receive a zero in this category.

Grouping the Documents (1 point): Documents should be grouped in at least three ways in order to earn a point in this category. You can group documents by matching two or more documents that hold some relevant feature in common. Each example grouping below represents documents that, when used together, can make up an argument that answers the prompt.

Groupings to show differences:

1. Documents 1 and 7 show differences between Mesopotamian and Egyptian religion and views of the afterlife.
2. Documents 3 and 6 show differences since Mesopotamia was conquered and Egypt was a conqueror.

Groupings to show similarities:

1. Documents 1, 5, and 6 show similarities in politics (kingship).
2. Documents 2 and 5 show similarities in economics (granaries, farming, boats and trade).
3. Documents 4 and 5 show similarities in economics (farming).

4. Documents 4 and 5 show similarities in society (slavery and hierarchy).
5. Documents 2 and 5 show similarities in technology (metalworking and grain storage).

Analyzing Point of View (1 Point): Many students find it challenging to earn the point in this category. The best way to earn the Point of View (POV) point is to go beyond the basic identity of the source author and the source itself, as described in the document source line. In order to write a successful POV statement, you should try to establish a better understanding of the identity of the author; you can do this by asking yourself questions about the author and the source. What is the author's gender or social class? What religion does the author follow? What is the author's profession? Does the author have an identifiable ethnicity, nationality, or other allegiance to a particular group? Is the source from a poem, essay, or novel? What was the source used for? Once you've asked these questions, go further and explain how some of these factors may have influenced the content of the source. Your complete POV statement should both identify the influences that may have shaped the author or source and explain how those particular influences have specifically affected the content of the document. Below are some examples of POV statements based on the documents from this question.

Examples of POV Statements:

Document 1: "Source: Mesopotamian epic poem the *Epic of Gilgamesh*, c. 2600 B.C.E."

✦ Epic poetry was passed orally for generations in the ancient world and included conventional wisdom through which people of a culture made sense of the world around them and their social order. The *Epic of Gilgamesh*, like other epic poetry of the ancient world, held explanatory power by illustrating Mesopotamian ideas about themselves. As a poem of a people with divine kingship, the *Epic of Gilgamesh* promotes kingship as sanctioned by the gods and supports the Mesopotamian government that was in place at the time.

Document 3: "Source: Mesopotamian poet, after the destruction of the city of Ur and the desecration of the city's temple, about 2000 B.C.E."

✦ This source reflects the loyalty of a Mesopotamian poet. As a resident of Mesopotamia, this poet describes the destruction of Ur as a tragic event. A poem from a conquering people might reflect a more celebratory tone, but this poem from a resident of the conquered place portrays the conquest as tragic.

Document 5: "Source: Egyptian school text copied by students training for positions as government administrators. Commonly titled 'Be a Scribe,' c. 1850 B.C.E."

✦ This text was created and used by teachers who sought to instruct students, so it reflects the goal of teaching. Its first priority was to teach writing, so it includes a variety of words. The text also speaks to the benefits of being educated and includes content aimed at persuading the student to continue his studies, which would also promote the work of the teacher. Teachers are likely to include ideas about why students should learn and unlikely to tell students why other pursuits are more rewarding than learning to write.

You should write as many POV statements as you are able to produce. You can earn the POV point with as few as two correct POV statements; however, it's not uncommon to make errors in writing POV statements. For that reason, it's safer to provide more than just two in order to make up for any errors. Additionally, if you earn all of the basic core points, an extra POV statement can earn you an expanded core point.

Additional Document Statement (1 Point): A good additional document statement identifies a missing document that, if added to the provided documents, would help make a better answer to the question. You are only required to make a single additional document statement to earn a point, but you should aim to identify a minimum of three additional documents. This allows room for mistakes, and after the first correct additional document statement, any extras can earn you bonus points in the expanded core if you earn all seven points in the basic core. You should be careful to avoid the common mistake of asking for a type of document that is already provided. Additional document statements must meet three standards to be considered successful:

- ✦ The document suggested must be historically plausible.
- ✦ The statement must include an explanation of **why** the additional document would be useful in answering the prompt.
- ✦ The analysis of **why** must speculate about the particulars of what the missing document might include. In other words, a successful additional document suggestion is historically possible given the time and place, includes an explanation of how the new source would help answer the prompt, and goes as far as speculating on arguments that the suggested source might support.

Document Analysis:

Document 1: "Source: Mesopotamian epic poem the *Epic of Gilgamesh*, c. 2600 B.C.E." This document can be used to show views of the afterlife in Mesopotamia and the existence of kingship. It portrays the afterlife as dreary where ". . . people sit in darkness; dust is their food and clay their meat." This use of Document 1 contrasts with the Egyptian afterlife portrayed in Document 7. And on kingship, "The father of the gods has given you kingship, such is your destiny," which is a feature shared with Egpyt, as shown by Documents 5 and 6.

Document 2: "Source: Sumerian poet describing Agade, the Akkadian capital, during its period of rule over Mesopotamia, c. 2200 B.C.E." Document 2 shows a similarity to Egypt in having granaries (Document 5), wealth, and trade conducted by boats.

Document 3: "Source: Mesopotamian poet, after the destruction of the city of Ur and the desecration of the city's temple, about 2000 B.C.E." Document 3 expresses sorrow at the sacking of Ur, which when used with Egyptian Document 6 shows a difference in the experience of these civilizations. Mesopotamian civilization suffered frequent wars and defeats, while Egypt was more isolated and less often conquered.

Document 4: "Source: *The Law Code of Hammurabi*, Mesopotamia, c. 1800 B.C.E." This document shows farming, which can be used by students to argue a similarity between Mesopotamia and Egypt. It shows farming in Mesopotamia in the line: "If any one agree with another to tend his field, give him seed, entrust a yoke of oxen to him, and bind him to cultivate the field. . . ." This document groups with Egyptian Document 5 to show similarity.

Document 5: "Source: Egyptian school text copied by students training for positions as government administrators. Commonly titled 'Be a Scribe,' c. 1850 B.C.E." This document illustrates a number of features of Egyptian civilization. It shows kingship, slavery, hierarchy, farming, metalworking, and grain storage—all of which a student may use in combination with Mesopotamian documents to make arguments of similarity.

Document 6: "Source: A hymn to the pharaoh, c. 1850 B.C.E." Document 6 shows Egypt as a conqueror in the line stating that the pharaoh "has trodden down foreign countries." This concept shows a difference when contrasted with Mesopotamian Document 3. Document 6 is also useful for showing a similarity in political kingship.

Document 7: "Source: A hymn to the pharaoh on the afterlife, c. 1500 B.C.E." This document when paired with Mesopotamian Document 1 shows a difference in views of the afterlife. The Egyptian afterlife promised that the pharaoh would "change into a living *Ba* [soul] and surely have the power to obtain bread and water and air. You shall take shape as a heron or swallow, as a falcon or a bittern, whichever pleases you." And further, the hymn claims, "You shall examine your body and find it whole and sound, no ill whatever adhering to you. Your own true heart shall be with you, and you shall have your former heart."

Answer Guide for Section II:
Part B

2. Analyze the continuities and changes that occurred as humans transitioned from hunting/foraging to early agricultural societies starting 10,000 years ago.

What Does the Question Ask?

This question deals with information from the first few days of a typical AP World History class. The transition from hunting and foraging to agricultural societies represents one of the greatest transformations covered in this course. You can use a broad range of evidence from potentially all of the major historical themes to answer this question, just as long as you address continuity and change over time.

Listed below is the scoring system used to grade continuity and change-over-time essays; also included are guidelines and examples for how to earn each point for this question.

Has Acceptable Thesis (1 point)

+ The thesis needs to correctly address both continuity and change during the transitions from hunting/foraging to agriculture.
+ The thesis should appear in the first paragraph (although it may also count if it is in the conclusion).
+ The thesis can be one sentence or multiple sentences.

Examples:

+ Example One: As humans moved from hunting and foraging to agriculture, they were much more likely to settle in one place. Even so, the size of these early settlements remained relatively small.
+ Example Two: Almost everyone was involved with food production throughout the time of hunter-gatherers and farmers. However, as agriculture became more established, people became more specialized in their labor.
+ Example Three: During the transition from Paleolithic hunting to Neolithic farming, people continued to create art that reflected their lives. The technologies that people used became much more sophisticated.

✦ Unacceptable Example: The main change that occurred during this time was the movement from hunting/foraging to agriculture.
   • This is an unacceptable thesis statement because it repeats information from the question without providing much else. Additionally, it also only addresses change without addressing continuity.

Addresses All Parts of the Question (2 points)

✦ The essay accurately addresses both a continuity (1 point) and a change (1 point).
✦ The statements of continuity and change may not appear in the thesis.

Examples:

✦ Example One: Most people still remained in small groups for many centuries after the Agricultural Revolution. With the Agricultural Revolution, people started living in settled communities where they farmed.
   • The first statement in the example above addresses continuity, while the second statement addresses change.

✦ Example Two: The vast majority of people throughout early history were involved with food production, whether through farming or foraging. As people started forming settled farming communities, social classes developed for craftsmen and ruling elites.
   • The first statement in the example above addresses continuity, while the second statement addresses change.

✦ Example Three: Fertility images were present both before and after the agricultural revolution. Settled agricultural people developed much more sophisticated tools, changing the way humans interacted with the environment.
   • The first statement in the example above addresses continuity, while the second statement addresses change.

Substantiates Thesis with Appropriate Historical Evidence (2 points)

✦ A piece of historical evidence is a fact that is correct and relevant to the time period.
✦ To earn the full two points in this category, an essay should have five or more pieces of evidence.
✦ To earn only one point in this category, an essay needs three or four pieces of evidence.
✦ Points for evidence can be earned even if the thesis point is not earned.

Examples:

✦ Example One: During hunter-gatherer times, people were nomadic, following seasonal animal movements and ripening plants. These small groups of people were most likely organized as clans with strong family connections. As people started farming, they built more permanent housing in areas that had fertile soil. Agricultural transitions occurred throughout the world in places as distant as the Fertile Crescent of the Middle East to the Andes of South America. These settlements first started small then grew to several hundred people over time.
✦ Example Two: Virtually everyone in Paleolithic cultures either hunted or foraged or did both. Social structure was most likely fairly equitable, and most people did work that was similar to what everyone else did. Farming produced surplus, such as grains, that could be stored. Some Neolithic people specialized in working specific crafts, such as basketry, pottery, or weaving. Religious and political elites emerged with the Agricultural Revolution.

✦ Example Three: Early humans before and after the agricultural transitions created art by carving bones, painting on cave walls, and molding clay. Ancient cave paintings in France and Spain show a fascination with hunting animals. Paleolithic people also made small stone carvings of female fertility objects. Once farming started, people developed more advanced ways of expressing themselves in art. Different patterns on clay pots showed the new ways of being creative.

Uses Relevant Historical Context (1 point)

✦ Historical context places the issue discussed in the essay into a broader global perspective.

Examples:

✦ Example One: Paleolithic people migrated out of Africa, across Eurasia, and into the Americas long before the discovery of agriculture.
✦ Example Two: Agriculture developed independently with wheat in the Middle East, rice in East Asia, and potatoes in South America.
✦ Example Three: Archeologists have found early carvings of fertility objects throughout Eurasia, from Europe to the Middle East and even in Asia.

Analyzes the Process of Continuity or Change (1 point)

✦ Analysis explains why the continuity or change occurred.

Examples:

✦ Example One: The reason why people settled into small villages at the beginning of the Agricultural Revolution was to look after the crops that they planted.
✦ Example Two: Since agricultural people could store surplus food, wealth was created. Political and religious rulers developed to take advantage of this wealth.
✦ Example Three: Art is a reflection of the values of the culture that made it. Therefore, early art throughout this time was concerned with fertility because people depended so greatly on the land for survival.

Expanded Core

You must earn all seven points in the basic core before earning any points in the expanded core. Points awarded in the expanded core reflect the general excellence of the essay. Any one aspect of your essay, such as the thesis or evidence, might be particularly insightful and earn a point in the expanded core. Essays that have a high degree of analysis and historical context often earn expanded core points if they have all of the other basic core points. Clarity of organization, strong cause-effect analysis, and particularly insightful ideas can make your essay stand out as excellent.

Examples:

✦ Example One: A discussion of specific archeological discoveries that relate to either Paleolithic or Neolithic sites could earn points in the expanded core.
✦ Example Two: A detailed description of the demographic changes, such as disease and life expectancy, that occurred as part of the Neolithic Revolution could earn points in the expanded core.
✦ Example Three: Abundant analysis explaining why early Paleolithic and Neolithic cultures adapted certain forms of art and technologies could earn points in the expanded core.

Answer Guide for Section II: Part C

3. Compare the cultural developments of TWO of the following early river valley civilizations.

- ✦ Shang in the Yellow or Huang He Valley
- ✦ Mesopotamia in the Tigris and Euphrates River Valleys
- ✦ Harappa in the Indus River Valley

What Does the Question Ask?

This question deals with developments relating to culture, which is a broad category for analysis. You can write an essay dealing with religion, belief systems, science, technology, art, and/or architecture. The essay also provides some choices for which river valley civilizations you can write about.

Listed below is the scoring system used to grade comparative essays; also included are guidelines and examples for how to earn each point for this question.

Has Acceptable Thesis (1 point)

- ✦ The thesis needs to correctly address both a similarity and a difference in cultural developments for two of the three civilizations.
- ✦ The thesis should appear in the first paragraph (although it may also count if it is in the conclusion).
- ✦ The thesis can be one sentence or multiple sentences.

Examples:

- ✦ Example One: Both Harappan of South Asia and Shang of East Asia used elaborate writing systems. They differed in how these writing systems were used.
- ✦ Example Two: The Shang set up tombs for their elites, whereas the civilization in the Indus River Valley focused on architecture for a broader range of their population. Both of these civilizations had elaborate structures in their cities.
- ✦ Example Three: Although little is known about the details of either civilization, both the Shang and the Harappans seemed to have complex religious philosophies. These religions differed in how they were practiced.
- ✦ Unacceptable Example: Both the Shang Dynasty and the Indus River Valley share interesting cultural similarities but differ in their governments.
  - This is an unacceptable thesis because the cultural similarity is not specific. The difference mentioned here is also a political difference and not a cultural difference called for in the question.

Addresses All Parts of the Question (2 points)

- ✦ The essay accurately addresses both a valid similarity (1 point) and a valid difference (1 point).
- ✦ The statements of comparison may not appear in the thesis.

Examples:

- ✦ Example One: Complex writing systems developed in both China and India with the first river valley civilizations. The oracle bones of China were used to foretell the future, while the seals of India were more for trade purposes.

- The first statement in the example above addresses similarity, while the second statement addresses difference.

✦ Example Two: Shang emperors were buried in luxurious tombs. Harappa, however, did not have palaces, tombs, or monuments for rulers. Both areas had monumental architecture.
  - The first statement in the example above addresses difference, while the second statement addresses similarity.

✦ Example Three: Complex religious rituals were practiced by both the Shang and Indus River peoples. However, Shang religion was based more on ancestor worship, and Indus River religion may have been more like ancient Hinduism.
  - The first statement in the example above addresses similarity, while the second statement addresses difference.

Substantiates Thesis with Appropriate Historical Evidence (2 points)

✦ A piece of historical evidence is a fact that is correct and relevant to the time period.
✦ To earn the full two points in this category, an essay should have five or more pieces of evidence.
✦ To earn only one point in this category, an essay needs three or four pieces of evidence.
✦ Points for evidence can be earned even if the thesis point is not earned.

Examples:

✦ Example One: During the Shang dynasty, the Chinese people developed the first writing system in East Asia. They would carve characters into bones and turtle shells. These were then used for predicting the future. Harappan seals were pushed into clay pottery. Although we cannot read the Harappan writing system, the seals probably represent words.
✦ Example Two: The cities of the early Indus River Valley civilization had advanced plumbing and sewage systems. One of their most impressive structures was a large pool that may have been used for bathing. Almost all of their structures were made of clay bricks. The Shang tombs had wonderful pieces of art buried with the emperors. Much of the surviving pieces from the Shang dynasty were made of bronze.
✦ Example Three: In the Shang dynasty, people focused much of their religious life on their ancestors and the emperors. They were concerned with the connection between heaven and earth. The Shang looked to art and mythology for messengers who could connect them to heaven. The Indus River people built a bathing pool that might have been used for religious purification. Some of their surviving art shows bulls, which could have been religiously symbolic.

Makes a Direct, Relevant Comparison (1 point)

✦ A direct comparison is an explicit, concrete, and factually correct statement of either similarity or difference.

Examples:

✦ Example One: The oracle bones of China and the clay seals of the Harappans both use pictographic symbols that represent words.
✦ Example Two: The surviving structures of the Indus River Valley civilization were mostly used for everyday activities. The surviving tomb structures of the Shang were meant for specific religious and political purposes.

✦ Example Three: Both the religious expressions of the Shang and Indus peoples contributed to the religious practices for later periods of Chinese and Indian cultures.

Analyzes at Least One Reason for a Similarity or Difference (1 point)

✦ Analysis explains a reason for the similarity or difference.

Examples:

✦ Example One: One reason why the writing systems differed could be that the oracle bones of China were used by the ruling elites, and the Harappan seals were used by merchants for trade purposes.
✦ Example Two: The architecture of Indus River Valley civilization differs from the Shang because the Indus society most likely did not have ruling emperors like the Shang. The social structure was flatter, so the buildings were constructed for the use of ordinary people.
✦ Example Three: Religious complexity emerged among both the Shang and Indus peoples because as early civilizations became more urbanized and sophisticated, religious elites were more likely to impose order.

Expanded Core

You must earn all seven points in the basic core before earning any points in the expanded core. Points awarded in the expanded core reflect the general excellence of the essay. Any one aspect of your essay, such as the thesis or evidence, might be particularly insightful and earn a point in the expanded core. Essays that have a high degree of analysis and historical context often earn expanded core points if they have all of the other basic core points. Clarity of organization, strong cause-effect analysis, and particularly insightful ideas can make your essay stand out as excellent.

Examples:

✦ Example One: An essay that relates the writing systems to broader issues of river valley civilization in general and to the specific structure of both the Shang and Harappan civilization could earn points in the expanded core.
✦ Example Two: Discussing specific pieces of art and multiple comparisons of their functions could earn points in the expanded core.
✦ Example Three: Providing multiple theories for the differences in religious expression between the Shang and Indus peoples could earn points in the expanded core.

Organization and Reorganization of Human Societies, c. 600 B.C.E. to c. 600 C.E.

PART TWO
Second-Wave Civilizations in World History, 500 B.C.E.–500 C.E.

AP World History Key Concepts

 2.1: **The Development and Codification of Religious and Cultural Traditions**

 2.2: **The Development of States and Empires**

 2.3: **Emergence of Transregional Networks of Communication and Exchange**

The Big Picture: After the First Civilizations: What Changed and What Didn't?

World history functions differently from other methods of studying history, partly because of the huge spans of time covered in the course and partly because of its comparative nature. *Ways of the World* uses the analogy of a camera lens zooming out to a panorama to cover large spans of time and zooming in to a middle or close view to look at some periods in more detail. Chapter 1 required the panoramic view; Chapter 2, a more mid-range view. This ability to shift "lenses" is a fundamental world history skill.

In order to consider the focus question, "After the First Civilizations: What Changed and What Didn't?" zoom out to consider the period from 3500 B.C.E. to 1750 C.E. The dominant development in this period is the spread of agriculture and civilizations based on agriculture. First-wave civilizations began the process around the globe

61

but largely in isolation from each other. Although First Civilizations developed large and complex societies, all these societies collapsed. Mesopotamian city-states were absorbed into empires (such as Babylon and Assyria). Civilizations faded in Central Asia, the Indus Valley, and Norte Chico. During the first millennium B.C.E., Egypt fell to foreign invaders, the Olmecs abandoned their cities, and the Zhou dynasty kingdom in China fragmented into warring states. However, these urban, state-based civilizations set patterns that continued to shape their regions, while new civilizations emerged in Ethiopia and West Africa, Japan, Indonesia, and Southeast Asia. Second-wave civilizations, such as the Roman Empire, Han China, and Mayan city-states, rose and eventually collapsed. Third-wave civilizations (500 to 1500 C.E.) appeared: some, such as China, re-envisioned older patterns; in other regions, such as Western Europe, Russia, Japan, and West Africa, newer civilizations emerged and borrowed from older civilizations. Civilizations continued to trade and communicate with each other and with neighboring pastoral peoples.

Identifying changes that take place between one period and another or within a period, and, at the same time, identifying enduring continuities are two of the most important historical thinking skills. Identifying continuity usually requires a panoramic lens, while observing change often requires a closer zooming in to study specific details.

Part Two focuses thematically and comparatively on second-wave era (500 B.C.E. to 500 C.E.) civilizations in Eurasia and North Africa. Chapter 3 examines political frameworks and empires; Chapter 4 analyzes and compares cultural and religious traditions; Chapter 5 compares social and gender organizations; and Chapter 6 analyzes the extent to which the development of civilizations in inner Africa and the Americas parallel those of Eurasia or offer alternative paths.

Continuities: No fundamental transformation of social or economic life took place.

- ✦ States and empires rose, expanded, and collapsed.
  - • Monarchs continued to rule most of them.
  - • Social and gender inequalities persisted, as did slavery.
- ✦ No technological breakthroughs produced new ways of organizing social or economic life.
  - • Land-owning elites saw little reason for innovation, while peasants also did not produce innovations that would profit the landowners or themselves.
  - • Merchants were dominated by the states and were often looked down on by ruling elites.

Changes: While not as transformative as the Agricultural Revolution, incremental changes altered human society in a variety of ways.

- ✦ Population grew more rapidly than in in the Paleolithic era, with interruptions for pandemic diseases.
- ✦ Second- and third-wave states were larger than those of the First Civilizations.
  - • States were more diverse.

✦ Rising and collapsing empires had consequences for the people under their dominion.

✦ Second- and third-wave civilizations generated many innovations within their spheres.
- Distinctive wisdom traditions developed, such as Confucianism and Daoism in China; Hinduism and Buddhism in South Asia; Judaism, Zoroastrianism, Christianity, and Islam in the Middle East; and the rational scientific philosophy of Greece.

✦ Technological changes allowed humans to manipulate the environment in more profound ways.
- China led the way with piston bellows, the draw-loom, silk-handling machinery, the wheelbarrow, draft harnesses for animals, the crossbow, iron casting, iron-chain suspension bridges, gunpowder and firearms, the magnetic compass, printing, paper, and porcelain.
- India produced techniques for manufacturing cotton textiles and crystallizing sugar.
- Roman achievements included building roads, bridges, aqueducts, the keystone arch, fortifications, and glassblowing.

✦ Some social hierarchies were modified.
- India's caste system became more complicated.
- Roman slaves and Chinese peasants sometimes rose in rebellion.
- Women were often less subject to restrictions at the beginnings of a civilization, but patriarchy became more intense as civilizations developed.
- Some Buddhist and Christian women found some opportunities for leadership and learning in convents.
- After the first-wave civilizations, networks of trade and communication grew more intense and far-flung.

✦ Long-distance trade routes became regional and transregional in caravan routes across northern Eurasia and the Sahara, maritime trade in the Indian Ocean, river-based commerce in the eastern woodlands of North American, and in Mesoamerica and the Andes.
- Trade routes carried goods as well as culture and religions.
- Diseases, such as the Black Death, also spread along the trade routes.

CHAPTER THREE

State and Empire in Eurasia/North Africa, 500 B.C.E.–500 C.E.

AP World History Key Concepts

2.1: The Development and Codification of Religious and Cultural Traditions

I. Codifications and further developments of existing religious traditions provided a bond among the people and an ethical code to live by.

II. New belief systems and cultural traditions emerged and spread, often asserting universal truths.

III. Belief systems affected gender roles. Buddhism and Christianity encouraged monastic life and Confucianism emphasized filial piety.

IV. Other religious and cultural traditions continued parallel to the codified, written belief systems in core civilizations.

V. Artistic expressions, including literature and drama, architecture, and sculpture, show distinctive cultural developments.

Long-distance trade flourished along the Silk Routes in northern Eurasia, the Mediterranean basin, the trans-Saharan routes, and the Indian Ocean. These networks allowed the spread of goods, technological innovations, and cultural traditions such as the "wisdom traditions" (Hinduism, Buddhism, Judaism, Zoroastrianism, and Christianity) and the rational philosophies of the Greek and Hellenistic world. *See Chapter 4 for more depth on this Key Concept.*

2.2: The Development of States and Empires

I. The number and size of key states and empires grew dramatically by imposing political unity on areas where previously there had been competing states.

II. Empires and states developed new techniques of imperial administration based, in part, on the success of earlier political forms.

III. Unique social and economic dimensions developed in imperial societies in Afro-Eurasia and the Americas.

IV. The Roman, Han, Persian, Mauryan, and Gupta empires created political, cultural, and administrative difficulties that they could not manage, which eventually led to their decline, collapse, and transformation into successor empires or states.

After the collapse of the first-wave civilizations, some new civilizations grew in the shadow of the original ones, borrowing from their earlier cultures and political systems, while new states also arose on the fringes of previous civilizations. This chapter focuses on the political development of empires in Eurasia and North Africa. You will need to know all of the following empires, as well as their locations:

- ✦ Qin and Han in China (See Map 3.5, p. 135)
- ✦ Mauryan and Gupta (See Map 3.6, p. 142)
- ✦ Greek city-states (See Map 3.2, p. 123)
- ✦ Persian (See Map 3.1, p. 121)
- ✦ Hellenistic (See Map 3.3, p. 127)
- ✦ Roman (See Map 3.4, p. 131)

The Chinese empires incorporated much of the traditions of the First Civilization in that region. Following the collapse of the original Indus Valley civilization and the migration of the Aryans to the Indian subcontinent, the Mauryan and Gupta empires arose in a politically and culturally fragmented South Asia. The Greek, Roman, and Persian cultures arose on the fringes of the old civilizations of the Fertile Crescent. All of these empires created strong militaries and administrative systems that would cope with the expanded size and multicultural nature of their conquered territories. Inevitably, these second-wave civilizations (also called classical civilizations) fell, often from a combination of invasions from peoples on the periphery of their control and internal problems they could not resolve. *See Chapter 5 for more depth on social issues in these empires and Chapter 6 for the empires outside Eurasia.*

2.3: Emergence of Transregional Networks of Communication and Exchange

I. Land and water routes became the basis for transregional trade, communication, and exchange networks in the Eastern Hemisphere.

II. New technologies facilitated long-distance communication and exchange.

III. Alongside the trade in goods, the exchange of people, technology, religious and cultural beliefs, food crops, domesticated animals, and disease pathogens developed across far-flung networks of communication and exchange.

You will need to know the long-distance trade routes: the Silk Routes in northern Eurasia, the Mediterranean basin routes, the trans-Saharan routes, and the Indian Ocean routes. Goods, technological innovations, cultural traditions, crops, and diseases spread along these new or intensified trade networks. The Roman, Chinese, and Indian empires had little direct contact but were linked loosely by trade networks. The Persians and Greeks were geographically close and engaged in direct conflict with each other. The Hellenistic empires, following the conquests by Alexander the Great, blended and spread the cultures of the old Greek territories through Egypt, the Middle East, and South Asia. The Romans later conquered much of the territory around the Mediterranean and incorporated many of the cultural traditions of Greek and blended Hellenistic cultures, which they spread in turn to Western Europe.

Theme 1: Interaction Between Humans and the Environment

Negative environmental impacts arose from the second-wave empires due to increasing populations and their exploitation of resources. More land and forests were cleared for cultivation, and the face of the land was changed by human activity. Greek cities deforested hillsides for wood to process metals, such as iron, creating erosion and thinning soil. On the other hand, the mountainous geography of the Peloponnesian peninsula meant that Greek city-states remained relatively small and diverse and did not combine to create an empire until conquered by Philip of Macedon. The Romans, Persians, and Chinese drained swamps, diverted rivers, built canals, and created aqueducts to help bring food and water to their growing cities. Mild Mediterranean climates allowed both Greeks and Romans to conduct public life outdoors in the agora or forum. Passes in the Hindu Kush mountains northwest of India allowed different groups to migrate, creating cultural and linguistic diversity and contributing to political fragmentation in the region. India enjoyed relatively brief periods of imperial rule under the Maurya and Gupta. Second-wave empires also built or expanded cities, especially as new bureaucratic and cultural centers or trade hubs, but these empires also might destroy the urban centers of conquered people (such as Carthage). The concentration of people and domesticated animals led to epidemic diseases, which also spread along the trade routes, like the plague that hit Athens during the war with Sparta. Even though population grew during this period because of more intensive agriculture, the rate of increase was slow due to disease and warfare. The fall of second-wave empires, especially in Europe, led to a decline in urban populations.

Theme 2: Development and Interaction of Cultures

The second-wave empires had a huge impact on culture. Linguistically, in some cases (like China and Rome) empires created unifying national languages. The Hellenistic empires spread Greek language and culture to the edges of India and created cultural centers such as Alexandria in Egypt. Classical Greek philosophy, literature, drama, and art influenced Rome, and through it, Western Europe. Despite many minorities and different spoken languages and dialects, China developed a common written language that enabled the government to extend its rule and laws. Rome also spread the use of Latin throughout its territories and made it the language of law and government.

Empires created monumental architecture, including palaces, temples, tombs, walls and fortifications, and public buildings, to reinforce the power and majesty of the empire. Greco-Roman temples, gymnasia, theaters, and racetracks sprang up in far-flung corners of the Hellenistic and Roman empires. China's Great Wall, which was built to keep out nomadic tribes who periodically invaded the northern part of the country, projected the power of the Qin and Han emperors, as did the construction of elaborate palaces and royal tombs. The Persians encouraged artistic, religious, and cultural expressions from their conquered peoples and, like the Hellenistic empires, created a fusion of architectural and artistic styles. Gupta rulers presided over a golden age, building temples and encouraging the study of literature, science, medicine, and mathematics (especially the number system using nine numerals and zero). *Chapter 4 will discuss the religions and wisdom traditions of classical Eurasia in more detail.*

Theme 3: State-Building, Expansion, and Conflict

This chapter focuses primarily on the techniques that second-wave empires used to conquer and consolidate territory, administer these large territories to maintain order, and extract economic gain and the internal failures that led to their collapse. The needs of empire produced some commonalities in state building, yet the different cultures and locations of the empires created some important differences. One of these differences concerned the amount of participation individuals had in their government. Greek city-states had the most direct participation of adult male citizens, followed by the Roman Republic. In contrast, Asian monarchies, such as the Persian Empire or the Qin dynasty, placed almost absolute power in the hands of the king. Romans held out the possibility of citizenship and the protection of the Roman legal system and military to encourage loyalty among conquered people. The Chinese accepted minorities who adopted Chinese language and culture. The Persian, Hellenistic, and Indian empires ruled diverse peoples with varying degrees of cultural, if not political, tolerance.

Second-wave empires created bureaucracies to administer their territories, common legal systems, and systems of taxation. Examples of bureaucratic systems included the satraps and "eyes and ears of the King" in Persia, the Han professional bureaucracy trained in royal academies, and Mauryan rule according to the *Arthashastra*, a manual for pragmatic and moral rule. Romans used a military basis for governing their empire, despite maintaining the ideals of "the Senate and people of Rome" from the days of the Republic. All empires relied on strong militaries, both to create and expand their empires and to maintain control over conquered peoples. All used architecture and art to reinforce imperial prestige. All used the support of religion to justify imperial rule: the Han Mandate of Heaven; the Roman deification of the emperor; the Persian absolute monarchy incorporating Zoroastrian imagery; and Alexander the Great allowing himself to be made a god by the Egyptians.

The second-wave civilizations in Western Europe, India, and China overextended themselves geographically for their level of technological development and became unable to effectively administer their empires. In addition, social conflict, political divisions, and financial problems also weakened second-wave civilizations. Ironically, the Huns (steppe nomads called the Huna in India and Xiongnu in China) invaded all three weakened empires. While the Gupta and Han dynasties fell, India and China changed little culturally. The Chinese culturally assimilated the nomads and relied on Confucian models to rebuild a centralized state after a period of collapse. In Western Europe, however, the advance of the Huns forced warlike Germanic tribes into the heartland of the empire. Once inside the weakened empire, these groups established small Germanic kingdoms, each with its own culture and identity, which at first controlled the Roman emperors and then eventually displaced them. Over time, the Germanic tribes adopted Christianity, and the Church played a unifying role in the hybrid civilizations that followed. However, Western Europe did not recover as a unified state.

Theme 4: Creation, Expansion, and Interaction of Economic Systems

The unification of large territories into empires promoted trade by creating roads and canals, providing uniform legal and tax codes, and creating common languages and currencies. Some empires, such as the Persian, Roman, and Chinese, fostered communication networks by creating thousands of miles of roads or canals, while also standardizing weights and measures, coinage, and tax systems. Expanded transregional trade routes, such as the Silk Routes, trans-Saharan routes, and Indian Ocean basin routes, allowed the diffusion of inventions, ideas, and goods. Some inventions, such as new saddles or harnesses, directly helped trade, as did stone bridges built by the Romans or suspension bridges built by the Chinese. The domestication of the camel created new options for crossing the Sahara or Taklamakan deserts. China was the center of much of this technological invention, including such items as the magnetic compass, gunpowder, new techniques for iron smelting, silk-handling machinery, new harnesses for draft animals, wheelbarrows, porcelain, paper, and printing. Roman innovation was largely in the area of construction and engineering, with the use of the keystone arch in bridges and aqueducts, cement, and durable roadbeds; Romans also excelled in glassblowing. India, the focus of the Indian Ocean trading system, led in the production of textiles, such as cotton, and the technology used to crystalize cane syrup into sugar crystals. With the collapse of the second-wave civilizations, long-distance trade declined.

Theme 5: Development and Transformation of Social Structures

Second-wave empires accelerated social stratification and the dominance of patriarchal gender systems. Wealth concentrated in the hands of a few, while conquered people often became slaves, driving out the small landholder. Sparta, for example, maintained a large population of helots, conquered people who lived in slave-like conditions. In some cases, the ideals of a warrior society led to increased domination of women. For example, in Rome, the masculinity of upper-class male citizens was defined in part by a man's role as a soldier; this meant that in private he exercised absolute control over his wife, children, and slaves. *Chapter 5 discusses the social consequences of classical empires in more detail.*

CHAPTER FOUR

Culture and Religion in Eurasia/North Africa, 500 B.C.E..–500 C.E.

AP World History Key Concepts

2.1: The Development and Codification of Religious and Cultural Traditions

I. Codifications and further developments of existing religious traditions provided a bond among the people and an ethical code to live by.

II. New belief systems and cultural traditions emerged and spread, often asserting universal truths.

III. Belief systems affected gender roles. Buddhism and Christianity encouraged monastic life and Confucianism emphasized filial piety.

IV. Other religious and cultural traditions continued parallel to the codified, written belief systems in core civilizations.

V. Artistic expressions, including literature and drama, architecture, and sculpture, show distinctive cultural developments.

2.3: Emergence of Transregional Networks of Communication and Exchange

III. Alongside the trade in goods, the exchange of people, technology, religious and cultural beliefs, food crops, domesticated animals, and disease pathogens developed across far-flung networks of communication and exchange.

Chapter Four zooms in on cultural developments in the second-wave or classical civilizations. Some religious traditions such as animism and polytheism, which often included female deities, persisted from earlier eras—especially in areas outside of the cities. Second-wave civilizations often modified existing traditions: Vedic traditions in India were the basis of Hinduism; the beliefs of the ancient Hebrews in the Middle East were the foundation of Judaism and Christianity (and, later, Islam); and the Mandate of Heaven and veneration of ancestors endured for centuries in China.

The period around the sixth century B.C.E. saw the seemingly unrelated development of new religious beliefs in many parts of Eurasia/North Africa, creating traditions that still influence the world today. New or reforming religious leaders include Siddhartha Gautama (the Buddha), Zarathustra, and the Hebrew prophets. Philosophical or "wisdom traditions" developed in Greece (especially Athens) and China (Confucianism, Daoism, and Legalism). These wisdom traditions tended to focus on secular concerns rather than on the divine. Buddhism, especially the historical Buddha, also focused on the enlightenment of the individual through right action and meditation instead of on the divine. Hinduism, Judaism, and Zoroastrianism all moved toward monotheism and remained associated with particular groups of people. They did not proselytize (seek converts) outside the original group. However, all three did spread by migration or through merchants to regions outside of their places of origin. Buddhism and, later, Christianity became proselytizing universal religions, spreading far beyond their origins in India and Judea respectively (see Map 4.1, p. 191). The Chinese wisdom traditions spread within China's sphere of influence in East Asia to places such as Korea, Vietnam, and Japan. The rational, logical philosophies of the Greeks spread throughout Alexander's Hellenistic Empire and were taken up by the Romans—and, later, the Arabs—with profound influences on scientific, philosophical, and political thought in the Western world and beyond. Use the Snapshot on page 168 to review the thinkers and philosophies of the second-wave era. You may also wish to add the names of the sacred literature or major works associated with each of these traditions.

Theme 1: Interaction Between Humans and the Environment

Refer to Chapter 3 for a more in-depth discussion of this theme.

Theme 2: Development and Interaction of Cultures

In Greece, an explosion of artistic and literary forms emerged in the early part of this period. In addition, Greeks assumed that through rational thought and scientific questioning humans could discover the explanation for natural phenomena instead of attributing them to the actions of divine beings. In Athens, philosophical questioning was also applied to social and political issues. The questioning and writings of Greek philosophers like Socrates, Plato, and Aristotle impacted Western thought long after Athens ceased to be independent.

The Warring States era in China led to different approaches to restoring order and tranquility. When the Qin reconstituted the empire following the Warring States era, the concept of the heavens favoring the ruler (known as the Mandate of Heaven) was already a tradition. Qin Shihuangdi, the first emperor, also adopted Han Fei's doctrine of Legalism to subdue all opposition. Legalism was based on a very negative view of humanity, featuring clear, strict laws with harsh punishments for anyone who broke the law or offended the emperor. Partly because of this harsh system, the Qin dynasty was very short-lived. The next dynasty, the Han, moved away from Legalism and adopted the philosophy of Confucius. Confucianism sought to restore the harmony of a past golden age through the governance of educated gentlemen who led through moral example and concern for their followers' well-being; the superior man demonstrated virtue and care for the inferior in the relationship, while the inferior person owed respect and obedience. Education was highly valued in China, partly because Confucius believed that humans were able to improve their moral lives through education. Later, the civil service would require rigorous examinations based on Confucian learning. The third solution to the turmoil of the Warring States period was Daoism. Its founder, Laozi, rejected the Confucian emphasis on education and service to the government. Instead, one would withdraw from the world and study the *dao*, the way of nature that governed all natural phenomena. Daoism became popular with the people, but instead of competing with each other, Daoism and Confucianism tended to be complementary.

Hinduism did not have a single founder. Like Judaism and Zoroastrianism, it was specific to a certain people and territory. The basis of religion in India was the Vedas, a collection of prayers, hymns, and rituals passed down in Brahmin families by oral tradition and later written down in Sanskrit. Brahmins were responsible for proper ritual observances, which they controlled through their knowledge of the Vedas, but dissatisfaction grew because of their exclusive control and the high fees they charged. The central philosophical concepts of Hinduism were outlined in the Upanishads. Brahman, the World Soul, was the unifying force that underlay all creation. The individual soul (*atman*) was a part of Brahman and could be reunited with the Brahman, according to the laws of *karma*, after many cycles of rebirth (reincarnation) if the individual followed pure action appropriate to his or her social station or caste. Hinduism became the underpinning of the caste system and gender inequality, as codified by the *The Laws of Manu*.

Siddhartha Gautama was the founder of Buddhism. He challenged the Brahmins' control of ritual and the caste system's control of individuals' attempts to achieve enlightenment. The core of Buddhist beliefs are found in the Four Noble Truths—essentially that suffering is inevitable, but that by ending attachment to material things and by meditation, one can achieve *nirvana* (enlightenment) in this lifetime. Buddhism became a universal religion and spread outward from India. In India itself, Buddhism gradually disappeared as it was reabsorbed into Hindu beliefs.

Around the sixth or seventh century B.C.E., Zarathustra (Zoroaster) created a monotheistic religion out of Persian polytheism. While Zoroastrianism did not become a universal religion, it had great influence on Judaism and, through it, Christianity. Zarathustra spoke of a benevolent deity, Ahura Mazda, who was in a cosmic struggle with the forces of evil. A savior would appear and, after a final judgment day, those who had aligned themselves with the forces of light would be rewarded with resurrection of the body and eternal life in paradise, while those who had aligned themselves with the evil forces of darkness would be condemned to eternal punishment.

The Hebrews worshipped one god (Yahweh) who had formed a covenant with their ancestor Abraham and had guided them out of Egypt to the Promised Land, Canaan. Yahweh was seen as the creator of the natural world, working through history and speaking directly to humans. Prophets like Isaiah and Amos helped transform rituals that were temple-based and controlled by priests into concern for social justice and moral action. Like Hinduism, the Jewish sacred text (the Torah) had first been passed down in oral tradition and was only written down after the Jews had returned to Jerusalem from captivity in Babylon. Like Hinduism and Zoroastrianism, Judaism did not become a proselytizing religion.

The founder of Christianity was Jesus, who came from a Jewish family in Roman-controlled Judea. He inherited the Jewish tradition of intense personal devotion to a single deity and its emphasis on moral action and social justice. After Jesus' death, his followers professed belief in his divinity. Paul, an early convert to Christianity, transformed Christianity from a local sect into a universal religion by his missionary activity in the eastern portion of the Roman Empire. Paul emphasized that all people, not just Jews, could follow Jesus' teachings. For the first 600 years, Christianity was predominantly found in the Asian and African portions of the Roman Empire—especially the area that is now Turkey and northern Africa. Later, the Germanic tribes in Western Europe that had defeated the western Roman Empire accepted Christianity, making it the dominant religion in Europe.

Theme 3: State-Building, Expansion, and Conflict

There are some ways in which religions and the wisdom traditions directly interacted with the state. In China, the Qin dynasty used Legalism as a way to secure rule and eliminate opposition. Confucian philosophy became the official belief of the Han dynasty and became the foundation for the civil service system that continued into the twentieth century. The Mandate of Heaven justified dynastic rule: the "heavens" approved of the ruler who behaved in the manner of a Confucian gentleman, seeing to the welfare of his people and conducting himself as a moral example. Zoroastrianism became the dominant religion of Persian kings of the Achaemenid dynasty. Judaism and, later, Christianity were persecuted by the polytheistic Roman Empire, which relied on the cult of divine caesars to legitimize Roman rule. Christianity later became the official religion of the Roman Empire, and in other areas, such as Armenia and Axum (Ethiopia). The desire to maintain a stable rule led some Roman emperors to encourage Christians to decide on one official or orthodox version among the many that arose in the first three centuries following the life of Jesus. The Eastern Empire, centered on Constantinople, rejected the supremacy of the Roman pope and developed into the Eastern Orthodox Church, which, in turn, supported the Byzantine Empire for the next 1,000 years. Pluralism and tolerance for different beliefs generally characterized India, although Emperor Ashoka converted to Buddhism and raised stupas (mound-like structures containing Buddhist relics) throughout his realm in an attempt to encourage people to follow his example. *Refer to Chapter 3 for a more in-depth discussion of this theme.*

Theme 4: Creation, Expansion, and Interaction of Economic Systems

Religions often spread along trade routes. Hinduism spread into Southeast Asia along land and sea routes. Buddhism followed later and also expanded along the Silk Road into China and East Asia. Buddhism also spurred trade in Buddhist religious artifacts and scriptures. Jewish merchants traveled along the trade routes to Asia, Europe, and Africa, especially after the destruction of Jerusalem and the Diaspora. Buddhism and Christianity, as universal religions seeking converts, profited especially from the ability to move along trade routes that were made relatively safe by the second-wave empires. *Refer to Chapter 3 for a more in-depth discussion of this theme.*

Theme 5: Development and Transformation of Social Structures

The tendency of monotheistic religions to envision God as male contributed to continued patriarchal dominance of women. The early Christian church reflected Jesus' acceptance of women in leading roles, but later conformed to prevailing patriarchal beliefs as articulated by Paul and later church fathers. Christianity and Buddhism both allowed women some autonomy in separate monastic communities, but not in secular life or religion outside the cloistered walls. In Confucian China, families were male dominated, with children (even adult children) owing filial piety toward their parents. Women were completely subservient to their fathers, husbands, and—when widowed— their sons. This view of women as subservient to male family members was shared by most of the religions of this period but was especially stringent in China and India. Even the Greek philosophers generally believed women to be inferior to men.

Religion and wisdom traditions also affected class identity. In China, the Qin favored warriors and farmers as essential to the state. The Han, shaped more by Confucian ideas, placed great emphasis on the scholar-gentry at the top of the class structure, followed by farmers who were essential to supporting the large population. Hinduism codified existing social groups into a more stringent caste system, with the Brahmins as the highest class, followed by warriors, merchants, and laborers. In contrast to the caste system in India, upward mobility was possible in China: even a peasant could, through diligent scholarship, rise to become part of the scholar-gentry class. Both Buddhism and Christianity opposed traditional class structures, so both drew significant numbers of early converts from the lower classes. Daoism was also popular among the people of China, and its philosophy underlay the Yellow Turban peasants' revolt. *Refer to Chapter 5 for a more in-depth discussion of this theme.*

CHAPTER FIVE

Society and Inequality in Eurasia/North Africa, 500 B.C.E.–500 C.E.

AP World History Key Concepts

2.1: The Development and Codification of Religious and Cultural Traditions

I. Codifications and further developments of existing religious traditions provided a bond among the people and an ethical code to live by.

II. New belief systems and cultural traditions emerged and spread, often asserting universal truths.

III. Belief systems affected gender roles. Buddhism and Christianity encouraged monastic life and Confucianism emphasized filial piety.

2.2: The Development of States and Empires

I. The number and size of key states and empires grew dramatically by imposing political unity on areas where previously there had been competing states.

II. Empires and states developed new techniques of imperial administration based, in part, on the success of earlier political forms.

IV. The Roman, Han, Persian, Mauryan, and Gupta empires created political, cultural, and administrative difficulties that they could not manage, which eventually led to their decline, collapse, and transformation into successor empires or states.

Second-wave (or classical) civilizations continued the social hierarchies and gender inequalities that arose in the First Civilizations. This chapter focuses on the different ways that empires in China, Rome, and India expressed these inequalities. The landowning classes achieved wealth by exploiting the labor of the mass population, a pattern that continued until the Industrial Revolution. Roman state religion moved from a polytheistic cult of the emperor to Christianity. Late Roman emperors ended persecutions against Christians and saw them as a group who were therefore loyal to the emperor. They chose Christians for administrative roles, even when Christians were still a minority in the empire. Two of the Eurasia civilizations suffered from rebellions of the lower classes against state control: Chinese peasants rose in the Yellow Turban Rebellion, while slaves like Spartacus rebelled against their masters in Rome. Perhaps because of strong deference to the *varnas* (four broad social groups set forth in *The Laws of Manu* and supported by Hindu beliefs), class rebellion—as opposed to regional attempts to throw off the control of the empire—was less likely in India. In addition, belief systems both supported and, in some cases, undercut the hierarchies of class and gender. For example, Confucian hierarchies and the Mandate of Heaven upheld the Han Empire, and Hinduism provided common beliefs throughout culturally diverse India, while upholding the social structure. Buddhism and Christianity cut across class and caste, holding all (males) to be equal within their beliefs. Patriarchy continued to be dominant in all three empires, with some lessening of restrictions on women in times of political crisis.

Concerning gender roles, women, such as Boudica in Britain or the Trung sisters in Vietnam, sometimes led resistance movements to both Roman and Han expansion. One woman, Empress Wu, became the ruler of China in the Tang dynasty, although her rule was such an affront to Chinese ideas about the proper role of women that no other woman was allowed to reign for centuries. Elite women were usually closely confined to the home and forbidden from assuming public roles. Again, belief systems tended to reinforce patriarchy, with women finding some small escape in Christian and Buddhist convents.

Theme 1: Interaction Between Humans and the Environment

Refer to Chapter 3 for a more in-depth discussion of this theme.

Theme 2: Development and Interaction of Cultures

Chinese scholar-gentry were often the creators of elite Chinese culture. They were highly educated and wrote books or painted nature scenes in addition to fulfilling the official duties of their positions. In Rome, slaves often held positions of teachers, artists, or scribes. Throughout second-wave civilizations, women rarely received an equal education to that of men in similar social classes. Greek city-states varied in their attitudes toward women. Sparta, for example, allowed women more freedom than Athens, but both retained patriarchy. A few exceptional women demonstrated learning and culture, such as Aspasia in Periclean Athens, but most were kept firmly inside the doors of their homes and not taught to read. Buddhism and Christianity both ignored class structure in seeking converts—a person from any class could achieve salvation or reach nirvana. All belief systems reflected strong gender biases. Women who became Christian or Buddhist nuns could, at least partially, escape from patriarchal control. *See Chapter 4 for more discussion of this theme.*

Theme 3: State-Building, Expansion, and Conflict

Slaves in all three empires most often were captured in warfare as the empire expanded. Of the three empires, only the Roman Empire based much of its economy on slave labor, leaving Rome open to frequent slave rebellions such as the Spartacus revolt. In India and China, peasants performed agricultural and other low-level labor. The Chinese state was often faced with peasant rebellions, such as the Yellow Turban Rebellion, which weakened the Han Empire. In India and Rome, warriors had relatively high prestige, but in China, scholar-gentry were favored and warriors were disdained because they did not contribute to the creation of food or goods. Occasionally, on the fringes of imperial expansion, women took leadership roles in defending their homes from Roman or Chinese conquest; but in general, women were not involved in the military or in governing. In China, state officials were chosen and promoted in rank by passing exams based on Confucian principles. Administrators in Rome came from the military and elite, but educated slaves held many lower offices. Empress Wu ruled China during the Tang dynasty, but all other rulers of these empires were male. *See Chapter 3 for more on this theme.*

Theme 4: Creation, Expansion, and Interaction of Economic Systems

Although merchants and trade were important to Qin and Han China, they were widely viewed as unproductive, greedy, and materialistic. In addition, merchants were often forced to loan large amounts of money to the state and were actively discriminated against. Neither India's nor China's economy benefitted much from slavery, unlike the Roman Empire, whose economy was based on slave labor. Slaves provided between 30 and 40 percent of the labor force, especially on the large estates (*latifundia*) and in the mines. In second-wave empires, the elites often found ways to avoid taxation, pushing the burden onto lower classes, leading to economic problems that helped destabilize the empires. Female slaves often served as domestic servants, actresses and entertainers, or simply as prostitutes. Male slaves filled a variety of roles including agricultural labor, skilled craftsmen, gladiators—even accountants, scribes, and teachers. *See Chapter 3 for more on this theme.*

Theme 5: Development and Transformation of Social Structures

All second-wave civilizations were sharply divided along class lines. Each civilization had slight differences, however. As in the First Civilizations, wealth meant access to and ownership of land. Classical China was able to offer some means of social mobility through the famous exam system. Although this system certainly favored the rich and well-connected, it was possible for intelligent young men from very limited means to rise to the level of a scholar and thus into the bureaucracy that administered the empire. Most often, the scholar-gentry class reflected the twin influences of education and wealth. The majority of people in China were peasants—some lucky enough to own their land, while others worked as tenants on large estates. Although peasants were exploited, they were lauded in official Chinese documents. Merchants, however, were often seen as unproductive and materialistic. Although there were relatively few slaves in Han China, they did exist, especially as status symbols for the wealthy.

In Mauryan and Gupta India, the caste system—the rigid, inherited hierarchy—developed over centuries. The four main groups, or varna, had religious justification and consisted of the Brahmins, priests and teachers; the Kshatriya, warriors and rulers;

Vaisya, the cultivators, merchants, or craftsmen; and the Sudras, who were laborers. Outside the caste system were the Untouchables, who performed tasks considered to be ritually polluting, such as slaughtering animals or burying the dead. These castes were divided into multiple sub-castes, known as *jatis*, which were based on occupation. There were also a small number of slaves, often criminals, debtors, or prisoners of war. Slaves did have some legal protection. Because the caste system was tied into religious beliefs about reincarnation, there was relatively little upward mobility or upheaval—in contrast to the peasant and slave revolts occurring in the other two empires. However, new migrants were incorporated into a *jati*, and entire *jati* could be upgraded into a higher caste, creating some mobility within the caste system.

In the Mediterranean region, however, slavery was common. The Greek city-states relied on slave labor, and some estimates state that 30 to 40 percent of the Roman Empire's population was slaves, mostly captured as prisoners of war. This large slave population worked the fields of the *latifundia* and competed with free laborers and craftsmen, ultimately undermining the economy and state. Romans sometimes manumitted (freed) their slaves, and slaves could save money and buy their freedom. Freed slaves could become full citizens. Members of Rome's upper class were known as patricians; they were landowners who controlled the Senate in the days of the Republic. Toward the end of the Republic, wealthy commoners could also join the elite. The widespread use of slaves severely limited the viability of artisans or other "middle" classes.

Patriarchy permeated the second-wave empires—although restrictions tended to be more pronounced in urban areas for elite women than for lower-class or rural women. In general, women were expected to be obedient to their fathers, then their husbands, and finally (as widows) to their sons. Women's subservience to men was justified by Confucian texts, Hindu religious writings (such as *The Laws of Manu*), or long-held ideals of the Greco-Roman matron. In China, women's roles fluctuated. When pastoral peoples invaded, society was in collapse, or order was threatened, women were able to expand their roles. Some, like the Empress Wu, were able to take over and rule. Within the Greek city-states, Spartan women were allowed more freedom relative to their sisters in other states, such as Athens. They married men who were closer to their own age, were expected to engage in athletics so they would have strong children, were respected for giving birth (a woman who died in labor was considered a warrior who had died in battle), and were not secluded.

CHAPTER SIX

Commonalities and Variations: Africa and the Americas, 500 B.C.E.–1200 C.E.

AP World History Key Concepts

2.1: The Development and Codification of Religious and Cultural Traditions

IV. Other religious and cultural traditions continued parallel to the codified, written belief systems in core civilizations.

V. Artistic expressions, including literature and drama, architecture, and sculpture, show distinctive cultural developments.

2.2: The Development of States and Empires

III. Unique social and economic dimensions developed in imperial societies in Afro-Eurasia and the Americas.

3.1: Expansion and Intensification of Communication and Exchange Networks

I. Improved transportation technologies and commercial practices led to an increased volume of trade, and expanded the geographical range of existing and newly active trade networks.

II. The movement of peoples caused environmental and linguistic effects.

3.2: Continuity and Innovation of State Forms and Their Interactions

I. Empires collapsed and were reconstituted; in some regions new state forms emerged.

3.3: Increased Economic Productive Capacity and Its Consequences

I. Innovations stimulated agricultural and industrial production in many regions.

Partly because the Agricultural Revolution (and its effect on population growth) began in Eurasia, the First Civilizations and their second-wave successors contained most of the population of the earth. This chapter explores both agricultural civilizations and smaller cultures that developed outside of Eurasia. Africa had significant contact with Eurasia through the Indian Ocean and Mediterranean trade routes, but the Americas developed without contact from the Afro-Eurasian world. The groups that developed urban sedentary civilizations—the Maya and Teotihuacán in Meso-america (see Map 6.2, p. 273), the Chavín, Moche, Wari, and Tiwanaku in the Andes (see Map 6.3, p. 278), Meroë and Axum in northeastern Africa (See Map 6.1, p. 266)—displayed many of the characteristics developed in First Civilizations: intensive agriculture, more complex political and religious life, monumental architecture and art, trade links with distant regions, stratified societies reflecting different specializations, and an explosion in technology. However, settled agriculture that was productive enough to support an urban population without being supplemented by hunting and foraging developed more slowly in the Americas and sub-Saharan Africa because they lacked the available grains and domesticable draft animals found in Eurasia. Some of these cultures did not share the stark social or gender hierarchies characteristic of Eurasian empires and developed their own ways of organizing agricultural villages and towns. The Bantu-speaking peoples spread their methods of agriculture, religious beliefs, and language throughout much of sub-Saharan Africa (see Map 6.1, p. 266). The Niger Valley was also the site of agricultural communities that did not turn into imperial states. In North America, the Pueblo peoples in the southwest and the mound builders in the southeast also developed agriculture and urban centers without an empire (see Map 6.4, p. 286).

Theme 1: Interaction Between Humans and the Environment

Eurasia was estimated to possess 80 percent of the population of second-wave civilizations, while Africa made up 11 percent and the Americas between 5 and 7 percent. In addition, with the exception of llamas and alpacas, draft animals were not available in either the Americas or (except by importation) in sub-Saharan Africa. This accounts for the continued use of hoes and digging sticks instead of plows in most regions (Meroë was a major exception). Metallurgy (especially iron) was also much less developed in these two areas, with Meroë and, later, West Africa being the main sites for iron technology. Ironworking caused environmental degradation as trees were cut down to provide fuel for smelters. While Meroë was blessed with sufficient rainfall to make it less dependent on irrigation agriculture, water control continued to be important in all these regions. In the Niger River delta, a group known collectively as the Bantu-speaking peoples slowly spread new agricultural techniques, domesticated animals such as cattle, and their tool-making technology southward and eastward from their ancestral home.

In Mesoamerica, civilizations such as the Maya and Teotihuacán in the Valley of Mexico relied on farming corn, chilies, beans, and squash in a variety of ecological regions from rain-forested lowlands to cold, high mountainous regions. The land was terraced, swamps were drained, mountain ridges were flattened, and water management systems developed — all in order to transform the land for intensive agriculture. Andean cultures also adapted to a wide variety of ecological regions, including high plateaus and mountains where potatoes and llamas were raised; mid-level valleys where crops such as cotton and food crops like maize, chilies, and cacao grew; and coastal regions that relied on fishing and bird guano (excrement) as fertilizer for crops. Farmers developed a raised-field system to drain water away from crops in swampy areas and dug canals that controlled rain water or snow melt from the mountains. In contrast to the urban civilizations of Mesoamerica and the Andes, most North American cultures were semi-sedentary. The mound builders (Hopewell culture) in eastern North America developed agriculture independently and relied on crops such as sunflower seeds, sumpweed, goosefoot, gourds, and squash for part of their staple food, augmented by hunting and gathering. Around 900 C.E., maize-based agriculture arrived from Mexico and allowed for larger settlements, such as Cahokia. Maize agriculture, supplemented by squash and beans, also reached the Pueblo people where it allowed for a very sudden rise in permanent villages in the deserts of the Southwest. Agricultural civilizations in the Americas and the Nile Valley struggled to cope with changes in climate (such as prolonged drought), deforestation, and soil exhaustion from over-farming, which hastened their demise.

Theme 2: Development and Interaction of Cultures

Many capital cities of these civilizations continued the pattern of monumental architecture and royal tomb art, which exemplified the power of the rulers. Meroë, in contact with Egyptian civilization up the Nile River, created monumental architecture like tombs, pyramids, and sculptures and was ruled by sacred monarchs. The kingdom of Axum created huge obelisks and adopted Coptic Christianity in the 400s. Their successor state, Ethiopia, continued to be a predominantly Christian country, even though Islam was sweeping the region. Bantu-speaking people spread their language, ancestor veneration, dancing, drum music, and respect for women as agricultural workers throughout much of sub-Saharan Africa. The people of Jenne-jeno produced elaborate masks and statues representing ancestral spirits.

In both Mesoamerica and Andean America, temple architecture, accurate solar calendars, complex mathematics, and ritual sacrifices performed by priests and sacred kings were important. The Hopewell culture was characterized by large earth mounds; some of them appear to be burial mounds, while others might have astronomical purposes. In the southwest, sunken houses and kivas (sunken religious spaces) were surrounded by multi-storied, interconnected, aboveground structures known as pueblos. While the Mesoamericans developed writing (the Maya used both glyphs and syllabic symbols), none of the other peoples in the Americas did. In the Andean region, the Chavín created a pan-Andean religious movement that became the basis for later civilizations. Moche warrior-priests performed shamanistic rituals and ruled a region along the northern coast of modern Peru. Tombs of the warrior-elite contained great riches and beautiful artifacts. Wari and Tiwanaku shared a cult of an Andean Staff God.

Theme 3: State-Building, Expansion, and Conflict

Civilizations in Sub-Saharan Africa and the Americas were not as large as those in Afro-Eurasia, but they nevertheless controlled quite a bit of territory. Teotihuacán, for example, controlled an area of around 10,000 square miles and over 100,000 people. In the Andean regions, several successive civilizations arose, such as the Chavín and Moche along the coast, and the Wari and Tiwanaku in the Andes. Later civilizations, such as the Inca, built on the administrative and military techniques their predecessors established. Meroë and Axum, linked in trade with the Eurasian empires, developed their own strong states in northeastern Africa. Meroë was ruled by sacred kings (and queens) similar to the pharaohs of Egypt. Axum, on the Horn of Africa, was built on controlling trade with Rome and the Indian Ocean trade routes. Monumental architecture, such as obelisks, reinforced the grandeur of these kings. In contrast, some civilizations, such as the Maya, existed as separate city-states that fought each other for prisoners to sacrifice in religious rituals. Archeology at Jenne-jeno in the Niger River region reveals central towns surrounded by smaller villages dedicated to specific crafts (such as iron smelting), which also did not unite into larger empires.

Theme 4: Creation, Expansion, and Interaction of Economic Systems

Each of these civilizations relied on agriculture and trade for economic success. The kingdom of Axum relied on very efficient plow-based agriculture, unlike the majority of sub-Saharan Africa that relied on hoes and digging sticks. Axum controlled the trade between the Indian Ocean ports along the African coast and the African interior by controlling Adulis, the largest port on the east African coast. Smaller civilizations such as the city-states along the Niger River valley flourished in small clusters of villages devoted to special economic activities such as ironsmiths, cotton weavers, leather workers, and potters. All three non-traditional second-wave civilizations—the mound builders, the pueblo, and the Bantu—seem to have traded over a large region for luxury items such as feathers, precious stones, animal hides, and ivory. The Bantu appear to have incorporated sugarcane and bananas from Indonesia and ironworking from the north (likely Meroë/Axum). The domestication of the camel allowed greater movement of trade goods across the Sahara. Mesoamericans had guilds of merchant traders who carried luxury goods from the hinterland and between cities by canoe and foot. Burial mounds in the Hopewell culture show evidence of trade goods coming from as far away as Yellowstone, the Gulf of Mexico, and the Great Lakes. Pueblo people traded with Mexico along the turquoise road. In the Andes, the Wari and Tiwanaku created roads where llama caravans allowed goods to be traded between regions.

Theme 5: Development and Transformation of Social Structures

Urban civilizations in these more remote areas continued the pattern of Eurasian empires, with stratified social classes consisting of ruling elites (often ruling as shamanistic mediators between humans and the gods), merchants, skilled artisans, servants, agricultural laborers, and slaves. However, Jenne-jeno in West Africa and the Bantu-speaking peoples did not seem to have major differences in wealth (and, we assume, social classes). Sub-Saharan Africa also seems to have been less sharply patriarchal than Eurasia. Meroë had at least ten women who ruled in their own right and, unlike Egypt, were portrayed as women and not as men (as Hatshepsut had been). Bantu-speaking people believed in separate spheres for men and women, but valued both; women continued to be respected as the primary agricultural workers, while men continued as hunters and warriors. The elite of Mesoamerica and Andean America were thought to be divine, similar to beliefs in Meroë.

PRACTICE EXAM 2

WORLD HISTORY
SECTION I

Note: This exam uses the chronological designations B.C.E. (before the common era) and C.E. (common era). These labels correspond to B.C. (before Christ) and A.D. (anno Domini), which are used in some world history textbooks.

TIME — 40 Minutes
50 Questions

Directions: Each of the questions or incomplete statements below is followed by four suggested answers or completions. Select the one that is best in each case.

1. Which of the following gave Indian civilization a distinctively unique identity and character NOT found in other second-wave civilizations?
    (A)   The tribute system
    (B)   The devshirme system
    (C)   The caste system
    (D)   The civil service

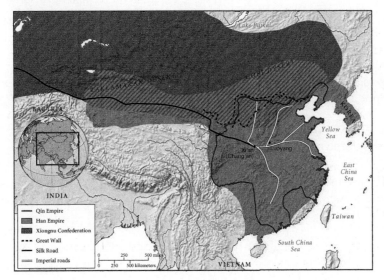

Questions 2–5 are based on Map 3.5.

2. What was the most likely purpose of the Great Wall depicted in Map 3.5?
    (A)   To keep the Xiongnu and other nomadic peoples from the northern steppes out of China
    (B)   To keep the Chinese from conquering the northern steppes in Central Asia
    (C)   To honor the emperors of the Qin and Han dynasties
    (D)   To protect travelers and merchants along the Silk Road

GO ON TO THE NEXT PAGE.

3. Map 3.5 suggests that the city of Xi'an (previously known as Chang'an) was an important center of

 (A) warfare
 (B) defense
 (C) religion
 (D) commerce

4. Map 3.5 suggests that Chinese expansion northwards was checked by the

 (A) lack of infrastructure
 (B) bandits along the Silk Road
 (C) Xiongnu Confederation
 (D) Qin and Han empires

5. Which of the following, shown in Map 3.5, highlights one way in which the Chinese state sought to establish centralized control over its territory?

 (A) Xiongnu Confederation
 (B) Great Wall
 (C) Silk Road
 (D) Imperial roads

Questions 6–7 are based on the following quote:

> It is true that we are called a democracy, for the administration is in the hands of the many and not of the few.
>
> *Pericles, a funeral oration delivered c. 430 B.C.E.*

6. In the quote above, Pericles is describing the government of

 (A) Athens
 (B) India
 (C) Persia
 (D) Sparta

7. Which of the following would weaken Pericles' claim that "the administration is in the hands of the many and not of the few"?

 (A) The extension of access to public office to a wider group of men
 (B) The exclusion of women, slaves, and foreigners from citizenship
 (C) The participation of all citizens in the Assembly
 (D) The compensation paid to all who held public office

8. The logging industry in Han dynasty China and the smelting of metals in the second-wave civilizations of Rome and Greece both led to

 (A) intensive agriculture
 (B) extensive deforestation
 (C) private industrialization
 (D) massive construction

GO ON TO THE NEXT PAGE.

9. Which of the following was a feature of both the classical Greek intellectual tradition and Confucian thought in China?

   (A) Mythology
   (B) Mysticism
   (C) Secularism
   (D) Superstition

10. Which of the following characteristics reflect the influence of Daoism on Chinese culture?

    (A) Landscape paintings showing tiny human figures dwarfed by the vastness of nature
    (B) The importance placed on the moral example of superiors
    (C) The belief in reincarnation
    (D) The emphasis on education

11. Which of the following was a new feature that was incorporated into Buddhism as it spread?

    (A) The paired concepts of *wen* and *wu*
    (B) The goal of achieving nirvana through self-effort
    (C) The belief in various levels of heavens and hells
    (D) The idea of a cosmic struggle between good and evil

12. Over the course of the two and a half millennia from 1500 B.C.E. to 1000 C.E., the religious traditions of South Asia that evolved into Hinduism featured all of the following EXCEPT

    (A) monotheistic belief
    (B) ritual sacrifice
    (C) philosophical speculation
    (D) devotional worship

13. Which of the following contributed to the preservation of Greek learning in the centuries following the fall of the Roman Empire?

    (A) The incorporation of the works of Socrates, Plato, and Aristotle into Christian doctrine
    (B) The cultural synthesis of Greek drama with Indian works of literature in the bhakti movement
    (C) The translations of Greek works of science and philosophy into Arabic in the Islamic world
    (D) The military conquests of Alexander the Great that initiated the Hellenistic era

14. Popular forms of all of the following religious traditions appealed to women and the lower classes EXCEPT

    (A) Buddhism
    (B) Daoism
    (C) Hinduism
    (D) Legalism

GO ON TO THE NEXT PAGE.

15. All of the following reflect the influence of Confucianism on China EXCEPT the

    (A) civil service examination system
    (B) preoccupation with the supernatural
    (C) view of the family as a miniature state
    (D) link between filial piety and political loyalty

16. Which of the following teachings of the Buddha would a Hindu find the most difficult to accept?

    (A) A person's caste has no effect on one's chances of attaining nirvana.
    (B) One should seek to overcome the incessant demands of the ego.
    (C) The practice of meditation offers a way to spiritual enlightenment.
    (D) The ultimate goal is to be released from the cycle of rebirth.

17. Which of the following reflects how Hinduism changed in response to the challenges posed by the emergence of Buddhism?

    (A) The idea of monotheism that gained widespread popularity and state support
    (B) The commitment to social equality that led to the abolition of the caste system
    (C) The belief that detached performance of caste duties provided a path to liberation
    (D) The view that human reason alone offered the means to understanding the world

18. Which of the following identifies a similarity between Buddhism and Christianity?

    (A) Both offered an alternative vision that rejected all existing religions.
    (B) Both emphasized belief based on reason rather than faith.
    (C) Both promoted political engagement as a path to spiritual enlightenment.
    (D) Both began as efforts to reform an existing religious tradition.

19. Which of the following reflects a Zoroastrian idea that was later incorporated into Judaism, Christianity, and Islam?

    (A) Hope for the arrival of a savior
    (B) Notions of rebirth and karma
    (C) The ultimate goal of liberation or moksha
    (D) The abandonment of education

20. What did Jesus of Nazareth, Siddhartha Gautama, and Muhammad Ibn Abdullah all share in common?

    (A) They were the historical founders of major world religions.
    (B) They introduced monotheism into their respective homelands.
    (C) They assumed roles as religious, political, and military leaders.
    (D) They claimed to be sons of God carrying God's message to humanity.

21. The earliest recorded Christian church building was located in what is today Syria. What does this suggest about early Christianity?

    (A) Jesus spent most of his time in the Middle East doing missionary work.
    (B) Christianity was a European-centered religion from the outset.
    (C) Most Christians lived in the non-European regions of the Roman Empire.
    (D) The earliest language of the Christian liturgy was Latin.

GO ON TO THE NEXT PAGE.

22. Which of the following philosophical traditions reflects a secular outlook?
    (A) Confucianism
    (B) Daoism
    (C) Zoroastrianism
    (D) Buddhism

23. In China, the practice of ancestor veneration was reinforced by the Confucian emphasis on
    (A) spiritual enlightenment
    (B) political disengagement
    (C) self-cultivation
    (D) filial piety

24. Which of the following describes a feature common to both Hinduism and Judaism?
    (A) Both disappeared from the land of their birth.
    (B) Both are associated with a particular group of people.
    (C) Both had historical founders.
    (D) Both are monotheistic religions.

25. All of the following have been identified as reasons why India, unlike many other second-wave civilizations, did not experience long periods of imperial rule EXCEPT the
    (A) absence of empires in India
    (B) cultural diversity of South Asia
    (C) frequent invasions from Central Asia
    (D) local loyalties to one's caste

26. All of the following reflect features of the infrastructure developed by the Persian Empire under the Achaemenid dynasty that would serve as a model for later states in the region EXCEPT the
    (A) levying of predictable taxes on each province
    (B) establishment of the imperial courier service
    (C) creation of the civil service examination system
    (D) construction of canals and roads

27. All of the following have contributed to peasant rebellions throughout Chinese history EXCEPT
    (A) natural disasters
    (B) high taxes and rents
    (C) state demands for labor
    (D) exemptions from military service

28. Which of the following justified and strengthened the caste system in India?
    (A) Hindu notions of karma, dharma, and rebirth
    (B) Buddhist notions of nirvana and enlightenment
    (C) Confucian notions of propriety and ritual
    (D) Daoist notions of the supernatural and immortality

GO ON TO THE NEXT PAGE.

29. Historians point to all the following as evidence of considerable social flux in the caste system in ancient Indian history EXCEPT the

   (A) assimilation of tribal peoples into the Brahmin and Kshatriya castes
   (B) theory that the castes were formed from the body of the god Purusha
   (C) inclusion of tribal medicine men and sorcerers as Brahmins
   (D) evolution of the Vaisya caste from cultivators to merchants

30. All of the following have been identified by scholars as providing the inspiration for the practice of slavery EXCEPT the

   (A) taming of animals
   (B) acquisition of women as concubines
   (C) capture of prisoners of war
   (D) campaigns against infidels

31. The practice of slavery was most widespread in which second-wave civilization?

   (A) Gupta Empire
   (B) Mauryan Empire
   (C) Roman Empire
   (D) Han dynasty China

32. In contrast to the social hierarchies of other second-wave civilizations, India's was the only one that was based on

   (A) notions of ritual purity
   (B) the civil service examination system
   (C) racially based views of outsiders as barbarians
   (D) landownership

33. "Most often, patriarchies were lighter and less restrictive for women in the early years of a civilization's development. . . ."

   Robert Strayer, world historian, 2012

   Which of the following offers evidence to support the above interpretation?

   (A) The participation of Vedic women in religious sacrifices
   (B) The writings of Ban Zhao explaining women's roles
   (C) The emergence of Neo-Confucianism in Song China
   (D) The writings of Greek thinkers like Aristotle

34. The Greek philosopher Aristotle stated, "A woman is, as it were, an infertile male. She is female in fact on account of a kind of inadequacy."

   Which of the following reflects the same view expressed by Aristotle?

   (A) The Daoist perspective on relations between men and women that emphasized complementarity and balance
   (B) The argument made in *The Laws of Manu* that all embryos are male and only weak semen produce female babies
   (C) The interpretation of Venus figurines as connecting the cycles of female fertility to the regeneration of life
   (D) The Legalist view that a uniform set of laws and a system of rewards and punishments was the basis of political control

GO ON TO THE NEXT PAGE.

35. How did slavery come to an end in the Greco-Roman world in the era of the second-wave civilizations?

    (A) Abolitionist movements gained momentum.
    (B) Industrialization made slave labor unnecessary.
    (C) Slavery was seen as incompatible with Christianity.
    (D) Slavery gradually transitioned to serfdom.

36. What new possibility did Christianity and Buddhism open up for some female converts?

    (A) Women assumed positions of leadership in the upper echelons of the church hierarchy.
    (B) Women identified as the most devout and selfless could own and inherit church lands.
    (C) Women who entered convents enjoyed some freedom from patriarchal control.
    (D) Women who married members of the clergy could preach to their own followers.

37. All of the following reflect how elite status in classical civilizations was gendered EXCEPT the

    (A) belief that women and men are born equal in the state of nature
    (B) exclusion of women from the civil service examination system in China
    (C) limitation of political office to men in the Roman Empire and Athens
    (D) seclusion of upper-class women in the private space of the home

38. "In childhood a female must be subject to her father, in youth to her husband, when her lord is dead to her sons; a woman must never be independent."

    The Laws of Manu, India, 200 B.C.E.–200 C.E.

    Which of the following reflects the same idea expressed in the above quote?

    (A) The *Epic of Gilgamesh*
    (B) The code of bushido
    (C) The "Pillars of Islam"
    (D) The "three obediences"

39. All of the following reflect similarities between China's civil service examination system and India's caste system EXCEPT the

    (A) maintenance of a social hierarchy that lasted for millennia
    (B) emphasis on equality in class and gender relations
    (C) invocation of universally accepted ideas to justify inequalities
    (D) promise of illusion of mobility within a rigid social hierarchy

GO ON TO THE NEXT PAGE.

Questions 40–41 are based on Visual Source 5.4, which shows a shrine from the Roman Empire in the first century C.E.

40. Which of the following offers an interpretation of the imagery in Visual Source 5.4 that would suggest that early Romans practiced ancestor veneration?

    (A) The three figures represent Apollo, Venus, and Jupiter.
    (B) The figures represent the emperor flanked by his two high priests.
    (C) The central figure represents the spirit of the male head of household.
    (D) The scene depicts the initiation rites associated with the cult of Dionysus.

41. Where would a shrine like the one shown in Visual Source 5.4 most likely be found in the Roman Empire in the first century C.E.?

    (A) In a wall niche in someone's home
    (B) In the altar of a Christian church
    (C) In a temple devoted to the imperial cult
    (D) In a tavern catering to the lower classes

42. The societies that emerged in the Chaco canyon region and the Mississippi valley in the ninth century were both sustained by the corn-based agriculture introduced from

    (A) the Andes region
    (B) Central Asia
    (C) Eurasia
    (D) Mesoamerica

43. All of the following reflect the effect of the vertical environment of the Andes region on the Wari and Tiwanaku empires that flourished between the fifth and eleventh centuries EXCEPT the

    (A) establishment of colonies at lower elevations by both empires
    (B) control over a continuous band of territory in both empires
    (C) Wari system of hillside terracing using snow melt from the Andes
    (D) Tiwanaku system of raised fields separated by irrigation canals

GO ON TO THE NEXT PAGE.

44. The societies referred to as the Mound Builders by archeologists left behind large earthen mounds that cover which region?

(A) Mesoamerica
(B) Andes Mountains
(C) The area east of the Mississippi River in North America
(D) The area along the Amazon River in South America

45. Which of the following provides evidence of contact between northeastern Africa and the Mediterranean world during the age of second-wave civilizations?

(A) A statue of the Roman emperor Augustus in Meroë
(B) A statue from Jenne-jeno in the Niger Valley
(C) The depictions of jaguars and snakes in Chavín artwork
(D) The corn-based agriculture of the Bantu migrants

46. Shamans were powerful leaders in all of the following societies EXCEPT

(A) Maya
(B) Chavín
(C) Moche
(D) Axum

47. Which of the following resulted from the spread of wheat and olives throughout the North African coastal region during the centuries it was under Roman rule?

(A) The wars between Meroë and Axum for control of trade routes
(B) The emergence of large estates based on slave labor
(C) The spread of agriculture throughout sub-Saharan Africa
(D) The rise of the Bantu peoples as the dominant group in North Africa

48. Which of the following cities operated as an important transshipment point in the long-distance commerce of West Africa between 300 B.C.E. and 900 C.E.?

(A) Carthage
(B) Ghat
(C) Jenne-jeno
(D) Taghaza

49. Which of the following was a central feature of Bantu religion that influenced the cultural traditions of sub-Saharan Africa?

(A) Ancestor veneration
(B) Religious monotheism
(C) Missionary zeal
(D) Secular universalism

50. Scholars use all of the following in their study of people who left behind no written record EXCEPT

(A) linguistic similarities
(B) geometric earthworks
(C) changes to the geographical landscape
(D) literature, poetry, and drama

STOP

END OF SECTION I

WORLD HISTORY
SECTION II

Part A
(Suggested writing time — 40 minutes)
Percent of Section II Score — 33 1/3

Directions: The following question is based on the accompanying Documents 1–7. (The documents have been edited for the purpose of this exercise.)

This question is designed to test your ability to work with and understand historical documents.

Write an essay that:

✦ Has a relevant thesis and supports that thesis with evidence from the documents.
✦ Uses all of the documents.
✦ Analyzes the documents by grouping them in as many appropriate ways as possible. Does not simply summarize the documents individually.
✦ Takes into account the sources of the documents and analyzes the authors' points of view.
✦ Identifies and explains the need for at least one additional type of document.

You may refer to relevant historical information not mentioned in the documents.

1. Using the following documents, analyze the methods employed by ancient empires to exert political power before 600 C.E. Identify an additional type of document and explain how it would help your analysis of these empires.

GO ON TO THE NEXT PAGE.

Document 1

Source: Greek historian Herodotus, 5th century B.C.E.

Of nations, [the Persians] . . . look upon themselves as very greatly superior in all respects to the rest of mankind, regarding others as approaching to excellence in proportion as they dwell nearer to them; whence it comes to pass that those who are the farthest off must be the most degraded of mankind. [Prior to the Persians,] the several nations of the [Median] Empire exercised authority over each other in this order. The Medes were lords over all, and governed the nations upon their borders, who in their turn governed the States beyond, who likewise bore rule over the nations which adjoined on them. And this is the order which the Persians also follow in their distribution of honor; for that people, like the Medes, has a progressive scale of administration and government.

There is no nation which so readily adopts foreign customs as the Persians. Thus, they have taken the dress of the Medes, considering it superior to their own; and in war they wear the Egyptian breastplate. As soon as they hear of any luxury, they instantly make it their own. . . . Next to prowess in arms, it is regarded as the greatest proof of manly excellence to be the father of many sons. Every year the king sends rich gifts to the man who can show the largest number: for they hold that number is strength. Their sons are carefully instructed from their fifth to their twentieth year, in three things alone—to ride, to draw the bow, and to speak the truth.

Document 2

Source: Pericles, Greek political leader and general of Athens and the Delian League, "Funeral Oration," 5th century B.C.E.

Our form of government does not enter into rivalry with the institutions of others. We do not copy our neighbors, but are an example to them. It is true that we are called a democracy, for the administration is in the hands of the many and not of the few. But while the law secures equal justice to all alike in their private disputes, the claim of excellence is also recognized; and when a citizen is in any way distinguished, he is preferred to the public service, not as a matter of privilege, but as the reward of merit. . . . A spirit of reverence pervades our public acts; we are prevented from doing wrong by respect for the authorities and for the laws. . . .

Because of the greatness of our city the fruits of the whole earth flow in upon us; so that we enjoy the goods of other countries as freely as of our own. . . .

Then, again, our military training is in many respects superior to that of our adversaries. . . .

For we have compelled every land and every sea to open a path for our valor, and have everywhere planted eternal memorials of our friendship and of our enmity. Such is the city for whose sake these men nobly fought and died; they could not bear the thought that she might be taken from them; and every one of us who survive should gladly toil on her behalf.

GO ON TO THE NEXT PAGE.

Document 3

Source: Han Fei, expressing Legalist philosophy, which was adopted as a doctrine of rule by Emperor Shihuangdi of Qin dynasty China in the 3rd century B.C.E.

Any ruler able to expel private crookedness and uphold public law, finds the people safe and the state in order; and any ruler able to expunge private action and act on public law, finds his army strong and his enemy weak. So, find out men following the discipline of laws and regulations, and place them above the body of officials. . . .

The law does not fawn on the noble. . . . Punishment for fault never skips ministers, reward for good never misses commoners. Therefore, to correct the faults of the high, to rebuke the vices of the low, to suppress disorders, to decide against mistakes, to subdue the arrogant, to straighten the crooked, and to unify the folk-ways of the masses, nothing could match the law. . . .

If rewards are high then what the ruler wants will be quickly effected; if punishments are heavy, what he does not want will be swiftly prevented. . . .

The means whereby the intelligent ruler controls his ministers are two handles only. The two handles are chastisement and commendation. What are meant by chastisement and commendation? To inflict death or torture upon culprits is called chastisement; to bestow encouragements or rewards on men of merit is called commendation.

GO ON TO THE NEXT PAGE.

Document 4

Source: Emperor Ashoka, Mauryan dynasty in India, from stone inscriptions called the "Rock Edicts," 3rd century B.C.E.

Beloved-of-the-Gods*, [Ashoka] conquered the Kalingas eight years after his coronation. One hundred and fifty thousand were deported, one hundred thousand were killed and many more died [from other causes]. After the Kalingas had been conquered, Beloved-of-the-Gods came to feel a strong inclination towards the Dhamma** [the teachings of Buddha], a love for the Dhamma and for instruction in Dhamma. Now Beloved-of-the-Gods feels deep remorse for having conquered the Kalingas. . . . Indeed, Beloved-of-the-Gods is deeply pained by the killing, dying and deportation that take place when an unconquered country is conquered. . . .

Now it is conquest by Dhamma that Beloved-of-the-Gods considers to be the best conquest. . . . I have had this Dhamma edict written so that my sons and great-grandsons may not consider making new conquests, or that . . . they consider making conquest by Dhamma only, for that bears fruit in this world and the next. . . .

Along roads I have had banyan trees planted so that they can give shade to animals and men, and I have had mango groves planted. At intervals . . . I have had wells dug, rest-houses built, and in various places, I have had watering-places made for the use of animals and men. . . .

Judicial officers in the city are to be told this: I wish to see that everything I consider to be proper is carried out in the right way. And I consider instructing you to be the best way of accomplishing this. I have placed you over many thousands of people that you may win the people's affection. . . . All men are my children. What I desire for my own children, and I desire their welfare and happiness both in this world and the next, that I desire for all men. . . . You must attend to this matter. While being completely law-abiding, some people are imprisoned, treated harshly and even killed without cause so that many people suffer. Therefore your aim should be to act with impartiality. It is because of these things—envy, anger, cruelty, hate, indifference, laziness or tiredness—that such a thing does not happen. Therefore your aim should be: "May these things not be in me." And the root of this is non-anger and patience. Those who are bored with the administration of justice will not be promoted; [those who are not] will move upwards and be promoted. . . .

That the judicial officers of the city may strive to do their duty and that the people under them might not suffer unjust imprisonment or harsh treatment. To achieve this, I will send out Mahamatras every five years who are not harsh or cruel, but who are merciful and who can ascertain if the judicial officers have understood my purpose and are acting according to my instructions.

*Ashoka is referred to as "Beloved-of-the-Gods."
**"Dhamma" is used here to signify "the teachings of Buddha."

GO ON TO THE NEXT PAGE.

Document 5

Source: Qin Emperor Shihuangdi ordered the carving of this stone inscription, which was set in a tower on Mount Langya in the 3rd century B.C.E.

A new age is inaugurated by the Emperor;
Rules and measures are rectified. . . .
Great are the Emperor's achievements,
Men attend diligently to basic tasks,
Farming is encouraged, secondary pursuit discouraged,
All the common people prosper;
All men under the sky
Toil with a single purpose;
Tools and measures are made uniform,
The written script is standardized;
Wherever the sun and moon shine,
Wherever one can go by boat or by carriage,
Men carry out their orders
And satisfy their desires;
For our Emperor in accordance with the time
Has regulated local customs,
Made waterways and divided up the land. . . .
He defines the laws, leaving nothing in doubt,
Making known what is forbidden.
The local officials have their duties,
Administration is smoothly carried out,
All is done correctly, all according to plan. . . .
Great is the virtue of our Emperor
Who pacifies all four corners of the earth,
Who punishes traitors, roots out evil men,
And with profitable measures brings prosperity. . . .
The universe entire
Is our Emperor's realm,
Extending west to the Desert,
South to where the houses face north,
East to the East Ocean,
North to beyond Dahsia;
Wherever human life is found. . . .

GO ON TO THE NEXT PAGE.

Document 6

Source: *The Analects*, as compiled by students of Confucius and expressive of the ruling philosophy of Han dynasty China starting in the 3rd century B.C.E.

The Master said, "To rule a country of a thousand chariots, there must be reverent attention to business, and sincerity; economy in expenditure, and love for men; and the employment of the people at the proper seasons."

The Master said, "He who exercises government by means of his virtue may be compared to the north polar star, which keeps its place and all the stars turn toward it."

The Master said, "If the people be led by laws, and uniformity sought to be given them by punishments, they will try to avoid the punishment, but have no sense of shame. If they be led by virtue, and uniformity sought to be given them by the rules of propriety, they will have the sense of shame, and moreover will become good."

Chi K'ang asked Confucius about government. Confucius replied, "To govern means to rectify. If you lead on the people with correctness, who will dare not to be correct?"

"Truly, if the ruler is not a ruler, the subject not a subject, the father not a father, the son not a son, then even if there be grain, would I get to eat it?"

Document 7

Source: Aelius Aristides, Greek-speaking Roman citizen from Smyrna in Anatolia, delivered "The Roman Oration" before the Roman emperor, 2nd century C.E.

Here is brought from every land and sea all the crops of the seasons and the produce of each land, river and lake. . . . So many merchant ships arrive here . . . that the city is like a factory common to the whole earth. It is possible to see so many cargoes from India and even from [southern] Arabia. . . . Your farmlands are Egypt, Sicily, and all of [North] Africa which is cultivated. The arrival and departure of ships never stops. . . .

You have divided into two parts all the men of your empire . . . and everywhere you have made citizens all those who are the more accomplished, noble, and powerful people, even if they retain their native affinities, while the remainder you have made subjects and the governed. . . . You have divided people into Romans [citizens] and non-Romans [subjects]. . . . [T]he most important and powerful people in each place guard their countries for you. . . .

And the whole inhabited world, as it were attending a national festival, has laid aside. . . . the carrying of weapons and has turned . . . to adornments and all kinds of pleasures. . . . Everything is full of gymnasiums, fountains, gateways, temples, handicrafts, and schools . . . and a boundless number of games. . . .

END OF PART A

WORLD HISTORY
SECTION II

Part B
(Suggested planning and writing time—40 minutes)
Percent of Section II score—33 1/3

Directions: You are to answer the following question. You should spend 5 minutes organizing or outlining your essay.

Write an essay that:

+ Has a relevant thesis and supports that thesis with appropriate historical evidence.
+ Addresses all parts of the question.
+ Uses world historical context to show continuities and changes over time.
+ Analyzes the process of continuity and change over time.

2. Analyze the continuities and changes in the roles of urban centers from circa 600 B.C.E. to 600 C.E. Be sure to include evidence from specific cities in your analysis of the roles of urban centers.

END OF PART B

WORLD HISTORY
SECTION II

Part C
(Suggested planning and writing time—40 minutes)
Percent of Section II score—33 1/3

Directions: You are to answer the following question. You should spend 5 minutes organizing or outlining your essay.

Write an essay that:

- Has a relevant thesis and supports that thesis with appropriate historical evidence.
- Addresses all parts of the question.
- Makes direct, relevant comparisons.
- Analyzes relevant reasons for similarities and differences.

3. Compare the effect on social structures of TWO of the following religious systems before 600 C.E.

- Hinduism
- Confucianism
- Buddhism
- Christianity

STOP

END OF EXAM

Answer Key for Practice Exam 2

Answers for Section I:
Multiple-Choice Questions

1. C	14. D	27. D	40. C
2. A	15. B	28. A	41. A
3. D	16. A	29. B	42. D
4. C	17. C	30. D	43. B
5. D	18. D	31. C	44. C
6. A	19. A	32. A	45. A
7. B	20. A	33. A	46. D
8. B	21. C	34. B	47. B
9. C	22. A	35. D	48. C
10. A	23. D	36. C	49. A
11. C	24. B	37. A	50. D
12. A	25. A	38. D	
13. C	26. C	39. B	

Rationales:

1. Answer: C

   Explanation: Although other civilizations had social hierarchies, the caste system in India was unique in a variety of ways. Indian society was organized into four castes. People remained permanently in the caste they were born in. Caste identity determined employment, marriage, and residency, among many other things.

   Page Reference: pp. 141, 225

KEY CONCEPT	THEME	SKILL
2.2.III.B	5: Development and Transformation of Social Structures.	Comparison

2. Answer: A

   Explanation: Construction of the Great Wall began in the Qin dynasty. Its purpose was to keep out northern "barbarians" like the Xiongnu, who posed a constant threat to the security of subsequent Chinese dynasties.

   Page Reference: pp. 135, 139

KEY CONCEPT	THEME	SKILL
2.2.IV.B	3: State-Building, Expansion, and Conflict.	Contextualization Interpretation

3. Answer: D

   Explanation: The map shows that the city of Xi'an/Chang'an was the point of origin of the Silk Road that traversed most of Central Asia. The Silk Road was the major land route in long-distance trade networks. An imperial road also passed through the city. It would be reasonable to infer that the city's location at the cross-roads of the Silk Road and an imperial road made it an important commercial hub.

Page Reference: p. 135

KEY CONCEPT	THEME	SKILL
2.2.III.A	4: Creation, Expansion, and Interaction of Economic Systems.	Interpretation

4.   Answer: C

Explanation: The presence of the Xiongnu Confederation effectively blocked Chinese expansion northwards. Although China launched intermittent military campaigns against the Xiongnu, none of them succeeded in bringing the Xiongnu under Chinese rule. At times, China was forced to pay tribute to the Xiongnu.

Page Reference: pp. 135, 139, 374–75, 518–19

KEY CONCEPT	THEME	SKILL
2.2.I	3: State-Building, Expansion, and Conflict.	Interpretation Contextualization

5.   Answer: D

Explanation: The map's designation of these roads as "imperial" indicates that the state was responsible for their construction. The state's construction of the imperial roads represents one way in which Chinese dynasties sought to integrate different parts of the empire. The roads not only promoted political integration but also facilitated economic integration.

Page Reference: pp. 135–36

KEY CONCEPT	THEME	SKILL
2.2.II.B-C	3: State-Building, Expansion, and Conflict.	Interpretation

6.   Answer: A

Explanation: Pericles was an important political figure from the Greek city-state of Athens, where more people had a direct role in government than any other part of the world at the time. The more dominant political form at the time was an imperial monarchy.

Page Reference: pp. 125, 146–48

KEY CONCEPT	THEME	SKILL
2.1.II.E	3: State-Building, Expansion, and Conflict.	Interpretation Contextualization

7.   Answer: B

Explanation: Together, women, slaves, and foreigners constituted more than half the population. These groups were denied status as citizens. Consequently, they held no political rights and could not participate in the political process. The "many" in Pericles's quote included less than the majority of the population.

Page Reference: pp. 125, 146–48

KEY CONCEPT	THEME	SKILL
2.1.II.E 2.2.III.B 2.2.III.D	3: State-Building, Expansion, and Conflict. 5: Development and Transformation of Social Structures.	Interpretation Synthesis

8. Answer: B

Explanation: Smelting metals requires an abundant supply of wood. The logging industry was based on wood. The demands of both smelting and logging led to entire forests being cleared.

Page Reference: pp. 123–24, 138

KEY CONCEPT	THEME	SKILL
2.2.IV.A	1: Interaction Between Humans and the Environment.	Causation Comparison

9. Answer: C

Explanation: The classical Greek intellectual tradition emphasized human rationality and elaborated a set of moral and ethical values. It sought to separate science and philosophy from religion. This secular emphasis was also pronounced in Confucian thought, which focused on present-day realities.

Page Reference: p. 183

KEY CONCEPT	THEME	SKILL
2.1.II.B 2.1.II.E	2: Development and Interaction of Cultures.	Comparison

10. Answer: A

Explanation: Daoist influence can be seen in landscape paintings that portray humans as insignificant compared with nature.

Page Reference: p. 174

KEY CONCEPT	THEME	SKILL
2.1.II.C	2: Development and Interaction of Cultures.	Interpretation Causation

11. Answer: C

Explanation: The concept of multiple levels of heavens and hells was a feature associated with Mahayana (Great Vehicle) Buddhism. This modified form of Buddhism emerged in the early centuries of the Common Era. The goal of achieving nirvana through intense self-effort was an idea associated with the historical Buddha; the paired concepts of *wen* and *wu* were associated with Confucianism, while the idea of a cosmic struggle between good and evil was found in Zoroastrianism.

Page Reference: pp. 177–79

KEY CONCEPT	THEME	SKILL
2.3.III.C	2: Development and Interaction of Cultures.	Continuity and Change

12. Answer: A

Explanation: Although the South Asian religious tradition changed during this period, it remained consistently polytheistic. The Vedas emphasized ritual sacrifice. The Upanishads focused on philosophical abstractions. The bhakti movement emphasized devotional worship.

Page Reference: pp. 175–76, 179–80

KEY CONCEPT	THEME	SKILL
2.3.III.C	2: Development and Interaction of Cultures.	Continuity and Change

13. Answer: C

Explanation: After the fall of the Roman Empire, much of Greek learning was neglected. The spread of Christianity throughout Europe led scholars to focus on religious texts rather than the more secular writings of Greek scholarship. Intellectuals in the growing Islamic world played a key role in preserving the Greek legacy by translating Greek works into Arabic.

Page Reference: pp. 186–87

KEY CONCEPT	THEME	SKILL
2.1.II.E	2: Development and Interaction of Cultures.	Continuity and Change

14. Answer: D

Explanation: Legalism was more of a political philosophy than a religious tradition. Mahayana Buddhism offered more ways for more people to find enlightenment. Daoism viewed gender relations as complementary rather than hierarchical. The bhakti movement that emerged in the Hindu tradition weakened the caste and gender hierarchies in India by making worship of the Divine open to all.

Page Reference: pp. 173, 178–79, 180

KEY CONCEPT	THEME	SKILL
2.1.III 2.3.III.C	2: Development and Interaction of Cultures. 5: Development and Transformation of Social Structures.	Comparison Continuity and Change

15. Answer: B

Explanation: Confucianism was a secular philosophy and did not deal with the supernatural. Confucian texts were the basis of the educational curriculum tested in the civil service examination system. The Confucian value of filial piety was extended to a subject's relationship to the emperor. Just as children should respect and obey their parents, so too should subjects respect and obey the emperor. In this respect, the family served as a metaphor for the state.

Page Reference: pp. 170–72

KEY CONCEPT	THEME	SKILL
2.1.III	2: Development and Interaction of Cultures.	Causation Interpretation

16. Answer: A

    Explanation: The caste system was a central part of Hinduism. Hindus believed that the higher one's caste, the better one's chances of achieving moksha, that is, liberation from the cycle of rebirth. Nirvana was the Buddhist equivalent of the Hindu concept of moksha. In Buddhism, everyone had an equal opportunity to achieve nirvana. All of the other choices represent ideas also found in Hinduism.

    Page Reference: pp. 175, 177, 178

KEY CONCEPT	THEME	SKILL
2.1.I.B 2.1.II.A	2: Development and Interaction of Cultures.	Comparison Interpretation

17. Answer: C

    Explanation: Buddhism had challenged the role of the caste system in determining one's ability to find spiritual enlightenment. A revived Hinduism responded to that challenge by reinterpreting caste as a means to finding liberation. Fulfilling the duties attached to one's caste offered a possible way to achieve liberation.

    Page Reference: p. 179

KEY CONCEPT	THEME	SKILL
2.3.III.C	2: Development and Interaction of Cultures.	Continuity and Change

18. Answer: D

    Explanation: The founders of both religions sought to revitalize the dominant religion in their respective societies. The Buddha sought to reform Hinduism, while Jesus sought to reform Judaism. Eventually, their ideas evolved into separate religions.

    Page Reference: p. 188

KEY CONCEPT	THEME	SKILL
2.1.II.A 2.1.II.D	2: Development and Interaction of Cultures.	Comparison

19. Answer: A

    Explanation: The idea of a savior found a place in Judaism, and later, Christianity and Islam. The notions of rebirth, karma, and moksha are associated with Hinduism and Buddhism. The abandonment of education was a characteristic of Daoism.

    Page Reference: pp. 181–82

KEY CONCEPT	THEME	SKILL
1.3.III.E	2: Development and Interaction of Cultures.	Continuity and Change Comparison

20. Answer: A

Explanation: Jesus founded Christianity. Siddhartha Gautama founded Buddhism. Muhammad founded Islam.

Page Reference: pp. 187, 414

KEY CONCEPT	THEME	SKILL
2.1.II.A 2.1.II.D 3.1.III.A	2: Development and Interaction of Cultures.	Comparison

21. Answer: C

Explanation: For the first six centuries following the birth of Christianity, most Christian converts lived on the outskirts of the Roman Empire. These regions included North Africa, Egypt, Anatolia, and Syria. There were also significant Christian communities in Arabia, Persia, Ethiopia, India, and China.

Page Reference: p. 189

KEY CONCEPT	THEME	SKILL
2.1.II.D	2: Development and Interaction of Cultures.	Interpretation Contextualization Synthesis

22. Answer: A

Explanation: Zoroastrianism, Daoism, and Buddhism were all religions, so by definition, they cannot be secular. Confucianism was a secular philosophy because it did not deal with the spiritual world but rather with practical matters involving political and social issues.

Page Reference: pp. 169, 172, 181, 184–85

KEY CONCEPT	THEME	SKILL
2.1.II.B 2.1.II.E	2: Development and Interaction of Cultures.	Comparison

23. Answer: D

Explanation: The practice of ancestor veneration was a part of Chinese popular culture. The Confucian value of filial piety also emphasized the importance of honoring one's ancestors and parents.

Page Reference: pp. 170–71

KEY CONCEPT	THEME	SKILL
2.1.III 2.1.IV.B	2: Development and Interaction of Cultures.	Interpretation

24. Answer: B

Explanation: Hinduism is associated with the people in India, conventionally referred to as the Aryans. Judaism is associated with the Hebrews.

Page Reference: pp. 174, 182

KEY CONCEPT	THEME	SKILL
2.1.I.A-B 1.3.III.E	2: Development and Interaction of Cultures.	Comparison

25. Answer: A

Explanation: The Mauryan and Gupta empires attest to the presence of empires in India; however, these were the exception rather than the rule. South Asia suffered more invasions from Central Asia than other civilizations. As a consequence, emerging states were destroyed before they had a chance to become empires. The cultural diversity of the people in South Asia, combined with the caste system, strengthened local loyalties.

Page Reference: p. 143

KEY CONCEPT	THEME	SKILL
2.2.I	3: State-Building, Expansion, and Conflict.	Causation Comparison

26. Answer: C

Explanation: The Persian Empire did not have a civil service examination system (China did). It did have an imperial courier service. It also created a tax system that enabled the empire to collect revenue from each province. The state also sponsored public works to facilitate commerce and transportation.

Page Reference: pp. 121–22

KEY CONCEPT	THEME	SKILL
2.2.I 2.2.II.B-C	3: State-Building, Expansion, and Conflict.	Continuity and Change

27. Answer: D

Explanation: The state conscripted peasant men for military service. This was a contributing cause of peasant rebellions. Other causes were the effect of natural disasters, high taxes and rents, and state demands for a month of labor on public projects.

Page Reference: pp. 221–24

KEY CONCEPT	THEME	SKILL
3.3.III.C 2.2.III.C	3: State-Building, Expansion, and Conflict.	Continuity and Change

28. Answer: A

Explanation: A person's caste was believed to be a reflection of one's deeds in a previous life (karma). The notion of rebirth held out the hope that those who faithfully and selflessly fulfilled their caste duties (dharma) could be reborn in a higher caste in the next lifetime. This justified caste inequalities and strengthened the caste system.

Page Reference: p. 227

KEY CONCEPT	THEME	SKILL
2.2.III.B	2: Development and Interaction of Cultures. 5: Development and Transformation of Social Structures.	Causation

29. Answer: B

Explanation: The varna theory postulated that the four castes were formed from the body of the god Purusha. Consequently, the caste system was eternal and changeless. The Brahmin and Kshatriya castes were theoretically Aryan, but both castes have incorporated non-Aryans. Members of the Vaisya caste were originally cultivators and later became identified with merchants.

Page Reference: pp. 225–26

KEY CONCEPT	THEME	SKILL
2.2.III.B	5: Development and Transformation of Social Structures.	Continuity and Change Argumentation

30. Answer: D

Explanation: Religious intolerance has not been identified as a factor in the emergence of slavery. Scholars have suggested that the domestication of animals provided a model for the enslavement of people. Others have noted that warfare produced prisoners of war who were then enslaved. Most female captives were enslaved as concubines.

Page Reference: p. 229

KEY CONCEPT	THEME	SKILL
2.2.III.B	5: Development and Transformation of Social Structures.	Causation Argumentation

31. Answer: C

Explanation: Slavery was practiced on a wide scale in the Roman Empire. Almost 40 percent of the population in the heartland of the Roman Empire were slaves. Most of the slaves came from the prisoners of war captured in the military conquests that created the Roman Empire.

Page Reference: p. 231

KEY CONCEPT	THEME	SKILL
2.2.III.B	5: Development and Transformation of Social Structures.	Comparison Contextualization

32. Answer: A

Explanation: The caste system in India was based on notions of ritual purity. The Brahmins were at the top because they were the most ritually pure. The untouchables were outside the caste system because they engaged in labor considered to be spiritually polluting.

Page Reference: p. 228

KEY CONCEPT	THEME	SKILL
2.2.III.B	5: Development and Transformation of Social Structures.	Comparison

33. Answer: A

Explanation: The Vedic period refers to the formative centuries of Indian civilization, from 1500–600 B.C.E. Although a patriarchal society, Vedic women enjoyed more opportunities than their counterparts in later periods. In addition to participating in religious sacrifices, Vedic women sometimes engaged in scholarship and religious debate and were allowed to wear the sacred thread that symbolized ritual purity. In later periods, women were forbidden to study the Vedas. They were considered "unclean" and banned from public religious rituals.

Page Reference: pp. 175–76, 233

KEY CONCEPT	THEME	SKILL
2.2.III.D	5: Development and Transformation of Social Structures.	Argumentation Interpretation Contextualization Synthesis

34. Answer: B

Explanation: The argument made in *The Laws of Manu* echoes the same view of female inadequacy expressed by Aristotle. Both assume the male to be the prototype. Aristotle's description of a woman as "an infertile male" highlights her inability to produce sperm. The argument made in *The Laws of Manu* blame the weakness of sperm for producing female babies.

Page Reference: p. 237

KEY CONCEPT	THEME	SKILL
2.2.III.D	5: Development and Transformation of Social Structures.	Interpretation

35. Answer: D

Explanation: Slavery was a widespread practice in ancient Greece and Rome. After the fall of the Roman Empire, however, a period of disunity characterized the next few centuries. In this changed political climate, slavery gave way to the practice of serfdom. Unlike slaves, serfs were not "owned," but they did owe fees, service, and a portion of their harvest to their lords in return for protection.

Page Reference: p. 241

KEY CONCEPT	THEME	SKILL
2.2.III.B	5: Development and Transformation of Social Structures.	Continuity and Change

36.　Answer: C

Explanation: Christianity and Buddhism both encouraged people to devote their lives to the religion by joining monasteries. Women who became Christian or Buddhist nuns were able to enjoy relative freedom from the patriarchal restrictions that characterized society. Some women were even able to rise to positions of leadership within the convent. Most gained literacy and other skills.

Page Reference: pp. 234, 483

KEY CONCEPT	THEME	SKILL
2.1.III	5: Development and Transformation of Social Structures.	Comparison

37.　Answer: A

Explanation: There were no discourses expounding the inherent equality of men and women in the classical era. Elite status was gendered masculine by the limitation of political power to men. Elite status was gendered feminine by the seclusion of women in the home. Lower-class women were unable to meet this expectation because of the necessity to go out and work; their public appearances marked them as lower class.

Page Reference: pp. 234–35, 237–38

KEY CONCEPT	THEME	SKILL
2.2.III.D	5: Development and Transformation of Social Structures.	Comparison Interpretation

38.　Answer: D

Explanation: The "three obediences" was a core teaching of Confucianism. It taught that women should obey their father, husband, and son. At all stages of her life, a woman was expected to follow a man related to her.

Page Reference: pp. 234–35, 246–47

KEY CONCEPT	THEME	SKILL
2.2.III.D	5: Development and Transformation of Social Structures.	Comparison Interpretation Synthesis

39.　Answer: B

Explanation: Both the civil service examination system and the caste system sustained hierarchies that justified and perpetuated class and gender inequalities for millennia. The civil service examination system drew from the Confucian discourse that, beginning with the Han dynasty, became the official ideology of China. The caste system was inseparable from Hindu cultural practices. Both held out the promise of mobility in an otherwise rigid social structure; talented men could elevate their status through success on the exams, and rebirth offered people the hope of being born in a higher caste in the next lifetime.

Page Reference: pp. 219, 228

KEY CONCEPT	THEME	SKILL
2.2.III.B	5: Development and Transformation of Social Structures.	Comparison

40. Answer: C

Explanation: Many Roman households had a shrine that housed paintings or sculptures depicting guardian spirits or deities. Occasions such as births, marriages, or deaths were marked by sacrifices and rituals in which food and wine were placed at the shrines. The portrayal of the spirit of the male household head in this shrine indicates that ancestor veneration was a central part of Roman popular beliefs.

Page Reference: p. 256

KEY CONCEPT	THEME	SKILL
2.1.IV.B	2: Development and Interaction of Cultures.	Interpretation Evidence

41. Answer: A

Explanation: Shrines like the one shown in Visual Source 5.4 were a common feature in Roman households. It reflects the popular practice of offering sacrifices and performing rituals centered around the shrine. The spirits of ancestors was a common feature in these shrines.

Page Reference: p. 256

KEY CONCEPT	THEME	SKILL
2.1.IV.B	2: Development and Interaction of Cultures.	Contextualization

42. Answer: D

Explanation: The cultivation of corn originated in Mesoamerica. From there, it spread slowly throughout the Americas. Agriculture in the Chaco canyon region and the Mississippi valley became dependent on corn, which allowed for population growth and the development of complex societies.

Page Reference: pp. 288–89

KEY CONCEPT	THEME	SKILL
2.3.III.A	4: Creation, Expansion, and Interaction of Economic Systems.	Comparison

43. Answer: B

Explanation: The varying elevations in the Andes region made it impossible for either empire to establish control over a continuous band of territory. Instead, both empires colonized areas at lower elevations and in the highlands. The vertical environment also shaped farming and irrigation practices, with the Wari practicing hillside terracing and the Tiwanaku employing a system of raised fields.

Page Reference: p. 281

KEY CONCEPT	THEME	SKILL
2.3.III.A	3: State-Building, Expansion, and Conflict. 4: Creation, Expansion, and Interaction of Economic Systems.	Comparison Causation

44. Answer: C

    Explanation: Large earthen mounds believed to be burial mounds dot the landscape of the region east of the Mississippi. The earliest of these mounds dates to around 2000 B.C.E. The most elaborate and widespread of the Mound Builders was the Hopewell culture in Ohio, which flourished between 200 B.C.E. and 400 C.E.

    Page Reference: p. 288

KEY CONCEPT	THEME	SKILL
2.1.V.B	2: Development and Interaction of Cultures.	Contextualization

45. Answer: A

    Explanation: Meroë was the center of Nubian civilization in northeastern Africa between 300 B.C.E. and 100 C.E. Scholars speculate that the statue of Augustus found in Meroë most likely came from a raid against the northern part of Egypt, which was at that time part of the Roman Empire.

    Page Reference: p. 267

KEY CONCEPT	THEME	SKILL
2.2.I 2.2.III.A	3: State-Building, Expansion, and Conflict.	Evidence Contextualization

46. Answer: D

    Explanation: Axum became a Christian state around the fourth century; shamanism was not a prominent feature of the political system. The political power of shamans stemmed from their key role in mediating between the human and supernatural worlds. The rulers of Maya civilization were considered "state shamans." In Chavín, shamans were religious leaders. The rulers of Moche were shaman-rulers.

    Page Reference: pp. 274, 278–79

KEY CONCEPT	THEME	SKILL
2.1.IV.A	2: Development and Interaction of Cultures. 3: State-Building, Expansion, and Conflict.	Comparison

47. Answer: B

    Explanation: The Roman Empire used the North African coastal region to produce the wheat and olives consumed throughout the empire. During the centuries this region was under Roman rule, large estates emerged that were dedicated to the production of wheat and olives. Slaves provided the principal source of labor.

Page Reference: p. 263

KEY CONCEPT	THEME	SKILL
2.3.III.A 2.2.III.C	4: Creation, Expansion, and Interaction of Economic Systems.	Causation

48. Answer: C

Explanation: Jenne-jeno is one of the most well-documented cities of the Niger Valley civilization in West Africa. Iron ore, copper, gold, stones, and salt—none of which are indigenous to the area—have been found in Jenne-jeno. Goods were transferred from boat to donkey and vice versa in Jenne-jeno.

Page Reference: pp. 270, 272

KEY CONCEPT	THEME	SKILL
2.2.III.A 2.3.I	4: Creation, Expansion, and Interaction of Economic Systems.	Contextualization

49. Answer: A

Explanation: The Bantu-speaking migrants spread their cultural practices throughout most of sub-Saharan Africa. A central feature of their religious beliefs was ancestor veneration. It was believed that the supernatural power of ancestral spirits could be tapped through the proper performance of rituals.

Page Reference: pp. 284–85

KEY CONCEPT	THEME	SKILL
2.1.IV.B	2: Development and Interaction of Cultures.	Causation

50. Answer: D

Explanation: Literature, poetry, and drama are all written forms of expression. The 400 distinct but related languages categorized as Bantu help scholars to trace the path of Bantu migration. Geometric earthworks like burial mounds help scholars understand the culture of people within the "Hopewell Interaction Sphere" in the Ohio River valley. The terraced hillsides of the Wari and Maya help scholars to understand farming practices.

Page Reference: pp. 274, 281, 282, 288

KEY CONCEPT	THEME	SKILL
2.1.V.B	2: Development and Interaction of Cultures.	Evidence

Answer Guide for Section II:
Part A

General Guidelines for Answering a Document-Based Question (DBQ):

1. Pre-Write. Create a brief outline before you start writing.
2. Write your DBQ in a multiple-paragraph structure. In your first paragraph, write an introduction that clearly states your thesis.
3. Present your arguments in body paragraphs. Body paragraphs should integrate groupings of documents, demonstrate understanding of documents, support the thesis using documents as evidence, analyze point of view, and possibly include additional relevant historical content. Present your arguments in body paragraphs that focus on a grouping of documents and that put forth a single argument centered on answering the prompt.
4. In your final paragraph, write a conclusion that includes a reworded restatement of your thesis.

AP World History DBQ essays are scored using a core scoring method with a maximum score of nine. In the basic core, you may earn the following seven points:

+   one point for a thesis
+   one point for addressing and understanding the documents
+   up to two points for using the documents as evidence to answer the prompt
+   one point for grouping the documents
+   one point for analyzing Point of View (POV)
+   one point for identifying and explaining the need for an additional document

If you earn ALL seven basic core points, you have the chance to earn up to two additional points in what is called expanded core. Expanded core points may be granted for the following features:

+   an excellent, sophisticated, and comprehensive thesis
+   insightful document analysis
+   analyzing POV in all or most documents
+   including extra document groupings or additional documents
+   incorporating relevant historical content not found in the documents

Below is a detailed description of what you will need to do in your answer to earn each basic core point.

Thesis (1 point): To earn a point in this category, you must write a thesis that responds to the entire prompt and outlines the specific arguments you will make based on a correct usage of the documents. You will need to mention the arguments you plan on making in your answer, and you will need to avoid generalizations that do not reflect reasonable interpretations of the documents. Thesis statements will only earn a point if they appear in the first or last paragraph of the essay. Common errors in thesis writing include merely rewriting the prompt or presenting an answer to only some parts of the prompt, so make sure you address the entire prompt and briefly present the specific arguments that you will use in your answer based on the documents.

> **Prompt:** Using the following documents, analyze the methods employed by ancient empires to exert political power before 600 C.E. Identify an additional type of document and explain how it would help your analysis of these empires.

Examples:

> Example Thesis: "In the period before 600 C.E., ancient empires exerted political power through various methods, including military conquest, making alliances

with people they conquered, promoting ideologies supporting their rule, promoting good government officials, and creating legal systems."

> ✦ This thesis earns the point by identifying the specific arguments based on the documents that the student will use to answer the prompt. It presents many methods used by ancient empires to exert political control. It answers the entire prompt.

Unacceptable Example: "Ancient empires exerted political power in a lot of different ways before 600 C.E."

> ✦ This thesis does little other than state the obvious given the prompt.

Addressing and Understanding Documents (1 point): To earn this point, you must address ALL of the documents and demonstrate understanding of "all but one." This means that throughout your answer, you must show understanding of at least six of the seven documents.

Using Documents as Evidence (2 points): To earn two points, you must correctly incorporate at least six documents (although seven would be better) into arguments that answer the prompt. You will earn only one point if you use five of the seven documents in your arguments. If you use four or fewer documents in your essay, you will receive a zero in this category.

Grouping the Documents (1 point): Documents should be grouped in at least three ways in order to earn a point in this category. You can group documents by matching two or more documents that hold some relevant feature in common. Each example grouping below represents documents that, when used together, can make up an argument that answers the prompt.

Grouping the Documents:

Military Conquest	Docs 1, 2, 4, 5, 7 (implied in Doc 3)
Alliances with Conquered	Docs 1, 7
Attitude of Superiority	Docs 1, 2, 5
Powerful Ideologies	Docs 2 (democracy); 3, 4 (Buddhism); 5 (Legalism); 6 (Confucianism)
Militant Society	Docs 1, 2
System of Law/Justice	Docs 2, 3, 4, 5, 6
Center of Trade/Promote Trade	Docs 2, 4, 5, 6, 7
Public Improvements	Docs 4, 5, 7
Promote Good Gov't/Officials	Docs 2, 4, 5, 6
Use of Coercion/Punishments	Docs 3, 4

Analyzing Point of View (1 Point): Many students find it challenging to earn the point in this category. The best way to earn the Point of View (POV) point is to go beyond the basic identity of the source author and the source itself, as described in the document source line. In order to write a successful POV statement, you should try to establish a better understanding of the identity of the author; you can do this by asking yourself questions about the author and the source. What is the author's gender or social class? What religion does the author follow? What is the author's profession? Does the author have an identifiable ethnicity, nationality, or other allegiance to a particular group? Is the source from a poem, essay, or novel? What was the source used for? Once you've asked these questions, go further and explain how some of these factors may have influenced the content of the source. Your complete POV statement should both identify the influences that may have shaped the author or source and explain how those particular influences have specifically affected the content of the document. Below are some examples of POV statements based on the documents from this question.

Examples of POV Statements:

Document 1: "Source: Greek historian Herodotus, 5th century B.C.E."

+ Historians write history and attempt to use the past as a way to illuminate the present or guide the ideas of their people. Herodotus may have written this history of Persia hoping to instruct the leaders of Greece to promote the success of Greece by adopting good ideas from foreigners and to teach the Greek people what successful government would do.

Document 2: "Source: Pericles, Greek political leader and general of Athens and the Delian League, 'Funeral Oration,' 5th century B.C.E."

+ Pericles led Greece and pointed out the greatness of Greece in his speech. In stating positives of Greece, Pericles in effect bragged about himself and his own successes as a ruler. Rulers typically highlight their own success hoping to secure support for their own rule.

Document 7: "Aelius Aristides, Greek-speaking Roman citizen from Smyrna in Anatolia, delivered 'The Roman Oration' before the Roman emperor, 2nd century C.E."

+ This document reflects the influence of the audience Aelius Aristides spoke before, and the goals of his speech. As a non-Roman from a land controlled by Rome speaking before the Roman emperor, he talked of the positives of Roman rule. He may not have been free to comment negatively, or it may have been dangerous for him to speak negatively of the emperor. It is also possible that he spoke before the emperor seeking some favor and so tried to create goodwill by noting the benefits of the rule of the emperor. He may have chosen to highlight positives by his manners and in a desire to avoid offending his host.

You should write as many POV statements as you are able to produce. You can earn the POV point with as few as two correct POV statements; however, it's not uncommon to make errors in writing POV statements. For that reason, it's safer to provide more than just two in order to make up for any errors. Additionally, if you earn all of the basic core points, then an extra POV statement can earn you an expanded core point.

Additional Document Statement (1 Point): A good additional document statement identifies a missing document that, if added to the provided documents, would help make a better answer to the question. You are only required to make a single additional document statement to earn a point, but you should aim to identify a minimum of three additional documents. This allows room for mistakes, and after the first correct additional document statement, any extras can earn you bonus points in the expanded core if you earn all seven points in the basic core. You should be careful to avoid the common mistake of asking for a type of document that is already provided. Additional document statements must meet three standards to be considered successful:

+ The document suggested must be historically plausible.
+ The statement must include an explanation of **why** the additional document would be useful in answering the prompt.

✦ The analysis of **why** must speculate about the particulars of what the missing document might include. In other words, a successful additional document suggestion is historically possible given the time and place, includes an explanation of how the new source would help answer the prompt, and goes as far as speculating on arguments that the suggested source might support.

Document Analysis:

Document 1: "Source: Greek historian Herodotus, 5th century B.C.E." This document shows methods of exerting political power, including military conquest, Persian alliances with conquered people, and the Persian attitude of superiority. The ideology of superiority appears in the statement from the passage that the Persians "look upon themselves as very greatly superior . . . to the rest of mankind." Persia as a militant society is shown in the passage, "Next to prowess in arms, it is regarded as the greatest proof of manly excellence to be the father of many sons. Every year the king sends rich gifts to the man who can show the largest number: for they hold that number is strength. Their sons are carefully instructed from their fifth to their twentieth year, in three things alone—to ride, to draw the bow, and to speak the truth."

Document 2: "Source: Pericles, Greek political leader and general of Athens and the Delian League, 'Funeral Oration,' 5th century B.C.E." The Athenian use of military conquest is seen in the passage "For we have compelled every land and every sea to open a path for our valor. . . ." Their attitude of superiority can be found in the passage "Our form of government does not enter into rivalry with the institutions of others. We do not copy our neighbors, but are an example to them. . . ." Athenians employed a powerful ideology of democracy as best promoting their rule. The Athenians promoted militant social values, arguing "our military training is in many respects superior to that of our adversaries. . . ." They employed a system of rule by law. They ruled through prosperity by being a center of trade and by taking the products of the conquered, as seen in the passage "Because of the greatness of our city the fruits of the whole earth flow in upon us; so that we enjoy the goods of other countries as freely as of our own. . . ." Lastly, they sought to promote good officials in the passage "when a citizen is in any way distinguished, he is preferred to the public service, not as a matter of privilege, but as the reward of merit. . . ."

Document 3: "Han Fei, expressing Legalist philosophy, which was adopted as a doctrine of rule by Emperor Shihuangdi of Qin dynasty China in the 3rd century B.C.E." The Qin dynasty used the powerful ideology of Legalism to rule. They set up a system of law and used coercion and punishments as illustrated in the passage "The means whereby the intelligent ruler controls his ministers are two handles only. The two handles are chastisement and commendation. What are meant by chastisement and commendation? To inflict death or torture upon culprits is called chastisement; to bestow encouragements or rewards on men of merit is called commendation."

Document 4: "Source: Emperor Ashoka, Mauryan dynasty in India, from stone inscriptions called the 'Rock Edicts,' 3rd century B.C.E." This document shows that the Mauryan dynasty was established when Ashoka "conquered the Kalingas. . . ." It especially shows the use of a powerful ideology in the form of promoting Buddhism, as described in the passage "Now it is conquest by Dhamma that Beloved-of-the-Gods considers to be the best conquest. . . . I have had this Dhamma edict written so that my sons and great-grandsons may not consider making new conquests, or that . . . they consider making conquest by Dhamma only, for that bears fruit in this world and the next. . . ." The document references laws and therefore shows use of a system of law. It notes public improvements in the statement "Along roads I have had banyan trees planted so that they can give shade to animals and men, and I have had mango groves planted. At intervals . . . I have had wells dug, rest-houses built, and in various places, I have had watering-places made for the use of animals and men. . . ." Ashoka showed concern for promoting good government officials, noting, "Those who are bored with the administration of justice will not be promoted; [those who are not] will move upwards and be promoted. . . ." He also used punishments to keep order, "That the judicial officers of the city may strive to do their duty and that the people under them might not suffer unjust imprisonment or harsh treatment. To achieve this, I will send out Mahamatras every five years who are not harsh or cruel, but who are merciful and who can ascertain if the judicial officers have understood my purpose and are acting according to my instructions."

Document 5: "Qin Emperor Shihuangdi ordered the carving of this stone inscription, which was set in a tower on Mount Langya in the 3rd century B.C.E." The Qin military conquest is implied by the statement that the Emperor "pacifies all four corners of the earth." The use of a system of law and justice is apparent in the lines "He defines the laws, leaving nothing in doubt,/Making known what is forbidden." The Qin used public improvements in the form of canals implied by the phrase "made waterways." Qin promotion of good government is shown by the lines "The local officials have their duties,/Administration is smoothly carried out,/All is done correctly, all according to plan."

Document 6: "*The Analects*, as compiled by students of Confucius and expressive of the ruling philosophy of Han dynasty China starting in the 3rd century B.C.E." This document illustrates the use of a powerful ruling ideology in the form of Confucianism. It promotes good government through the use of good officials: "The Master said, 'He who exercises government by means of his virtue may be compared to the north polar star, which keeps its place and all the stars turn toward it.'"

Document 7: "Aelius Aristides, Greek-speaking Roman citizen from Smyrna in Anatolia, delivered 'The Roman Oration' before the Roman emperor, 2nd century C.E." Document 7 shows military conquest in the line "You have divided people into Romans [citizens] and non-Romans [subjects]" and shows alliances with conquered people in the passage "You have divided into two parts all the men of your empire . . . and everywhere you have made citizens all those who are the more accomplished, noble, and powerful people, even if they retain their native affinities, while the remainder you have made subjects and the governed." This document shows rule can be reinforced by acting as a center of trade, as seen in the passage "Here is brought from every land and sea all the crops of the seasons and the produce of each land, river and lake." The document also shows the use of public improvements used to justify rule when it states: "Everything is full of gymnasiums, fountains, gateways, temples, handicrafts, and schools. . . ."

Answer Guide for Section II: Part B

2. Analyze the continuities and changes in the roles of urban centers from circa 600 B.C.E. to 600 C.E. Be sure to include evidence from specific cities in your analysis of the roles of urban centers.

What Does the Question Ask?

This question provides you with a broad opportunity to discuss how different cities developed and transformed throughout the Classical Age. Note that the prompt asks you to mention at least two cities in your essay.

Listed below is the scoring system used to grade continuity and change-over-time essays; also included are guidelines and examples for how to earn each point for this question.

Has Acceptable Thesis (1 point)

+ The thesis needs to correctly address both continuity and change.
+ The thesis should appear in the first paragraph (although it may also count if it is in the conclusion).
+ The thesis can be one sentence or multiple sentences.

Examples:

+ Example One: Cities continued to be the political centers of classical empires from 600 B.C.E. to 600 C.E. As empires collapsed, however, certain cities changed their roles.
+ Example Two: Trade remained an important factor in urbanization during the Classical Age. Shifting trade routes led to the rise of cities in different parts of the world.
+ Example Three: Cities continued to serve as significant centers for the practice of religion. New religions that emerged from 600 B.C.E. to 600 C.E. meant that the role of the urban centers in religious worship shifted considerably.
+ Unacceptable Example: A large number of cities changed their roles during the Classical Age. Many of the roles stayed the same.
  • This is an unacceptable thesis because it does not provide any information other than what is stated in the question prompt.

Addresses All Parts of the Question (2 points)

+ The essay accurately addresses both a continuity (1 point) and a change (1 point).
+ The statements of continuity and change may not appear in the thesis.

Examples:

+ Example One: The area around the Mediterranean Sea had a number of political capitals throughout this period. Rome emerged as the major city in this region but collapsed dramatically by the end of the Classical Age.
  • The first statement in the example above addresses continuity, while the second statement addresses change.

+ Example Two: Long-distance trade continued to encourage the formation of large urban centers. As trade expanded across Eurasia, however, new cities developed to take advantage of new trade networks.
  • The first statement in the example above addresses continuity, while the second statement addresses change.

+ Example Three: The rise of Christianity meant that Rome and Constantinople became places for large churches. Big religious centers were constructed throughout this time period.
  • The first statement in the example above addresses change, while the second statement addresses continuity.

Substantiates Thesis with Appropriate Historical Evidence (2 points)

- A piece of historical evidence is a fact that is correct and relevant to the time period.
- To earn the full two points in this category, an essay should have five or more pieces of evidence.
- To earn only one point in this category, an essay needs three or four pieces of evidence.
- Points for evidence can be earned even if the thesis point is not earned.

Examples:

- Example One: The city of Athens in Greece was the center of a city-state that eventually set up colonies throughout the Mediterranean. Unlike cities in the rest of the world, Athens was ruled through a form of democracy. Rome replaced Athens as a center of a powerful empire before the Common Era. All roads seemed to lead to Rome since the Roman emperors used it as the focal point of their power. Enormous buildings like the Coliseum displayed the power of imperial Rome.
- Example Two: Many classical cities were located on water. For example, Byzantium, which later became Constantinople, sat on a vital waterway connecting Europe to Asia. This connection to water was important for trade. Plenty of cities in China could be found on the Yangzi River and Yellow River. Other cities, such as Samarkand, developed in Central Asia to take advantage of the new Silk Road trade.
- Example Three: As Christianity developed, Rome became the center for the new religion. The bishop of Rome was the pope, who was the head of the church. When Constantine moved the Roman Empire to Constantinople, it also became an important city for Christianity. The Byzantines built Hagia Sophia, the largest church in the world. Pagan temples that were in both cities were either destroyed or converted into Christian churches.

Uses Relevant Historical Context (1 point)

- Historical context places the issue discussed in the essay into a broader global perspective.

Examples:

- Example One: As the Roman Empire became larger, stretching from Britain to the Middle East to Africa, the city of Rome became increasingly more important.
- Example Two: Trade networks in the Mediterranean and along the Silk Road led to the founding of new cities that took advantage of the wealth of the long-distance trade.
- Example Three: The spread of Christianity from the Middle East into Europe transformed the role of Rome and other cities that became important centers for the new religion.

Analyzes the Process of Continuity or Change (1 point)

- Analysis explains why the continuity or change occurred.

Examples:

- Example One: New urban centers were founded and became more cosmopolitan because of the conquests of Alexander the Great.
- Example Two: Since the Han Dynasty and the Roman Empire were connected though the Silk Roads, many cities in Central Asia developed as rest stops along the way.

✦ Example Three: As the Christian Church became more centralized, cities such as Constantinople and Rome became more important.

Expanded Core

You must earn all seven points in the basic core before earning any points in the expanded core. Points awarded in the expanded core reflect the general excellence of the essay. Any one aspect of your essay, such as the thesis or evidence, might be particularly insightful and earn a point in the expanded core. Essays that have a high degree of analysis and historical context often earn expanded core points if they have earned all of the other basic core points. Clarity of organization, strong cause-effect analysis, and particularly insightful ideas can make your essay stand out as excellent.

Examples:

✦ Example One: An essay that uses several cities as examples of the political role of specific empires could earn points in the expanded core.
✦ Example Two: Connecting the changing nature of global trade systems to the rise and fall of specific cities could earn points in the expanded core.
✦ Example Three: A detailed description of how Christianity influenced the role of Rome and Constantinople could earn points in the expanded core.

Answer Guide for Section II:
Part C

3. Compare the effect on social structures of TWO of the following religious systems before 600 C.E.

✦ Hinduism
✦ Confucianism
✦ Buddhism
✦ Christianity

What Does the Question Ask?

This question deals with social structures, which could include gender roles, family relationships, and economic classes. The essay also allows you to choose which religious systems to write about.

Listed below is the scoring system used to grade comparative essays; also included are guidelines and examples for how to earn each point for this question.

Has Acceptable Thesis (1 point)

✦ The thesis needs to correctly address both a similarity and a difference in social structures for two of the four religious systems.
✦ The thesis should appear in the first paragraph (although it may also count if it is in the conclusion).
✦ The thesis can be one sentence or multiple sentences.

Examples:

✦ Example One: Both Confucianism and Christianity emphasized family relationships. The Christian faith focused on the spiritual equality of all classes of people, while Confucianism focused on rules for dealing with those in a superior or inferior social position.

- ✦ Example Two: In both Hinduism and Buddhism, the issue of reincarnation was significant in how social roles developed. They differ greatly because in Hinduism a person was born into a social caste, and in Buddhism a person from any social class could achieve salvation through his or her devotion.
- ✦ Example Three: Confucianism provided a great deal more social mobility than Hinduism, but both supported patriarchy.
- ✦ Unacceptable Example: Hinduism and Buddhism both started in India and spread to parts of Southeast Asia. Siddhartha Gautama was a Hindu prince who founded Buddhism.
  - • This is an unacceptable thesis because the similarity does not relate to social structures. The sentence about Siddhartha Gautama is not comparative.

Addresses All Parts of the Question (2 points)

- ✦ The essay accurately addresses both a valid similarity (1 point) and a valid difference (1 point).
- ✦ The statements of comparison may not appear in the thesis.

Examples:

- ✦ Example One: Patriarchy played a large role in Christianity and Confucianism. The message of Jesus of Nazareth stressed the blessedness of the poor and meek, while Confucius stressed the importance of respecting those above you.
  - • The first statement in the example above addresses similarity, while the second statement addresses difference.

- ✦ Example Two: Buddhism was generally much more equitable in how it dealt with social and gender differences than Hinduism. However, both religions had people who were considered socially more important because of their religious positions.
  - • The first statement in the example above addresses difference, while the second statement addresses similarity.

- ✦ Example Three: The Hindu caste system set up a more rigid social hierarchy than the Confucian educational system. However, men were considered dominant within both Hindu and Confucian families.
  - • The first statement in the example above addresses difference, while the second statement addresses similarity.

Substantiates Thesis with Appropriate Historical Evidence (2 points)

- ✦ A piece of historical evidence is a fact that is correct and relevant to the time period.
- ✦ To earn the full two points in this category, an essay should have five or more pieces of evidence.
- ✦ To earn only one point in this category, an essay needs three or four pieces of evidence.
- ✦ Points for evidence can be earned even if the thesis point is not earned.

Examples:

- ✦ Example One: Confucianism based itself on the five relationships. The Chinese government used Confucianism as a way of creating an elite class of educated bureaucrats. Filial piety strengthened the bond that held families together. Christianity looked down on divorce and adultery. The message of Christianity appealed greatly to the lower classes.

✦ Example Two: In Buddhism, men and women could join monasteries, although male and female were separated. Buddhism said that the spiritual path could be followed by people from any social class. In Hinduism, separate castes separated people into four groups: priests, warriors, craftsmen, and servants. Subgroups known as *jati* also regulated social relationships. A rigid patriarchy also existed in Hinduism.

✦ Example Three: The Chinese civil service exam was part of the Confucian structure of China, which encouraged social mobility. The filial piety of China emphasized the relationship between son and father and the relationship between brother and brother. Women were considered through the five relationships only as subservient wives. In Hindu mythology, female deities served as loyal wives. The dramatic Hindu practice of *sati* also showed dramatically how women were expected to be loyal to their husbands.

Makes a Direct, Relevant Comparison (1 point)

✦ A direct comparison is an explicit, concrete, and factually correct statement of either similarity or difference.

Examples:

✦ Example One: Unlike Confucianism, the collapse of empire allowed Christianity to play a larger role in government.

✦ Example Two: Siddhartha, the founder of Buddhism, rejected Hindu notions of caste.

✦ Example Three: The writings of Confucius and the Hindu scriptures both stress social order.

Analyzes at Least One Reason for a Similarity or Difference (1 point)

✦ Analysis explains a reason for the similarity or difference.

Examples:

✦ Example One: Confucianism was used as a tool of government control and therefore was more concerned with social order. Christianity, on the other hand, developed more on the margins of the Roman Empire and drew its early followers from the lower end of the social scale; for this reason, Christianity became more focused on social equality.

✦ Example Two: The emphasis on the personal journey toward nirvana in Buddhism led to a kind of equality that was not present in the social structure of Hinduism.

✦ Example Three: Since the written traditions of both Confucianism and Hinduism stressed the responsibilities of social classes, both systems had a strong social hierarchy.

Expanded Core

You must earn all seven points in the basic core before earning any points in the expanded core. Points awarded in the expanded core reflect the general excellence of the essay. Any one aspect of your essay, such as the thesis or evidence, might be particularly insightful and earn a point in the expanded core. Essays that have a high degree of analysis and historical context often earn expanded core points if they have all of the other basic core points. Clarity of organization, strong cause-effect analysis, and particularly insightful ideas can make your essay stand out as excellent.

Examples:

- Example One: An essay that describes the social changes that occurred within Christianity and/or Confucianism as they spread and became more centralized could earn points in the expanded core.
- Example Two: A description of gender roles with specific references for both Buddhism and Hinduism could earn points in the expanded core.
- Example Three: A discussion of the various types of social divisions within Hinduism and a discussion of the different relationships within Confucianism could earn points in the expanded core.

PERIOD THREE
Regional and Transregional Interactions, c. 600 C.E. to c. 1450 C.E.

PART THREE
An Age of Accelerating Connections, 500–1500

AP World History Key Concepts

3.1: Expansion and Intensification of Communication and Exchange Networks

3.2: Continuity and Innovation of State Forms and Their Interactions

3.3: Increased Economic Productive Capacity and Its Consequences

The Big Picture: Defining a Millennium

How do scholars decide what defines the ending of one stage of history and the beginning of another? This question corresponds to the AP historical thinking skill of periodization—the ability to categorize historical events into meaningful epochs and to determine transitional phases in the historical narrative. For this textbook, the period chosen is roughly a millennium: 500 C.E. (the fall of the second-wave civilizations) to 1500 C.E. (the voyages of Columbus). Scholars do not have a very accurate way of describing this period; "postclassical" or "medieval" are terms that are often used, but apply most specifically to Europe. *Ways of the World* has chosen to call this era before the beginning of the modern world the era of third-wave civilizations.

Third-Wave Civilizations: Something New, Something Old, Something Blended

One of the reasons why scholars do not have a very accurate way of describing this period is because of the "rather different trajectories of various regions of the world during this millennium." This means that it is difficult to find ways to characterize this period without violating the reality for regions outside Eurasia. However, there are some regional patterns that emerge.

First, the globalization of civilizations that were unique yet still drew on that of their predecessors continued. Common features included states and cities, specialized economies, social stratification, and gender inequality.

✦ New, smaller civilizations arose along the East African coast (like the Swahili city-states) and engaged in the Indian Ocean trade.
✦ In West Africa, the kingdoms of Ghana, Mali, and Songhay controlled the trans-Saharan trade.
✦ Kievan Russia borrowed culture from the Mediterranean region and controlled trade between the Baltic and the Black Sea.
✦ In East Asia, Japan, Korea, and Vietnam borrowed from China.
✦ Srivijaya and the Angkor kingdom borrowed from the Hindu and Buddhist traditions of South Asia.

Next, a new civilization arose: Islam, a civilization defined by its religion, began in the seventh century in Arabia and expanded rapidly (see Map 9.2, p. 309) to control much of North Africa and the Middle East.

Another pattern was the persistence or reconstitution of second-wave civilizations into the third-wave era.

✦ The Byzantine Empire continued the pattern of Roman Christian civilization until 1453.
✦ After a period of fragmentation, the Sui, Tang, and Song Chinese dynasties restored political unity and Confucian traditions.
✦ Indian civilization continued patterns of cultural diversity, caste, and Hinduism.
✦ In Mesoamerica, the collapse of the Maya and Teotihuacán led to the success of the Mexica (Aztec) empire.
✦ In the Andes, the Incas incorporated previous centers of civilization into a large empire.

A final pattern followed the collapse of the Roman Empire in Western Europe: the decentralized rule of smaller successor states, which created a civilization that blended Greco-Roman and Germanic elements where kings and church leaders attempted to maintain links with the religion and culture of the classical Mediterranean world. Western Europe, a backwater in the first part of this millennium, began to emerge after 1000 as a group of competitive, expansive states.

The Ties That Bind: Transregional Interaction in the Third-Wave Era

The variety of regional developments makes it difficult to identify truly transregional patterns, but clearly there was an increased rate and degree of exchange between cultures, whether through trade, migration, or conquest. In some areas, "local cosmopolitan regions" emerged: island Southeast Asia, the Swahili states, Central Asian cities, the Islamic Middle East, parts of Western Europe, and the Inca Empire. Accelerating trade had several consequences.

+ **Long-distance trade** routes such as the Silk Roads in Eurasia, the Indian Ocean basin, the trans-Saharan routes, and along the Mississippi and other rivers grew considerably during this period. Trade passed along not only goods, but people, religious ideas, technology, and even pathogens. New products became known through the trade routes, and in some regions, people began to produce goods for that trade instead of for a local market. People who controlled trade often became quite wealthy.
+ **Larger empires** were another characteristic of the third-wave civilizations. The empires often provided stability and security and encouraged trade, such as the West African savanna empires or the Tang dynasty. Large empires also meant more diversity, as different groups of people came under the sway of one state, such as the Inca or the Islamic empire. The largest empires were created by pastoralists or nomadic peoples: Arabs, Berbers, Turks, Mongols, or Aztecs.
+ **Religions spread** along the trade routes protected by large empires. Hinduism, Buddhism, Christianity, and Islam all expanded outside their original location to become world religions.
+ **Technologies spread** to different regions. Technology such as silk manufacturing, the sugar crystallization process, cotton textile manufacturing, the Hindu-Arabic number system, the concept of zero, and corn (maize) production diffused to regions far beyond their original creation.
+ **Diseases spread** to become transregional pandemics, such as the Black Death.
+ **Travelers along the trade routes** become a major focus of historical interest, whether merchants, missionaries, migrants, soldiers, or bureaucratic administrators. This focus on travel raises the following questions:
    • What happens when strangers from different cultures meet?
    • How did external stimuli cause change within societies?
    • How did societies or individuals choose what to accept and what to reject from other cultures, and what modifications did they make to the foreign ideas or technologies?

A masculine, warrior culture meant that much of the "work" of building empires and administering them, establishing trade routes, spreading religions, and so on was predominantly the realm of men, and most of our historical sources from this time come from men. Third-wave civilizations mostly provide "men's history"; however, women often had a stronger local role, and their labor contributed to making goods that entered long-distance trade. Gender roles varied over time and between regions and groups of people.

CHAPTER SEVEN

Commerce and Culture, 500–1500

AP World History Key Concepts

3.1: Expansion and Intensification of Communication and Exchange Networks

I. Improved transportation technologies and commercial practices led to an increased volume of trade, and expanded the geographical range of existing and newly active trade networks.

II. The movement of peoples caused environmental and linguistic effects.

III. Cross-cultural exchanges were fostered by the intensification of existing, or the creation of new, networks of trade and communication.

The primary focus of this chapter is the development and intensification of trans-regional trade networks: the Silk Roads across Central Asia (see Map 7.1, p. 319), the Indian Ocean Basin (see Map 7.2, p. 325), the trans-Saharan routes (see Map 7.4, p. 336), and the less dense trade routes in the Americas (see Map 7.5, p. 340). Also, make sure to review the Snapshot charts of goods traded in the different regions, such as the goods traded on the Silk Roads on page 320 and across the Indian Ocean basin on page 327. Trade routes most often connected different environmental regions—the goods or agricultural products produced in one area might not be able to be found in another area with a different geography. All of these routes generated wealth and led to the development or expansion of urban centers like the Swahili city-states or Cahokia. This expanded trade relied on new technology like the sternpost rudder, magnetic compass, astrolabe, lateen sail, and the domestication of camels. Expanded trade also facilitated the exchange of more than just trade goods; religions, culture, languages, agricultural products, human populations (whether merchants, travelers, or slaves), and disease were all transported along the trade routes. Much of the trade was conducted by independent merchants, who often lived in diaspora communities along the trade routes, but in some cases, as with the Incas, trade was strictly controlled by the state. Languages spread with the merchants, such as Sanskrit into Southeast Asia or Arabic into East Africa. New languages also developed, such as Swahili—based on the Bantu language group, but written in Arabic and using Arabic loan words. Environmental effects include the dissemination of new crops, such as bananas, maize, yams, or sugar to new locations; the exploitation of forests for rare woods, animals and birds, or ivory; or the spread of diseases such as the Black Death.

3.2: Continuity and Innovation of State Forms and Their Interactions

I. Empires collapsed and were reconstituted; in some regions new state forms emerged.

II. Interregional contacts and conflicts between states and empires encouraged significant technological and cultural transfers.

The expansion of trade encouraged urban growth along important junctures in trade routes, such as the Swahili city-states in East Africa or Gao and Timbuktu in West Africa, as well as creating opportunities for new kinds of states like Srivijaya (see Map 7.3, p. 329), built on the Strait of Malacca, a choke point in the sea trade routes between the South China Sea and the Indian Ocean. Culture, including technology, traveled along the trade routes. Some technological transfers aided exploration, such as the stern-post rudder and lateen sail or the spread of camel domestication from Asia to northern Africa. Others included transferring the special products of one region to another, sometimes by "industrial espionage." For example, silk production technology was a closely guarded secret in China, but was transferred to other regions such as Korea or the Byzantine Empire, dispersing silk manufacturing. Sometimes agricultural products were transferred, such as sugarcane to India; maize to the Ancestral Pueblo people, the Mound Builders, or the Andean region; or bananas to Madagascar and Eastern Africa.

Religion also spread through the travels of merchants. Judaism, Christianity, Hinduism, Buddhism, and Islam were all carried to distant lands by merchants. Buddhism traveled the eastern ends of the Silk Roads between India and China and followed Hinduism into Southeast Asia. Conversion to Buddhism was voluntary and demonstrated the symbiotic relationship between the trade and religion; wealthy Buddhists spent quite a bit of money promoting Buddhist traditions and acquiring Buddhist artifacts, while Buddhist travelers, whether monks or merchants, helped fuel long-distance trade. Similarly, the cultures of peripheral regions in East and Southeast Asia were influenced by dominant trading partners. For example, Vietnam, Japan, and Korea became part of China's sphere of influence. Other areas in Southeast Asia were influenced by Indian culture because of the trading relationship between those areas and the Hindu kingdoms of South Asia. The temple of Angkor Wat is a prime example of Hindu and, later, Buddhist cultural influence in Southeast Asia. Islam spread throughout the Indian Ocean basin and in Western Africa in much the same way as Buddhism did along the Silk Roads; conversion was voluntary and offered advantages to local rulers in terms of trade and culture, including a written language. Islam also cemented societal hierarchies and inherited kingship lines.

3.3: Increased Economic Productive Capacity and Its Consequences

I. Innovations stimulated agricultural and industrial production in many regions.

II. The fate of cities varied greatly, with periods of significant decline, and with periods of increased urbanization buoyed by rising productivity and expanding trade networks.

III. Despite significant continuities in social structures and in methods of production, there were also some important changes in labor management and in the effect of religious conversion on gender relations and family life.

Cities contracted or became extinct in the face of over-extended agriculture (Chaco Canyon), shifting of trade routes due to combat or invasion (inner Asian cities after the breakup of the Han and invasion of pastoral peoples), or exposure to trade-borne diseases (such as the Black Death, which devastated many cities in Eurasia and northern Africa). Trade also contributed to the creation of cities or their expansion, such as Dunhuang along the Silk Road, Venice in the Mediterranean trade, or the Swahili city-states in East Africa. Long-distance trade also permitted the transportation of slaves from one region to another. Women were most often used as domestic servants or concubines, while men were often agricultural laborers, miners, porters, or even government officials. Some African slaves even ended up in the Abbasid caliphate.

Theme 1: Interaction Between Humans and the Environment

Since Eurasia is on an east–west axis, much of the agricultural products or domesticated animals available in one region could be grown or raised in another along the same lines of latitude. In the Americas and Africa, all continents on a north–south axis, much modification was needed to transport animals or crops into totally different zones; rain forest, deserts, high mountains — all served to limit trade and the transfer of crops or animals. This explains the more rapid expansion of crops across Eurasia and the relatively long time it took for maize to spread beyond its origins in Mesoamerica to the Andes or northeastern woodlands. One of the most important environmental issues in the increased trade was when Malay sailors learned to use the monsoons (seasonal winds in the Indian Ocean region) to travel over open sea instead of hugging the coastline (see Map 7.2, p. 325). Along with new navigation technology and shipbuilding techniques, the Indian Ocean became a "common highway" for traders from China to the Swahili cities.

Theme 2: Development and Interaction of Cultures

Cultures interacted in unprecedented ways as the intensity of economic exchanges increased. The most obvious example is the spread of religions. Specifically, Buddhism, Islam, Hinduism, and even Christianity came to new areas via trade routes, and linked far-flung people with a common belief system. Great monumental structures, such as the Hindu temples of Angkor Wat, Buddhist temples such as Borobudur in Indonesia, or the mosques and Islamic universities of Timbuktu, speak to cultural diffusion along trade routes. Similarly, intellectual knowledge such as mathematics, medical innovations, and hydrologic technology spread. Foodstuffs, such as rice, noodles, sugar, and citrus, spread across Eurasia, while Malay sailors spread bananas, coconuts, and cocoyams to Madagascar. Kings in East African city-states converted to Islam, wore silk and used porcelain dishes from China, and used a language composed of Bantu words written in Arabic script. Lastly, travelers recorded their journeys and gave new insight into the cultures they encountered, such as Ibn Battuta and Marco Polo.

Theme 3: State-Building, Expansion, and Conflict

State expansion was often linked to controlling needed trade routes. States garnered wealth from trading and taxing those who traded. West African states such as Ghana and Mali became extremely wealthy because they controlled the gold–salt trade across the Sahara. Their gold monopoly allowed them to create armies to take over more territory and to protect the trade routes. Srivijaya controlled the strategic straits of Malacca and also became incredibly wealthy by charging ships that passed through the narrow strait. Pastoralists (such as the Mongols or Berbers) controlled trade through steppes and desert regions. The Mongols (see Chapter 11) created a huge land empire stretching from China to Eastern Europe, and a rejuvenated Silk Road trade flourished under their protection.

Theme 4: Creation, Expansion, and Interaction of Economic Systems

Along with the much-coveted silks, commodities such as cotton textiles from India, hides and furs from Russia, lapis lazuli from the Middle East, and olive oil and wine from the Mediterranean region traveled across the land routes collectively known as the Silk Roads. These trails stretched in various directions from Luoyang in the east to Tyre in the west. They circumvented the Taklamakan desert to the north and to the south, linked with routes going northward for Baltic amber and furs and timber from Siberia, and stretched southward into Barygaza in India as well as into the Persian Gulf.

The goods traded within the Indian Ocean basin (the Sea Roads) included many of the same goods that were transmitted overland along the Silk Roads; however, because ships could carry more than camels or donkeys, nonluxury goods such as rice, pepper, sugar, wheat, and timber traveled via the Indian Ocean trade network. As new technology was employed, the volume of trade across land and sea increased. In addition, traders engaged in economic warfare and espionage by smuggling trade secrets from one area to another. For example, knowledge of how to raise silk worms was smuggled out of China and helped the Byzantines, Persians, Japanese, and Koreans learn how to produce the much-coveted silk cloth, thus expanding the silk industry. Malay sailors learned how to use the seasonal monsoon winds to navigate the Indian Ocean, therefore connecting the east coast of Africa with Asia.

The trans-Saharan trade routes across Africa (or Sand Roads) originated as trade routes between the various cities in Sudanic Africa and were transformed by the importation of the camel. Once the camel came to West Africa, regional trade expanded into a large network of trade routes that exchanged salt, gold, ivory, and slaves within West Africa and to the cities around the Mediterranean Sea.

In the Americas, long-distance trade routes became increasingly important. These American trade routes were not as direct or well-established as those in the Afro-Eurasian area, but luxury goods such as obsidian and turquoise traveled their way southward from North America into Mesoamerica, while the knowledge of the cultivation of maize traveled northward to the Ancestral Pueblo people and the Mississippi Valley, and indirectly travelled south to the Andes. The pochteca (independent merchant guild) controlled trade in the Aztec Empire. In the Andean region, however, the Inca state created thousands of miles roads and exerted absolute control over trade.

Theme 5: Development and Transformation of Social Structures

Interregional trade affected social structures. One of the most obvious is that although men often undertook the trade, women often created the items that were traded. This was especially true in silk. Women were responsible for raising silk worms and creating silk cloth. Trade also increased the social complexity in areas that had previously not been a central part of the trade network. Also, because of expanded long-distance trade, slaves could be taken long distances from their homes—even to different continents. For example, slaves from non-Islamic stateless societies in Africa were used as agricultural laborers by the Abbasid in the modern region of southern Iraq. Finally, access to coveted luxury goods from distant lands cemented the differences between the ruling elite and the commoners. Rulers were almost always male, and traditional matrilineal descent patterns changed in favor of patriarchal forms of political, economic, and social powers.

In the Aztec Empire, the pochteca (independent merchants' guild) lived separately from the permanent residents of cities, married only among themselves, and sometimes served as spies for rulers. In the Inca Empire of South America, the state controlled the storage and dispersion of food and other goods, requiring a system of recordkeeping by a highly trained class of accountants.

CHAPTER EIGHT
China and the World: East Asian Connections, 500–1300

AP World History Key Concepts

3.1: Expansion and Intensification of Communication and Exchange Networks

I. Improved transportation technologies and commercial practices led to an increased volume of trade, and expanded the geographical range of existing and newly active trade networks.

II. The movement of peoples caused environmental and linguistic effects.

III. Cross-cultural exchanges were fostered by the intensification of existing, or the creation of new, networks of trade and communication.

The fall of the Han dynasty led to several hundred years of political fragmentation. Large numbers of Han Chinese migrated southward during these unsettled years, which were marked by frequent incursion from steppes pastoralists such as the Xiongnu and Jurchen, who intermarried with the northern Chinese. Buddhism grew rapidly in China as Confucianism lost favor. Large populations in the south were possible because of improved agricultural techniques and water management, as well as the importation of new strains of rice. Old-growth forests were felled and hillsides were terraced, all in an effort to grow enough to feed the ever-increasing population.

During the Tang and Song dynasties, China led the world in technology and was once again the center of transregional trade. China took control of the Silk Roads and also opened or expanded many interior trade systems along canals and rivers. Using advanced shipbuilding and navigational techniques, Chinese merchants ranged throughout Southeast Asia and the Indian Ocean. Uniform taxes and tariffs and the use of paper money and bank drafts, as well as China's openness to foreign merchants, led to significant improvements in trade. China learned to deal with people they considered to be barbarians through a system of tribute exchanges or through military conflict when all else failed. China remained the "superpower" of the region and affected the political, social, cultural, and economic systems of nearby Korea, Vietnam, and Japan.

3.2: Continuity and Innovation of State Forms and Their Interactions

I. Empires collapsed and were reconstituted; in some regions new state forms emerged.

II. Interregional contacts and conflicts between states and empires encouraged significant technological and cultural transfers.

The Sui dynasty rebuilt a centralized state in China, followed closely by the Tang and Song dynasties. Confucian and Daoist ideals were reinvigorated and absorbed many aspects of Buddhism, which came to be seen as a foreign religion and associated with conquest. The Confucian examination system was reestablished, and the political system endured (with a brief Mongol interruption) until the twentieth century. China's technological advances—such as printing, porcelain making, steel making, the magnetic compass, shipbuilding techniques, medical advances, and gunpowder—found their way across Afro-Eurasia along the trade routes, often disseminated by Muslim merchants.

3.3: Increased Economic Productive Capacity and Its Consequences

I. Innovations stimulated agricultural and industrial production in many regions.

II. The fate of cities varied greatly, with periods of significant decline, and with periods of increased urbanization buoyed by rising productivity and expanding trade networks.

III. Despite significant continuities in social structures and in methods of production, there were also some important changes in labor management and in the effect of religious conversion on gender relations and family life.

As Song Chinese moved south to escape the invasions of steppes nomads, they greatly modified the land around the Yangzi River valley through intensive agriculture to accommodate the higher population level; they brought in new, high-yield rice strains from Vietnam (Champa rice), improved water control over river flooding and irrigation, cut down trees, terraced hillsides, and dug canals. China could support the highest population in the world and at the time was the most urbanized country. Large cities rose further south, away from invaders, while the northern population dropped. Cities included large administrative capitals and growth was also fueled by increased industrialization and foreign trade. Social structures reflected the traditional values established under the Han; the scholar-gentry class continued to be in charge, but merchants could become exceedingly wealthy because of the reestablished trade networks. While Chinese agriculture continued to be based on the labor of free peasants and tenant farmers, some changes did occur. For example, requiring cash payments of rents instead of payment in kind meant that peasant households had to produce something to sell, often goods that could be traded to the growing internal urban markets or on long-distance trade networks. Gender roles in the Song dynasty also returned to what was perceived as proper Confucian submission of women, especially women of the upper class. It was at this time that the practice of foot binding began. While aspects of Chinese culture and its political and economic structure influenced Korea, Japan, and Vietnam, these nations on China's periphery often retained much of their own traditions on social and gender roles.

Theme 1: Interaction Between Humans and the Environment

China saw both population increases and decreases during this period. Invasions from steppes nomads and warfare caused populations to decline or move south to escape warfare; raging epidemic diseases such as the Black Death also took their toll. Overall, more intensive agriculture was made possible by improved techniques, such as terracing, using fertilizer (night soil or human feces), canal and flood control, and the importation of new crops, such as Champa rice, led to rapidly rising population numbers as well as increased population density and urbanization. This intensive agriculture, in addition to clear-cutting forests to provide power for kilns and metalworking, tended to destroy the original ecology of a region. Some farmers switched to cash crops instead of growing food, which they now purchased from expanded internal markets.

Theme 2: Development and Interaction of Cultures

China had a complicated relationship with cultures on its periphery. When China was strong, its expansion and control strongly impacted surrounding peoples such as the nomadic and seminomadic steppes people to the north, non-Han southern peoples, and surrounding states such as Vietnam, Korea, and Japan. China, as the middle kingdom, believed that their emperor ruled "all under heaven." Non-Chinese people could become accepted as civilized if they adopted Chinese language and writing, dress, customs, and cultural beliefs. Peripheral states often took part in a tribute system where they acknowledged both the cultural and military superiority of the Chinese and offered elaborate gifts or tribute to the emperor, who would reciprocate with token gifts. When China was weak, however, as in the period following the collapse of the Han dynasty and during the Tang dynasty, it paid vast amounts of tribute to its northern neighbors to prevent invasion, even offering Chinese princesses to barbarian leaders as wives to try to maintain peaceful borders.

China's cultural impact on its neighbors led to the adoption of Confucian values and education in Vietnam, Korea, and Japan. These regions also learned Buddhism from Chinese monks, adopted Chinese ideograms for their local languages, modeled their governments, economic systems, and, in the case of Japan, their cities, on Chinese models. However, this cultural borrowing was piecemeal; for example, Japanese and Korean landowners and nobility retained control of their governments without adopting a merit-based system, women often retained slightly more independence (for example, Japanese samurai women were expected to learn martial arts; Vietnamese women like the Trung sisters led rebellions against Chinese rule; and none adopted foot binding), and Chinese ideograms were adapted to local language phonetics.

Chinese philosophy within China changed. Confucianism was devalued following the fall of the Han and ensuing political fragmentation, and Buddhism became an alternative that promised solace. However, when central rule was restored under the Sui, Tang, and Song, a new form of Confucianism was restored as the center of government. This new form, called Neo-Confucianism, incorporated elements of Buddhism and stressed even stronger submission for women and adherence to Confucian hierarchies. The examination system was expanded with the help of printing, which made more texts available.

Theme 3: State-Building, Expansion, and Conflict

China regained its central governmental unity under the Sui dynasty. It rebuilt and extended canals (see Map 8.1, p. 368 for the location of the Grand Canal) and attempted to expand its borders to include Korea. This military venture was unsuccessful and exhausted the dynasty's finances, leading to its collapse. The Tang dynasty continued traditional Chinese models: strong central control by an emperor supported by a theoretically merit-based bureaucracy trained through a strenuous Confucian academic tradition and civil service examinations (though in actuality, the landed gentry still had a significant role in governing). Six ministries were established (personnel, rites, finance, army, justice, and public works), and a Censorate oversaw the operations of the other branches. This basic system remained intact until the twentieth century, despite changes in dynasties. Tang China was considered the best-run state in the world and expanded its control along the Silk Roads. The Tang suppressed Buddhism in China, partly because it conflicted with Confucian hierarchical support for dynastic rule and partly because it was seen as a foreign religion at a time when China was recovering the core of Chinese culture expressed through Neo-Confucianism. Toward the end of Tang rule, Vietnam managed to win its independence from direct Chinese rule. As northern nomadic tribes such as the Khitan and Jurchen took over regions along the northern border, the next dynasty, the Song, moved southward. By the end of the thirteenth century, another group of steppes nomads, the Mongols, seized control of the entire empire and ruled until the mid-fourteenth century. Japan copied many aspects of China's culture and governance but remained more feudal than the centralized middle kingdom.

Theme 4: Creation, Expansion, and Interaction of Economic Systems

After the restoration of centralized government with the Sui dynasty, and continuing with the Tang and Song dynasties, China regained its dominance in world trade and industry. Constructing the Grand Canal and other internal waterways allowed more direct trade within the country. Low-cost transportation allowed bulk materials, not just luxury goods, to be shipped and permitted farmers to specialize in production of items for trade because they could buy food in the local market instead of having to grow it themselves. Silk cloth and other handicrafts were produced for internal and interregional trade. The production of iron for armor, arrowheads and other weapons, monastery bells, and agricultural tools soared not only in large-scale, state-run smelters but also in small backyard furnaces. Production of paper and printing presses increased the volume of information and scholarly texts. Gunpowder, new navigational techniques, and improved designs for shipbuilding all added to China's growth and strength. China was the most commercialized country in the world under the Tang and Song. In addition, the Tang took control of the eastern half of the Silk Roads into Central Asia through the Tarim basin (see Map 8.1, p. 368). Large amounts of trade goods, such as Chinese silks and porcelain, traveled westward; tribute arrangements also increased the amount of Chinese goods flowing west and north to the pastoral people of the steppes, as well as other goods being imported into China from the west and Central Asia. This trade greatly influenced cultures on China's periphery.

Theme 5: Development and Transformation of Social Structures

The influence of pastoral nomads—during the period after the fall of the Han, the rise of Turkic empires during the Tang, and the collapse of the Song under the Mongols—led to some loosening of traditional Confucian hierarchies, especially the subordination and confinement of women. However, the traditional Chinese values expressed in Neo-Confucianism meant that during most of this period women were forced into submission, and the social hierarchy established under the Han remained relatively constant.

The Song practice of foot binding was a new factor that demonstrated the renewed subordination of women and was thought to create beautiful, tiny feet that distinguished upper-class Chinese women from the barbarians. Women also lost control of silk weaving, but they continued to be the major producers of silk worms and thread. Women did have increased opportunities running restaurants, selling fish and vegetables, or working as domestic servants, dressmakers, concubines, or performers. In contrast, women's property rights expanded, as did their education (at least for elite women).

In Korea, Chinese influence saw a regression of women's freedom as the Confucian system became more popular. Also, the landowning gentry in Korea maintained far more control than did their counterparts in China; the meritocracy was less effective in providing social mobility in Korea. Vietnam, in contrast, more heartily adopted the civil service examination system and thus maintained greater social mobility than Korea.

While Japan copied Chinese bureaucratic principles, the Japanese did not adopt China's social structure or views on the role of women. Unlike Song China, Japanese women escaped foot binding and had considerably more freedom. Also, the warrior virtues of the samurai were at the core of Japanese feudal society, whereas warriors were not highly regarded in China's social structure.

CHAPTER NINE

The Worlds of Islam: Afro-Eurasian Connections, 600–1500

AP World History Key Concepts

3.1: Expansion and Intensification of Communication and Exchange Networks

I. Improved transportation technologies and commercial practices led to an increased volume of trade, and expanded the geographical range of existing and newly active trade networks.

II. The movement of peoples caused environmental and linguistic effects.

III. Cross-cultural exchanges were fostered by the intensification of existing, or the creation of new, networks of trade and communication.

The expansion of Islamic empires created the first hemisphere-wide trading and communication network involving Africa, Asia, South Asia, and Europe (see Map 9.3, p. 429). Distant regions such as Central Asia and sub-Saharan Africa became more closely linked to the major trading systems (Indian Ocean, Mediterranean, Silk Roads, and Saharan routes) through the spread of Islamic empires. Muslim merchants continued advances in shipbuilding and navigation, such as improving the astrolabe by adding azimuths for determining location at sea. Islam was friendly to merchants and trade if conducted fairly, unlike the more hostile attitude toward merchants in other cultures (such as China and Christian Europe). The economic system of the *Dar al-Islam* (land under Islamic rule) often borrowed from the Persians and employed many commercial techniques that facilitated trade, in addition to enjoying the advantages of a common language (Arabic), system of taxation, and laws. The spread of Islam, whether by armies, merchants, or Sufi mystics, was accompanied by the spread of Arabic, the language used in the sacred texts of the Quran and *hadiths* (sayings of the prophet Mohammed). Arabic became a common trade language, and many previously unwritten languages, such as Swahili, came to be written in Arabic script. The creation of a hemisphere-wide trade network also contributed to the spread of different crops, agricultural and water management techniques, and agricultural implements. In some areas, such as Muslim Spain, Central Asia, or sub-Saharan Africa, syncretism or cultural blending occurred alongside the diffusion of Islam and Arabic culture.

3.2: Continuity and Innovation of State Forms and Their Interactions

I. Empires collapsed and were reconstituted; in some regions new state forms emerged.

II. Interregional contacts and conflicts between states and empires encouraged significant technological and cultural transfers.

The rapid expansion of Islam (see Map 9.2, p. 420 and Map 9.3, p. 429), first through conquest by Arab armies and later through conversion, brought the core of Afro-Eurasia under the control of one group. State rule evolved from military conquest to the creation of new forms of governance. The military forces sweeping out of Arabia led to the ultimate downfall of the Byzantine Empire, Christian kingdoms in Spain, and the Sassanid Empire (Persia) before moving to take control of the trade routes and confronting China at the Battle of Talas River in Central Asia in 751. This rapid expansion led to an empire that was united by a common faith, with no separation of religion and governance.

The first four Rightly Guided Caliphs had all been companions of the prophet Mohammed. After their deaths, a split emerged in Islam between the Sunni and the Shia. The Sunnis believed that the caliphs should be chosen by the Islamic community; the Shia held that leadership should derive from the blood relatives of Muhammad. While Persia became Shia and maintained Farsi as their language, much of the rest of northern Africa, Spain, and the Middle East were Sunni Arabs and used Arabic as the language of government. The Umayyad caliphate following the Rightly Guided Caliphs was replaced by the Abbasids, who were strongly influenced by Persian traditions. Persian culture, architecture, administrative techniques, and court ritual had a huge impact on Muslim rule in Iran, India, Central Asia, and the Ottoman Empire. The Abbasids soon lost all but nominal control over outlying regions and were ultimately conquered by the Mongols, who destroyed their capital of Baghdad.

3.3: Increased Economic Productive Capacity and Its Consequences

I. Innovations stimulated agricultural and industrial production in many regions.

II. The fate of cities varied greatly, with periods of significant decline, and with periods of increased urbanization buoyed by rising productivity and expanding trade networks.

III. Despite significant continuities in social structures and in methods of production, there were also some important changes in labor management and in the effect of religious conversion on gender relations and family life.

Persian water management techniques helped increase agricultural production throughout the Dar al-Islam. Crops, including sugar, cotton, and citrus, were widely diffused. Urban areas grew as administrative, religious, or trade centers. Mecca, for example, saw millions of pilgrims each year during the hajj. Baghdad was built as the capital of the Abbasid caliphate. Gao became a religious and educational center in West Africa, and the Swahili city-states grew in East Africa as a result of trade in the Indian Ocean basin.

Islam also brought changes to social and gender roles. All believers were equal in the eyes of Allah, so there was no distinction in prayer and no rigid caste system. This encouraged conversion of lower-caste people in South Asia, for example, and encouraged slaves to adopt Islam as a means to end their servitude. Women were also considered to be equal religiously and gained more property rights under the Quran. However, women were still clearly subordinate to their husbands. Some regional traditions of veiling and sequestration of women became more common and widespread and were later identified as Muslim customs.

Theme 1: Interaction Between Humans and the Environment

Because of the arid environment in the Arabian Peninsula, Arab culture originated with nomadic tribes who searched for pastures and oases with water and shade for their animals (usually sheep, goats, and camels). Some oases developed into agricultural villages and trading centers that later developed into cities. Islamic empires united Afro-Eurasia in trade networks, leading to great environmental change. New agricultural products and practices became widespread; rice, sugarcane, sorghum, "hard" wheat, citrus, bananas, and other tropical fruits found their way westward. In addition, water management systems (such as the qanat system—drilling into a mountainside to create a tunnel to bring water for irrigation and drinking to distant places) and plantation systems with slave labor created an "Islamic Green Revolution" that increased the food supply and caused an increase in population density and urbanization. New technology that entered the Islamic world from the east (like gunpowder, water drilling, cotton and silk textile manufacturing, and papermaking) was passed through to other regions under Islamic control.

Theme 2: Development and Interaction of Cultures

The founder of Islam, Muhammad Ibn Abdullah, was originally a trader along the routes that connected Arabia with the Levant and Mesopotamia, where Judaism, Christianity, and Zoroastrianism were all practiced. Consequently, he was familiar with several spiritual concepts that were later found in Islam, such as an all-powerful male Creator God, spiritual warfare between good and evil, an eternal heaven for the faithful as well as hell for nonbelievers. As Islam developed from a tribal religion into a universal religion, Islamic culture and the Arabic language spread as well. The Islamic world tolerated other monotheistic religious followers, particularly Christians and Jews as *dhimmis*, or "people of the book," which was unusual for this period. However, because of its tolerance, Islam looked quite different in the various regions it conquered.

Not long after Muhammad's death, a split developed in the *umma* (community of believers). Some followers, later known as Sunnis, believed the caliph should be selected by the entire Islamic community; those who believed that leadership should come from the line of Ali and Husayn, who were related to the prophet Mohammad, became known as the Shia. The division has never been reconciled. Other subgroups also developed, including the mystical Sufis (who served as missionaries and traders) and, much later, the Sikhs, who blended Islam with Hinduism.

Islam created the first truly international, hemispheric empire in history; its network reached from Spain to India, from the Mediterranean across the Sahara into West Africa and along the East African trading coastline. Its principles of faith, sometimes condensed into the Pillars of Islam (belief in one all-powerful God, obligations for prayer, charity, fasting during Ramadan, and completing a hajj [pilgrimage] to Mecca), wove a web of interconnectedness; yet, local traditions also shaped Islamic civilization outside of the Arab-controlled areas of the Middle East and North Africa.

Islam reached India via Turkic warriors invading from the Asia steppes. Although Islam proved attractive to disillusioned Buddhists and the lower castes of Hinduism and provided some tax relief, Muslims remained a minority population. In the early sixteenth century, Sikhism, a new religious movement developed; it incorporated elements of Islam (monotheism) with Hindu concepts (reincarnation and karma). Hinduism, however, remained dominant in South Asia.

The Byzantine Empire was defeated by Muslim Ottoman Turks with the fall of Constantinople in 1453. The Turkish conquerors offered many benefits to the conquered population, and Islam was not as foreign to monotheistic Christians, Jews, and Zoroastrians as it had been to Hindus and Buddhists. Sufis facilitated conversion as they established schools, hospitals, and other public works. Perhaps because a much larger proportion of the population was Turkish, as opposed to the smaller Turkic population in India, the Ottoman Empire emerged with a distinctive Turkish culture; the language was Turkish, and elements of Turkish shamanism found their way into the cultural fabric.

A different pattern of expansion and conversion occurred in West Africa where traders instead of warriors carried the message across the Sahara into Ghana, Mali, Songhay, and Kanem-Bornu. The earliest converts to Islam were the ruling elites of these kingdoms because Islam provided a source of literate officials to assist with administration and bureaucracy. Islam also offered African merchants important trade ties. In West Africa, cities became centers of government administration and trade as well as centers of Islamic religious and intellectual life. Islam did not spread quickly to rural areas, which clung to the ancient African religions and traditions.

Islam penetrated the Iberian Peninsula from North Africa early in the eighth century. To a great degree, Muslims, Christians, and Jews lived in better harmony here than elsewhere. The fine arts and sciences flourished, including medicine, astronomy, architecture, literature, and art. By 1000, Spain was perhaps 75 percent Islamic, and many of its cultural practices had spread to others, whether they converted or not. By the late tenth century, toleration began to fade. Christians began to invade from the north in an effort to reclaim Spain, and Crusaders' armies attempted to retake Jerusalem in the East. A more strict and fundamental form of Islam entered Spain from North Africa, and relationships among the three religions changed as Muslims avoided contact with Christians and imposed several limitations on them. The Reconquista (the reconquest of Muslim Spain by the Christian monarchs Ferdinand and Isabella) was completed in 1492. Possibly the most important impact of Muslim Spain was its intellectual activity, making an abundance of Islamic and classical Greek learning available to backward Europe.

Theme 3: State-Building, Expansion, and Conflict

The creation and rapid spread of the Islamic Empire was remarkable; by 750, Islam encompassed all of the Arabian Peninsula, stretched across North Africa and into the Iberian Peninsula, across Persia into South Asia, and northward into the Central Asian steppes. The defeat of the Chinese at the Battle of the Talas River halted Chinese westward expansion. Muslim military might began as a defense against other Arabs hostile to the new religion and gradually grew into an imperial army. New lands, rich agricultural areas, and profitable trading networks were brought under Muslim rule.

As the Arab Empire grew, its caliphs were transformed from tribal leaders into absolute rulers, often patterning themselves after the political administration of the

Byzantine or Sassanid (Persian) emperors they had recently fought. Included in this transformation was the acquisition of a bureaucracy, standing armies, taxes, and currency, as well as dynastic rivalries and succession disputes. The Umayyad (630–750) and the Abbasid (750–1258) dynasties followed the first caliphs. The empire did not distinguish between secular and religious rule; the caliph was the leader of both the religion and the government. Sharia (Islamic law) was developed to create a way to govern justly, behave properly, and create a good society following the teachings of the Quran and *hadith*. The unity of the *umma* did not last long; different regions broke away as local rulers became strong enough to assert individual control over their particular territory, while maintaining nominal allegiance to the caliph in Baghdad. By the tenth century, little political unification remained, even as the religion and culture it created continued to spread to different parts of the Eastern Hemisphere. The Abbasids were conquered by the Mongols, who swept down from the steppes and destroyed Baghdad. *See Chapter 11 for more detailed discussion of the Mongols.*

Theme 4: Creation, Expansion, and Interaction of Economic Systems

As Islam spread throughout Arabia, across the North African coast, and northeast into Southwest Asia and beyond, it created an immense network of economic and cultural exchanges. Commercial activity was respected in the Islamic world (Muhammad had himself been a trader) as opposed to Christendom, China, and South Asia. The pilgrimage to Mecca also encouraged travel and exchange among the faithful, and the desire of urban elites for luxury goods stimulated craftsmanship and trade. Baghdad, the Abbasid capital, became a cosmopolitan city with goods and services from across the hemisphere. Arab and Persian merchants became the dominant players in such exchanges across the third-wave civilizations and were active in the Mediterranean, across the Silk Roads and Saharan routes, and in the Indian Ocean basin. Agricultural production in Spain was the highest in Europe during the early centuries of Islamic rule, and Córdoba was one of the most splendid and cosmopolitan in the world at this time. Many new economic tools, often of Persian origin, helped expand trade, such as forms of banking, letters of credit, business partnerships, and contracts.

Theme 5: Development and Transformation of Social Structures

Socially, Islam assumed the equality of all believers before Allah. This religious egalitarianism encouraged conversion among some groups, such as lower-caste people in India. Although the Quran offered women specific protections—such as property and inheritance rights and the prohibition of female infanticide or marriage by capture—less freedom was allowed in other areas—such as ending polyandry (the practice of taking multiple husbands) or freedom of movement in public. Early Arab Muslim practices were also more liberal toward women than those of the Abbasid Empire, where elite women were confined not only in public but also in private areas of the home called harems.

Strict seclusion was not possible for women of lower economic status, whose economic activity was needed outside the home. Some Sufi groups, however, allowed women as equal members or had separate groups for women similar to the nuns of Buddhism and Christianity. A few educated women were poets or became teachers of the faith; these teachers were also called *mullahs*, the same term that was applied to male teachers of the faith. However, most women were limited to a narrow sphere that centered on their family obligations.

At first, there was little attempt to convert conquered peoples to Islam, only to bring them under Islamic rule. People from monotheistic religions were promised freedom of worship, if not political equality. The *dhimmis* were granted protected status and incurred a special tax. In some areas, such as the Iberian Peninsula and the Ottoman Empire, Christians and Jews could rise to prominent positions in government and society.

CHAPTER TEN

The Worlds of Christendom: Contraction, Expansion, and Division, 500–1300

AP World History Key Concepts

3.1: Expansion and Intensification of Communication and Exchange Networks

I. Improved transportation technologies and commercial practices led to an increased volume of trade, and expanded the geographical range of existing and newly active trade networks.

II. The movement of peoples caused environmental and linguistic effects.

III. Cross-cultural exchanges were fostered by the intensification of existing, or the creation of new, networks of trade and communication.

After the collapse of the Roman Empire in the West, long-distance trade plummeted as Roman roads fell into disrepair and social order disintegrated leaving small chiefdoms competing for control. Additionally, there was a series of invasions from groups such as the Muslims, Magyar/Huns, and Vikings (see Map 10.3, p. 481). Recovery began after 1000 when the invasions ended, partly stimulated by the Crusades (see Map 10.4, p. 487), which reintroduced a taste for Eastern luxury goods. Contact with Muslims in Spain and elsewhere led to improvements in shipbuilding and knowledge of gunpowder. In the eastern Mediterranean, the Byzantine Empire (see Map 10.1, p. 471) maintained trade ties with Asia and, along with the Italian city-states (such as Genoa, Florence, and Venice), was responsible for most of Asian or African goods entering Europe. Another trading network stretching from the Atlantic, to the Baltic, into Russia, and south to Constantinople was created by the Vikings. An indigenous trade network slowly grew in Western Europe; the Hanseatic cities in the north and the trade fairs centered in France helped begin the rebuilding process.

3.2: Continuity and Innovation of State Forms and Their Interactions

I. Empires collapsed and were reconstituted; in some regions new state forms emerged.

II. Interregional contacts and conflicts between states and empires encouraged significant technological and cultural transfers.

The Byzantine Empire continued the existence of Greco-Roman culture and ruled for a thousand years after the fall of the western Roman Empire until it was conquered by the Ottoman Turks in 1453. The Byzantines continued the Roman struggle against the Persian Empire, which weakened both and contributed to their losses to Muslim armies.

In Western Europe, the collapse of Rome created a power vacuum in which competing Germanic chiefs attempted to carve out kingdoms. Ultimately, the need to fend off outside invaders, such as the Arabs, Magyars, and Vikings, led to improved military techniques and the adoption of feudalism, a decentralized form of governance where individual fighters swear allegiance to a lord, promising to provide warriors at the lord's need in exchange for protection, land, and justice. Except for a brief attempt to reconstitute the Roman Empire in the West under Charlemagne (see Map 10.2, p. 478), decentralized government remained the norm until the High Middle Ages (1000–1300) when new centralized states like England, France, and Spain began to emerge. Unlike China, European states remained separate and competed against each other (see Map 10.3, p. 481). Some areas saw the rise of new, hybrid states; for example, Kiev was created by Vikings (Rus) and Slavic people but adopted Byzantine ideas of absolute power in the hands of an emperor, the Cyrillic writing system based on Greek, and Eastern Orthodox Christianity. New trade goods entering Europe, funneled through the Byzantine Empire and Muslim sources, also brought new ideas and technology (see Snapshot: European Borrowing, p. 490), which fueled the European economy and intellectual thought.

3.3: Increased Economic Productive Capacity and Its Consequences

I. Innovations stimulated agricultural and industrial production in many regions.

II. The fate of cities varied greatly, with periods of significant decline, and with periods of increased urbanization buoyed by rising productivity and expanding trade networks.

III. Despite significant continuities in social structures and in methods of production, there were also some important changes in labor management and in the effect of religious conversion on gender relations and family life.

The economy and agricultural practices declined during the years following the fall of the Roman Empire in the West. Long-distance trade virtually disappeared in the regions conquered by Germanic tribes and agricultural land turned into wasteland. Population dropped, and most of the remaining population was rural, tied to the land in an effort to grow enough to survive. Contact with Muslim Spain, the Crusades, and the rise of Italian trading city-states (as well as trade through Constantinople) led to significant borrowing in technology; new plows, horse collars, wheelbarrows, and spinning wheels increased rural productivity.

A generally warming trend in weather, the use of crop rotation, and new agricultural implements led to a gradual population increase. Some cities also began to increase in size for the first time since the fall of Rome. Kiev, as capital of the empire created by the Rus, was also a trade link between the Baltic and Constantinople. Italian city-states continued to prosper based on trade with the Byzantines and the Muslim world, and cities such as Córdoba and Granada rose in Muslim occupied Spain. Paris, Bologna, and other cities became university centers.

Both the social and gender structure changed after the fall of Rome as Germanic and Greco-Roman influences blended into a new entity. Women remained under patriarchal control but were able to participate in many craft guilds; however, by the fifteenth century, they were pushed out of most guilds.

Theme 1: Interaction between Humans and the Environment

The fall of Rome led to vast areas of land falling into disuse. Disease, warfare, and invasion led to a 25 percent drop in population in urban centers outside of the Italian peninsula. The monastery movement stimulated the reclamation of wasteland and intensification of agriculture. Gradually, as order was restored, peasant and serf-based agriculture began to revive.

By the High Middle Ages, a more efficient feudal labor system, relative freedom from invasion, a warming climate, and technological innovations (such as the heavy wheeled plow, improved horse collar and iron horseshoes, wheelbarrow, and the three-field system of crop rotation) provided sufficient food to cause a population rebound. Towns along old Roman trade routes began to grow, as did centers for secular and church administration (including universities and cathedral towns). Italian cities continued to grow to service the Mediterranean trade.

Theme 2: Development and Interaction of Cultures

Much of northern Africa was Christian when Muslim armies swept out of Arabia. Gradually, much of the population converted to Islam, recognizing similar beliefs in one God and an afterlife of reward or punishment, as well as similar rituals of purification. Some groups, such as the Coptic-speaking Christians in Egypt, remained as minority *dhimmis* under Muslim rule. Others, such as the Ethiopian Church in Axum, maintained their allegiance to Christianity, even though Muslim-ruled territories cut them off from much exchange with other Christians.

The Mediterranean world was a cultural crossroads where Germanic invaders, Muslim Arabs, Byzantine Greeks, and the remainder of Rome in the West as personified by the Catholic Church mixed and merged. Missionaries continued to spread Christianity into the northern parts of Europe and to convert Germanic and Nordic rulers. Christian practices were melded with local traditions, and traditional pagan sacred sites often became the location for new churches.

Both the Byzantine Empire and Muslim Spain were areas of cultural contact, but in different ways. The Byzantine Empire continued the practice of ancient Greek learning and transmitted this cultural heritage to the Islamic world and the Christian West. Byzantine religion spread north and east into the Balkans and Russia. Muslim Arab conquerors of Spain tolerated Christians and Jews as *dhimmis*, some of whom rose quite high in the court. Cultural interchange in the Muslim world produced advances in medicine, science, and mathematics, as well as an attempt to rationalize Aristotelian science and religious belief. European intellectuals travelled to places such as Córdoba to learn.

In Western Europe, a new culture was being created, combining remnants of Greco-Roman culture, the culture of Germanic tribes, and influences from the Roman Catholic Church. Latin continued as the language of the Church and of all literate people in Western Europe. Members of the Church also provided expertise for the new Germanic rulers to draw on to create their governments, legal systems, and taxation systems. Medieval scholars, such as Thomas Aquinas, also attempted to reconcile the natural philosophy of the classical world with Christian beliefs. Europeans also demonstrated a passion for new technology borrowed from the East and often improved upon these advancements. Key figures such as Roger Bacon stimulated empirical scientific thought, leading ultimately to the Scientific Revolution and the Enlightenment.

Theme 3: State-Building, Expansion, and Conflict

The eastern half of the Roman Empire, later known as the Byzantine Empire, continued to preserve Greco-Roman culture and governance for a thousand years after the fall of Rome. Their Eastern Orthodox version of Christianity was closely linked to the emperor, combining leadership of both church and state in a relationship known as caesaropapism. The Byzantine court was filled with elaborate rituals, separating the emperor from the people and even from other nobles. The capital, Constantinople, was a lynchpin in the trade between Asia and the Mediterranean, and that trade provided revenue for the empire.

While the more densely populated and more strategically situated Byzantine Empire was not taken over by the Germanic tribes or the Huns, they did mount a centuries' long rear-guard action against the forces of Islam. First the Byzantines lost North Africa and the Middle East, then Muslim armies gradually chipped away at Anatolia, the Byzantine heartland, and southeastern Europe until only the city of Constantinople remained. The Byzantines were helped by strong fortifications around their capital and the use of weapons such as Greek fire and artillery. Their war with Persia and later the destruction left by the Crusaders, who destroyed part of Constantinople's fortifications and attacked its people whom they considered to be heretics, further weakened the empire until the Ottoman Turks finally took the city in 1453, using superior cannon and siege technology to destroy the remaining walls.

Western Europe suffered a series of invasions that drastically altered the culture and forced the urbanized people of the Roman Empire into decline. First, the Germanic tribes overthrew the last Roman emperor, dividing the territory among the tribes such as the Franks, Lombards, Visigoths, and Vandals (see Map 10.1, p. 471). Gradually, these tribal chiefdoms incorporated elements of Roman rule, preserved by the Church. Charlemagne and his Carolingian dynasty attempted to restore unified rule under one king and one God in the Roman model; the unification did not outlast Charlemagne. As a new hybrid system of governance was developing, more invasions from Muslims, Magyars, and Vikings occurred until approximately 1000 (see Map 10.3, p. 481). The need to repel frequent invasions led to decentralized rule based on mutual obligations between landed nobles and their rulers; this system is known as feudalism. By the eleventh century, new national states had begun to emerge like France, England, the Scandinavian states, and Spain as it reconquered the Iberian Peninsula. The Holy Roman Empire remained a more traditional and decentralized collection of local feudal nobles owing allegiance to a common monarch.

Christian Europeans were also invaders; the Crusades and the Reconquista (see Map 10.4, p. 487) were attempts to retake lands in the hands of Muslims. While the Reconquista was ultimately successful in driving Muslims and Jews from Spain, the Crusades had little effect on the Middle East. However, the taste for Eastern luxuries, such as spices and silks, stimulated European interest in long-distance trade. New states, like Kiev in southern Russia, also arose on the periphery of the old Roman Empire. Kievan Russia shared more than religion with the Byzantine Empire; it also adopted Byzantine attitudes toward absolute rule uniting state and religion as well as elaborate court rituals. When the Byzantine Empire fell to the Ottoman Turks (1453), Russia considered itself the "third Rome," the direct inheritors of the Roman Empire.

Theme 4: Creation, Expansion, and Interaction of Economic Systems

The fall of Rome to Germanic tribes and the emergence of Arab Muslims sundered the unified Mediterranean trading system, plunging much of Europe into a "dark age" where virtually all long-distance trade ceased. A trickle of goods still made its way through Constantinople and to the Italian city-states such as Venice and Genoa where some goods were traded across the Alps. In Western Europe, the feudal political structure was paralleled by manorialism, characterized by local agricultural estates that were virtually self-sufficient and worked by serfs. Gradually, order was restored, and a taste for Asian luxuries stimulated by the Crusades helped the European economy rebuild. New trade routes were created by the Vikings, linking the Baltic and Russia with Constantinople. Powerful craft guilds controlled production of commodities such as textiles and metalworking. Chartered towns, independent from local feudal lords, grew as trade and economic centers. Free-trade towns, such as the Hanseatic cities, flourished in northern Europe. Technology spread from Asia, often through Muslim merchants, which Europeans used and adapted to stimulate economic growth in the High Middle Ages. After the fall of Constantinople, all trade with Asia and Africa had to pass through Muslim-controlled lands, where Christian merchants were subject to extra taxes. Merchants and princes began to look to the Atlantic instead of the Mediterranean for possible long-distance trade.

Theme 5: Development and Transformation of Social Structures

A new society, blended from Germanic, Greco-Roman, and Christian traditions, was created in Western Europe after the fall of Rome. Unlike China, a much-glorified military elite emerged at the top of the social classes. The need to support armed men and horses for heavy cavalry (knights) without much cash or trade revenues led to the creation of the feudal system, where lords gave land (to be worked by peasants or serfs) to their retainers in exchange for mutual obligations of defense and loyalty. A small middle class of university-educated men, like doctors, lawyers, and church theologians, grew, while guildsmen and merchants populated the towns.

The basis of the society was agricultural labor bound to the land as serfs. Unlike slaves, serfs could not be sold but were passed along with the land as chattel. The Church had its own hierarchy, also based on land worked either by monks or by serfs, from the Pope, through cardinals and bishops, to abbots, monks, and priests.

Women had more freedom in the earlier part of the period, both in convents and in craft guilds, such as spinning, weaving, brewing, and baking. They had obligations to their feudal lord to be paid by labor or in kind. By the High Middle Ages, women were pushed out of most of the crafts, except for spinning and midwifery (and prostitution), and lost much of the independence that they had previously enjoyed in convents.

CHAPTER ELEVEN
Pastoral Peoples on the Global Stage: The Mongol Movement, 1200–1500

AP World History Key Concepts

3.1: Expansion and Intensification of Communication and Exchange Networks

I. Improved transportation technologies and commercial practices led to an increased volume of trade, and expanded the geographical range of existing and newly active trade networks.

II. The movement of peoples caused environmental and linguistic effects.

III. Cross-cultural exchanges were fostered by the intensification of existing, or the creation of new, networks of trade and communication.

The major new empires in Eurasia during this period did not come from the core or foundational First Civilizations, but from pastoral nomads who lived in dry grasslands or steppes, areas unsuitable for agriculture. For centuries, pastoralists had facilitated trade with and between settled peoples, had provided innovations in transportation and weaponry (such as the stirrup, camel saddle, and compound recurve bow), and had originated religions such as Judaism and Islam.

In West Africa, the Almoravids took control of the gold trade and then crossed the Mediterranean to take control southern Spain. Turkic tribes spread westward from Central Asia, becoming a major force in the spread of Islam. The Ottoman Turks took Anatolia from the Byzantines and replaced much of the local culture; the Turkish language replaced Greek, and Islam replaced Christianity.

The most impressive pastoral empire was that of the Mongols, who created the largest land empire ever seen in Eurasia. The Mongols, however, had little long-term impact on culture or language in most of the regions they conquered; instead, they often adapted to the civilizations of the settled peoples they defeated. The Mongols did have a huge impact on Eurasian trade, however. They protected and taxed merchants across their realms and contributed to the rebirth of the Silk Routes, allowing crops, technology, religions, and knowledge to flow across Eurasia at a greater rate than ever before.

Environmentally, the Mongols destroyed agricultural resources and irrigation systems when conquering a region, and new crops were dispersed to different regions following the *pax Mongolica* (Mongol peace). The most significant environmental impact was the spread of the Black Death from Central Asia across the Mongol trade routes, creating a pandemic reaching much of Eurasia and northern Africa.

3.2: Continuity and Innovation of State Forms and Their Interactions

I. Empires collapsed and were reconstituted; in some regions new state forms emerged.

II. Interregional contacts and conflicts between states and empires encouraged significant technological and cultural transfers.

The collapse of the second-wave empires had huge consequences; in particular, they created opportunity for peoples on the periphery of empires to assert themselves on a larger stage. Often, these groups were pastoralists (see Snapshot: Varieties of Pastoral Societies, p. 516). Pastoralists, like the Xiongnu, Turkic peoples, or Mongols, often raided and harassed settled states, such as China. When the Chinese state was strong, the pastoral incursions were a nuisance, not a threat. When the Chinese state was weak, it was forced to pay tribute to the tribes in order to prevent invasion. During the Tang dynasty, the northern part of China was ruled by pastoralists, and the greatest pastoral empire of all—the Mongols—captured Song China and ruled as the Yuan dynasty. For the most part, the Mongols in China remained culturally distinct and had little lasting effect on China. Other pastoral empires included the Seljuk Turks, who took military control of the Persian Empire and adopted the title of sultan (the Abbasids remained in nominal control); they were defeated by the Mongols to form the Il-Khanate of Persia.

The Mongol conquest was devastating to the heavily populated agricultural region and cities such as Baghdad. The Mongols themselves were changed by this conquest; they adopted Islam, drew heavily on Persian administrative techniques, and some became farmers and intermarried with local people.

In Russia, the Mongols of the Golden Horde destroyed the Kievan Rus. However, because the rich steppes to the southeast provided ample pasture for Mongol horses and livestock, they continued a pastoral life, requiring tribute from Russian princes instead of governing them directly. This indirect rule allowed the princes of Moscow to become powerful and eventually throw off Mongol control. There was little cultural transfer between the Christian Russians and the Mongols, who assimilated with the Kipchaks and adopted Islam. Mongol control of the major trade routes in Eurasia promoted cultural transfer. The Mongol capital, Karakorum, became a multicultural center open to craftsmen and merchants of many far-flung regions. Chinese technology, art, and medicine moved westward, Muslim astronomy and crops moved east to influence the Chinese, and the comparatively backward Western Europe benefitted from new crops, technology, and knowledge without having to undergo Mongol conquest. *See Chapters 8, 9, and 10 for discussion of this Key Concept for East Asia, the Arab empires, and Europe.*

3.3: Increased Economic Productive Capacity and Its Consequences

I. Innovations stimulated agricultural and industrial production in many regions.

II. The fate of cities varied greatly, with periods of significant decline, and with periods of increased urbanization buoyed by rising productivity and expanding trade networks.

III. Despite significant continuities in social structures and in methods of production, there were also some important changes in labor management and in the effect of religious conversion on gender relations and family life.

In some regions, such as the Middle East, Mongol invasion meant great destruction to both urban centers and the agricultural system that supported them. The overall effect of the interchange along Mongol-protected trade routes stimulated trade and technology. One of the most significant transfers, however, was disease; the Black Death (bubonic plague) swept along the trade routes, killing between 25 percent and 50 percent of the populations of Eurasia and northern Africa. The social consequences were huge in some regions. For example, much of Western Europe experienced a significant drop in population among the serfs and laborers, leading to changes in the social system; laborers demanded higher wages and freedom from serfdom. Another, shorter-term impact of the pastoral invasions was a lessening of patriarchy. Mongols and other steppes people allowed women much more active social and economic roles and even participation in political and military power.

Theme 1: Interaction Between Humans and the Environment

The most important role of nomads to the global historical record was their ability to adapt to environments unsuitable for agriculture. The domestication of the horse and the development of skilled horseback riding were pivotal for the success of pastoralists in Eurasian grasslands. Camels provided the same advantages in arid environments such as Arabia and the Sahara. Ranges and herd sizes (usually goats, sheep, horses, or camels) increased, as did the ability to transport shelters and goods. Pastoral skills such as hunting and riding, along with improved technology (such as horse and camel saddles, stirrups, smaller compound or laminated bows that could be fired while on horseback or camelback) provided military advantages over sedentary civilizations. Mongol trade routes fostered the spread of religions, agricultural products (such as carrots and lemons to China from the Middle East), and technology (such as the stirrup and gunpowder).

At the same time, Mongol attacks devastated local populations who resisted. Khwarizm, Kievan Russia, and the Abbasid Empire were crushed by the Mongols, their people were killed or enslaved, and their cities were destroyed. The Mongols had different priorities than those of settled civilizations and often converted agricultural land into pasture. As a result, Persian and Iraqi irrigation systems were neglected and destroyed, causing immense damage to these agricultural societies. On the other hand, new cities were built, such as the Mongol capitals of Karakorum in Mongolia and Khanbalik in China, or existing cities grew in response to renewed trade across the Silk Roads. Another environmental impact of the vast Mongol trading system was the ease with which epidemic disease could be spread. The Black Death began in Central Asia and spread outward to affect most of the hemisphere except Sub-Saharan Africa or the tundra regions of northern Eurasia (see Map 11.2, p. 535).

Theme 2: Development and Interaction of Cultures

Nomads are often seen as the world's first connectors between various cultures as they migrated from one pastureland to another. They carried exotic commodities, unique plants and seeds, technology, and religions from place to place; as a result, they spurred innovation and creativity among sedentary civilizations. With the development of horseback and camel riding, nomads were able to travel farther than before and expand their realm of influence. The Xiongnu (see Map, p. 518) in the third and second centuries B.C.E., provoked by Chinese incursions into their territory, created a military confederacy that was instrumental in the demise of both the Roman and Han empires. Later nomadic groups performed similar functions (Huns, Turks, Germans, Arab Bedouins, Magyars, Vikings, Almoravids). A major turning point in history was the conversion of Turks to Islam, which gave these nomadic Central Asian tribal peoples cultural cohesion that afforded them the ability to create one of the major third-wave Islamic civilizations and become a major source of spreading Islam and Turkic languages as they penetrated Afro-Eurasia.

The most expansive pastoralist people, the Mongols, had a small cultural impact, leaving behind no new universal faith, language, or organizational skills. To control conquered populations, the Mongols distributed population clusters of one culture among those of another culture or sent them to other areas of the empire where their services as skilled craftsmen, bureaucrats, or military experts were required. In China, some Mongols sampled Daoism or Buddhism, though most remained true to their ancient animistic beliefs. While they adopted many Chinese luxuries, such as wearing silk, the Yuan dynasty did not attempt to assimilate into Chinese society. The Mongolian occupation, however, impacted the succeeding Ming dynasty, which attempted to return to a pure Chinese culture and reestablish Confucian values.

In Persia, members of the Mongolian court assimilated much of the Persian culture, and a number of Mongols actually became farmers, married local people, and converted to Islam. When the Mongolian dynasty in Persia collapsed in 1330, the Mongols were not driven out (as they were in China and Russia) because they had become so assimilated into Persian culture that divisions among the cultures no longer existed.

After the Mongols destroyed Kiev, they collected tribute from but did not occupy Russia. The nearby grasslands allowed the Mongols to continue their nomadic culture, near the Kipchak people from whom they adopted Islam. The center of Russian culture, however, shifted from Kiev to Moscow. In addition, the tolerant Mongolian attitude toward religion allowed the Eastern Orthodox Church to flourish as it received exemption from many taxes.

Theme 3: State-Building, Expansion, and Conflict

The traditional pastoral unit was the clan or tribe, and different clans or tribes were often at war with each other. Sometimes a charismatic leader would be able to unite the tribes to create new empires, but because steppes tribes were organized around family and kinship relationships, maintaining unification was a challenge. The Xiongnu north of China established perhaps the earliest such nomadic empire. The largest nomadic empire was that of the Mongols, who united the steppes tribes and attacked established civilizations such as Song China and Abbasid Persia (see Map 11.1, p. 522).

The charismatic leader Chinggis Khan created the most powerful military in the world at the time, defeating neighboring tribes and harnessing their skills as cavalry to create a Mongol Empire. Continued expansion kept his warriors unified and provided loyalty through the distribution of wealth and other rewards. Although he and his descendants created the largest Eurasian land empire, they were not successful in every military venture; they withdrew from Eastern Europe, were defeated by the Mamluks at

Ain Jalut in 1260, failed twice to invade Japan due to typhoons, and failed to penetrate the tropical jungles of Southeast Asia. Chinggis organized his army in groups of hundreds, thousands, and ten thousands (similar to the Roman legions), dispersed warriors from defeated steppes tribes among Mongolian warriors, and borrowed military techniques developed by other cultures, such as gunpowder, battering rams, and catapults from the Chinese. Chinggis's terrifying reputation preceded him; many cities surrendered rather than fight and be annihilated. As his territory expanded, Chinggis created Karakorum, a capital city in the Mongolian homeland. A centralized bureaucracy evolved, staffed with scholars from all reaches of the growing empire, as did a type of "Pony Express" system to relay messages, information, and decrees that also helped facilitate unification and trade. Mongol rulers often continued or drew on the governmental administration already in place at the time of conquest.

In China, the southern Song dynasty was not conquered until Chinggis's grandson, Khubilai, became the Great Khan. The Mongols initiated practices that irritated the Chinese, such as using foreigners (particularly Muslims) as administrators, bypassing Confucian scholars at the highest levels of government (positions which were reserved for Mongols), eliminating the civil service examinations, and allowing women to sit in councils. In addition, Mongols favored merchants and artisans over scholar-bureaucrats. As a result of social resentment, rising taxes, floods and famine (which created peasant rebellions), endemic outbreaks of plague and disease, and increasing factionalism among the Mongols themselves, the Chinese were able to combine forces and push the Mongols back north to the steppes.

The weakened Abbasid Empire collapsed in 1258 with the conquest and slaughter of Baghdad, the capital. The Mongols made use of institutions already in place, including the bureaucratic system, leaving much of the political administration in Persian hands. The demise of the Mongols in Persia was the result of cultural assimilation rather than military or political conquest. Kievan Rus was also in a state of decline at the time, with regional princes unable or unwilling to unite against a common enemy. Mongol weaponry and siege tactics had become increasingly more sophisticated after coming into contact with the Chinese. Mongolian control of Russia was basically indirect; taxes were extensive and frequent. The degree of control and exploitation was unequal, however, allowing some areas of Russia to prosper while devastating others. Moscow became the new governmental and military center, with the Muscovite princes eventually throwing off Mongol rule.

Theme 4: Creation, Expansion, and Interaction of Economic Systems

Mongols loved the products of artisans from settled areas; one of the motivating factors for expansion was the desire to take these products from the cultures that produced them. They consistently promoted commerce and the exchange of goods in various ways, like standardizing weights and measures, providing financial assistance for caravans, and offering tax breaks for merchants. In addition, the Mongol peace (*pax Mongolica*) brought the two ends of Eurasia in closer contact than ever before and created a vibrant new phase of trade along the various Silk Roads. It created sub-networks in the process and overland trade networks that linked with maritime systems through the South China Sea and the Indian Ocean. When the vast land empire of the Mongols collapsed and land-based trade became dangerous again, trade and travel shifted to a maritime system, utilizing connections already established during Mongolian control.

Theme 5: Development and Transformation of Social Structures

Social relationships in nomadic societies differed from those in sedentary civilizations; populations were smaller and were composed of kinship-based groups. In times of crisis, these kinship-based groups or clans would sometimes come together into larger tribes. The mobility required for nomadic life prevented rigid social or political stratification, but the leader was usually the most talented in whatever skills were considered the most important to the clan. One of Chinggis Khan's greatest challenges was figuring out how to override the tribalism that would have torn his newly unified Mongolian state apart. He accomplished this by scattering members of different tribes among members of other tribes. Loyalty was inspired by Mongol commanders sharing experiences, food, clothing, sleeping quarters, hardships, and victories with their warriors. Mongol military commanders were at the front of the battle, leading and inspiring their men, and merit and valor were quickly rewarded. The flow of wealth from conquered peoples benefitted all involved, although not all equally, and the standard of living rose for almost all participants.

Status in Mongolian society rested upon talents, abilities, or skills. Consequently, those of lesser status in settled cultures suddenly found themselves valuable under Mongol rule, particularly if they were unusually skilled in language, trade, scholarship, or craftsmanship. However, a skilled individual could be relocated hundreds of miles away from home and family to serve the Mongols. The Mongols usually kept a distinct division between them and their conquered peoples, though Mongol assimilation in Persia serves as an obvious exception. The Kievan Rus had little to offer the Mongols, and the Mongols maintained their cultural identity by living outside that civilization and maintaining their pastoral way of life. Mongols also went to great efforts to remain culturally and socially detached from the Chinese, forbidding intermarriage and prohibiting Chinese scholars from learning Mongolian script.

Mongolian women always had more independence and freedom of movement than women in agriculturally based societies. As much as possible, they continued their lifestyle of the steppes, freely associating with men, riding their own horses, participating in hunting excursions with their husbands, sitting in council, or becoming warriors. Foot binding and seclusion, characteristic of Chinese women, were not adopted by the Yuan dynasty.

CHAPTER TWELVE
The Worlds of the Fifteenth Century

AP World History Key Concepts

3.1: Expansion and Intensification of Communication and Exchange Networks

I. Improved transportation technologies and commercial practices led to an increased volume of trade, and expanded the geographical range of existing and newly active trade networks.

II. The movement of peoples caused environmental and linguistic effects.

III. Cross-cultural exchanges were fostered by the intensification of existing, or the creation of new, networks of trade and communication.

Chapter 12 provides an overview of the world in the fifteenth century—just as the hemispheres were about to be permanently linked. Much of the world was not governed by empires; people in Australia, Siberia, the Arctic coastal regions, and parts of Africa (see Map 12.3, p. 574) and the Americas (see Map 12.5, p. 581) continued to use stone-age technology. Some people, particularly in Australia and along the northwest coast of North America, lived in hunter-forager bands or villages, while other people, such as the Igbo in West Africa and the Iroquois in eastern North America, lived in agricultural villages. Still others were nomadic pastoralists, such as the Turkic tribes in Central Asia and the Fulbe of West Africa. However, the dominant story of this period resides with civilizations in both hemispheres.

Both hemispheres witnessed an intensification of trade networks, such as the *pochteca* of the Aztecs, Andean trade controlled by the Incas, Indian Ocean trade under Islamic control, trans-Saharan trade under the Songhay, and trade between the Safavid, Mughal, and Ottoman Islamic empires. The expansion or destruction of empires, however, damaged trade; the collapse of Mongol empires hurt trade on trans-Eurasia land routes, while the fall of Constantinople to the Ottoman Turks damaged Christian European trade with Asia. In other regions, migrations led to new connections, such as the Fulbe in Africa and the continued Polynesian migrations in Oceania. Some trade existed between North and South America by ocean-going canoe, but trade routes were mostly limited to regional trade. Environmental effects of trade included not only the diffusion of food crops but also of diseases. Technological improvements in shipbuilding and navigation, exemplified by the Chinese and Portuguese, rendered ships more capable of open-ocean voyaging and prepared the way for global connections in the sixteenth century. Cultural changes included the continued expansion of Islam in Africa, following merchants and Sufis in West Africa and the migration of the Fulbe in

Central Africa, and the adoption of Quechua and the cult of the Incas throughout the Andean empire.

3.2: Continuity and Innovation of State Forms and Their Interactions

I. Empires collapsed and were reconstituted; in some regions new state forms emerged.

II. Interregional contacts and conflicts between states and empires encouraged significant technological and cultural transfers.

In the Americas, new state forms emerged. The Mexica (Aztecs) took control of much of Mesoamerica, imposing tributary relationships with existing city-states (such as the Maya and Toltec) for luxury goods, textiles, clothing, weapons, and slaves for sacrificing to the Aztec gods. In the Andes, the Incas also asserted control over preexisting cultures such as the Chavín, Moche, Wari, and Tiwanaku, but asserted more direct, bureaucratic rule under an emperor believed to be divine. In contrast, in North America the Iroquois League created limited government. In Africa, the Igbo created a stateless society. *See Chapters 7 through 11 for discussion of this Key Concept for Afro-Eurasia.*

3.3: Increased Economic Productive Capacity and Its Consequences

I. Innovations stimulated agricultural and industrial production in many regions.

II. The fate of cities varied greatly, with periods of significant decline, and with periods of increased urbanization buoyed by rising productivity and expanding trade networks.

III. Despite significant continuities in social structures and in methods of production, there were also some important changes in labor management and in the effect of religious conversion on gender relations and family life.

The Americas experienced many economic improvements during the fifteenth century. In Mesoamerica, the Aztecs/Mexica transformed the lake and swampy area around their capital, Tenochtitlán, with canals, causeways, and floating islands (*chinampas*) where food and flowers were grown. The Incas continued the Quechua practiced of raised-bed agriculture (called *waru-waru*) with channels between the beds to control rainwater. Aztec trade was managed by the *pochteca*, an independent guild, while the Incas directly controlled trade in the Andes. Social roles for men and women were clearly defined, but patriarchy was less entrenched than it was in Eurasia. For example, women could be local rulers among the Aztecs, and descent was reckoned from both father and mother. In the Inca culture, women could be priestesses, and descent was traced through the mother for women and through the father for men. *See Chapters 7 through 11 for discussion of this Key Concept for Afro-Eurasia.*

4.1: Globalizing Networks of Communication and Exchange

III. Remarkable new transoceanic maritime reconnaissance occurred in this period.

After the expulsion of the Mongols, Ming Emperor Yongle sent his admiral Zheng He on a series of voyages around the Indian Ocean to reestablish lapsed tributary relations. The Chinese fleet of "treasure ships" was huge and sophisticated, dominating East Asian and Indian Ocean trade routes. However, when Yongle died, the voyages ceased. Improved naval technology and restriction of trade through Constantinople encouraged Europeans to explore the oceans in an attempt to forge new trade routes with the East. The Portuguese sponsored voyages along the coast of Africa, eventually leading to contact with Indian Ocean trade, and the Spanish sponsored Columbus, who seemingly by chance ran into the Americas while seeking Asia and forged permanent transatlantic ties.

Theme 1: Interaction Between Humans and the Environment

Some groups of people continued to follow pre-agricultural lifestyles. The inhabitants of Australia manipulated their environment by burning off brush and grass to facilitate hunting and to promote the growth of species of plants and animals they favored. Peoples such as the Chinookan, Skagit, and Tulalip of the northwest coast of North America lived in a rich environment where hunting, fishing, and gathering allowed them to build permanent villages without agriculture. Agricultural villages in what is now New York State adopted corn and bean farming from Mesoamerica. The Aztecs brought control of their environment to a high art by draining swamps, creating floating islands, and building bridges and causeways around their capital city. The Incas had to create an empire across many ecological zones from rocky mountains to deserts and rain forests.

In China, the Ming dynasty attempted to cultivate lands ravaged by the Mongols and by plague. They rebuilt canals, reservoirs, and irrigation systems and planted an estimated one billion trees in order to reforest China.

Theme 2: Development and Interaction of Cultures

A major goal of the Ming dynasty was to restore a pure Chinese culture following the end of Mongol rule; in many ways, China attempted to return to an idealized past or golden age. The Ming revitalized the examination system, based on Confucian learning, for choosing and promoting bureaucrats. Emperor Yongle ordered 2,000 scholars to create an encyclopedia to record or summarize all previous Chinese knowledge. Gender roles also returned to Confucian norms. The Emperor ordered the construction of a new capital and the palace complex, the Forbidden City. On the other end of Eurasia, Europeans also looked to the past, that of classical Greece and Rome, to create a new cultural movement called the Renaissance. Renaissance humanists pursued secular learning based on rational thought and empiricism, glorified the individual, and used classical models for art and architecture.

In the Islamic world (see Map 12.4, p. 577), the Turkic Safavid dynasty enforced Shia Islam, unlike the other Eurasian Islamic empires (like Ottoman and Mughal), which were Sunni. Both the Ottoman and Mughal empires also controlled large populations that were not Muslim and at times handled them with great toleration. Vijayanagara, a Hindu state south of the Mughal Empire, borrowed architectural styles from the Mughals. In the Songhay Empire of West Africa, Islam was infused with local traditions, although Timbuktu became a major center for Islamic learning.

In the Americas, the Aztec religion required sacrifices of human blood to its patron deity, Huitzilopochtli, to maintain cosmic order. Sacrificial victims were frequently prisoners of war, and the need for ever-increasing numbers to sacrifice led to continued warfare. Aztec poetry focused on the transience of human life. The Incas required their subjects to worship the major Incan deities but also allowed them to worship their own gods. While Aztec men and women worshipped deities of both sexes, Incan women worshipped the moon and men the sun.

Theme 3: State-Building, Expansion, and Conflict

The civilizations of the fifteenth century were poised to become linked in global, instead of regional, networks (see Snapshot: Major Developments around the World in the Fifteenth Century, p. 562). A major contrast in state building existed between the centralized bureaucracy of the Ming dynasty in China, which asserted unitary rule over a large region, and the separate, often competing and warring, independent states of Europe (see Maps 12.1, p. 567 and 12.2, p. 570). Some of the individual states, especially in Western Europe, were developing more efficient bureaucracies and centralized control under their monarchs.

Other states, especially in Eastern Europe, still followed a feudal model of decentralized control with the nobles and Church exercising considerable power. The princes of Moscow freed themselves from Mongol rule and began the process of expansion that would eventually create the Russian Empire.

The Ming dynasty in China, also having thrown off Mongol rule, proceeded to establish a Confucian state. At first, there was a struggle for political power between the eunuchs, who were more innovative, progressive, and directly loyal to the emperor, and the conservative Confucian scholar-bureaucrats, who were dedicated to restoring past values and methods. The resolution of this feud can be seen in the decision to end the voyages of Zheng He (who was himself a eunuch) and the dismantling of his fleet. China looked inward, "perfecting" itself and returning to traditional virtues and concerns about its traditional pastoralist enemies in the north. Competing European states, such as Portugal and Spain, on the other hand, funded exploratory voyages, which ultimately led to European empires in the Americas and control of the lucrative Indian Ocean trade system.

The Islamic world of the Ottoman, Mughal, and Safavid empires was controlled by descendants of pastoral Turkic people (see Map 12.4, p. 577). Competition could be found between these Islamic empires; the Sunni Ottoman Empire was often at war with the Shia Safavids. Ottoman sultans claimed the title of caliph (successor to the prophet Muhammad) and asserted both secular and religious authority. The Ottomans effectively used gunpowder and cannon to defeat the last vestiges of the Byzantine Empire in 1453. They ruled a population composed of many non-Muslims, protecting (most of the time) the *dhimmi* status of Christians and Jews. The Ottoman Empire, along with China and the Incas, was one of the largest and wealthiest empires in this era. The Mughals also controlled a large non-Muslim population, composed mostly of Hindus, in southern Asia. The Empire of Songhay, successor to Mali and Ghana in controlling the gold-salt trade in West Africa, represented the further expansion of Islam in Africa.

In the Americas (see Map 12.5, p. 581), the Mexica, a semi-nomadic group in northern Mexico, gradually asserted military control over much of Mesoamerica. The new rulers claimed descent from the Toltecs in order to give themselves legitimacy and respect. They governed loosely, primarily using a tributary system bolstered by a religious justification; only the blood of sacrificed humans could keep the gods from destroying the world.

The Incas in South America, on the other hand, exercised more direct bureaucratic control. They also added religious justification in that the Inca emperor was an absolute, divine ruler. While the empire was ruled as a centralized bureaucratic state, the Incas delegated authority to local bureaucrats in regions that had previously possessed a bureaucracy and created administrative systems where none had previously existed. They exacted labor (*mita*) from their subjects to create goods, such as textiles, or to work on building projects.

In North America, the Iroquois developed a unique solution to tribal feuds and bloodshed; an agreement known as the Great Law of Peace established a confederacy where a council of clan leaders had the power to settle disputes by consensus. This creation of limited government, not imposed from the outside but mutually agreed upon, was much-admired by the creators of the United States Constitution. In Africa, the Igbo represent an agricultural society with kings; power was balanced among kinship groups, ritual experts who provided mediation, women's associations, and wealthy men. *See Chapter 13 for more detailed discussion of Eurasian empires.*

Theme 4: Creation, Expansion, and Interaction of Economic Systems

Much of the wealth of fifteenth-century states was created by controlling commerce or by producing specialized goods, such as silk, for trade. The Afro-Eurasian trade systems were discussed previously in this unit. Changes in the fifteenth century include the Ming dynasty's decision to concentrate on internal, rather than maritime, trade networks. However, the Ming still traded across their huge internal market and with foreign merchants who came to them for the goods that China produced. In addition, much of the trade in Afro-Eurasia was under control of Muslim merchants and empires (see Map 12.6, p. 588). Malacca, located on a strategic strait (see Map 12.1, p. 567), grew into a major Muslim port and was instrumental in spreading Islam to Southeast Asia.

Another fifteenth-century landmark was the fall of Constantinople, which ended direct trade between Christian Europe and Asia. Control of the trade hub previously occupied by the Byzantines created immense wealth for the Ottomans and encouraged Europeans to begin looking to the Atlantic to find trade routes with Asia.

Beginning in the 1450s, the Portuguese funded voyages south along the western coast of Africa, seeking an alternate route into the Indian Ocean and the wealth of spices, silk, and gems that could be found there. Beginning later than the Portuguese, the Spanish sponsored Columbus's attempt to reach Asia by sailing west across the Atlantic. In the Americas, Aztec trade was under the control of the *pochteca*, an independent guild of merchants. Active markets were held in the major cities, where food and goods from throughout the region were exchanged. The Incas assumed direct control of trade along thousands of miles of roads built in the Andes, uniting the trade links between different ecological regions forged by previous cultures. *See Chapter 7 for more detailed discussion of Eastern Hemisphere trade systems.*

Theme 5: Development and Transformation of Social Structures

As discussed in previous chapters from Part Three, society remained hierarchical and most often patriarchal in most settled agricultural empires. A repeated pattern, however, was that pastoralists had fewer gender restrictions than did the agricultural peoples; as pastoral peoples assimilated into settled life, however, more gender restrictions arose (see Chapter 11).

In the Americas, women were not as subjugated to men as in Eurasia. For example, the Iroquois practiced matrilineal descent, and men lived with their wives' families. Iroquois women also were involved in selecting or deposing leaders. Aztec women could be priestesses, crafts workers, officials, traders, and teachers. In the Andes, gender parallelism (women and men operating in separate but equally valued spheres) had formed part of the culture before the rise of the Incas. For example, men worshipped the sun and women the moon with their own separate priesthoods. The *sapay Inca* (Inca ruler) and his *coya* (female consort) governed side by side, claiming descent from the sun and the moon, respectively.

PRACTICE EXAM 3

WORLD HISTORY
SECTION I

Note: This exam uses the chronological designations B.C.E. (before the common era) and C.E. (common era). These labels correspond to B.C. (before Christ) and A.D. (anno Domini), which are used in some world history textbooks.

TIME—45 Minutes
60 Questions

Directions: Each of the questions or incomplete statements below is followed by four suggested answers or completions. Select the one that is best in each case.

1. In the period between 500 and 1500, the expansion of commercial networks in the Afro-Eurasian world contributed to the rise of states in all of the following regions EXCEPT
   - (A) West Africa
   - (B) East Africa
   - (C) Siberia
   - (D) Southeast Asia

2. All of the following reflect the influence of the culture of the northern steppes on northern Chinese elites in the Tang dynasty EXCEPT the
   - (A) greater freedom women enjoyed
   - (B) drinking of yogurt
   - (C) Turkic style of battle
   - (D) tribute system

3. All of the following were technological innovations that spread from China to the rest of Eurasia by the eleventh century EXCEPT
   - (A) papermaking
   - (B) printing
   - (C) cannons
   - (D) cast iron

4. Which of the following is an example of how Japan, Korea, and Vietnam combined elements of Chinese culture with local traditions in the pre-modern period?
   - (A) The development of a writing system that combined Chinese characters with phonetic symbols
   - (B) The merging of Shinto and Daoist views of humanity's relationship to the natural world
   - (C) The assimilation of Hindu and Buddhist reincarnations into the local pantheon of gods
   - (D) The incorporation of the civil service examination system into the tribute system

GO ON TO THE NEXT PAGE.

5. Which of the following describes the conditions under which Chinese culture was initially introduced into Korea and Vietnam?

   (A) Marriages and alliances
   (B) Migration and disease
   (C) Trade and diplomacy
   (D) Conquest and colonization

6. Which of the following did Japan and Europe share in common in the tenth century?

   (A) A cultural tradition regarded as universal
   (B) A selective borrowing of Confucianism
   (C) A belief in the divinity of the emperor
   (D) A decentralized political structure

7. "As you do not understand the Arts of Peace your skill in the Arts of War will not, in the end, achieve victory."

   Imagawa Ryoshun, Japan, 1412

   This statement suggests that the ideal samurai was one who

   (A) preferred diplomacy to warfare
   (B) rejected bushido and embraced Shintoism.
   (C) achieved both literary and martial excellence
   (D) knew when to surrender and admit defeat

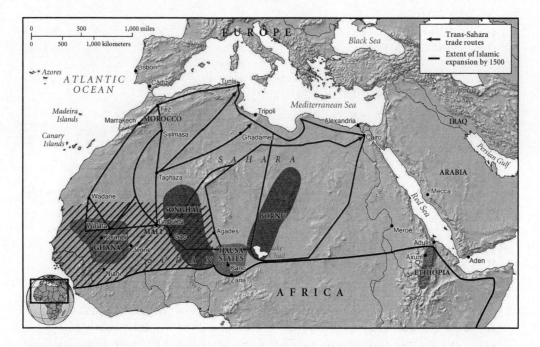

8. The information shown in Map 9.6 supports all of the following conclusions EXCEPT

   (A) the trans-Saharan trade facilitated the spread of Islam
   (B) Islam entered North Africa through military conquest and forced conversions
   (C) the presence of Islam was strongest in the empires of West Africa
   (D) commerce and Islam connected West Africa to the Islamic world

GO ON TO THE NEXT PAGE.

9. The expansion of Islamic civilization before the sixteenth century introduced agricultural goods and innovations into the Middle East from

   (A) South and Southeast Asia
   (B) North and South America
   (C) Australia and the South Pacific
   (D) Western Europe and South Africa

10. Military conquest by Arab and Berber forces in the eighth century resulted in a predominantly Muslim population in Spain by the

    (A) tenth century
    (B) thirteenth century
    (C) fifteenth century
    (D) sixteenth century

The following quote is for questions 11–13.

> Thus the Lord made Himself known to the people of Israel in Egypt; and yet He allowed them the use of the sacrifices which they were wont to offer to the Devil, in his own worship; so as to command them in his sacrifice to kill beasts, to the end that, changing their hearts, they might lay aside one part of the sacrifice, while they retained another; that while they offered the same beasts which they were wont to offer, they should offer them to God, and not to idols; and thus they would no longer be the same sacrifices.
>
> *Pope Gregory, giving advice to the bishop of England, 601*

11. The pope's strategy to convert the people of England is based on the assumption that

    (A) idolatry and animal sacrifice are fundamentally different
    (B) only those customs followed by the ancient Israelites are followed
    (C) existing cultural practices conflict with Christian doctrine
    (D) local customs will acquire a Christian meaning

12. Based on the pope's attitude toward the local customs of the people in England, which of the following would he mostly likely support?

    (A) The destruction of temples devoted to the worship of idols
    (B) The desecration of wells and springs regarded by the locals as sacred
    (C) The designation of festivals honoring ancient gods as Christian holy days
    (D) The confiscation of amulets and charms believed to ward off evil

13. Which of the following characterizes the pope's attitude towards the practices of the local people?

    (A) Intolerant
    (B) Accommodating
    (C) Condescending
    (D) Indifferent

14. In contrast to the Roman Catholic Church in Western Europe, the Byzantine Church was closely tied to the state in a relationship called

    (A) caesaropapism
    (B) fundamentalism
    (C) neoliberalism
    (D) pastoralism

GO ON TO THE NEXT PAGE.

15. Which of the following replaced slavery as the dominant form of unfree labor in Europe after the fall of the Roman Empire?

 (A) Indentured servitude
 (B) Corvée labor
 (C) Serfdom
 (D) Chiefdom

16. All of the following increased agricultural productivity in northern Europe beginning in the sixth century EXCEPT the

 (A) horse collar
 (B) heavy wheeled plow
 (C) iron horseshoes
 (D) spinning wheel

17. Between the ninth and thirteenth centuries, classical Greek philosophy influenced the intellectual traditions of all of the following civilizations EXCEPT

 (A) Western Europe
 (B) Song dynasty China
 (C) the Byzantine Empire
 (D) the Islamic world

18. Scholars point to all of the following policies as evidence of the Mongols' interest in promoting interregional trade EXCEPT the

 (A) incentives given to Mongol traders
 (B) financial backing for caravans
 (C) standardization of weights and measures
 (D) tax breaks granted merchants

19. Chinese medical practices like acupuncture and taking a patient's pulse to make a diagnosis reached the Middle East by the thirteenth century as a result of policies promoted by the

 (A) Ottomans
 (B) Mughals
 (C) Mongols
 (D) Romans

20. All of the following reflect similarities between the Mongols in the thirteenth century and Europeans in the sixteenth century EXCEPT

 (A) Both were more economically developed than the Chinese and Islamic civilizations.
 (B) Both exhibited a tendency to plunder the wealth of civilizations they encountered.
 (C) Both were on the periphery of the major, established civilizations.
 (D) Both created a network of communication and exchange over a vast area.

GO ON TO THE NEXT PAGE.

21. In recent decades, some historians have challenged negative images of pastoral societies in world history. Which of the following evidence would best support this historical reinterpretation?

    (A)   Nomadic peoples were by nature pacifist and have been exploited and manipulated by agrarian civilizations.

    (B)   The Turkic states raided nearby civilizations and extorted tribute payments from established states.

    (C)   The Arabs had a reputation for ruthless brutality and destroyed all civilizations that resisted conquest.

    (D)   The Mongol capital at Karakorum had places of worship for Buddhists, Daoists, Muslims, and Christians.

22. Compared to women in agricultural civilizations, women in pastoral societies before the sixteenth century

    (A)   did not engage in productive labor
    (B)   had no domestic responsibilities
    (C)   enjoyed a greater role in public life
    (D)   could not remarry or divorce

The following quote is for questions 23–24.

> At that time the harvest failed for several years in a row. . . . Menggu ordered the officials to travel around announcing that those who returned to their property would be exempt from taxes and services for three years.
>
> *Chinese epitaph for the Honorable Menggu, 1274*

23. The exemption from taxes and labor service during times of bad harvest by Menggu reflects the influence of which set of ideas?

    (A)   Christianity
    (B)   Confucianism
    (C)   Hinduism
    (D)   Islam

24. Based on the information provided, it can be reasonably inferred that Menggu served as an official during the dynasty ruled by the

    (A)   Mongols
    (B)   Arabs
    (C)   Turks
    (D)   Manchus

25. Some scholars have argued that of all the areas that came under Mongol rule, Russia was the most affected. Which of the following evidence would support this historical interpretation?

    (A)   Mongol migrants settled in Russia and established themselves as an aristocracy.

    (B)   Mongol herdsmen converted farmland into pastures, permanently destroying soil fertility.

    (C)   Russian peasants converted to Islam in great numbers and married Mongol soldiers.

    (D)   Russian princes adopted the diplomatic rituals, court practices, and military draft of the Mongols.

GO ON TO THE NEXT PAGE.

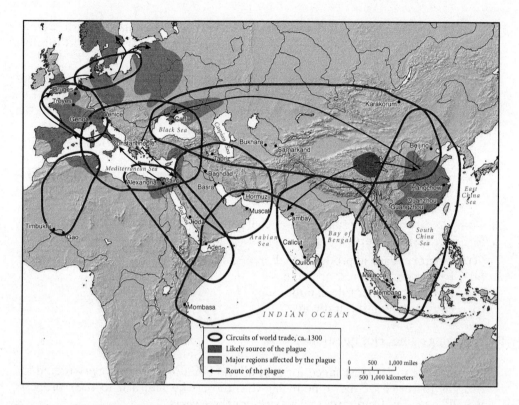

Questions 26–27 are based on Map 11.2.

26. The spread of the plague was facilitated and accelerated by the networks of exchange created by the empire established by the

    (A) Europeans
    (B) Xiongnu
    (C) Mongols
    (D) Uighurs

27. Which of the following can be inferred based on the information shown in Map 11.2?

    (A) Central Asia was protected from the spread of the plague because of its marginalized position in the circuits of world trade.
    (B) The trade circuits of the fourteenth century linked Europe to the long-established trading networks of Eurasia.
    (C) The major circuits of world trade in the fourteenth century operated independently and did not overlap.
    (D) The plague broke out independently in different parts of Eurasia and did not spread beyond the immediate vicinity.

28. Which of the following policies of Mongol rulers facilitated the exchange of ideas and techniques throughout Eurasia in the thirteenth and fourteenth centuries?

    (A) The forcible transfer of skilled and educated people to distant parts of the empire
    (B) The use of siege warfare and cannons in their military conquests
    (C) The creation of an imperial bureaucracy that excluded the local population
    (D) The establishment of a taxation system that significantly increased state revenues

GO ON TO THE NEXT PAGE.

29. The rulers of which of the following pairs of civilizations shared a common religion?

    (A) The Aztecs and the Incas
    (B) The Songhay Empire and the Ottoman Empire
    (C) The Mughal Empire and Vijayanagara Kingdom
    (D) The Safavid Empire and Ethiopia

30. The Byzantine Empire incorporated the road system, tax-collecting methods, military organization, government administration, imperial court, and laws of the

    (A) Ottoman Empire
    (B) Persian Empire
    (C) Holy Roman Empire
    (D) Roman Empire

31. Which of the following can be used as evidence of the influence of the Byzantine Empire on the civilization of Kievan Rus in the late tenth century?

    (A) The ban on the use of icons
    (B) The celibacy of priests
    (C) The use of the Cyrillic alphabet
    (D) The acceptance of papal authority

32. Which of the following is a useful source of evidence for research on how Christianity was transformed by the cultures within which it took root?

    (A) The Jesus Sutras
    (B) *Epic of Gilgamesh*
    (C) Code of Hammurabi
    (D) Venus figurines

33. Which of the following is a belief of Islam that reflects the influence of Christianity and Judaism?

    (A) Jesus as a divine being
    (B) Muhammad as the last prophet
    (C) Arabs as a chosen people
    (D) The Kaaba as God's house

34. Which of the following represents Islam's departure from the prevailing beliefs and practices of the local population in the Arabian Peninsula where Islam emerged?

    (A) Social identity was based on family, clan, and tribal status.
    (B) Religious, military, and political authority were clearly separated.
    (C) A professional clergy emerged to mediate people's relationship with God.
    (D) Membership in the Islamic community was based exclusively on belief.

35. All of the following contributed to the rapid spread of Islam in the centuries following its birth EXCEPT

    (A) military conquest
    (B) benefits attached to Muslim identity
    (C) a clean break from all existing religions
    (D) commerce-friendly policies

GO ON TO THE NEXT PAGE.

36. Although they have no basis in the Quran, all of the following patriarchal controls on Muslim women came to be identified as Islamic as a result of the absorption of local traditions into Islamic practice EXCEPT

   (A) polygyny
   (B) "honor killings"
   (C) seclusion of women
   (D) female clitorectomy

37. Islam was introduced to all of the following regions through military conquest EXCEPT

   (A) India
   (B) Anatolia
   (C) Spain
   (D) West Africa

38. The founders of Buddhism, Christianity, and Islam shared all of the following EXCEPT

   (A) spiritual revelations
   (B) military responsibilities
   (C) the key to salvation
   (D) a belief that all believers were equal

39. Which of the following would support the argument that the Islamic world was more fractured than it was unified?

   (A) The Sunni/Shia split
   (B) The Catholic/Protestant divide
   (C) The Mahayana/Theravada branches
   (D) The Confucian/Legalist conflict

40. Which of the following would scholars point to as evidence of an "Islamic Green Revolution" in the centuries following the Muslim conquest of northwestern India?

   (A) The conversion of agricultural fields into pastureland for animals to graze
   (B) The policies of Islamic states that promoted sustainability and environmentalism
   (C) The introduction of rice, sugarcane, and cotton from India to the Middle East and Africa
   (D) The dependence on renewable sources of energy like wind, water, and solar power

41. In the ninth century, Arab scholars developed algebra based on the numerical notation invented by the

   (A) Indians
   (B) Aztecs
   (C) Protestants
   (D) English

42. All of the following show the greater extent of state penetration and regulation of local society in the Inca Empire than in the Aztec Empire EXCEPT the

   (A) "chosen women"
   (B) "sun farms"
   (C) system of *mita*
   (D) practice of human sacrifice

GO ON TO THE NEXT PAGE.

Questions 43–44 are based on Visual Source 7.4, which is a Kushan pendant from the fourth century. The figure depicted is Hariti, a Hindu goddess.

43. The pendant shows the influence of all of the following cultures EXCEPT

  (A) Greek
  (B) Olmec
  (C) Indian
  (D) Buddhist

44. All of the following help to explain the cultural cosmopolitanism of the pendant EXCEPT

  (A) The official language of the Kushan Empire was derived from India.
  (B) The Kushan Empire was linked to the Silk Road trading network.
  (C) Parts of the Kushan Empire had once been part of the empire established by Alexander the Great.
  (D) The Mongols were descendants of the founder of the Kushan Empire.

45. Which of the following offers evidence of the cultural impact made by diasporic communities of merchants from the Roman world on southern India and East Africa in the first few centuries of the Common Era?

  (A) The cultivation of maize in Mesoamerica
  (B) The launching of the gunpowder revolution
  (C) The spread of Christianity in Axum and Kerala
  (D) The synthesis of Hinduism and Buddhism

46. What was a key difference in the conduct of trade in the Aztec and Inca Empires?

  (A) Trade in the Aztec Empire was in private hands; trade in the Inca Empire was controlled by the state.
  (B) Trade in the Aztec Empire was limited to basic supplies; trade in the Inca Empire focused on precious metals.
  (C) Aztec rulers used trade as a means to spread their religion; Inca rulers used trade as a way to appease the gods.
  (D) Aztec rulers promoted trade by building a complex infrastructure; Inca rulers discouraged commercial activities.

GO ON TO THE NEXT PAGE.

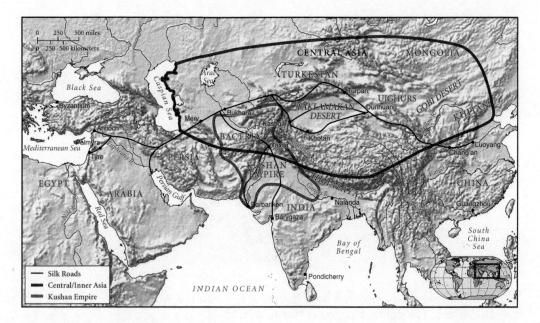

Questions 47–48 are based on Map 7.1.

47. Which of the following cities shown on the map would most likely have a caravanserai?

   (A)   Pondicherry

   (B)   Dunhuang

   (C)   Nalanda

   (D)   Byzantium

48. Which of the following best describes the societies that lived along the trade routes of the Silk Roads?

   (A)   Agricultural settlements

   (B)   Industrialized societies

   (C)   Hunting and gathering societies

   (D)   Pastoral peoples

49. Which of the following describes how the preference for luxury items in the Silk Road trade affected ordinary people?

   (A)   People from the lower classes could live the lifestyles of the powerful and wealthy.

   (B)   Artisans in India began mass-producing wool and linen textiles to satisfy local demand.

   (C)   Peasants in China shifted from the cultivation of crops to the production of silk, porcelain, and iron tools.

   (D)   Merchants focused on local trade where the volume was higher, the profits more predictable, and the risks minimal.

50. The spread of diseases along trade routes weakened all of the following civilizations EXCEPT

   (A)   Mohenjo Daro in 2000 B.C.E.

   (B)   Athens in the fifth century B.C.E.

   (C)   Byzantium in the sixth century

   (D)   the Mongol Empire in the fourteenth century

GO ON TO THE NEXT PAGE.

51. All of the following contributed to the dominance of the Malay kingdom of Srivijaya in the Indian Ocean trade between 670 and 1025 EXCEPT

    (A)   its abundance of gold
    (B)   its access to spices
    (C)   the practice of intensive agriculture
    (D)   the taxes it levied on passing ships

52. All of the following provide evidence of the influence of Indian culture on Southeast Asia in the first millennium EXCEPT the

    (A)   adoption of Confucianism in Vietnam
    (B)   Buddhist monument known as Borobudur in Java
    (C)   use of Sanskrit and Pallava in Southeast Asian languages
    (D)   wide circulation of *Ramayana* in Southeast Asia

53. Which best describes the attitude of the fourteenth-century Arab traveler Ibn Battuta toward the cultural traditions of West African societies he encountered in the Islamic world?

    (A)   Appreciative
    (B)   Critical
    (C)   Dismissive
    (D)   Mocking

54. In its political structure, Maya civilization was most similar to the

    (A)   imperial systems of Rome, Persia, and China
    (B)   maritime empires of Britain and France
    (C)   bureaucratic state of the Inca Empire
    (D)   competing city-states of ancient Mesopotamia

55. Recent scholarship on the collapse of the Maya civilization identifies all of the following as contributing causes EXCEPT

    (A)   rapid population growth
    (B)   climate change
    (C)   the Spanish invasion
    (D)   increased warfare

56. Which of the following reflects a similarity between the Aztec Empire's treatment of conquered peoples and the Mongol Empire's treatment of the Russian principalities it conquered?

    (A)   Both demanded tribute from conquered peoples.
    (B)   Both enslaved the entire conquered population.
    (C)   Both assimilated the conquered peoples into their society.
    (D)   Both used conquered peoples in human sacrifice rituals.

57. Which of the following would be the most useful source of evidence for research about the Mongol Empire?

    (A)   Encyclopedia articles about pastoral societies that became world empires
    (B)   Biographies about Marco Polo, Ibn Battuta, and Xuanzang
    (C)   The writings of those who participated in the Crusades
    (D)   The reports of European delegations to the Mongol capital

GO ON TO THE NEXT PAGE.

58. Which of the following sources from the fifteenth century have been used by historians to argue that artisan opportunities for women were declining?

   (A) Tax laws
   (B) Guild regulations
   (C) Birth records
   (D) Marriage certificates

59. Historians have used all the following terms to describe the period during which the Byzantine Empire, the Islamic world, and the Mongol Empire flourished EXCEPT the

   (A) early modern era
   (B) postclassical era
   (C) medieval period
   (D) age of third-wave civilizations

60. All of the following are generally acknowledged as the most powerful civilizations in the world in the eleventh century EXCEPT

   (A) China
   (B) Byzantium
   (C) Western Europe
   (D) the Islamic world

STOP

END OF SECTION I

WORLD HISTORY
SECTION II

Part A
(Suggested writing time—40 minutes)
Percent of Section II score—33 1/3

Directions: The following question is based on the accompanying Documents 1–7. (The documents have been edited for the purpose of this exercise.)

This question is designed to test your ability to work with and understand historical documents.

Write an essay that:

+ Has a relevant thesis and supports that thesis with evidence from the documents.
+ Uses all of the documents.
+ Analyzes the documents by grouping them in as many appropriate ways as possible. Does not simply summarize the documents individually.
+ Takes into account the sources of the documents and analyzes the authors' points of view.
+ Identifies and explains the need for at least one additional type of document.

You may refer to relevant historical information not mentioned in the documents.

1. Using the following documents, analyze the problems confronted by Japanese leaders seeking to establish political order and the methods they adopted to solve those problems from 600 C.E. to 1450 C.E. Identify an additional type of document and explain how it would help your analysis of the problems faced and methods adopted by Japanese leaders.

GO ON TO THE NEXT PAGE.

Document 1

Source: Shotoku, Regent of Japan under Empress Suiko, *The Seventeen Article Constitution*, 604 C.E.

1. Harmony is to be valued, and an avoidance of wanton opposition to be honored. All men are influenced by class feelings, and there are few who are intelligent. Hence there are some who disobey their lords and fathers, or who maintain feuds with the neighboring villages. But when those above are harmonious and those below are friendly, and there is concord in the discussion of business, right views of things spontaneously gain acceptance. . . .

2. Sincerely reverence the three treasures . . . the Buddha, the Law [teachings], and the Priesthood [community of Buddhist monks]. . . .

3. When you receive the Imperial commands . . . scrupulously obey them. The lord is Heaven, the vassal is Earth. Heaven overspreads, and Earth upbears. . . . [W]hen the superior acts, the inferior yields compliance.

6. Chastise that which is evil and encourage that which is good. This was the excellent rule of antiquity. . . .

7. Let every man have his own charge, and let not the spheres of duty be confused. When wise men are entrusted with office, the sound of praise arises. If unprincipled men hold office, disasters and tumults are multiplied. In this world, few are born with knowledge: wisdom is the product of earnest meditation. In all things, whether great or small, find the right man, and they will surely be well managed. . . .

12. Let not the provincial authorities or the [local nobles] levy exactions on the people. In a country, there are not two lords. . . . The sovereign is the master of the people of the whole country. . . .

GO ON TO THE NEXT PAGE.

Document 2

Source: Sei Shonagon, imperial court member as lady-in-waiting to Empress Sadako, *Pillow Book*, c. 1000 C.E.

That parents should bring up some beloved son of theirs to be a priest [Buddhist monk] is really distressing. No doubt it is an auspicious thing to do; but unfortunately most people are convinced that a priest is as unimportant as a piece of wood, and they treat him accordingly. A priest lives poorly on meager food, and cannot even sleep without being criticized. . . .

A preacher ought to be good-looking. For, if we are properly to understand his worthy sentiments, we must keep our eyes on him while he speaks; should we look away, we may forget to listen. Accordingly an ugly preacher may well be the source of sin. . . .

It is very annoying, when one has visited Hase Temple and has retired into one's enclosure, to be disturbed by a herd of common people who come and sit outside in a row, crowded so close together that the tails of their robes fall over each other in utter disarray. I remember that once I was overcome by a great desire to go on a pilgrimage. Having made my way up the log steps, deafened by the fearful roar of the river, I hurried into my enclosure, longing to gaze upon the sacred countenance of Buddha. To my dismay I found that a throng of commoners had settled themselves directly in front of me, where they were incessantly standing up, prostrating themselves, and squatting down again. They looked like so many basket-worms as they crowded together in their hideous clothes, leaving hardly an inch of space between themselves and me. I really felt like pushing them all over sideways.

Document 3

Source: Twelfth-century painting depicting the famous naval battle of Dan-no-ura in which the samurai warriors of the Taira clan fought the Minamoto clan in 1185.

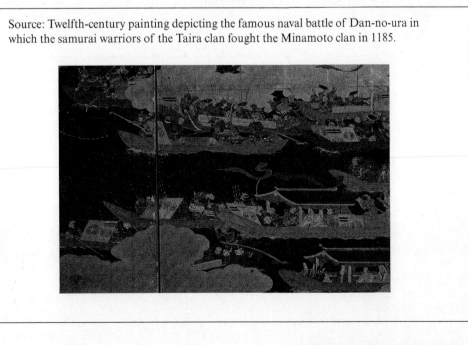

GO ON TO THE NEXT PAGE.

Document 4

Source: Dōgen, Japanese Buddhist who introduced and popularized Zen Buddhism in Japan, *Writings on Zen Buddhism*, c. 1227 C.E.

We teach: For all the Buddha dharma-preserving Zen ancestors and Buddhas, sitting upright in the practice of self-actualizing *sama-dhi* [concentration] is the true path of awakening. Both in India and in China, all who have attained awakening did so in this way. . . .

In the correctly transmitted Zen lineage we teach: This directly transmitted, authoritative Buddha dharma is the best of the best. Once you start studying under a good teacher, there is no need for lighting incense, worshipful prostrations . . . repentance, or chanting scripture. Just sit and slough off body-mind. . . .

When I stayed at T'ien-t'ung monastery [in China], the venerable Ching used to stay up sitting until the small hours of the morning and then after only a little rest would rise early to start sitting again. In the meditation hall he went on sitting with the other elders, without letting up for even a single night. Meanwhile many of the monks went off to sleep. The elder would go around among them and hit the sleepers with his fist or a slipper, yelling at them to wake up. If their sleepiness persisted, he would go out to the hallway and ring the bell to summon the monks to a room apart, where he would lecture to them by the light of a candle.

"What use is there in your assembling together in the hall only to go to sleep? Is this all that you left the world and joined holy orders for? . . . Great is the problem of birth and death; fleeting indeed is our transitory existence. Upon these truths both the scriptural and meditation schools agree. What sort of illness awaits us tonight, what sort of death tomorrow? While we have life, not to practice Buddha's Law but to spend the time in sleep is the height of foolishness. Because of such foolishness Buddhism today is in a state of decline."

GO ON TO THE NEXT PAGE.

Document 5

Source: Kitabatake Chikafusa, court official and member of Japan's imperial family, *The Chronicle of the Direct Descent of Gods and Sovereigns,* 1339.

Japan is the divine country. The heavenly ancestor it was who first laid its foundations, and the Sun Goddess [Amaterasu] left her descendants to reign over it forever and ever. This is true only of our country, and nothing similar may be found in foreign lands. That is why it is called the divine country.

Japan is the land of the Sun Goddess. Or it may have thus been called because it is near the place where the sun rises. . . . Thus, since Japan is a separate continent, distinct from both India and China and lying in a great ocean, it is the country where the divine illustrious imperial line has been transmitted.

Only in our country has the succession remained inviolate from the beginning of heaven and earth to the present. It has been maintained within a single lineage, and even when, as inevitably has happened, the succession has been transmitted collaterally, it has returned to the true line. This is due to the ever-renewed Divine Oath and makes Japan unlike all other countries. . . .

Because our Great Goddess is the spirit of the sun, she illuminates with a bright virtue which is incomprehensible in all its aspects but dependable alike in the realm of the visible and invisible. All sovereigns and ministers have inherited the bright seeds of the divine light, or they are descendants of the deities who received personal instruction from the Great Goddess. Who would not stand in reverence before this fact? The highest object of all teachings, Buddhist and Confucian included, consists in realizing this fact and obeying in perfect consonance its principles. It has been the power of the dissemination of the Buddhist and Confucian texts which has spread these principles. . . . Since the reign of the Emperor Ōjin, the Confucian writings have been disseminated, and since Prince Shotoku's time Buddhism has flourished in Japan. Both these men were sages incarnate, and it must have been their intention to spread a knowledge of the way of our country, in accordance with the wishes of the Great Sun Goddess.

GO ON TO THE NEXT PAGE.

Document 6

Source: General Shiba Yoshimasa, feudal lord and government official, *Advice to Young Samurai,* c. 1400 C.E.

Wielders of bow and arrow should behave in a manner considerate not only of their own honor, of course, but also of the honor of their descendants. They should not bring on eternal disgrace by solicitude for their limited lives.

That being said, nevertheless to regard your one and only life as like dust or ashes and die when you shouldn't is to acquire a worthless reputation. A genuine motive would be, for example, to give up your life for the sake of the sole sovereign, or serving under the commander of the military in a time of need; these would convey an exalted name to children and descendants. Something like a strategy of the moment, whether good or bad, cannot raise the family reputation much.

Warriors should never be thoughtless or absentminded but handle all things with fore-thought. . . . It is said that good warriors and good Buddhists are similarly circumspect. Whatever the matter, it is vexing for the mind not to be calm. . . .

Even if one doesn't perform any religious exercises and never makes a visit to a shrine, neither deities nor buddhas will disregard a person whose mind is honest and compassionate. In particular, the Great Goddess of Ise [Amaterasu, the sun goddess] the great bodhisattva Hachiman [a Japanese deity who came to be seen as a Buddhist bodhisattva], and the deity of Kitano [Japanese patron god of learning] will dwell in the heads of people whose minds are honest, clean, and good.

GO ON TO THE NEXT PAGE.

Document 7

Source: Imagawa Ryoshun, samurai military leader and poet, "The Imagawa Letter," addressed to his successor, and later widely published and used to teach young samurai, 1412 C.E.

As you do not understand the Arts of Peace [literary skills including poetry, history, philosophy, and ritual] your skill in the Arts of War [horsemanship, archery, swordsmanship] will not, in the end, achieve victory.

You live in luxury by fleecing the people and plundering the shrines.

You permit yourself to forget the kindness that our lord and father showed us; thus you destroy the principles of loyalty and filial piety.

You disregard other people's viewpoints; you bully them and rely on force.

You ought to show utmost respect to Buddhist monks and priests and carry out ceremonies properly.

Whether you are in charge of anything—such as a province or a district—or not, it will be difficult to put your abilities to any use if you have not won the sympathy and respect of ordinary people.

Just as the Buddhist scriptures tell us that the Buddha incessantly strives to save mankind, in the same way you should exert your mind to the utmost in all your activities, be they civil or military, and never fall into negligence.

It should be regarded as dangerous if the ruler of the people in a province is deficient even in a single [one] of the cardinal virtues of human-heartedness, righteousness, propriety, wisdom, and good faith.

You were born to be a warrior, but you mismanage your territory, do not maintain the army, and are not ashamed although people laugh at you.

It is, indeed, a mortifying situation for you and our whole clan.

END OF PART A

WORLD HISTORY
SECTION II

Part B
(Suggested planning and writing time—40 minutes)
Percent of Section II score—33 1/3

Directions: You are to answer the following question. You should spend 5 minutes organizing or outlining your essay.

Write an essay that:

+ Has a relevant thesis and supports that thesis with appropriate historical evidence.
+ Addresses all parts of the question.
+ Uses world historical context to show continuities and changes over time.
+ Analyzes the process of continuity and change over time.

2. Analyze the continuities and changes in the development of political states in ONE of the following regions from circa 600 C.E. to 1450 C.E.

+ Central Asia
+ East Asia
+ Middle East

END OF PART B

WORLD HISTORY
SECTION II

Part C
(Suggested planning and writing time — 40 minutes)
Percent of Section II score — 33 1/3

Directions: You are to answer the following question. You should spend 5 minutes organizing or outlining your essay.

Write an essay that:

+ Has a relevant thesis and supports that thesis with appropriate historical evidence.
+ Addresses all parts of the question.
+ Makes direct, relevant comparisons.
+ Analyzes relevant reasons for similarities and differences.

3. Analyze the similarities and differences in trade dynamics between the Indian Ocean trading system and the Silk Roads up to 1450 C.E.

STOP

END OF EXAM

Answer Key for Practice Exam 3

Answers for Section I:
Multiple-Choice Questions

1. C	16. D	31. C	46. A
2. D	17. B	32. A	47. B
3. C	18. A	33. B	48. D
4. A	19. C	34. D	49. C
5. D	20. A	35. C	50. A
6. D	21. D	36. A	51. C
7. C	22. C	37. D	52. A
8. B	23. B	38. B	53. B
9. A	24. A	39. A	54. D
10. A	25. D	40. C	55. C
11. D	26. C	41. A	56. A
12. C	27. B	42. D	57. D
13. B	28. A	43. B	58. B
14. A	29. B	44. D	59. A
15. C	30. D	45. C	60. C

Rationales:

1. Answer: C

   Explanation: States like Srivijaya (670–1025) in Southeast Asia owed their power to control of key points in the Indian Ocean commercial networks. Commerce in the Indian Ocean basin also contributed to the rise of the Swahili city-states in East Africa as early as the eighth century. Between the sixth and seventeenth centuries, the trans-Saharan trade gave rise to numerous states in West Africa, including Ghana, Mali, Songhay, Kanem, and the Hausa city-states.

   Page Reference: pp. 307, 328, 332–33, 335

KEY CONCEPT	THEME	SKILL
3.1.I.A	3: State-Building, Expansion, and Conflict. 4: Creation, Expansion, and Interaction of Economic Systems.	Contextualization Comparison Causation

2. Answer: D

   Explanation: Women in the northern steppes enjoyed greater freedom. During the Tang dynasty, elite Chinese women in the northern part of the empire also enjoyed greater freedom, as suggested in paintings and sculptures featuring aristocratic women riding horses. Drinking yogurt was also customary among the nomadic peoples, a practice picked up by the Chinese elite in the north. Chinese military leaders adopted the battle styles of Turkic warriors.

   Page Reference: pp. 371, 376

KEY CONCEPT	THEME	SKILL
3.2.II	2: Development and Interaction of Cultures.	Causation

3. Answer: C

    Explanation: Although the Chinese were the first to arrive at a formula for gunpowder, the development of cannons occurred in Europe in the early fourteenth century. All the other innovations listed first emerged in China. The first use of cast iron dates to the fourth century B.C.E., papermaking was developed by the second century B.C.E., and printing was developed by 1045.

    Page Reference: p. 386

KEY CONCEPT	THEME	SKILL
3.2.II	2: Development and Interaction of Cultures.	Contextualization

4. Answer: A

    Explanation: Japan, Korea, and Vietnam all used classical Chinese as the basis of their writing systems. However, each society also incorporated an indigenous writing system. Korea developed hangul, Vietnam developed chu nom, and Japan developed hiragana.

    Page Reference: pp. 379, 381, 383

KEY CONCEPT	THEME	SKILL
3.2.I.C	2: Development and Interaction of Cultures.	Comparison

5. Answer: D

    Explanation: Chinese influence first entered Korea when the Han dynasty conquered northern Korea and Chinese migrants began to settle in the area. Although Korea eventually gained political independence, Vietnam was absorbed into the Chinese empire for more than a millennium (111 B.C.E.–939 C.E.). During this long period of direct colonization, the Chinese state pursued a policy of political integration and cultural assimilation.

    Page Reference: pp. 377, 379–80

KEY CONCEPT	THEME	SKILL
3.2.II	2: Development and Interaction of Cultures. 3: State-Building, Expansion, and Conflict.	Comparison

6. Answer: D

    Explanation: In both Europe and Japan, political power was decentralized. The king/emperor was a figurehead. Real power was in the hands of the great lords who commanded their own army of soldiers. The knights of Europe and the samurai of Japan pledged an oath of loyalty to their lords. As a reward for their military service, they received grants of land.

    Page Reference: pp. 382, 478

KEY CONCEPT	THEME	SKILL
3.2.I.B	3: State-Building, Expansion, and Conflict.	Comparison

7. Answer: C

Explanation: This conception of the model samurai reflects the synthesis of Confucianism, borrowed from China, and bushido, indigenous to Japan. Confucianism emphasized education and the arts, referred to in the quote as "the Arts of Peace." Bushido is the warrior code that samurai followed, referred to in the quote as "the Arts of War." It emphasized martial skills, honor, loyalty, and bravery.

Page Reference: pp. 382, 402

KEY CONCEPT	THEME	SKILL
3.2.I.C	2: Development and Interaction of Cultures.	Interpretation Contextualization

8. Answer: B

Explanation: The map contains no information about military conquest or forced conversions. Rather, the map suggests that the spread of Islam followed trade routes and was adopted by the states in the West African empires. It can also be reasonably inferred that trade and Islam linked West Africa to the Islamic world.

Page Reference: p. 432

KEY CONCEPT	THEME	SKILL
3.1.III.A	2: Development and Interaction of Cultures.	Comparison Contextualization Interpretation Synthesis

9. Answer: A

Explanation: Muslim invaders conquered northwestern India and at their peak, controlled most of the subcontinent. Islam also spread throughout Southeast Asia, a process facilitated by Muslim merchants. Crops indigenous to those areas gradually diffused throughout the Islamic world in the Middle East and North Africa.

Page Reference: p. 439

KEY CONCEPT	THEME	SKILL
3.1.I.E 3.1.IV.A	3: State-Building, Expansion, and Conflict. 4: Creation, Expansion, and Interaction of Economic Systems.	Contextualization

10. Answer: A

Explanation: By the tenth century, about 75 percent of the population in Spain was Muslim. After the thirteenth century, Spain returned to the world of Western Christendom. With the unification of Spain following the marriage of Ferdinand

and Isabella in the late fifteenth century, Muslim Granada reverted to Christian control.

Page Reference: pp. 434–35

KEY CONCEPT	THEME	SKILL
3.1.III.A	3: State-Building, Expansion, and Conflict.	Causation Contextualization

11. Answer: D

    Explanation: The pope invokes the story of the Lord revealing himself to the people of Israel in Egypt as a model for the conversion of the "pagan" Anglo-Saxons to Christianity. The basic point is that church leaders should tolerate local customs rather than eliminate them. The pope expresses the hope that in time, such customs will acquire a Christian meaning.

    Page Reference: pp. 479, 501–02

KEY CONCEPT	THEME	SKILL
3.2.I.C 2.3.III.C	2: Development and Interaction of Cultures.	Interpretation

12. Answer: C

    Explanation: As Christianity spread across Europe, it acquired many elements from local cultures. Church leaders usually pursued a policy of accommodation and tolerance when confronted with the "pagan" practices of the people they wished to convert. The incorporation of festivals centered on ancient gods as Christian holy days is one example of this synthesis of local traditions and Christian practices.

    Page Reference: pp. 479, 501–02

KEY CONCEPT	THEME	SKILL
3.2.I.C 2.3.III.C	2: Development and Interaction of Cultures.	Interpretation Synthesis

13. Answer: B

    Explanation: The pope reflects the Church's tolerance of local customs and even its willingness to adopt some of the existing practices of non-Christians. As Christianity spread, it acquired some of the features of the local cultures it encountered. The interaction between Christianity and "paganism" was a two-way street.

    Page Reference: pp. 479, 501–02

KEY CONCEPT	THEME	SKILL
3.2.I.C 2.3.III.C	2: Development and Interaction of Cultures.	Interpretation

14. Answer: A

    Explanation: The concept of caesaropapism was a political innovation unique to the Byzantine Empire. The emperor was not only the head of the state but of the Church as well. Church leaders, called patriarchs, were appointed by the emperor.

    Page Reference: p. 472

KEY CONCEPT	THEME	SKILL
3.2.I.A	3: State-Building, Expansion, and Conflict.	Comparison

15. Answer: C

Explanation: The emergence of feudalism in Europe after the collapse of the Roman Empire introduced a new form of labor servitude known as serfdom. Serfs were peasants who were legally tied to their lords' estates. In return for some land to cultivate and protection, serfs owed their lords labor service and various dues.

Page Reference: p. 478

KEY CONCEPT	THEME	SKILL
3.3.III.A	5: Development and Transformation of Social Structures.	Continuity and Change

16. Answer: D

Explanation: The development of the heavy wheeled plow enabled farmers to tackle the dense soils in northern Europe better than the light or "scratch" plow borrowed from the Mediterranean. As horses replaced oxen as the main source of animal muscle, iron horseshoes and a more efficient horse collar were developed. These innovations enabled Europeans to pull heavier loads. Together, these innovations contributed to higher yields, which could support a growing population.

Page Reference: p. 491

KEY CONCEPT	THEME	SKILL
3.3.I.A	1: Interaction Between Humans and the Environment.	Causation

17. Answer: B

Explanation: Muslim scholars translated many of the Greek works into Arabic. In the Byzantine Empire, scholars preserved and transmitted Greek knowledge. Western Europe received the heritage of Greek learning from the Byzantine Empire and the Islamic world and applied that knowledge to the development of natural philosophy.

Page Reference: pp. 494–96

KEY CONCEPT	THEME	SKILL
3.1.III.E	2: Development and Interaction of Cultures.	Comparison

18. Answer: A

Explanation: The Mongols themselves did not actively trade since their products were not in demand. They sought instead to tax trade and in that way extract wealth from agricultural societies. The Mongols sought to promote trade by providing financial backing for caravans, giving tax breaks to merchants, and standardizing weights and measures. These policies encouraged and facilitated interregional trade.

Page Reference: p. 534

KEY CONCEPT	THEME	SKILL
3.2.I.A	4: Creation, Expansion, and Interaction of Economic Systems.	Interpretation Argumentation

19. Answer: C

Explanation: The Mongol Empire spanned most of Eurasia, with China on one end and Eastern Europe on the other end. The Mongol rulers promoted the transmission of ideas and practices throughout their empire. Chinese medical practices and technological innovations spread as far as Europe.

Page Reference: p. 536

KEY CONCEPT	THEME	SKILL
3.2.II	2: Development and Interaction of Cultures.	Contextualization Causation

20. Answer: A

Explanation: The Mongols in the thirteenth century and the Europeans in the sixteenth century were marginalized societies. In both centuries, the Chinese and Islamic civilizations were more developed than their counterparts in Central Asia and Europe. Both the Mongols and the Europeans enriched themselves by using their military superiority to plunder the wealth of societies they encountered. As a result of their expansionist activities, they created a vast network of communication and exchange.

Page Reference: p. 539

KEY CONCEPT	THEME	SKILL
3.1.I.E 4.3.II.C	3: State-Building, Expansion, and Conflict.	Comparison

21. Answer: D

Explanation: The Mongol rulers tolerated the religions followed by its diverse population, provided that religious activity did not become politically subversive. Scholars have emphasized the more positive aspects of Mongol rule to balance the overwhelmingly negative portrayals of nomadic peoples in past scholarship.

Page Reference: pp. 536, 540

KEY CONCEPT	THEME	SKILL
3.1.I.E	1: Interaction Between Humans and the Environment. 3: State-Building, Expansion, and Conflict. 4: Creation, Expansion, and Interaction of Economic Systems.	Argumentation Interpretation

22. Answer: C

Explanation: Women in pastoral societies had greater freedom and fewer limitations than women in agricultural societies. Mongol women, for instance, often served as political advisers. Some participated in the military as well.

Page Reference: p. 515

KEY CONCEPT	THEME	SKILL
3.3.III.B	5: Development and Transformation of Social Structures.	Comparison

23. Answer: B

Explanation: Confucianism had long shaped Chinese civilization. When the Mongols conquered China, they incorporated some elements of Confucian statecraft. To relieve a village of tax and labor obligations during hard times was in keeping with the Confucian ideals of benevolent, just, and humane governance.

Page Reference: pp. 172, 527–28, 547–48

KEY CONCEPT	THEME	SKILL
3.2.I.C	2: Development and Interaction of Cultures. 3: State-Building, Expansion, and Conflict.	Interpretation Contextualization Synthesis

24. Answer: A

Explanation: The Mongols ruled over China from the late thirteenth century to the middle of the fourteenth century. The date of the epitaph—1274—falls within the period of Mongol rule in China. It can be inferred then that Menggu was an official serving the Mongol rulers.

Page Reference: pp. 527–29, 547–48

KEY CONCEPT	THEME	SKILL
3.1.I.E	3: State-Building, Expansion, and Conflict.	Contextualization

25. Answer: D

Explanation: Although the Mongols did not directly rule over Russia, opting instead to collect tribute and taxes, their rule did shape the emergent Russian state. Moscow's rise owed much to its role as tribute collector for the Mongols. Russians also adopted the weaponry, diplomatic rituals, court practices, taxation system, and military draft of the Mongols.

Page Reference: pp. 533–34

KEY CONCEPT	THEME	SKILL
3.2.II	3: State-Building, Expansion, and Conflict.	Argumentation Interpretation Comparison

26. Answer: C

    Explanation: By the fourteenth century, when the plague known as the Black Death began to spread, much of the Eurasian continent was under Mongol rule. The Mongols created an efficient infrastructure to facilitate trade and communication between the different parts of their empire. When the plague broke out in China, its spread throughout Eurasia was accelerated by those networks.

    Page Reference: pp. 535, 537

KEY CONCEPT	THEME	SKILL
3.1.IV.B	1: Interaction Between Humans and the Environment.	Interpretation Contextualization Causation

27. Answer: B

    Explanation: Because of its peripheral position on the Eurasian continent, Europe had long been marginalized in the circuits of world trade. With the Mongol conquest of much of Eurasia in the thirteenth century, Europe was linked to those trading networks for the first time. As Europeans traveled along the trade routes, they realized the full extent of the networks of which they had long been ignorant.

    Page Reference: pp. 534–35

KEY CONCEPT	THEME	SKILL
3.1.I.E	3: State-Building, Expansion, and Conflict. 4: Creation, Expansion, and Interaction of Economic Systems.	Interpretation Contextualization

28. Answer: A

    Explanation: The Mongol rulers actively promoted the exchange of ideas and techniques within the different parts of their empire. To achieve this, they forced the skilled and educated segments of the conquered population to relocate to distant locations throughout the empire. As a result, Chinese technology made its way to the Middle East and Europe, and Islamic knowledge made its way to China.

    Page Reference: p. 536

KEY CONCEPT	THEME	SKILL
3.2.II	2: Development and Interaction of Cultures.	Causation

29. Answer: B

    Explanation: The rulers of both the Ottoman and Songhay empires converted to Islam and established distinctly Islamic states. The Aztecs and Incas developed their own unique religious systems. The Mughal rulers were Muslim, while the rulers of the Vijayanagara Kingdom were Hindu. The rulers of the Safavid Empire were Muslim, while the rulers of Ethiopia were Christian.

    Page Reference: pp. 576–79

KEY CONCEPT	THEME	SKILL
3.1.III.A	3: State-Building, Expansion, and Conflict.	Comparison

30. Answer: D

Explanation: The rulers of the Byzantine Empire self-consciously styled themselves as the heirs to the Roman Empire. They referred to themselves as "Romans," and viewed the Byzantine capital at Constantinople as a "New Rome." They also retained the road system, tax-collecting methods, military organization, government administration, imperial court, and laws of the late Roman Empire.

Page Reference: p. 470

KEY CONCEPT	THEME	SKILL
3.2.I.A	3: State-Building, Expansion, and Conflict.	Continuity and Change

31. Answer: C

Explanation: In the late tenth century, Prince Vladmir of Kiev promoted the Eastern Orthodox Christianity of the Byzantine Empire. Besides religious ideas, Kievan Rus also borrowed other elements of Byzantine culture, including the use of the Cyrillic alphabet. The Cyrillic alphabet had been created by two Byzantine missionaries and was used to write the Slavic languages.

Page Reference: pp. 475–76

KEY CONCEPT	THEME	SKILL
3.2.II	2: Development and Interaction of Cultures.	Evidence Contextualization Synthesis

32. Answer: A

Explanation: The Jesus Sutras refers to the collected works of the Nestorian church that established itself in Tang dynasty China. By that time—the seventh century—Buddhism was a popular religion among the Chinese population. The characterization of the Christian texts as "sutras" highlights the influence of Buddhism.

Page Reference: p. 467

KEY CONCEPT	THEME	SKILL
3.1.III.D 2.3.III.C	2: Development and Interaction of Cultures.	Evidence Contextualization Synthesis

33. Answer: B

Explanation: Muslims believe that Muhammad was the last in a long series of prophets. Muslims believe that the prophets in the Jewish and Christian traditions—Abraham, Moses, and Jesus—were also sent by God. Muslims, however, believe that Islam represents the only true path.

Page Reference: p. 415

KEY CONCEPT	THEME	SKILL
3.1.III.A	2: Development and Interaction of Cultures.	Comparison

34. Answer: D

Explanation: The local Arab population was divided into clans and tribes that often feuded with one another. Islam broke away from that tradition by emphasizing belief rather than birth. Membership in the *umma*, the community of believers, replaced tribal, ethnic, and racial identities.

Page Reference: pp. 416–18

KEY CONCEPT	THEME	SKILL
3.1.III.A	2: Development and Interaction of Cultures.	Continuity and Change

35. Answer: C

Explanation: Islam was influenced by Judaism, Christianity, Zoroastrianism, and the popular beliefs of the Arab community. Many features of Islam—monotheism, ritual prayer, cleansing ceremonies, fasting, divine revelation, conceptions of heaven, hell, and final judgment—were familiar to Jews, Christians, and Zoroastrians. This made the process of conversion much easier as it was not a radical break from existing belief systems.

Page Reference: p. 421

KEY CONCEPT	THEME	SKILL
3.1.III.A	3: State-Building, Expansion, and Conflict.	Causation

36. Answer: A

Explanation: Although practiced in many local cultures, polygyny was sanctioned in the Quran through the stipulation that limited a man to four wives. The other choices have no basis in the Quran or Islamic law. They reflect local practices that were incorporated into the Islamic belief system.

Page Reference: p. 427

KEY CONCEPT	THEME	SKILL
3.3.III.D	5: Development and Transformation of Social Structures.	Continuity and Change Causation

37. Answer: D

Explanation: Islam entered West Africa via the trans-Saharan trade routes in the eleventh century. By that time, North Africa was already part of the Islamic world. Muslim traders crossing the Sahara found a receptive audience in the empires of West Africa, especially the Songhay Empire.

Page Reference: p. 432

KEY CONCEPT	THEME	SKILL
3.1.III.A	3: State-Building, Expansion, and Conflict.	Comparison

38. Answer: B

    Explanation: Only Muhammad assumed military responsibilities in addition to his role as religious leader. Like Jesus and the Buddha, Muhammad also had a powerful religious experience that led him to found a religion. All three also articulated a path to salvation and espoused the principle of the equality of the community of believers.

    Page Reference: pp. 415, 418

KEY CONCEPT	THEME	SKILL
3.1.III.A	2: Development and Interaction of Cultures.	Comparison

39. Answer: A

    Explanation: After Muhammad's death, a violent dispute erupted over who should be the rightful successor. The Sunni Muslims sided with the caliphs, while the Shia branch favored the blood relatives of Muhammad. Over time, the split evolved into differences of opinion on who held religious authority. Sunni Muslims emphasized the *ulama*, while Shia Muslims privileged the *imams*.

    Page Reference: p. 423

KEY CONCEPT	THEME	SKILL
3.1.III.A 4.1.VI.A	2: Development and Interaction of Cultures.	Argumentation

40. Answer: C

    Explanation: Crops indigenous to South and Southeast Asia spread throughout the Islamic world following the Muslim conquest of northwestern India. These new crops—rice, sugarcane, cotton, hard wheat, bananas, lemons, limes, watermelons, coconut palms, spinach, artichokes, and new strains of sorghum—made their way to the Middle East, Africa, and eventually, Europe.

    Page Reference: p. 439

KEY CONCEPT	THEME	SKILL
3.1.IV.A	4: Creation, Expansion, and Interaction of Economic Systems.	Argumentation Evidence

41. Answer: A

    Explanation: Networks of exchange in the ninth century linked the Islamic world to Asia. Indian numerical notation traveled along the trade routes and reached the Middle East, enabling Arab scholars to develop algebra.

    Page Reference: p. 441

KEY CONCEPT	THEME	SKILL
3.1.III.E	2: Development and Interaction of Cultures.	Causation Contextualization

42. Answer: D

Explanation: The Aztec Empire demanded from conquered populations tribute and victims for sacrificial rituals. In contrast, the Inca Empire controlled local society to a greater extent. In the system of *mita*, every household was expected to regularly contribute labor service to the state. Some worked on state farms called "sun farms." Specially selected women, the "chosen women," were trained at an early age to work at state production centers.

Page Reference: pp. 585–86

KEY CONCEPT	THEME	SKILL
3.3.III.C	3: State-Building, Expansion, and Conflict.	Comparison

43. Answer: B

Explanation: The Olmec civilization flourished around 1200 B.C.E. in Mesoamerica, so it is the wrong place and the wrong time. The depiction of a Hindu goddess indicates Indian influence. The lotus flower is a Buddhist symbol. The short tunic tightened with a belt shows Greek or Hellenistic influence.

Page Reference: pp. 359–60

KEY CONCEPT	THEME	SKILL
3.1.III.D 2.2.V.C	2: Development and Interaction of Cultures.	Interpretation Contextualization Synthesis

44. Answer: D

Explanation: For much of the first millennium, the Silk Roads that crisscrossed central Eurasia operated as a main conduit not only for commercial exchange but also for cultural interactions. Buddhism made its way throughout Asia along the Silk Roads. The Kushan Empire's proximity to the Silk Road network exposed it to Buddhism. Portions of the Kushan Empire fell under Alexander the Great's empire, exposing those regions to Hellenistic culture. Although the Kushan used the Greek alphabet to write their language, the language originated in India.

Page Reference: pp. 359–60

KEY CONCEPT	THEME	SKILL
3.1.III.D 2.2.V.C	2: Development and Interaction of Cultures.	Contextualization

45. Answer: C

Explanation: Axum is in East Africa, and Kerala is in southern India. Christianity was introduced into both areas by traveling merchants from the Roman world. Many of these merchants settled in southern India and along the East African coast and facilitated the spread of Christianity.

Page Reference: p. 327

KEY CONCEPT	THEME	SKILL
3.1.III.B	2: Development and Interaction of Cultures.	Contextualization

46. Answer: A

Explanation: In the Aztec Empire, trade was largely in the hands of professional merchants, called *pochteca*. Although they sometimes served the state, they also conducted trade on behalf of the nobility or for themselves. In contrast, the Inca state regulated trade, and no distinctive merchant group emerged.

Page Reference: p. 341

KEY CONCEPT	THEME	SKILL
3.1.I.B	4: Creation, Expansion, and Interaction of Economic Systems.	Comparison

47. Answer: B

Explanation: The caravanserai were stopping points along the Silk Roads. They offered travelers food, lodging, storage, and opportunities for trade. Dunhuang is the only city that lies in the path of the Silk Roads.

Page Reference: pp. 322, 355, 357

KEY CONCEPT	THEME	SKILL
3.1.I.C	4: Creation, Expansion, and Interaction of Economic Systems.	Evidence

48. Answer: D

Explanation: The map shows that the majority of the trade routes of the Silk Road network were within inner Eurasia. The harsher and drier climate in this region could not support agriculture, so most societies that emerged in this region were pastoral or nomadic societies.

Page Reference: p. 318

KEY CONCEPT	THEME	SKILL
3.1.I.A	4: Creation, Expansion, and Interaction of Economic Systems.	Contextualization Synthesis

49. Answer: C

Explanation: The long distances and high transportation costs associated with the Silk Road trade meant that only trade in expensive luxury items would be profitable. In response to the higher demand for luxury goods such as silk, porcelain, and iron tools, peasants in the Yangzi River delta of southern China turned from the cultivation of crops to the production of the goods that would garner higher prices on the market.

Page Reference: p. 321

KEY CONCEPT	THEME	SKILL
3.1.I.C 3.3.I.C	4: Creation, Expansion, and Interaction of Economic Systems.	Causation

50. Answer: A

Explanation: Not much is known about what contributed to the collapse of the city of Mohenjo Daro in the Indus Valley. Evidence does exist, however, that disease weakened Athens, Byzantium, and the Mongol Empire. The seaborne trade with Egypt introduced a new disease into ancient Greece, which contributed to the decline of Athens. An outbreak of the bubonic plague in the sixth century that came via the seaborne trade with India weakened the Byzantine Empire. And the Black Death traveled along the routes of the Silk Roads, from its point of origin in China and spreading across Eurasia. This contributed to the eventual collapse of the Mongol Empire.

Page Reference: pp. 323–24, 537

KEY CONCEPT	THEME	SKILL
3.1.IV.B 3.3.II.A	1: Interaction Between Humans and the Environment.	Comparison

51. Answer: C

Explanation: Srivijaya's strength was in seaborne commerce, not agriculture. Easy access to gold and spices like cloves, nutmeg, and mace placed Srivijaya in a strong position. Its control over a critical choke point of Indian Ocean trade also enabled it to increase state revenues by taxing passing ships.

Page Reference: pp. 328–29

KEY CONCEPT	THEME	SKILL
3.1.I.A 3.1.I.D 3.3.II.B	3: State-Building, Expansion, and Conflict. 4: Creation, Expansion, and Interaction of Economic Systems.	Causation

52. Answer: A

Explanation: Confucianism was a Chinese cultural export. Buddhism originated in India. Sanskrit and Pallava are Indian languages. *Ramayana* is an Indian epic.

Page Reference: pp. 329–30

KEY CONCEPT	THEME	SKILL
3.1.III.D 3.1.II.C	2: Development and Interaction of Cultures.	Synthesis

53. Answer: B

Explanation: In his account of his impressions of Mali, Ibn Battuta criticized what he considered the excessive freedom African women enjoyed. In his eyes, African women failed to abide by the rules that governed Muslim women in his society.

Page Reference: pp. 336, 350–53

KEY CONCEPT	THEME	SKILL
3.1.III.C	2: Development and Interaction of Cultures. 5: Development and Transformation of Social Structures.	Interpretation

54. Answer: D

Explanation: The Maya civilization was highly fragmented and composed of a variety of different structures. These ranged from city-states to regional kingdoms. Rivalry and warfare characterized the nature of relations within various centers of Maya civilization.

Page Reference: p. 274

KEY CONCEPT	THEME	SKILL
3.2.I.D	3: State-Building, Expansion, and Conflict.	Comparison

55. Answer: C

Explanation: Although there were still Maya when the Spanish arrived in the sixteenth century, the Maya civilization is considered to have fallen by the tenth century. Population growth beginning in the seventh century began to outstrip available resources. Climate changes in the ninth century produced prolonged droughts that further strained limited resources. The fragmented political structure of Maya civilization contributed to internecine warfare.

Page Reference: p. 275

KEY CONCEPT	THEME	SKILL
3.3.II.A	1: Interaction Between Humans and the Environment. 3: State-Building, Expansion, and Conflict.	Argumentation Causation

56. Answer: A

Explanation: In contrast to other parts of their empire, the Mongols did not occupy Russia. Instead, they demanded that Russian princes regularly send tribute to the Mongol capital at Sarai. Similarly, in the Aztec, imperial tribute collectors supervised the delivery of tribute from conquered regions to the Aztec capital at Tenochtitlán.

Page Reference: pp. 533, 582

KEY CONCEPT	THEME	SKILL
3.2.I.D 4.3.I.E	3: State-Building, Expansion, and Conflict.	Comparison

57.   Answer: D

Explanation: Western Europe escaped Mongol conquest, although the threat was ever-present. Both rulers and the pope sent numerous diplomatic missions to the Mongol court. The purpose of these missions was to probe Mongol intentions, secure Mongol assistance in the Crusades, and spread Christianity. The reports of the missions have been used by historians to learn about the Mongol Empire.

Page Reference: p. 536

KEY CONCEPT	THEME	SKILL
3.1.I.E	3: State-Building, Expansion, and Conflict.	Evidence

58.   Answer: B

Explanation: Most guilds by the fifteenth century were male-dominated. Guild regulations sought to exclude or restrict female members. Regulations in England prohibited women from manufacturing certain fabrics and denied women the opportunity to learn how to use new weaving machines.

Page Reference: p. 483

KEY CONCEPT	THEME	SKILL
3.3.III.A 3.3.III.B	5: Development and Transformation of Social Structures.	Evidence Interpretation

59.   Answer: A

Explanation: The early modern era generally refers to the period between 1450 and 1750. All the other terms have been used to refer to the millennium between 500 and 1500. The Byzantine Empire flourished during most of those centuries. The birth of Islam in the seventh century spawned a number of Islamic states and empires that created the Islamic world. The Mongol Empire flourished during the thirteenth century.

Page Reference: p. 307

KEY CONCEPT	THEME	SKILL
3.1.I.E	3: State-Building, Expansion, and Conflict.	Periodization

60.   Answer: C

Explanation: In the eleventh century, Western Europe was only beginning to emerge as a distinctive new civilization. Compared to the Byzantine Empire, the Islamic empires and China, Western Europe was still a backwater. Western Europe borrowed extensively from these more advanced and developed civilizations.

Page Reference: p. 309

KEY CONCEPT	THEME	SKILL
3.1.III.A 3.2.I.A	3: State-Building, Expansion, and Conflict.	Contextualization

Answer Guide for Section II:
Part A

General Guidelines for Answering a Document-Based Question (DBQ):

1. Pre-write. Create a brief outline before you start writing.
2. Write your DBQ in a multiple-paragraph structure. In your first paragraph, write an introduction that clearly states your thesis.
3. Present your arguments in body paragraphs. Body paragraphs should integrate groupings of documents, demonstrate understanding of documents, support the thesis using documents as evidence, analyze point of view, and possibly include additional relevant historical content. Present your arguments in body paragraphs that focus on a grouping of documents and that put forth a single argument centered on answering the prompt.
4. In your final paragraph, write a conclusion that includes a reworded restatement of your thesis.

AP World History DBQ essays are scored using a core scoring method with a maximum score of nine. In the basic core, you may earn the following seven points:

*   one point for a thesis
*   one point for addressing and understanding the documents
*   up to two points for using the documents as evidence to answer the prompt
*   one point for grouping the documents
*   one point for analyzing Point of View (POV)
*   one point for identifying and explaining the need for an additional document

If you earn ALL seven basic core points, you have the chance to earn up to two additional points in what is called expanded core. Expanded core points may be granted for the following features:

*   an excellent, sophisticated, and comprehensive thesis
*   insightful document analysis
*   analyzing POV in all or most documents
*   including extra document groupings or additional documents
*   incorporating relevant historical content not found in the documents

Below is a detailed description of what you will need to do in your answer to earn each basic core point for this essay.

Thesis (1 point): To earn a point in this category, you must write a thesis that responds to the entire prompt and outlines the specific arguments you will make based on a correct usage of the documents. You will need to mention the arguments you plan on making in your answer, and you will need to avoid generalizations that do not reflect reasonable interpretations of the documents. Thesis statements will only earn a point if they appear in the first or last paragraph of the essay. Common errors in thesis writing include merely rewriting the prompt or presenting an answer to only some parts of the prompt, so make sure you address the entire prompt and briefly present the specific arguments that you will use in your answer based on the documents.

> **Prompt:** Using the following documents, analyze the problems confronted by Japanese leaders seeking to establish political order and the methods they adopted to solve those problems from 600 C.E. to 1450 C.E. Identify an additional type of document and explain how it would help your analysis of the problems faced and methods adopted by Japanese leaders.

Examples:

Example Thesis: "In the period from 600 C.E. to 1450 C.E., Japanese political leaders seeking to establish political order confronted problems including poor leadership, disharmony, and general disrespect for Buddhism. They attempted to solve these problems by increasing support for Buddhism, applying Confucianism, and finding good men to promote in government positions."

✦ This thesis earns the point by identifying the specific arguments based on the documents that will be used to answer the prompt. It presents BOTH problems and solutions, so it answers the entire prompt. Thesis statements can be longer than a single sentence. A multi-sentence thesis should, however, be presented in contiguous sentences.

Unacceptable Example One: "Japanese political leaders faced problems and tried to establish political order by solving these problems creatively."

✦ This thesis does little other than state the obvious given the prompt.

Unacceptable Example Two: "Japanese leaders tried to use Buddhism, Confucianism, and their own traditions to solve their problems."

✦ This thesis improves upon the first example by including some specific solutions, but it would NOT earn a thesis point because it does not answer the entire prompt.

Addressing and Understanding Documents (1 point): To earn this point you must address ALL of the documents and demonstrate understanding of "all but one." This means that throughout your answer, you must show understanding of at least six of the seven documents.

Using Documents as Evidence (2 points): To earn two points, you must correctly incorporate at least six documents (although seven would be better) into arguments that answer the prompt. You will earn only one point if you use five of the seven documents in your arguments. If you use four or fewer documents in your essay, you will receive a zero in this category.

Grouping the Documents (1 point): Documents should be grouped in at least three ways in order to earn a point in this category. You can group documents by matching two or more documents that hold some relevant feature in common. Each example grouping below represents documents that, when used together, can make up an argument that answers the prompt.

Grouping the Documents:

Problems:

Disharmony	Docs 1, 3, 7
Class Divisions	Docs 1, 2, 7
People Disobeying Lords	Docs 1, 7
Poor Leadership	Docs 1, 6, 7
National Rule vs. Local Rule	Docs 1, 3
Lack of Respect for Buddhism	Docs 2, 4, 6, 7

Solutions:

Buddhism	Docs 1, 4, 5, 6, 7
Use of Confucianism	Docs 1, 5, 6
Calls on Japanese Tradition	Docs 1, 5, 6
Find Good Men for Gov't	Docs 1, 6, 7
Ideologies Supporting Rule	Docs 5, 6

Analyzing Point of View (1 Point): Many students find it challenging to earn the point in this category. The best way to earn the Point of View (POV) point is to go beyond the basic identity of the source author and the source itself, as described in the document source line. In order to write a successful POV statement, you should try to establish a better understanding of the identity of the author; you can do this by asking yourself questions about the author and the source. What is the author's gender or social class? What religion does the author follow? What is the author's profession? Does the author have an identifiable ethnicity, nationality, or other allegiance to a particular group? Is the source from a poem, essay, or novel? What was the source used for? Once you've asked these questions, go further and explain how some of these factors may have influenced the content of the source. Your complete POV statement should both identify the influences that may have shaped the author or source and explain how those particular influences have specifically affected the content of the document. Below are some examples of POV statements based on the documents from this question.

Examples of POV Statements:

Document 1: "Source: Shotoku, Regent of Japan under Empress Suiko, *The Seventeen Article Constitution*, 604 C.E."

✦ As ruler of Japan, Shotoku sought to concentrate political authority in the imperial government. He wanted to diminish the rival political authority of provincial lords or clans and so advocated a constitution that invested more authority with the imperial government. As an imperial ruler, he wouldn't reduce his own power and give more to local lords.

Document 4: "Source: Dōgen, Japanese Buddhist who introduced and popularized Zen Buddhism in Japan, *Writings on Zen Buddhism*, c. 1227 C.E."

✦ Dōgen was a Buddhist, and as a Buddhist, he would promote and support Buddhism in Japan. His *Writings on Zen Buddhism* support and promote his idea of Buddhism.

Document 5: "Source: Kitabatake Chikafusa, court official and member of Japan's imperial family, *The Chronicle of the Direct Descent of Gods and Sovereigns*, 1339."

✦ As a member of Japan's imperial family, Chikafusa pushed for the divine origins of the line of the imperial family. He presents ideas that reinforce the rule of the imperial family and as a member of government, would not offer ideas undermining the basis for his rule, or the rule of his family.

You should write as many POV statements as you are able to produce. You can earn the POV point with as few as two correct POV statements; however, it's not uncommon to make errors in writing POV statements. For that reason, it's safer to provide more than just two in order to make up for any errors. Additionally, if you earn all of the basic core points, an extra POV statement can earn you an expanded core point.

Additional Document Statement (1 Point): A good additional document statement identifies a missing document that, if added to the provided documents, would help make a better answer to the question. You are only required to make a single additional document statement to earn a point, but you should aim to identify a minimum of three additional documents. This allows room for mistakes, and after the first correct additional document statement, any extras can earn you bonus points in the expanded core if you earn all seven points in the basic core. You should be careful to avoid the common mistake of asking for a type of document that is already provided. Additional document statements must meet three standards to be considered successful:

  ✦ The document suggested must be historically plausible.
  ✦ The statement must include an explanation of **why** the additional document would be useful in answering the prompt
  ✦ The analysis of **why** must speculate about the particulars of what the missing document might include. In other words, a successful additional document suggestion is historically possible given the time and place, includes an explanation of how the new source would help answer the prompt, and goes as far as speculating on arguments that the suggested source might support.

Document Analysis:

Document 1: "Source: Shotoku, Regent of Japan under Empress Suiko, *The Seventeen Article Constitution*, 604 C.E." This document shows that Japanese leaders faced problems of disharmony, class divisions, people disobeying elites, poor leadership, and a conflict between those favoring national rule or local clan rule. It offers solutions explicitly in promoting Buddhism and implicitly, in advocating Confucian ideas. (You will have to recognize Confucian ideas in order to make this argument since Shotoku doesn't explicitly label them as "Confucian"; for example, #3 of the constitution expresses Confucian ideology.) He also seeks good men for government.

Document 2: "Source: Sei Shonagon, imperial court member as lady-in-waiting to Empress Sadako, *Pillow Book*, c. 1000 C.E." Shonagon expresses an elitist distaste for the peasantry, which might be used to show class divisions as a problem faced by Japanese leaders. Shonagon also disrespects Buddhism if the monks are less than pleasing to the eye, which reflects another problem faced by Japanese rulers who viewed Buddhism as a potential solution.

Document 3: "Source: Twelfth-century painting depicting the famous naval battle of Dan-no-ura in which the samurai warriors of the Taira clan fought the Minamoto clan in 1185." The painting shows warfare between rival Japanese clans, which illustrates disharmony and suggests that imperial Japanese rule had less than full national authority. These local rulers pursued their own interests in the conflict, which would have damaged national unity.

Document 4: "Source: Dōgen, Japanese Buddhist who introduced and popularized Zen Buddhism in Japan, *Writings on Zen Buddhism*, c. 1227 C.E." Dōgen notes a lack of respect for Buddhism and in lamenting this decline, implies that a return to a better practice of Buddhism would increase respect for the religion.

Document 5: "Source: Kitabatake Chikafusa, court official and member of Japan's imperial family, *The Chronicle of the Direct Descent of Gods and Sovereigns*, 1339." Chikafusa merges Japanese tradition and belief in the Sun Goddess along with the teachings of Buddhism and Confucianism in order to justify the good and divine rule by the imperial line of Japan. Chikafusa then illustrates Japanese leaders' use of ideologies to support their rule. Chikafusa indicates a support for Buddhism, Confucianism, and also uniquely Japanese traditions as positive goods in seeking an orderly society.

Document 6: "Source: General Shiba Yoshimasa, feudal lord and government official, *Advice to Young Samurai*, c. 1400 C.E." Yoshimasa instructs Japan's young samurai to follow Japanese tradition, particularly in deference to their superiors and their family elders. He also encourages young samurai to follow Buddhism. Both Japanese and Buddhist traditions are referenced in the line, "the Great Goddess of Ise [Amaterasu, the sun goddess] the great bodhisattva Hachiman [a Japanese deity who came to be seen as a Buddhist bodhisattva], and the deity of Kitano [Japanese patron god of learning]."

Document 7: "Source: Imagawa Ryoshun, samurai military leader and poet, "The Imagawa Letter," addressed to his successor, and later widely published and used to teach young samurai, 1412 C.E." Ryoshun identifies poor leadership, class divisions, people's lack of respect for elites and for Buddhism as problems faced by Japanese leaders. He then advocates for Buddhism, which will help shape better men to rule in government. He advises a poor leader that "Just as the Buddhist scriptures tell us that the Buddha incessantly strives to save mankind, in the same way you should exert your mind to the utmost in all your activities, be they civil or military, and never fall into negligence." He also states, "It should be regarded as dangerous if the ruler of the people in a province is deficient even in a single [one] of the cardinal virtues of human-heartedness, righteousness, propriety, wisdom, and good faith."

Answer Guide for Section II: Part B

2. Analyze the continuities and changes in the development of political states in ONE of the following regions from circa 600 C.E. to 1450 C.E.

- ✦ Central Asia
- ✦ East Asia
- ✦ Middle East

What Does the Question Ask?

This question deals with political developments, which could include the forms of government, political rulers, imperial expansion, and conflict within or among political states.

Listed below is the scoring system used to grade continuity and change-over-time essays; also included are guidelines and examples for how to earn each point for this question.

Has Acceptable Thesis (1 point)

- ✦ The thesis needs to correctly address both continuity and change in the political states of Central Asia, East Asia, or the Middle East between 600 C.E. and 1450 C.E.
- ✦ The thesis should appear in the first paragraph (although it may also count if it is in the conclusion).
- ✦ The thesis can be one sentence or multiple sentences.

Examples:

- ✦ Example One: The political state of China varied from 600 C.E. to 1450 C.E. in how centralized it was. However, throughout the entire period, they emphasized a bureaucratic form of government.
- ✦ Example Two: From around 600 C.E. to 1450 C.E., the politics of the Middle East continued to focus on Islam. There were several different empires during this time.
- ✦ Example Three: Central Asia was under the control of pastoral groups from 600 C.E. to 1450 C.E. One of those groups, the Mongols, was able to unify the pastoral groups under one ruler.
- ✦ Unacceptable Example: The Five Pillars of Islam were important to the Muslims during this period. People would go to mosques and pray. New artistic values emerged as Islam spread throughout the Middle East.
  - • This is an unacceptable thesis because it exclusively addresses cultural issues rather than the development of political states.

Addresses All Parts of the Question (2 points)

- ✦ The essay accurately addresses both a continuity (1 point) and a change (1 point).
- ✦ The statements of continuity and change may not appear in the thesis.

Examples:

- ✦ Example One: Following Mongol rule, China returned to its tradition of a strong, unified state. Even during Mongol rule, the emperors of China continued to use a bureaucracy to run the vast country.
  - • The first statement in the example above addresses change, while the second statement addresses continuity.

- ✦ Example Two: The Middle East remained majority Islamic from Muhammad's time through 1450. However, the center of the Islamic state moved several times during this period, from Mecca to Damascus to Baghdad and eventually to Istanbul.
  - • The first statement in the example above addresses continuity, while the second statement addresses change.

- ✦ Example Three: Nomadic people controlled much of Central Asia during the postclassical era. At times, they invaded urban areas and were able to exercise political control through their military skills.
  - • The first statement in the example above addresses continuity, while the second statement addresses change.

Substantiates Thesis with Appropriate Historical Evidence (2 points)

- ✦ A piece of historical evidence is a fact that is correct and relevant to the time period.
- ✦ To earn the full two points in this category, an essay should have five or more pieces of evidence.
- ✦ To earn only one point in this category, an essay needs three or four pieces of evidence.
- ✦ Points for evidence can be earned even if the thesis point is not earned.

Examples:

- ✦ Example One: China emerged as a centralized state during this time period. The Chinese used a civil service exam system focused on Confucianism to select their government leaders. The Grand Canal and Great Wall were reconstructed and expanded. The Mongols invaded, starting a new dynasty known as the Yuan. They did away with the Confucian civil servants, replacing them with their own non-Chinese bureaucrats.

✦ Example Two: The cities of Mecca and Medina were vital in the early years of Islam. In addition to being a religious prophet, Muhammad was also a ruling political figure. Early caliphs were the successors of Muhammad and ruled under Islamic law. The Sunnis were the main group controlling much of the politics of early Islamic empires. In the short-lived Umayyad Empire, non-Arabs and Shia were politically marginalized.

✦ Example Three: Chinggis Khan unified the Mongol clans in the thirteenth century. His enormous armies were able to expand dramatically across Eurasia. The areas under Mongol control split into different empires after the death of Chinggis Khan. Other Central Asian groups like the Turks also expanded their political influence. Tamerlane conquered much of Central Asia including many Silk Road cities.

Uses Relevant Historical Context (1 point)

✦ Historical context places the issue discussed in the essay into a broader global perspective.

Examples:

✦ Example One: The Mongols invaded from Central Asia and established a new dynasty in China.
✦ Example Two: Soon after the founding of Islam, Arab states spread dramatically throughout the Middle East and beyond to Asia, and even Europe. This created a united Muslim world known as Dar al-Islam.
✦ Example Three: The Ottoman Turks united under Islamic rule and spread their influence into the Middle East and Europe by 1450.

Analyzes the Process of Continuity or Change (1 point)

✦ Analysis explains why the continuity or change occurred.

Examples:

✦ Example One: Since the Mongols were not Chinese, they preferred to use non-Chinese people as administrators in their government.
✦ Example Two: Conflict over succession caused the split between the Shia and the Sunni factions of Islam.
✦ Example Three: Mongols were able to control such an enormous empire because they maintained control of a vast system of roads.

Expanded Core

You must earn all seven points in the basic core before earning any points in the expanded core. Points awarded in the expanded core reflect the general excellence of the essay. Any one aspect of your essay, such as the thesis or evidence, might be particularly insightful and earn a point in the expanded core. Essays that have a high degree of analysis and historical context often earn expanded core points if they have earned all of the other basic core points. Clarity of organization, strong cause-effect analysis, and particularly insightful ideas can make your essay stand out as excellent.

Examples:

✦ Example One: An essay that has a high amount of relevant, detailed information about the transformations that occurred in China during this time period could earn points in the expanded core.

- ✦ Example Two: Analyzing the differences among the various Islamic empires throughout this period could earn points in the expanded core.
- ✦ Example Three: Discussing the rise and fall of different Central Asian empires could earn points in the expanded core.

Answer Guide for Section II: Part C

3. Analyze the similarities and differences in trade dynamics between the Indian Ocean trading system and the Silk Roads up to 1450 C.E.

What Does the Question Ask?

This question does not offer a choice in what areas you can write about; you must address the Silk Roads and Indian Ocean trade systems. However, your essay could involve much more than just economics if other topics, such as religion or politics, are linked to the dynamics of the trade systems.

Listed below is the scoring system used to grade comparative essays; also included are guidelines and examples for how to earn each point for this question.

Has Acceptable Thesis (1 point)

- ✦ The thesis needs to correctly address both a similarity and a difference in trade dynamics between the Indian Ocean and Silk Road systems.
- ✦ The thesis should appear in the first paragraph (although it may also count if it is in the conclusion).
- ✦ The thesis can be one sentence or multiple sentences.

Examples:

- ✦ Example One: Both the Indian Ocean and the Silk Road trade systems linked different world regions together. The Silk Road, however, had greater religious diversity among its merchants than the Indian Ocean trade system.
- ✦ Example Two: China and India provided valuable trade goods for both the Indian Ocean and Silk Road systems. Certain trade items, like ivory, were more prevalent along the Indian Ocean than along the Silk Roads.
- ✦ Example Three: The Silk Road and the Indian Ocean systems both spread technological innovations, yet the ways in which merchants traveled differed.
- ✦ Unacceptable Example: Europeans were dominant in both the Silk Road and the Indian Ocean trade systems. For example, the Roman Empire was connected to Han China as a result of the Silk Roads, and the Portuguese eventually dominated the Indian Ocean trade.
  - • This is an unacceptable thesis because both the Roman Empire and the Portuguese role in the Indian Ocean trade are outside of the time period.

Addresses All Parts of the Question (2 points)

- ✦ The essay accurately addresses both a valid similarity (1 point) and a valid difference (1 point).
- ✦ The statements of comparison may not appear in the thesis.

Examples:

+ Example One: Islamic merchants connected the different regions involved in both trade systems. Merchants who were Buddhist and Christian were more common on the Silk Roads.
  • The first statement in the example above addresses similarity, while the second statement addresses difference.

+ Example Two: Merchants traded textiles as part of both the Indian Ocean and Silk Road trade routes. The main cloth traded along the Silk Road was obviously silk, whereas cotton from India was the most important textile shipped through the Indian Ocean.
  • The first statement in the example above addresses similarity, while the second statement addresses difference.

+ Example Three: Trade systems like those of the Indian Ocean and the Silk Road helped to disperse new ideas and technological information. The technologies involved in the actual traveling differed greatly.
  • The first statement in the example above addresses similarity, while the second statement addresses difference.

Substantiates Thesis with Appropriate Historical Evidence (2 points)

+ A piece of historical evidence is a fact that is correct and relevant to the time period.
+ To earn the full two points in this category, an essay should have five or more pieces of evidence.
+ To earn only one point in this category, an essay needs three or four pieces of evidence.
+ Points for evidence can be earned even if the thesis point is not earned.

Examples:

+ Example One: Silk Road cities, such as Samarkand, were centers for the mixing of different people and the exchange of trade goods. Muslims and Buddhists who traveled in these trade networks helped to spread their religion to people far outside of the areas where these religions were founded. For example, Islam came to the coastal cities of East Africa as a result of the influence of Muslim merchants. The Silk Roads connected the Mediterranean region with the great markets of China. Africa, Europe, and Asia were all more closely connected as a result of these trade routes.
+ Example Two: The Indian Ocean trade system was an overseas trade linking India and Southeast Asia to Africa and the Middle East. The Silk Roads stretched from China to the Mediterranean coast. Gold, ivory, and precious woods came out of Africa into India. India shipped textiles and spices to the African coast. Chinese trade items included silk cloth, lacquer wood items, and porcelain.
+ Example Three: The Indian Ocean trade was conducted on wooden ships called dhows. Most of the trade along the Silk Road was carried by caravans of horses and camels. The technology of compasses and astrolabes were important in helping the merchants get from one place to another. The new language of Swahili developed because of the Indian Ocean trade. Other technologies like paper and silk making also spread through the Silk Roads.

Makes a Direct, Relevant Comparison (1 point)

+ A direct comparison is an explicit, concrete, and factually correct statement of either similarity or difference.

Examples:

- ✦ Example One: The religion of Islam spread with the trade goods that were traded along both the land routes of Central Asia and the water routes of the Indian Ocean.
- ✦ Example Two: Trade along both the Indian Ocean and Silk Roads involved high-value luxury items like gold, silver, and spices.
- ✦ Example Three: Technological innovations, such as lateen sails and special saddles for camels, improved travel and increased trade along both the Silk Road and Indian Ocean trade systems.

Analyzes at Least One Reason for a Similarity or Difference (1 point)

- ✦ Analysis explains a reason for the similarity or difference.

Examples:

- ✦ Example One: Islamic merchants were prevalent in both trade systems because of the global span of Islam and its focus on traveling for religious pilgrimage.
- ✦ Example Two: Merchants traded luxury products along these trade routes because the long distances involved increased the transportation costs. The more the item was worth and the less it weighed, the more profit they could get from the trade.
- ✦ Example Three: Since the Silk Roads were mostly overland routes and the Indian Ocean trade relied on sailing boats, the types of innovation differed greatly. The Silk Roads, for example, developed new saddles, and the Indian Ocean trade spurred the development of new types of ships.

Expanded Core

You must earn all seven points in the basic core before earning any points in the expanded core. Points awarded in the expanded core reflect the general excellence of the essay. Any one aspect of your essay, such as the thesis or evidence, might be particularly insightful and earn a point in the expanded core. Essays that have a high degree of analysis and historical context often earn expanded core points if they have all of the other basic core points. Clarity of organization, strong cause-effect analysis, and particularly insightful ideas can make your essay stand out as excellent.

Examples:

- ✦ Example One: Since religion was a major feature of the trade dynamics, it counts for credit if it is linked to the trade system, even though it is not strictly considered economic. An essay that analyzes how religion and economics are linked in both of these trade systems could earn points in the expanded core.
- ✦ Example Two: A detailed analysis of why certain goods were desired by different regions involved in both trade systems could earn points in the expanded core.
- ✦ Example Three: A discussion of many different types of innovation, such as language, engineering, manufacturing, and other aspects of culture could earn points in the expanded core.

PERIOD FOUR
Global Interactions, c. 1450 to c. 1750

PART FOUR
The Early Modern World, 1450–1750

AP World History Key Concepts

4.1: Globalizing Networks of Communication and Exchange

4.2: New Forms of Social Organization and Modes of Production

4.3: State Consolidation and Imperial Expansion

The Big Picture: Debating the Character of an Era

Historians have found it useful to create a descriptive label for a period, but that practice often oversimplifies or assumes that certain trends are equally valid in all parts of the world.

Chapter 13 examines the new empires of this era in Europe, the Middle East, and Asia. The globalization of trade and the economy are analyzed in Chapter 14. Chapter 15 deals with new cultural trends within religious traditions and in the newly emerging scientific worldview.

An Early Modern Era?

The term most often used to describe this period, "early modern," spotlights globalization, modernity, and the transformation of Europe into a major actor in world affairs.

✦ Globalization:
  • Oceanic voyages by European explorers led to the conquest and colonization of the Americas and linked Africa to the Americas through the transatlantic slave trade.
  • Precious metals, such as silver, extracted from the Americas allowed Europeans to change the markets in Asia.
  • The Columbian exchange, the transfer of flora, fauna, people, ideas, and pathogens, altered the entire world.
  • Christianity spread to become a global religion.
  • Russia expanded east to the Pacific Ocean, China expanded into inner Asia, and the Ottoman Empire ruled from the Indian Ocean to Northern Africa to southeastern Europe.
✦ Modernity:
  • The Scientific Revolution in Europe changed the way people (at least some of them) understood the world, approached knowledge, and thought about religion.
  • World population doubled between 1400 and 1800; food from the Americas (such as corn and potatoes), the end of Mongol invasions, and recovery from the Black Death led to increasing population growth in Europe, China, India, and Japan. The Americas faced a catastrophic drop in the Native American population caused by the introduction of diseases from Africa and Eurasia, while African populations were limited by the transatlantic slave trade.
  • Commercial, urbanizing societies developed in parts of Eurasia and the Americas; Japan, for example, was the most urbanized society in the world. In some regions, such as in China, Southeast Asia, India, and the Atlantic basin, people began to produce primarily for distant markets.
  • States became stronger and more centralized; they promoted trade, manufacturing, and a common culture. Some states, particularly in Asia and the Middle East, also often incorporated local societies, using gunpowder and superior military forces to take over surrounding territories to build large empires. Some European states created overseas colonial empires.
  • Population pressure and plantation agriculture led to deforestation, draining swamps, and encroachment on the traditional grounds of hunter-gatherers and pastoralists.

A Late Agrarian Era?

In 1750, it was not clear that the forces of modernization would win, as most people in the world continued to live in traditional ways. The developments of this period often seemed to be those of a late agrarian age.

✦ European power was limited in much of Asia and Africa. China and Japan strictly limited European missionaries and merchants in their societies. African leaders set the rules under which the slave trade operated. Islam was the most rapidly growing religion. India and China were equivalent in their manufacturing output to Europe in 1750. European power might have seemed to be yet another cyclical pattern of surge and collapse.
✦ Nothing hinted that the Industrial Revolution was coming. Human and animal power, wind, and water still supplied almost all energy. Handicrafts had not been replaced by factory-based production. Landowning elites, not the middle class,

still held the reins of power; rural peasants, not urban workers, made up the primary social group among the lower classes. Social inequalities were still dominant; government was predominantly in the hands of kings and landowning nobles, not parliaments or the middle class, and women were still subject to patriarchal controls.

✦ Traditional values prevailed, such as Confucianism, Hinduism, and the caste system.

✦ Islam continued to spread in Southeast Asia and Africa.

✦ Some individuals in Chinese, European, and Islamic societies rejected new and untried ideas and urged a return to traditional ways.

CHAPTER THIRTEEN
Political Transformations: Empires and Encounters, 1450–1750

AP World History Key Concepts

4.1: Globalizing Networks of Communication and Exchange

V. The new connections between the Eastern and Western hemispheres resulted in the Columbian Exchange.

VI. The increase in interactions between newly connected hemispheres and intensification of connections within hemispheres expanded the spread and reform of existing religions and created syncretic belief systems and practices.

One of the most important changes in human history was the connection of the Eastern and Western Hemispheres; it allowed people, plants, animals, technology, and culture to move freely from one part of the world to another, often with extreme consequences for the receiving region. Food (such as corn and potatoes) from the Americas allowed populations to rise in Eurasia and helped mitigate the population loss due to the slave trade in Africa. Plants and animals from the Eastern Hemisphere changed the Americas, where there were often no local competitors. In addition, the Europeans often set up plantations where single crops were grown for export, eliminating biodiversity.

More than just plants and livestock made the journey across the Atlantic; humans arrived with their diseases and their cultures. Native Americans had little immunity to Eurasian diseases such as measles or smallpox, and in some areas, nearly 90 percent of the population died within a hundred years of European arrival. Western Europeans came to settle, to get rich, or to convert natives to Christianity, often while exploiting the labor of Native Americans in mines and fields. Africans were imported as slave labor when the "great dying" left few Native Americans to work in lucrative plantations growing sugar or cotton. Europeans promoting Christianity suppressed the beliefs of Native Americans and African slaves, but in many regions (especially those with high populations before the conquest, such as Mexico and the Andes), Christianity blended some of the local traditions to create new practices. *See Chapter 12 for the discussion of the voyages of reconnaissance and exploration, and Chapter 14 for more extensive analysis of the economic implications of the global age.*

4.2: New Forms of Social Organization and Modes of Production

I. Traditional peasant agriculture increased and changed, plantations expanded, and demand for labor increased. These changes both fed and responded to growing global demand for raw materials and finished products.

II. As new social and political elites changed, they also restructured new ethnic, racial, and gender hierarchies.

Most people still made their livings as agricultural laborers in various forms, ranging from serfdom in Russia, to peasant farmers in China, to people bound by the *encomienda* in Spanish America, to African slaves in the sugar plantations of Brazil and the Caribbean. Agricultural laborers more frequently worked to create products (such as sugar, tea, and tobacco) for global markets, not to produce food for themselves and local markets. In addition, demands for furs led to new exploitation of the environment in North America and Siberia.

In the Americas, new social orders emerged based on blending peoples from the Americas with those from Africa and Europe. For example, while pure Europeans were at the top of the social class system in Spanish colonies, people of mixed race — European and Indian or European and African — were accepted as racially mixed and identified in different groups (*mestizos* or *mulattoes*). In the British North American and Caribbean colonies, in contrast, strict racial attitudes led to people of mixed race being classified as black if they had any African ancestry. Women among the conquered indigenous people tended to fare even worse than men — in addition to harsh labor requirements, they often had to submit to the sexual advances of European men. The same was true for African women imported as slaves, but they suffered even further in that their families could be broken up and their children could be sold.

4.3: State Consolidation and Imperial Expansion

I. Rulers used a variety of methods to legitimize and consolidate their power.

II. Imperial expansion relied on the increased use of gunpowder, cannons, and armed trade to establish large empires in both hemispheres.

III. Competition over trade routes, state rivalries, and local resistance all provided significant challenges to state consolidation and expansion.

The era from 1450 to 1750 has often been called the age of gunpowder states; land-based Eurasian empires — such as the Mughal Empire, Ottoman Empire, Russian Empire, and Qing China — used their superior militaries and weapons, including cannons, to expand their empires over their neighbors. Western European states, starting with Spain and Portugal and continuing with France, England, and Holland, used superior military technology to acquire overseas empires in the Americas. These European states adapted ships to carry cannons, which allowed them to dominate sea trade, especially in the Indian Ocean. Cannon and gunpowder also helped European states overpower both the Aztec and Inca empires and more loosely populated regions in North America and Central Asia.

The conquests were also furthered by the spread of pathogens that nearly annihilated the peoples of the Americas and the small, isolated tribes in Siberia. For the first time, states ruled over vast territories that were separated by oceans from the "mother country," requiring new methods of governance. In Spanish and Portuguese colonies, rule was directly tied to the mother country. In settler colonies like British North America, somewhat more local government took place under charters granted by the king for particular groups, such as the Puritans, Catholics, or Quakers. In the Americas, indigenous governments were eradicated and replaced by European governors and European laws, conducted by European courts in European languages.

Eurasia saw the last surge of the pastoralist empires (the Mughal, Ottoman, and Qing dynasties all traced their ancestry to the steppes). At the same time, the Russian Empire, recently freed from Mongol rule, expanded into Siberia and the tundra regions to the north (as well as south and west from Moscow), subjugating nomadic hunters and herders and replacing their sparse populations with ethnic Russians. The Qing dynasty annexed the steppes from the south, as well as Tibetan and Muslim groups on the western frontiers. China and Russia thus incorporated and marginalized previously feared nomadic peoples into their empires and divided the old Silk Roads—one of the factors leading to the overland route's demise as the major east–west trade route. These empires all developed varying methods of incorporating people of different ethnic and religious groups into their empires.

Theme 1: Interaction Between Humans and the Environment

Linking the two hemispheres of the earth in the sixteenth century created the most significant environmental consequences since beginning of settled agriculture. This link, called the Columbian exchange, was the beginning of an unprecedented movement of flora, fauna, people, and pathogens between the Eastern and Western Hemispheres. Since the Western Hemisphere had been isolated, its plants, animals, and people encountered species and diseases against which they had no natural defenses. The most obvious consequence has been called "the great dying," the death of millions of native peoples to disease borne by Afro-Eurasians. In some areas, nearly 90 percent of the pre-Columbian population died from diseases (such as measles, small pox, typhus, influenza, or yellow fever) or from starvation. This series of epidemics was one of the reasons that numerically smaller Europeans were able to conquer the Aztec and Inca empires. In addition, plants—especially food crops such as wheat, rice, sugarcane, grapes, and vegetable and fruit crops—were brought to the Americas by Europeans eager to recreate their previous diet or to farm cash crops for sale on the global market. These crops replaced local forests, grasslands, and fields at an alarming rate and required different types of agricultural labor from the digging stick technology used by Native Americans. European animals—such as sheep, goats, cattle, horses, and pigs—also had a huge impact, creating new ways of life in ranching or herding, all while destroying local habitats. Food crops from the Americas—corn, potatoes and sweet potatoes, and cassava—fueled population increases in Eurasia and ameliorated the population loss in Africa from the transatlantic slave trade. Other New World crops such as tobacco and chocolate became fashionable in European markets (as did tea from China and coffee from the Muslim world). Plantations where sugarcane, tobacco, or cotton were grown led to further environmental degradation as local flora and fauna were destroyed to create monocultures of selected, lucrative crops, often grown using forced or slave labor.

Theme 2: Development and Interaction of Cultures

Europeans imposed their culture on conquered people in the Americas or Central Asia. Where the population was larger, as in Mexico or the Andes, significant cultural remainders endured and became part of a new syncretic culture. Where the population was small or had been relocated, "little Europes" grew. In some remote regions, traditional culture survived.

The most obvious cultural transplants were language and religion. Government was conducted in the languages of Europe, and conquered people had to adapt. In Mexico, zealous priests had most of the existing Maya and Aztec books destroyed to prevent people from returning to their old culture and religion. Christianity was also a major source of cultural transformation; Russian Orthodox Christianity spread in the newly forming empire and competed with Islam, while Roman Catholicism was brought to Spanish and Portuguese empires. In addition to being spread by conquering forces, Christianity was also spread by missionaries and Jesuit priests to China and Japan (where it later became suspect as a foreign religion). In the Americas, local beliefs became syncretized with the new faith. For example, in the Andes, sacred processions of the mummies of dead Inca kings were replaced with the processions of images of Christian saints.

Different solutions to cultural mixing occurred in the Asian empires, where much larger populations of different ethnic groups were absorbed into growing Mughal, Ottoman, and Qing empires. The Qing, hailing from Manchuria, attempted to remain separated from the conquered Han Chinese. Intermarriage was forbidden, and Manchurian dress was retained. As part of attempting to legitimize their conquest, however, the Qing adopted Confucian social and gender attitudes and bureaucracy. When they conquered Mongolia, Tibet, and Xinjiang, the Qing did not attempt to incorporate Muslim and Buddhist populations into Chinese culture (see Map 13.3, p. 641), in contrast to the practice of previous dynasties to reward assimilation to Han culture.

In the Mughal dynasty, Turkic Islamic rulers faced a large population of mostly Hindu Indians. Some leaders, such as Akbar, respected the cultures of local people and rewarded loyalty with government positions. Religious toleration prevailed. His heirs, such as Aurangzeb, reversed Akbar's policies and enforced Islamic law, destroyed some Hindu temples, and reinstituted the special tax (*jizya*) on non-Muslims. The art and architecture of the empire, however, continued to reflect a cultural blending of Hindu, Persian, and Arabic traditions (such as seen in the Taj Mahal, a tomb for the wife of a Mughal Shah).

The Ottoman Turks also took control of a region with a large population. As they conquered the Balkans, the Ottomans did not send large numbers of Turkic Muslim settlers; instead, they gave local religious groups (such as Armenian, Eastern Orthodox, and Roman Catholic Christians and Jews) an amount of local autonomy. Non-Muslims were required to contribute children to the *devshirme,* where they were trained to become janissaries (elite Ottoman warriors) or bureaucrats. The Ottomans also welcomed Jews fleeing from expulsion in Spain and Portugal. Like the Mughals, the Ottomans were influenced by Persian culture—poetry, painting, and court rituals. *See Chapter 15 for more depth on this theme.*

Theme 3: State-Building, Expansion, and Conflict

The possession of superior military training and technology, including gunpowder and cannons, allowed several Eurasian empires to flourish. The Russians threw off the last vestiges of Mongol rule and spread their influence to create the largest Eurasian land-based empire. Like the British in North America, they imposed their culture on the relatively sparse population of the steppes. Russia continued to be an autocracy, ruled by the tsar with the support of the Russian Orthodox Church; much of the actual power, though, rested in the hands of the large landowning *boyars* who controlled the labor of large numbers of serfs (people bound to the land). Peter the Great and Catherine the Great recognized that they were lagging behind Western Europe and began a policy of Westernization.

The Ottoman sultan claimed the title of caliph, giving him religious sanction as well as secular authority. Government was divided between regions and was, to some extent, based on local custom. Both the military and civilian bureaucracy took in young men from the *devshirme*, the tax of young boys levied on Christian communities. Court practices took their lead from the elaborate rituals of the Persians. Some women secluded in the harem also influenced the court in an attempt to promote their sons as possible future sultans.

The Qing dynasty adopted the Confucian civil service and examination system, while maintaining firm control for the Manchu elite. Han Chinese were required to wear distinctive hairstyles and clothing, and intermarriage with Manchus was forbidden. Newly conquered territories—Mongolia, Tibet, Xinjiang—were administered differently, without the usual Chinese attempt to assimilate the people into Chinese culture and without large resettlements of Chinese to the regions. In a similar manner to the Ottoman rule of its conquests, local authorities were often left in place, with Buddhist and Muslim authorities, monasteries, and nobles exempted from tax or labor obligations.

The Mughal dynasty succeeded in politically unifying most of South Asia. Akbar, who completed the conquest of this mostly Hindu region, attempted to rule in an enlightened and tolerant manner by bringing Hindus into important roles in government and military, ending the *jizya*, a special tax on non-Muslims, and ensuring religious toleration. His successors, such as Aurangzeb, reinstituted strict sharia law and the *jizya*, and destroyed some Hindu temples. Resistance by Hindu Rajputs against increasingly harsh Mughal rule weakened the empire and paved the way for British takeover.

Spanish and Portuguese colonies were ruled directly under viceroys appointed by the king and by a few *peninsulares*, men born in the Iberian Peninsula (not in the New World). The *peninsulares'* rule was aided by large royal grants (*encomienda*) giving, in addition to the land itself, control over indigenous people. This included the right to demand labor in order to produce crops or extract resources that were shipped back to the mother country. The *encomienda* often simply transferred to colonial rulers labor duties already owed to the state (such as the *mita* in Peru or labor owed to the Aztec Empire). British North American settlers came from a different environment than that of the Spanish and Portuguese; England had a limited monarchy with Parliament, a tradition of individual rights, a large and influential commercial middle class, and a history of conflicts between Catholic and Protestant (and between different Protestant groups). Attracted by readily available land, groups such as Puritans, Catholics, and Quakers came to North America. The British government paid little direct attention to the colonies in the seventeenth century, leaving the colonists to elect colonial assemblies to protect their "rights as Englishmen." Later, the colonists often resisted the governors' attempts to reassert control.

Theme 4: Creation, Expansion, and Interaction of Economic Systems

See Chapter 14 for a full analysis of this theme.

Theme 5: Development and Transformation of Social Structures

The Columbian exchange replaced social and political systems in the Americas with new societies that blended Native American, European, and African people. In Spanish colonies, there were relatively few European women, leading to intermingling of Europeans and Native Americans. Society distinguished between people born in Spain and those of pure Spanish ancestry born in the Americas (*peninsulares* and *creoles*), people of mixed Spanish and Native American ancestry (*mestizos*), people of mixed Spanish or Portuguese and African ancestry (*mulattoes*) and people of pure Native American or African ancestry. In general terms, these racial hierarchies also reflected social hierarchies and political control; in Peru and Mexico, *peninsulares* alone could hold the job of governor or viceroy, while creoles tended to be the large land owners and fill the top military, church, and professional roles. Mestizos mostly adopted Spanish culture and worked in skilled trades, as supervisors, and in lower-level positions in government bureaucracy, the church, or the military. Indians were at the bottom of the social hierarchy, subject to abuse and required to provide labor for the Spanish colonizers.

In the Caribbean and Brazilian sugar plantations, a similar structure developed, with enslaved Africans at the bottom of the social structure. Most of the Native Americans had either died (in the Caribbean) from European diseases or fled inland (Brazil). The populations were predominantly of African ancestry, but many were mulattoes; as many as forty groups composed of different degrees of racial mixing were identified.

In the plantation colonies of North America, different attitudes toward race prevailed; anyone with African ancestry was considered to be black, in contrast to the wide range of racial groups identified in Spanish and Portuguese colonies. Fewer slaves were freed in North America, and free blacks or mulattoes in Brazil had more economic opportunities. Settler colonies in North America had a higher ratio of Europeans than did the plantation colonies. In addition, British colonists had access to "free" land with relatively few native inhabitants and found it easier to set up family farms and businesses, relatively free from interference by elites from Europe.

Women continued to languish under patriarchal attitudes. In the Americas, indigenous women and African women were also subjected to the same social factors as their men—conquest, forced labor, slavery—but they were also subjected to the forced sexual advances of their conquerors. Some women among the native elites married Spanish men in order to maintain some control of their ancestral lands and social status. In the Qing dynasty, rulers adopted and enforced strict Confucian attitudes toward gender roles. Under Akbar, the Mughals acted to mitigate some of the Hindu restrictions on women by forbidding child marriage or *sati* (the immolation of a widow on her husband's funeral pyre) and by allowing separate market days for women. In addition, some royal women exerted power "behind the throne." After Akbar died, his successors reinstated sharia laws. Turkic women at first enjoyed many of the liberties of pastoral women, but as the Ottomans established their empire, they adopted the more restrictive patriarchal practices of the Mediterranean world; women were secluded, veiled, and not even counted in the census.

CHAPTER FOURTEEN
Economic Transformations: Commerce and Consequence, 1450–1750

AP World History Key Concepts

4.1: Globalizing Networks of Communication and Exchange

I. In the context of the new global circulation of goods, there was an intensification of all existing regional trade networks that brought prosperity and economic disruption to the merchants and governments in the trading regions of the Indian Ocean, Mediterranean, Sahara, and overland Eurasia.

II. European technological developments in cartography and navigation built on previous knowledge developed in the classical, Islamic, and Asian worlds, and included the production of new tools, innovations in ship designs, and an improved understanding of global wind and currents patterns—all of which made transoceanic travel and trade possible.

See Chapter 10 for a discussion of European borrowing and innovation.

III. Remarkable new transoceanic maritime reconnaissance occurred in this period.

See Chapter 12 for a more detailed discussion of this concept.

IV. The new global circulation of goods was facilitated by royal chartered European monopoly companies that took silver from Spanish colonies in the Americas to purchase Asian goods for the Atlantic markets, but regional markets continued to flourish in Afro-Eurasia by using established commercial practices and new transoceanic shipping services developed by European merchants.

V. The new connections between the Eastern and Western hemispheres resulted in the Columbian Exchange.

See Chapter 13 for a more detailed discussion of these concepts.

VI. The increase in interactions between newly connected hemispheres and intensification of connections within hemispheres expanded the spread and reform of existing religions and created syncretic belief systems and practices.

See Chapter 15 for a more detailed discussion of this topic.

VII. As merchants' profits increased and governments collected more taxes, funding for the visual and performing arts, even for popular audiences, increased.

See Chapter 12 for a more detailed discussion about the Renaissance.

Voyages of reconnaissance and exploration (such as Columbus's to the Americas, da Gama's to the Indian Ocean, and Magellan's circumnavigation of the earth) created permanent trade networks that linked the two hemispheres for the first time. The Portuguese and Dutch in Africa and the Indian Ocean began by creating trading ports, called entrepôts; the Spanish in the Americas and the Philippines and the Portuguese in Brazil established larger colonies (see Map 14.1, p. 672). The ability of Europeans to use cannons from shipboard changed the trading patterns in the Indian Ocean, allowing the Portuguese to demand exclusive trading rights. New or improved mercantile practices allowed private trading companies, like the British East India Company and the Dutch East India Company, to prosper and enrich their shareholders, while other trade was controlled by governments (such as Spain and Portugal) under the mercantilist economic theory. At first, European presence in the Indian Ocean trade system was relatively small; European trade goods were not valued by Asians (who felt that European goods were shoddy), so European ships carried Asian trade goods from port to port for Asian merchants. Profits from this "carrying trade" could later be reinvested by European merchants in trade goods such as spices, silk, and porcelain. Eventually, silver and other bullion from the mines of the Americas became a global commodity (see Map 14.2, p. 679). Silver from the Americas poured into China, exchanged for many valued trade items such as silk, tea, and porcelain. Ultimately, the glut of New World silver led to inflation and destroyed some of the economies that first were enriched by it (such as Spain). India remained the source of cotton textiles and gems as the Portuguese, then the British, established toeholds on the subcontinent. Much of the trade in Asia remained in the hands of traditional Asian merchants (such as Southeast Asians and Indian merchant families). Europeans primarily controlled the transatlantic trade, especially the trade of African slaves to the Americas to work in profitable sugar plantations (see Map 14.4, p. 687 and Snapshot: The Slave Trade in Numbers, p. 692).

Other trading systems also emerged, such as the fur trade in North America and Siberia (see Map 14.3, p. 684), where indigenous people often trapped furs and brought them to trading posts set up by Europeans, including the French, Dutch, and British in North America and the Russians in Siberia.

The spread of Christianity was a major component of European expansion and colonization. Missionaries often followed or arrived with the explorers, carrying with them royal charters that included not only the right of landowners to use the labor of local people but also the obligation to baptize locals. In the Spanish Philippines, Christianity came up against Islam on the island of Mindanao. In both China and Japan, Christian missionaries were seen as agents of foreign powers; in Tokugawa Japan, Christian missionaries were expelled for fear that the growing movement would lead to foreign takeover, as had happened in the Philippines, while Japanese converts were executed. In the Americas, Christianity frequently became a syncretic religion. *See Chapter 15 for a more detailed discussion of Christianity in this period.*

4.2: New Forms of Social Organization and Modes of Production

I. Traditional peasant agriculture increased and changed, plantations expanded, and demand for labor increased. These changes both fed and responded to growing global demand for raw materials and finished products.

See Chapter 13 for a more detailed discussion.

II. As new social and political elites changed, they also restructured new ethnic, racial, and gender hierarchies.

See Chapter 13 for a more detailed discussion.

One of the most significant changes in labor during this period was the extension of plantation agriculture to the Americas. Most of the Native Americans in tropical coastal regions either died from European diseases and warfare or fled inland, leaving a need for labor on the sugar plantations and, in North America, cotton and tobacco plantations. This void was filled by importing Africans as slaves; the slave trade functioned with the cooperation of local African leaders who brought slaves from the interior of Africa to European trading forts along the coast where slaves were sold to European traders for weapons, luxury goods, and other goods such as pots and textiles.

In Asia, peasant agriculture also underwent changes because of globalization. In China, the influx of silver from the Americas exchanged for Chinese goods allowed the government to require that all taxes be paid in cash, not goods or labor. Therefore, peasants had to produce crops or goods for sale in order to obtain the silver needed to pay their taxes. This disrupted local agricultural customs; for example, some villages devoted themselves to growing mulberry trees on which silkworms fed, but then had to import rice for their own food from another village.

In Japan, the *daimyos* (feudal lords) and their samurai warriors fought each other and welcomed European weapons and knowledge. However, under unification by the Tokugawa shogunate, contact with Europeans was greatly restricted and the ability of daimyos to possess their own armies and weapons was eliminated. European traders, except the nonproselytizing Dutch, were banned and contact with foreign goods and ideas was carefully controlled by the government.

In some regions, such as Southeast Asia, European merchants relied on local women to conduct trade within their countries. As in the Americas, some of the European traders and trappers found it helpful to take local wives who could be their interface with the native people.

4.3. State Consolidation and Imperial Expansion

I. Rulers used a variety of methods to legitimize and consolidate their power.

II. Imperial expansion relied on the increased use of gunpowder, cannons, and armed trade to establish large empires in both hemispheres.

III. Competition over trade routes, state rivalries, and local resistance all provided significant challenges to state consolidation and expansion.

When Europeans entered Asian markets, they discovered large, ancient, and well-defended empires such as the Qing, the Mughals, and the Ottomans. In addition, trade routes were already controlled by local merchants. The European advantage lay in superior ships and cannons. These advantages allowed some European states, such as Portugal, England, and Holland, to establish empires of commerce or "trading post empires."

The Portuguese captured or bought ports along the east coast of Africa, in India, and in Southeast Asia. At first, they sold their shipping services, carrying Asian goods to Asian ports, and attempted to monopolize trade. As Portugal became overextended, other European powers challenged them for control of the lucrative spice routes.

The British East India Company and Dutch East India Company received charters from their governments granting trade monopolies, the power to make war, and the power to govern conquered peoples. Both the British and Dutch established competing trading posts. The Dutch conquered some of the small Spice Islands in what is now Indonesia, placing the remaining people under the control of Dutch planters and using slave labor to grow nutmeg, mace, and cloves. The Dutch became wealthy, but the local people were reduced to starvation because they were not given sufficient land to grow food for their families. Excluded from the Dutch-controlled Spice Islands, the British set up trading bases in India, where they purchased pepper and Indian cotton textiles. The demand for cotton turned many interior villages to the production of textiles for the British trade. Gradually, the British and Dutch transformed their trading posts into colonies. In North America, the British, French, and Dutch competed for the fur trade (see Map 14.3, p. 684), making alliances with local Native American tribes. As European empires clashed, Native Americans were drawn into British and French wars.

Spain followed a different path and took over the Philippines, which was close to trade with China and the Spice Islands. They followed a similar pattern to the one established in their American colonies by enforcing tribute, taxes, unpaid labor, and conversion to Christianity on their new subjects. The capital of the Philippines, Manila, became a major multicultural trade center—the silver from the Americas was brought there to be exchanged for goods and spices from Asia. *See Chapter 12 for the establishment of the "gunpowder empires" in the Eastern Hemisphere and Chapter 13 for the European colonial empires in the Americas.*

Theme 1: Interaction Between Humans and the Environment

Key environmental impacts followed from globalizing trade networks. First, land degradation and deforestation followed mining (such as the silver mine at Potosí in modern Bolivia) and intensive single-crop agriculture to produce exports for the world market (such as sugar, nutmeg, cotton, mulberry trees for silkworms, and tea), not only in the Americas but also in China and other regions. Movement of people—voluntary or forced—created other environmental impacts, such as the transatlantic slave trade, relocation of Native Americans from coastal regions, European colonies and trading centers, or the Dutch East India Company's transportation of large numbers of ethnic Chinese to Taiwan to grow rice and sugar for export. Africa's population growth slowed because of the slave trade, even while new food crops from the Americas provided more nutrition. By 1900, Africa represented 6 percent of the world's population, while in 1600 it had possessed 18 percent. Along with the movement of people came the catastrophic spread of disease into regions where people had long been isolated from contact with the diseases of Eurasian agricultural people. In some cases, the death rate was near 90 percent after a century of contact. Cities grew as trade and administrative centers; one of the most spectacular was Manila, capital of the Spanish Philippines, where Spanish and Filipinos were joined by Japanese and Chinese traders, artisans, and mariners. Further environmental dislocation followed the fur trade; after depleting the populations of fur-bearing animals in Western Europe, French, English, Dutch, and Russian trappers and traders spread out into Siberia and North America, trading with local peoples, and driving many species (such as beaver, sable, and deer) nearly to extinction. *See Chapter 13 for discussion of the environmental impact of the Columbian exchange.*

Theme 2: Development and Interaction of Cultures

See Chapter 15 for discussion of cultural transformations in this period.

Theme 3: State-Building, Expansion, and Conflict

Europeans did not have the overwhelming political impact on the Indian Ocean basin as they had had in the Americas; they faced much more populous and organized empires, like the Mughal and Qing, and did not have the advantage of a severe local population decline due to disease. Some regions in Asia, such as parts of the Philippines, resisted Spanish attempts at mass conversion and subjugation of local people to Spanish rule. Chinese rebellions in the Philippines led to repressive responses by the Spanish, though Chinese rebellions against the Dutch in Taiwan were more successful. In Indonesia, the Dutch were more successful in controlling the local population, but not without shattering the economy and allowing thousands to die of starvation. The British were able to play upon the divisions within the Mughal Empire to secure trading bases in India. *See Chapters 12 and 13 for discussion of the political transformation in this time period.*

Theme 4: Creation, Expansion, and Interaction of Economic Systems

Commerce in the Eastern Hemisphere had been based on trading systems that transported luxury goods from China (such as porcelain, tea, and silk), India (such as cotton textiles), and Southeast Asia (such as spices). The two main systems involved overland trade through the Silk Routes in Central Asia and maritime routes that took advantage of the monsoon winds in the Indian Ocean basin. The land routes had been divided by Qing dynasty China and the expanding Russian Empire. The maritime routes were under the control of small-scale Asian merchants.

Several factors brought Western Europeans into this trading system. First, some regions, such as the northern Italian city-states, had been involved in bringing goods from Asian markets to Europe after the goods arrived in Egypt or Constantinople. These cities had developed economies based on market exchange, private ownership, and accumulation of capital. When Muslim armies captured Constantinople, Egypt, and the Indian Ocean trade routes, European merchants had to trade at a disadvantage. The Portuguese, facing the Atlantic and not the Mediterranean, funded voyages of reconnaissance along the African coast to seek a sea route to the Indian Ocean. When da Gama arrived in the Indian Ocean in 1498, Europeans found that the East Asians did not want the inferior European goods—only silver or gold could be traded for Asian spices and silks, which created a negative trade balance for mercantilist Europeans.

The Spanish and Dutch quickly followed the Portuguese (see Map 14.1, p. 672), taking over coastal regions or establishing outposts to conduct trade. Their superior ship technology and use of shipboard mounted cannons gave them the ability to set up "trading post empires" and carry Asian goods between Asian ports. The Dutch captured land in the Spice Islands, creating a monopoly in nutmeg production and destroying the local economy. The influx of bullion, mostly silver, from Spanish-controlled mines in the Americas altered the balance between European and Asian merchants, despite the fact that Japan was also a major exporter of silver. The flow of silver into the region affected both Asian and European economies, where inflation and rising prices led to political instability and rebellions. Ultimately, Spain did not invest its profits wisely. The monarchy chose to invest in European dynastic struggles instead of commerce and industry.

In China, the need to pay taxes in silver led to increased specialization of local economies and changes in traditional peasant life; now peasants often had to import rice from other regions because they were growing cash crops such as mulberry trees. Chinese and Indian goods remained the center of the global trading system; Europeans were a conduit of American silver and competed against each other for Chinese silk and Indian cotton.

Europeans dominated the transatlantic trade, especially the slave trade. As in Asia, Europeans did not take over large territories of Africa, but instead traded European and Indian textiles, cowrie shells, metal goods, guns and gunpowder, tobacco, alcohol, and decorative items to African tribal leaders in exchange for slaves. Silver from the Americas was used to purchase the cowrie shells, some of the other decorative items, and Indian cotton, linking the slave trade with the trade in silver and textiles. European imports added to the wealth of elite groups but did not destroy local African skilled crafts.

Slavery in the Americas differed in key ways from traditional slavery: the scale of the transatlantic slave trade dwarfed earlier trade; slaves were used mostly in plantation agriculture and were treated inhumanely; the children of slaves remained slaves, with little hope of eventual freedom; and slavery in the Americas was distinctively racial. Most slaves destined for plantations in the Americas were males; however, traditional slave-trading routes controlled by Muslims continued to transport mostly female slaves across the Sahara and into the Indian Ocean.

The transatlantic slave trade affected African societies. Slaves were often taken from marginal groups, such as prisoners of war or debtors, within these societies. The gender imbalance in the slave trade meant an increase in polygamy in Africa, as well as increasing the number of female slaves in Africa itself in regions such as the kingdom of Kongo. Some women in Senegambia married European men, which provided the men with access to African-operated trade networks. In West Africa, women such as Queen Nzinga resisted Portuguese imperialism, while women in the kingdom of Kongo held lower-level administrative positions. Small, kinship-based societies often were disrupted, while Kongo and Oyo disintegrated partly because other ethnic groups gained access to European weapons and rebelled. The kingdom of Dahomey created a government monopoly in trading slaves, which contributed to its success.

Theme 5: Development and Transformation of Social Structures

See Chapter 13 for discussion of this theme.

CHAPTER FIFTEEN

Cultural Transformations: Religion and Science, 1450–1750

AP World History Key Concepts

4.1: Globalizing Networks of Communication and Exchange

VI. The increase in interactions between newly connected hemispheres and intensification of connections within hemispheres expanded the spread and reform of existing religions and created syncretic belief systems and practices.

As the Eastern and Western Hemispheres came into sustained contact, religions spread and adapted. Christianity underwent internal divisions and reforms in the Protestant Reformation and the Catholic Counter-Reformation (see Map 15.1, p. 724, and Snapshot: Catholic/Protestant Differences in the Sixteenth Century, p. 725) and spread to new regions (see Map 15.2, pp. 726–727), where local cultures selectively adopted and adapted the new faith. Islam also underwent a period of renewal in Arabia under al-Wahhab (see Map 15.3, p. 737) and Mughal India under Aurangzeb, even as it spread further into Africa and Southeast Asia, where local cultures often modified its practices.

China attempted to revitalize and purify traditional Chinese culture after the expulsion of the Mongols in a movement called Neo-Confucianism. In addition, syncretic religions arose, such as Sikhism, which incorporated elements of Hinduism and Islam, and Vodou or Candomble, which incorporated elements of African religions and Christianity.

Encouraged by contact with science transmitted by the Muslim world, the Scientific Revolution in Europe rediscovered texts from ancient Greece, challenged traditional beliefs, and sought to understand the natural world by employing reason, empirical observation, collection of data, experimentation, and skepticism (See Snapshot: Major Thinkers and Achievements of the Scientific Revolution, p. 743). Many cultures practiced selective borrowing for both religious and scientific ideas that they encountered.

5.3: Nationalism, Revolution, and Reform

I. The rise and diffusion of Enlightenment thought that questioned established traditions in all areas of life often preceded the revolutions and rebellions against existing governments.

224

The Scientific Revolution spawned the Enlightenment in the eighteenth century. The Enlightenment attempted not only to popularize science but also to apply the principles of the scientific method and notions of progress in an attempt to find the natural laws governing human society. New ideas such as capitalism and government as a contract between the people and the rulers furthered new revolutionary thinking. In addition, many Enlightenment philosophers became deists or pantheists.

Theme 1: Interaction Between Humans and the Environment

See Chapter 13 for discussion of the environmental impact of the Columbian exchange.

Theme 2: Development and Interaction of Cultures

Western European Christianity fragmented beginning in 1517 when Martin Luther issued his Ninety-five Theses, condemning clerical abuses, such as corruption, immorality, luxurious lifestyles, and the sale of indulgences. Protestants also rejected the traditional Catholic belief in the authority of the Church fathers and salvation by good works. Instead, Luther proposed that man was saved by faith alone, while religious authority lay solely in the Bible. Protestants also believed that all vocations, not just monastic or religious vocations, had equal merit, which appealed to the rising urban and commercial classes. The Protestant Reformation spread rapidly because of the invention of the printing press and translations of the Bible into the vernacular, or everyday spoken language, as opposed to Latin, which was the official language of the Church but not spoken by the common people. Protestants emphasized that each person should read the Bible for him- or herself, creating an upsurge in literacy and individual thought, which also helped the Scientific Revolution.

The Catholic Church responded to the Reformation by initiating reforms, called the Catholic Counter-Reformation, and by opposing the spread of Protestantism. In addition, the Church reaffirmed the doctrines of papal authority, clerical celibacy, the veneration of saints, and the importance of church traditions and good works. Dissidents were accused of heresy and sometimes burned at the stake, and books and ideas were censored. New religious groups, such as the Jesuits (Society of Jesus), emerged, dedicated to the renewal of the Church and its spread abroad, especially to East Asia.

The missionary expansion of Christianity in the Americas and East Asia began with Spain and Portugal. Both countries conducted their voyages of discovery in the context of crusading traditions and the *Reconquista*. Catholic orders such as the Dominicans, Franciscans, and Jesuits led the missionary work, with the Portuguese focusing on Africa and Asia and the Spanish and French on the Americas. The Russian Orthodox Church followed the Russian Empire into Siberia. In these regions, new converts merged local beliefs with Christian beliefs and practices, often to the frustration of European Catholic priests who repeatedly attempted to end "backsliding" by destroying local shrines, religious artifacts and images, ancestral mummies in Peru, and books in Mexico.

Sometimes resistance to forced conversion was direct, as with the Peruvian movement known as Taki Onqoy (dancing sickness). More often, however, local people blended the new and local religious systems; for example, Aztec or Incan deities continued to be worshipped under new names, identified with Christian saints or the Virgin Mary. Syncretic religions in the Americas also formed around Africanized versions of Christianity, such as Vodou (Vodun), Candomble, Macumba, or Santeria, incorporating West African traditions such as drumming, dancing, animal sacrifice, and spirit possession.

In Asia, with its large populations and intact religious, societal, and governmental institutions, Christianity made less headway. Jesuit priests adopted the dress and language of China and chose to deal primarily with the Chinese official elite, emphasizing the similarities between Christianity and Confucian beliefs. Jesuits also passed along recent European gains in science, technology, astronomy, mapmaking, and geography, while withholding aspects such as Copernicus's heliocentric theory because it conflicted with official Church policy. Christian missionaries made few inroads in the total Chinese population for several reasons: they offered little that the Chinese needed, Christianity required converts to abandon much of traditional Chinese culture, and monogamy would require many Chinese men to abandon wives and concubines.

Islam was carried to sub-Saharan Africa by Sufi mystics, merchants, or scholars, who often intermarried with local women and did not require the total abandonment of traditional religious practices. Elites gained advisers, literacy in Arabic, the establishment of schools, and connections to the wider Islamic world. In Southeast Asia, in general, the common people also adopted a more syncretic form of Islam, while merchants aligned with stricter Middle Eastern traditions. The *bhakti* movement in India sought union with one of the Hindu deities through dance, song, prayer, and poetry; caste and gender distinctions were often set aside. The *bhakti* movement was similar to Sufi mysticism, blurring the distinction between Hinduism and Islam. Sikhism, a new syncretic religion, was developed by Guru Nanak in the Punjab region of South Asia. The new religion blended aspects of Hinduism and Islam but drew hostility from both. Among Javanese people, traditional animistic practices continued after conversion.

At the same time, Islamic renewal movements criticized what they considered to be lax Islamic practices. In West Africa, the descendants of the Fulbe led religiously based uprisings (jihads) to purify Islam. Some regions in Southeast Asia (such as the Sultanate of Acheh) attempted to enforce stricter adherence to dietary codes and almsgiving practices. In Mughal India, the emperor Aurangzeb reversed the tolerant policies of early Mughal leaders, such as Akbar. In Arabia itself, the birthplace of Islam, Muhammad ibn Abd al-Wahhab argued that the Ottoman Empire was declining because it was falling away from the pure faith of early Islam; he proclaimed that the veneration of Sufi saints and their tombs, Muhammad's tomb, or other natural sites was idolatrous and a violation of the monotheistic message of Islam. He gained the support of Ibn Saud, and they razed tombs and shrines, destroyed books on logic, and condemned using hashish, tobacco, or musical instruments.

In China, the Ming dynasty returned to Confucianism, but Neo-Confucianism incorporated insights of Buddhism and Daoism into traditional Confucian practices. In late Ming times, Wang Yangming suggested that anyone could lead a virtuous life through introspection and by studying nature, eliminating the need for traditional Confucian pursuits such as studying classical texts, intensive academic study, and constant moral striving. Later, critics argued that Wang Yangming's lax ideas were responsible for Ming decline and conquest by the Manchus. Chinese Buddhists also made their religion more accessible to laypeople. The *kaozheng* movement in China based research on evidence, paralleling the development of the Scientific Revolution in Europe. However, *kaozheng* was used more to examine old texts instead of making new scientific discoveries.

Western Europe entered a dynamic period of scientific discovery that had major long-term consequences not only for Europe but the entire world. New experimental techniques were built on Muslim science, the Hindu number system, and rediscovered

Greek texts, as well as the shock to traditional patterns of knowledge caused by information from the "new" world. Fundamental views about humans' place in the universe were altered, challenging religious teachings and the authority of both the Church and cultural traditions. The Scientific Revolution—based on empirical observation, data collection, experimentation, and logical reasoning and expressed in mathematical terms—began with astronomy. Copernicus changed centuries-old beliefs by using mathematics and observation to show that the sun, not the earth, was the "center" of the universe. This observation was followed by other astronomical insights and, finally, by Newton using calculus to describe the role of gravity as the force that governs planetary motion (see Snapshot: Major Thinkers and Achievements of the Scientific Revolution, p. 743). Medicine, anatomy, and other areas also utilized the scientific approach. Further, the interest in science led to the creation or improvement of new tools, such as the telescope, that extended human senses. In the eighteenth century, some tried to extend new scientific knowledge to broader audiences.

Building on the advancement of the Scientific Revolution, Enlightenment *philosophes* attempted to look for universal laws that governed politics and social structures. Other thinkers, such as Adam Smith, challenged the prevalent economic system of mercantilism with a new economic theory that eventually became known as capitalism. Englishman John Locke rejected the idea that government rested on the divine right of kings and suggested instead that government was a contract between the governed and the ruler. A core Enlightenment belief that continues to affect Western thought today is the idea of progress, or the belief that human society can be changed or improved by human reason and is not determined by divine plan or tradition. Other societies, such as in China and Japan, selectively chose what aspects of this new scientific movement would be allowed to enter their cultures.

Theme 3: State-Building, Expansion, and Conflict

See Chapter 13 for discussion of political transformations in the early modern world.

Theme 4: Creation, Expansion, and Interaction of Economic Systems

See Chapter 14 for discussion of economic transformations in the early modern world.

Theme 5: Development and Transformation of Social Structures

Religious reforms in this period affected gender roles. For example, Protestants destroyed convents and denigrated the cloistered life, which reduced the independent power of women in these communities. Protestantism also ended the veneration of Mary and female saints. Women were still not allowed to be members of the new Protestant clergy (except in the Quaker sect) but instead were subject to male supervision and viewed first and foremost as wives and mothers. The conversion to Christianity of large numbers of people in the Americas also altered the traditional role of native women as priests, shamans, or ritual specialists, as there was no corresponding role in the male-only Christian clergy. In Southeast Asia, women, who had been rulers in Sumatra, were forbidden to govern under stricter interpretations of Islamic law. In Java, however, women continued to serve in royal courts and as merchants in local markets. In India, the *bhakti* movement appealed to women as well as lower-caste men. In Arabia, ibn-Wahhab protected some rights of women within Islam, like the right to consent to marriage and to control dowries, to divorce, and to engage in commerce. He did not require head-to-toe covering of women in public places.

Many leaders of the Scientific Revolution in Western Europe adopted restrictive attitudes toward women. Even when women were able to perform research under the protection of husbands or fathers, they had their names removed from papers and books before publication. Occasionally, women of wealth and prestige, such as Margaret Cavendish, Duchess of Newcastle, managed to force their way into meetings of scientific societies. During the Enlightenment, women were often the sponsors of salons where *philosophes* met to discuss the issues of the day but were still subject to discriminatory treatment when they tried to publish their own works. Jean-Jacque Rousseau, for example, believed that women were innately inferior to men. Mary Wollstonecraft in England challenged his views by arguing that rational education of women was essential to progress.

PRACTICE EXAM 4

WORLD HISTORY
SECTION I

Note: This exam uses the chronological designations B.C.E. (before the common era) and C.E. (common era). These labels correspond to B.C. (before Christ) and A.D. (anno Domini), which are used in some world history textbooks.

TIME — 55 Minutes
70 Questions

Directions: Each of the questions or incomplete statements below is followed by four suggested answers or completions. Select the one that is best in each case.

Questions 1–3 are based on the following pair of quotes about Christopher Columbus.

> "[Columbus was a] pioneer of progress and enlightenment. . . ."
>
> *from a U.S. presidential address, 1892*

> "Columbus was a perpetrator of genocide. . . ."
>
> *Winona LaDuke, president of the Indigenous Women's Network, 1992*

1. What accounts for the different view of Columbus by the late twentieth century?
   (A) The discrediting of imperialism
   (B) The pseudo-scientific basis of racism
   (C) The resurgence of European dominance
   (D) The rejection of the Columbian exchange

2. How would the speaker of the first quote portray Columbus's arrival in the Americas in 1492?
   (A) As marking the beginning of the Enlightenment
   (B) As signaling the moral decline of the West
   (C) As paving the way for greater tolerance and equality
   (D) As initiating an era of American achievements

3. How would the speaker of the second quote portray Columbus's arrival in the Americas in 1492?
   (A) As proof of European dominance
   (B) As a sign of Native American resistance
   (C) As an invasion
   (D) As a blessing

GO ON TO THE NEXT PAGE.

4. Which of the following made possible transoceanic voyages in the Western Hemisphere by the late fifteenth century?

(A) Mastery of wind and current patterns in the Atlantic
(B) Understanding of the alternating monsoon winds
(C) Sponsorship by the Aztec king Montezuma
(D) Unification of the Inca and Maya civilizations

5. In the fifteenth century, European innovations in mapmaking, navigation, and shipbuilding were based on knowledge developed in earlier civilizations in all of the following regions EXCEPT

(A) the Mediterranean
(B) the Indian Ocean
(C) the Americas
(D) China

6. Which of the following is a phrase that historians use to emphasize certain aspects of the early modern era?

(A) Age of Reason
(B) Age of Empire
(C) New Imperialism
(D) Decolonization

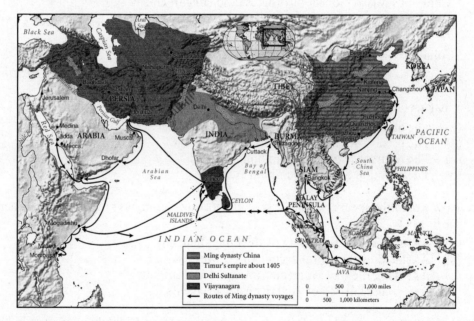

Questions 7–9 are based on Map 12.1.

7. Which of the following conclusions is supported by the information in Map 12.1?

(A) Ming dynasty China reached the Americas a century before the Europeans.
(B) The voyages of Ming dynasty China were undertaken to conquer new territories.
(C) The Chinese maritime expeditions facilitated long-distance trade in the Indian Ocean basin.
(D) China lost control of most of the trade routes in the Indian Ocean after the European arrival.

GO ON TO THE NEXT PAGE.

8. Which of the following cities shown on Map 12.1 emerged as an important trading port in the fifteenth century as a result of the growing communities of Muslim merchants in the Indian Ocean region?

    (A) Beijing
    (B) Baghdad
    (c) Delhi
    (D) Malacca

9. Of the civilizations shown on Map 12.1, which represents the last significant military conquest of pastoral societies from Central Asia?

    (A) Ming dynasty China
    (B) Timur's empire
    (c) Delhi Sultanate
    (D) Vijayanagara

10. Which of the following identifies a similar pattern in the spread of Islam in West Africa and Southeast Asia?

    (A) Islam was introduced by traveling merchants and consolidated by Sufi missionaries.
    (B) Islam emerged independently in both regions and had no link to the Middle East.
    (c) The spread of Islam was facilitated by state adoption of the Shia version of Islam.
    (D) The spread of Islam was accompanied by military conquest and forced conversions.

11. Which of the following offers evidence of the religious tolerance and cultural eclecticism common in China during the Ming dynasty?

    (A) Emperor Kangxi's expulsion of Jesuit missionaries from the imperial court
    (B) The incorporation of Andean deities into the Christian pantheon of saints
    (c) Zheng He's construction of a trilingual tablet in Ceylon praising the Buddha, Allah, and Vishnu
    (D) The development of a new writing system based on a hybrid form of the Roman alphabet

GO ON TO THE NEXT PAGE.

Questions 12–13 are based on Visual Source 12.3.

12. The illuminated page in Visual Source 12.3 was painted in the late fifteenth century by an Italian painter to serve as the frontispiece for a volume containing a Latin translation of Aristotle's writings along with commentaries by the twelfth-century Muslim scholar Ibn Rushd. Both men are depicted at the top, with Ibn Rushd on the left and Aristotle on the right. What does the image suggest about the relationship between Aristotle and Ibn Rushd?

   (A) Aristotle convinced Ibn Rushd to convert to Christianity.
   (B) Ibn Rushd rejected the secular elements of Aristotle's thoughts.
   (C) Aristotle made Ibn Rushd's works available to later generations.
   (D) Ibn Rushd made Aristotle's works available to later generations.

13. The illuminated page in Visual Source 12.3 offers evidence that would support which conclusion?

   (A) Europeans sought to reconcile Greek rationalism with Christian humanism.
   (B) Renaissance artists sought inspiration from the Greco-Roman and Islamic civilizations.
   (C) Italian thinkers sought to purge all Muslim influence from the writings of Aristotle.
   (D) Muslims sought to break the European intellectual monopoly on natural philosophy.

14. Which of the following describes the demographic implications of three centuries of Spanish rule in Peru and Mexico?

   (A) A mestizo population emerged.
   (B) The majority of the population was Spanish.
   (C) Spanish women outnumbered indigenous women.
   (D) Racial identity was defined as either Spanish or indigenous.

GO ON TO THE NEXT PAGE.

15. All of the following represent forms of labor servitude in Spanish-ruled Mexico and Peru EXCEPT the

   (A)   encomienda system
   (B)   repartimiento system
   (C)   factory system
   (D)   hacienda system

16. What accounts for the greater dependence on African slave labor in Brazil and the Caribbean than in Mexico and Peru?

   (A)   Large-scale sugar production
   (B)   Dependence on mining
   (C)   The infertility of the soil
   (D)   The strength of labor unions

17. Which of the following terms first emerged as a designation for the children of mixed-race unions in Portuguese-ruled Brazil?

   (A)   Creoles
   (B)   Mulattoes
   (C)   *Peninsulares*
   (D)   Mestizos

18. In what respect was the Russian empire different from the empires of the Western European countries?

   (A)   Russia had already established itself as a distinct state before embarking on expansion.
   (B)   Long distances separated Russia from its colonies, making the Russian empire the weakest.
   (C)   The Russian Empire was the only maritime empire that did not exploit its colonies.
   (D)   The processes of state building and imperial expansion occurred simultaneously.

19. By the mid-eighteenth century, the once-vital trade routes of which region declined in importance?

   (A)   Indian Ocean
   (B)   Mediterranean
   (C)   Overland Eurasia
   (D)   Sahara

Questions 20–21 are based on the following quote:

> The carousel, which has furnished me the subject of these reflections, had only been conceived at first as a light amusement, but little by little, we were carried away, and it became a spectacle that was fairly grand and magnificent . . . .it ought to represent in some way the duties of a prince. . . . For the device they chose the sun, which . . . is the most striking and beautiful image of a great monarch.
>
> *Louis XIV, French king, 1670*

GO ON TO THE NEXT PAGE.

20. Which of the following reflects Louis XIV's view of the relationship between "spectacle" and monarchy?

(A) The spectacle was a public display and celebration of the exalted role of the monarch.

(B) The spectacle enabled ordinary people to interact with the monarch in a carnival setting.

(C) The spectacle was a wasteful extravagance that drained the royal treasury.

(D) The spectacle was the monarch's way to create jobs and generate revenue.

21. Which of the following explains why Louis XIV believed that the sun was "the most striking and beautiful image of a great monarch"?

(A) A monarch's reign begins and ends, just as the sun rises and sets.

(B) Both the sun and the monarch are God's gift to humanity.

(C) Just as the sun can burn those who are exposed, so can the monarch punish those who do wrong.

(D) Just as the sun brings light to all it touches, so the monarch governs over all.

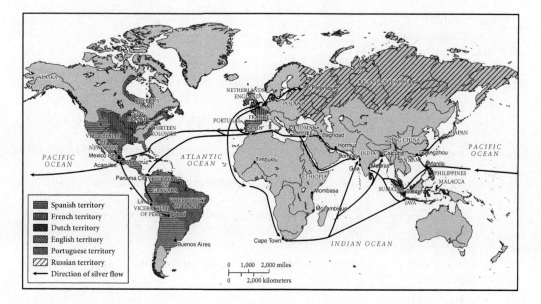

22. Based on the information provided in Map 14.2, which of the following cities was a source of the silver that made its way around the world?

(A) Calcutta

(B) Manila

(C) Potosí

(D) Guangzhou

23. The intensive mining of silver in Spanish America contributed to all of the following EXCEPT

(A) earthquakes

(B) deforestation

(C) soil erosion

(D) flooding

GO ON TO THE NEXT PAGE.

24. Which of the following is most similar to the Ottoman practice of *devshirme*?

    (A) The incorporation of Hindus into the political–military elite of the Mughal Empire under Akbar
    (B) The wars waged by the Aztec Empire to capture prisoners for the human sacrifices
    (C) The Inca practice of leaving in place local rulers in areas recently conquered
    (D) The Mongol policy of forced migration to disperse people throughout the empire

25. How did Russian expansion in the seventeenth century affect Siberia?

    (A) A mixed-race population emerged that acquired a distinctive identity.
    (B) Indigenous people were driven into reservations or enslaved.
    (C) Agricultural settlements replaced hunting grounds and pasturelands.
    (D) The nomadic lifestyle was adopted by Russian migrants.

26. In what respect was the scientific approach to knowledge emphasized in the *kaozheng* movement in China different from the Scientific Revolution in Europe?

    (A) The Chinese movement was more practical, while the European movement was more abstract.
    (B) The Chinese movement focused on the past, while the European movement focused on nature.
    (C) The Chinese movement focused on metaphysics, while the European movement focused on theory.
    (D) The Chinese movement focused on politics, while the European movement focused on religion.

27. In what respect was the Qing dynasty conquest of Central Asia different from the Russian Empire's conquest of Siberia?

    (A) Prior to conquest, the Chinese had never had contact with Central Asian people, while the Russians had interacted with Siberian peoples for centuries.
    (B) The Qing conquest was completed within a year, while the Russian conquest took two centuries to complete.
    (C) The Qing conquest was completed with minimal resistance, while the Russian conquest was never able to completely control the entire region.
    (D) The Qing dynasty restricted Chinese migration into Central Asia while the Russian Empire encouraged the mass migration of Russian settlers into Siberia.

28. All of the following empires gave opportunities to conquered peoples to serve in the bureaucracy and military EXCEPT the

    (A) Qing dynasty
    (B) Russian Empire
    (C) Mughal Empire
    (D) Ottoman Empire

GO ON TO THE NEXT PAGE.

29. What did the rulers of Qing China, Mughal India, and the Ottoman Empire share in common?

   (A) They waged wars to capture prisoners for the human sacrifices that were central to their religions.
   (B) They challenged Spain's monopoly of the silver trade in the Indian Ocean basin and South Pacific.
   (C) They created secular and constitutional forms of government that inspired the Enlightenment.
   (D) They ruled as absolute monarchs who promoted a cosmopolitan culture and generally favored religious tolerance.

30. All of the following empires demanded tribute from the conquered peoples identified EXCEPT the

   (A) British Empire from the Japanese
   (B) Russian Empire from Siberian peoples
   (C) Spanish Empire from the indigenous peoples in the Americas
   (D) Mongol Empire from Russian princes

31. Which of the following pairs reflects a division within the Spanish community in the Americas during the colonial era that was based solely on birth?

   (A) Creoles and *peninsulares*
   (B) Conquistadores and immigrants
   (C) Landowners and merchants
   (D) Missionaries and friars

32. All of the following describe the effect of the transatlantic slave trade on African society EXCEPT

   (A) an unbalanced sex ratio
   (B) an increase in female slaves
   (C) women marrying multiple husbands
   (D) higher labor demands on women

33. Unions between European men and local women occurred in all of the following regions EXCEPT

   (A) West African societies involved in the Atlantic slave trade
   (B) Central Asian societies involved in the Silk Road trade
   (C) North American societies involved in the fur trade
   (D) Latin American societies during the Spanish colonial era

34. Which of the following is most similar to the power struggle between the monarchy and the nobility in early modern Europe?

   (A) The Hindus and the Sikhs in Mughal India
   (B) The Manchus and the Chinese in the Qing dynasty
   (C) The plebeians and the patricians in the Roman Empire
   (D) The shogun and the daimyo in Tokugawa Japan

35. The political ideologies of the Aztec Empire and the various Chinese dynasties shared the belief that the public performance of rituals was critical to

   (A) maintaining cosmic order and averting catastrophe
   (B) fostering good relations with the population
   (C) cementing ties with neighboring societies
   (D) launching successful military campaigns

GO ON TO THE NEXT PAGE.

36. Which of the following is indicative of the European state system around the fifteenth century?

    (A) The unification of Aragon and Castile
    (B) The North Atlantic Treaty Organization
    (C) The Hundred Years' War between France and England
    (D) The emergence of Germany and Italy as new states

37. Which of the following offers evidence of the competitive nature of the political rivalries in the Italian city-states in the fifteenth and sixteenth centuries?

    (A) Niccolò Machiavelli's *The Prince*
    (B) William Shakespeare's *Macbeth*
    (C) Miguel de Cervantes's *Don Quixote*
    (D) Dante's *Inferno*

38. Which of the following shares the same view as that expressed in the Renaissance writer Christine de Pizan's *Book of the City of Ladies*?

    (A) Betty Friedan's *The Feminist Mystique*
    (B) Simone de Beauvoir's *The Second Sex*
    (C) Virginia Woolf's *A Room of One's Own*
    (D) Mary Wollstonecraft's *Vindication of the Rights of Woman*

39. All of the following represent syncretic religions that blended elements of African beliefs and practices with those of Christianity EXCEPT

    (A) Vodou in Haiti
    (B) Zoroastrianism in Persia
    (C) Santeria in Cuba
    (D) Macumba in Brazil

40. How did the Qing dynasty and Inca Empire treat local elites in the regions they conquered?

    (A) They executed them to instill fear in the population.
    (B) They formed marriage alliances with them.
    (C) They used them to govern the regions.
    (D) They signed formal treaties with them.

41. Which of the following provides evidence of the global circulation of silver in the early modern world?

    (A) The use of the Spanish silver coin in southern China
    (B) The search for silver mines in the South Pacific
    (C) The minting of silver in the southern regions of Africa
    (D) The low exchange rates in the international silver trade

42. All of the following contributed to the Columbian exchange and marked a new period in world history EXCEPT the

    (A) cultivation of corn, potatoes, and cassava in the Eastern Hemisphere
    (B) introduction of horses, pigs, cattle, goats, and sheep in the Americas
    (C) spread of smallpox, measles, typhus, and influenza in the Americas
    (D) immunity to Afro-Eurasian diseases among Native American populations

GO ON TO THE NEXT PAGE.

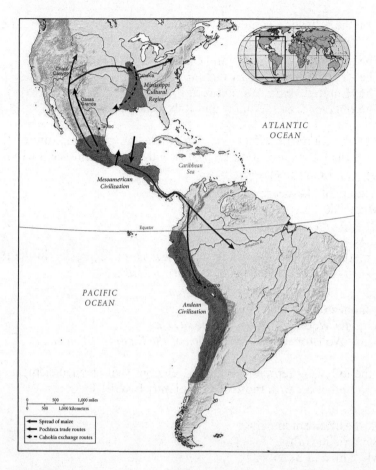

43. Which of the following conclusions can be made based on the information shown in Map 7.5?

(A) There were no long-distance trade routes connecting the Mesoamerican and Andean civilizations.

(B) The cultivation of maize occurred independently in North and South America.

(C) The isthmus at Panama operated as the center for trade between North and South America.

(D) The Mesoamerican and Andean civilizations engaged in frequent warfare to control the trade in luxury goods.

44. All of the following reflect how the original concepts of Buddhism were modified after its introduction into China EXCEPT the translation of

(A) "dharma" as "the way"

(B) "husband supports wife" as "husband controls wife"

(C) "morality" as "filial submission and obedience"

(D) "nirvana" as "tribute"

45. In contrast to their counterparts in China and Korea, elite women in Japan in the tenth century

(A) attained legal equality

(B) enjoyed greater freedom

(C) gained the right to vote

(D) joined the military

GO ON TO THE NEXT PAGE.

46. All of the following describe the effect of the Crusades on Europe EXCEPT

    (A) European demand for luxury goods from Asia increased
    (B) Europeans learned how to grow sugar on plantations worked by slaves
    (C) Eastern Orthodoxy was absorbed into Roman Catholicism
    (D) Islamic and Greek learning spread throughout Europe

47. Sufi missionaries facilitated the conversion to Islam of people living in Anatolia and India by

    (A) using local rulers to enforce the sharia
    (B) emphasizing a literal interpretation of the Quran
    (C) incorporating elements of local belief and practice
    (D) freeing slaves who agreed to convert

48. Which of the following describes an alternative lifestyle that both Christianity and Buddhism offered women in the pre-modern era?

    (A) Women who joined a convent were able to escape direct male supervision.
    (B) Women could hold high positions in the church hierarchy and shape policy.
    (C) The emphasis on poverty made begging a respectable occupation for women.
    (D) Female missionaries were able to travel abroad.

49. All of the following groups of people contributed to the spread of Islam through their military conquests EXCEPT the

    (A) Arabs
    (B) Persians
    (C) Turks
    (D) Xiongnu

50. The writings of which traveler would be a useful source of evidence for research on the communication infrastructure of the Mongol Empire?

    (A) Ban Zhao
    (B) Marco Polo
    (C) Xuanzang
    (D) Voltaire

51. The fourteenth-century Arab historian Ibn Khaldun described pastoral peoples in the following way: "It is their nature to plunder whatever other people possess." Which of the following evidence would counter the view of pastoral societies expressed by Ibn Khaldun?

    (A) The Xiongnu Empire extorted tribute payments from Han dynasty China.
    (B) Nomadic Bedouin Arabs regularly raided nearby agrarian societies.
    (C) Mongol rulers offered merchants 10 percent or more above their asking price.
    (D) The Seljuk Turks spread Islam throughout the Middle East by military conquest.

52. Which city emerged as the center of a new Russian state in the fifteenth century due in part to its role as a tribute collector for the Mongols?

    (A) Moscow
    (B) Kiev
    (C) Riazan
    (D) Sarai

GO ON TO THE NEXT PAGE.

53. Which of the following explains why nomadic pastoralism emerged only in Africa and Eurasia but not in the Americas?

   (A) The north–south orientation of the Americas
   (B) The rapid spread of agriculture in the Americas
   (C) The absence of large animals that could be domesticated in the Americas
   (D) The technological backwardness of the civilizations in the Americas

54. All of the following reflect motivations for European expansion but not for Chinese expansion in the fifteenth century EXCEPT

   (A) to enroll distant peoples and states in the tribute system
   (B) to gain direct access to the goods and wealth of the Indian Ocean basin
   (C) to spread Christianity and find Christian allies in the world
   (D) to monopolize the commerce of the Indian Ocean basin

55. All of the following Islamic empires accommodated the different religions of their subject populations EXCEPT the

   (A) Ottoman Empire
   (B) Safavid Empire
   (C) Songhay Empire
   (D) Mughal Empire

56. The Inca and Aztec civilizations practiced what scholars characterize as "gender parallelism." Which of the following evidence supports this interpretation of gender relations?

   (A) The restriction of male activities to the home
   (B) The feminization of political authority
   (C) Military units that integrated men and women
   (D) Separate religious cults for men and women

57. In recent decades, some historians have questioned past views that emphasize the role of the Aryans in the creation of a new civilization along the Ganges River on India's northern plain. According to this interpretation, the Aryans invaded and destroyed the Indus Valley civilization and created a completely new one. All of the following reflect recent reinterpretations that challenge this view EXCEPT

   (A) The Aryan invasion was sudden and destructive, leaving behind no remnants of the Indus Valley civilization.
   (B) The Aryans were already part of the population living in the Indus River valley before 600 B.C.E.
   (C) The Aryans migrated slowly into the Indus River valley and gradually assimilated into the local population.
   (D) The Indus Valley civilization contained many elements that have been attributed to the Aryan invaders.

58. Which of the following supports the historical portrayal of the Mauryan ruler Ashoka as a peace loving and tolerant ruler?

   (A) *Arthashastra* (*The Science of Worldly Wealth*)
   (B) Ashoka's repudiation of Buddhism
   (C) Ashoka's edicts carved on rocks and pillars
   (D) The tax imposed on Muslims within the empire

GO ON TO THE NEXT PAGE.

59. All of the following were undertaken by the second-wave civilizations of Persia and China to establish centralized governments EXCEPT

    (A) creation of an imperial bureaucracy
    (B) adoption of Islam
    (C) construction of infrastructure
    (D) standardization of currency

60. The imperial traditions of which second-wave civilization emphasized the importance of having good men in power rather than having a good set of laws?

    (A) Roman Empire
    (B) Persian Empire
    (C) Confucian China
    (D) Hindu India

61. The architectural style of which of the following became an inspiration for Renaissance artists?

    (A) Parthenon
    (B) Monticello
    (C) Hagia Sophia
    (D) Eiffel Tower

62. In what respect was the Mauryan ruler Ashoka's endorsement of Buddhism different from the Roman Empire's support of Christianity beginning with Emperor Constantine?

    (A) State support of Buddhism led to a wave of forced religious conversions, while state support of Christianity had no effect on the population.
    (B) State support of Buddhism was strengthened by military conquest, while state support of Christianity ended imperial expansion.
    (C) State support of Buddhism contributed to the demise of Hinduism, while state support of Christianity contributed to the emergence of Islam.
    (D) State support of Buddhism was accompanied by a policy of religious tolerance, while state support of Christianity led to a suppression of other religions.

63. All of the following were cultural traditions that strengthened patriarchy EXCEPT

    (A) Christianity
    (B) Confucianism
    (C) Dreamtime
    (D) Hinduism

64. Slaves constituted at least a third of the population in all of the following second-wave civilizations EXCEPT

    (A) Athens
    (B) Han dynasty China
    (C) the Roman Empire
    (D) Sparta

GO ON TO THE NEXT PAGE.

65. In which second-wave civilization was elite status associated with education and success in the civil service examination system?

   (A) China
   (B) Egypt
   (C) India
   (D) Persia

66. All of the following were advantages Bantu-speaking migrants had over the peoples they encountered as they spread throughout sub-Saharan Africa EXCEPT

   (A) ironworking technology
   (B) immunity to a wider range of diseases
   (C) a well-trained military and unified leadership
   (D) a larger population sustained by agriculture

67. City-states were the dominant feature of the political systems that emerged in all of the following EXCEPT

   (A) classical Greece
   (B) ancient Mesopotamia
   (C) Maya civilization
   (D) imperial China

68. All of the following mark the transition from the Paleolithic era to the Neolithic Revolution EXCEPT the

   (A) domestication of animals
   (B) human use of fire
   (C) deliberate cultivation of plants
   (D) intensification of agriculture

69. What did the rulers of the First Civilizations in China, Mesopotamia, and Egypt invoke to legitimize their power?

   (A) The gods
   (B) Reason
   (C) Social contract
   (D) Natural spirits

70. The development of writing in the First Civilizations was associated with

   (A) literature
   (B) poetry
   (C) accounting
   (D) science

STOP

END OF SECTION I

WORLD HISTORY
SECTION II

Part A
(Suggested writing time — 40 minutes)
Percent of Section II score — 33 1/3

Directions: The following question is based on the accompanying Documents 1–7. (The documents have been edited for the purpose of this exercise.)

This question is designed to test your ability to work with and understand historical documents.

Write an essay that:

+ Has a relevant thesis and supports that thesis with evidence from the documents.
+ Uses all of the documents.
+ Analyzes the documents by grouping them in as many appropriate ways as possible. Does not simply summarize the documents individually.
+ Takes into account the sources of the documents and analyzes the authors' points of view.
+ Identifies and explains the need for at least one additional type of document.

You may refer to relevant historical information not mentioned in the documents.

1. Using the following documents, evaluate the factors that contributed to the success of the Spanish conquest of the Aztec Empire in the early 1500s. Identify an additional type of document and explain how it would help your evaluation of the Spanish conquest.

GO ON TO THE NEXT PAGE.

Document 1

Source: King Moctezuma I, Aztec emperor, *Laws, Ordinances, and Regulations*, c. 1450 C.E.

The following laws were decreed:

1. The king must never appear in public except when the occasion is extremely important and unavoidable.

4. Only the king is to wear the final mantles of cotton brocaded with designs and threads of different colors and adorned with featherwork. . . .

5. The great lords, who are twelve, may wear special mantles of certain make and design, and the minor lords, according to their valor and accomplishments, may wear others.

7. The commoners will not be allowed to wear cotton clothing, under pain of death, but can use only garments of maguey fiber. . . .

8. Only the great noblemen and valiant warriors are given license to build a house with a second story; for disobeying this law a person receives the death penalty. . . .

12. An order of judges is to be established, beginning with the judges of the supreme council. After these would come regular court judges, municipal judges, district officials, constables, and councilmen, although none of them may give the death sentence without notifying the king. Only the sovereign can sentence someone to death or pardon him. . . .

14. There is to be a rigorous law regarding adulterers. They are to be stoned and thrown into the rivers or to the buzzards.

15. Thieves will be sold for the price of their theft, unless the theft be grave, having been committed many times. Such thieves will be punished by death.

16. Great privileges and exemptions are to be given those who dedicate themselves to religion, to the temples and the gods. Priests will be awarded great distinction, reverence, and authority.

GO ON TO THE NEXT PAGE.

Document 2

Source: Diego Durán, Dominican friar fluent in the Aztec language Nahuatl, *Book of the Gods and Rites*, 1574–1576 C.E.

I wish to tell of the way in which the natives sacrificed. . . .

Smeared with black, the six sacrificers appeared. . . . Seeing them come out with their ghastly aspect filled all the people with dread and terrible fear! The high priest carried in one hand a large stone knife, sharp and wide. Another carried a wooden yoke carved in the form of a snake. They humbled themselves before the idol and then stood in order next to a pointed stone, which stood in front of the door of the idol's chamber. . . .

All the prisoners of war who were to be sacrificed upon this feast were then brought forth. . . .

They seized the victims one by one, one by one foot, another by the other, one priest by one hand, another by the other hand. The victim was thrown on his back, upon the pointed stone, where the wretch was grabbed by the fifth priest, who placed the yoke upon his throat. The high priest then opened the chest and with amazing swiftness tore out the heart, ripping it out with his own hands. Thus steaming, the heart was lifted toward the sun, and the fumes were offered up to the sun. . . . After the heart had been extracted, the body was allowed to roll down the steps of the pyramid. . . .

All the prisoners and captives of war brought from the towns we have mentioned were sacrificed in this manner, until none were left. After they had been slain and cast down, their owners—those who had captured them—retrieved the bodies. They were carried away, distributed, and eaten, in order to celebrate the feast. There were at least forty or fifty captives, depending upon the skill which the men had shown in seizing and capturing men in war. . . .

GO ON TO THE NEXT PAGE.

Document 3

Source: Manuscript images depicting Spanish forces on the left and Aztecs on the right by anonymous Aztec authors and artists, supervised by friar Bernardino de Sahagún, *General History of the Things of New Spain*, also known as the *Florentine Codex*, 16th century C.E.

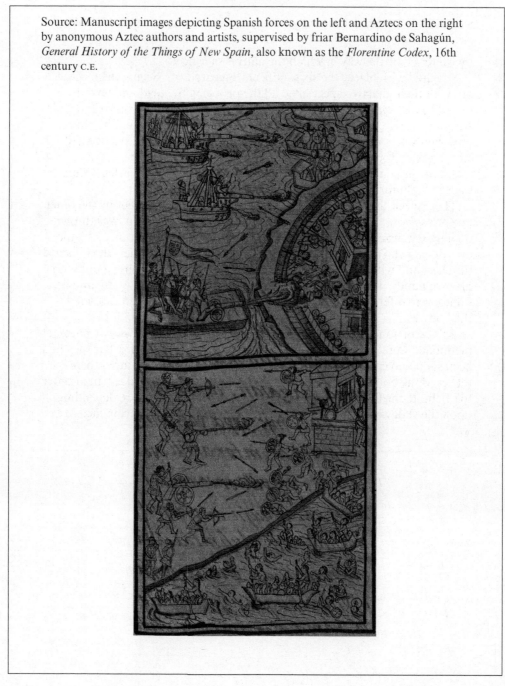

GO ON TO THE NEXT PAGE.

Document 4

Source: Bernal Diaz del Castillo, Spanish soldier, *conquistador*, and one of Cortés's officers, *The Conquest of New Spain*, 16th century C.E.

Moctezuma welcomed our Captain, and Cortés, speaking through Doña Marina, answered by wishing him very good health.

On our arrival we entered the large court, where the great Moctezuma was awaiting our Captain. Taking him by the hand, the prince led him to his apartment in the hall where he was to lodge, which was very richly furnished in their manner. . . .

Moctezuma said: ". . . [Y]ou and your brothers are in your own house. Rest a while. . . ."

We all thanked him heartily for his . . . good will, and Moctezuma replied with a laugh, because in his princely manner he spoke very gaily . . . "I know that these people of Tlaxcala with whom you are so friendly have told you that I am a sort of god. . . . It is true that I am a great king, and have inherited the riches of my ancestors, but the lies and nonsense you have heard of us are not true. You must take them as a joke, as I take the story of your thunders and lightnings."

Cortés answered also with a laugh that enemies always speak evil and tell lies about the people they hate. . . .

[F]our of our most valiant captains took Cortés aside in the church, with a dozen soldiers . . . and asked him to consider the net or trap in which we were caught, to look at the great strength of the city and observe the causeways and bridges, and remember the warnings we had received in every town we had passed through that [the Aztec God] Huichilobos had counseled Moctezuma to let us into the city and kill us there. We reminded him that the hearts of men are very fickle, especially among the Indians, and begged him not to trust the good will and affection that Moctezuma was showing us, because from one hour to another it might change. If he should take it into his head to attack us, we said, the stoppage of our supplies of food and water, or the raising of any of the bridges, would render us helpless. Then, considering the vast army of warriors he possessed, we should be incapable of attacking or defending ourselves. And since all the houses stood in the water, how could our Tlaxcalan allies come in to help us? We asked him to think over all that we had said, for if we wanted to preserve our lives we must seize Moctezuma immediately, without even a day's delay.

With two very dangerous alternatives before us, the better and more profitable thing, they said, would be to seize Moctezuma rather than wait for him to attack us. Once he did so, what chance would we have? Two of our Tlaxcalan allies had, moreover, secretly observed . . . that for the last two days the Mexicans had appeared less well disposed to us.

GO ON TO THE NEXT PAGE.

Document 5

Source: Anonymous Tlaxcalan artists, mural in the royal house of Tlaxcalans depicting a meeting between Moctezuma, Cortés, and Doña Marina, *Lienzo de Tlaxcala*, 1560 C.E.

GO ON TO THE NEXT PAGE.

Document 6

Source: Anonymous Aztec illustrated histories translated from the Nahuatl language, *The Broken Spears: The Aztec Account of the Conquest of Mexico*, 1500s C.E.

When Moctezuma had given necklaces to each one, Cortés asked him: "Are you Moctezuma?"

And the king said: "Yes, I am Moctezuma...."

When Moctezuma had finished, Doña Marina translated his address into Spanish so that the Captain could understand it. Cortés replied in his strange and savage tongue, speaking first to Doña Marina: "Tell Moctezuma that we are his friends. There is nothing to fear. We have wanted to see him for a long time, and now we have seen his face and heard his words. Tell him that we love him well and that our hearts are contented. "

Then he said to Moctezuma: "We have come to your house in Mexico as friends. There is nothing to fear...."

When Moctezuma was imprisoned [by the Spanish, the Aztec nobles]... all went into hiding. They ran away to hide and treacherously abandoned him!

Then the Spaniards fired one of their cannons, and this caused great confusion in the city. The people scattered in every direction.... It was as if they had eaten the mushrooms that confuse the mind, or had seen some dreadful apparition. They were all overcome by terror, as if their hearts had fainted. And when night fell, the panic spread through the city and their fears would not let them sleep.

The Aztecs begged permission of their king to hold the festival of Huitzilopochtli.

The [festival] procession began, and the celebrants filed into the temple patio to dance the Dance of the Serpent. When they were all together in the patio, the songs and the dance began.

At this moment in the festival, when the dance was loveliest and when song was linked to song, the Spaniards... all ran forward, armed as if for battle. They closed the entrances and passageways.... They posted guards so that no one could escape, and then rushed into the Sacred Patio to slaughter the celebrants.

They attacked the man who was drumming and cut off his arms. Then they cut off his head, and it rolled across the floor.

They attacked all the celebrants, stabbing them, spearing them, striking them with their swords. They attacked some of them from behind, and these fell instantly to the ground with their entrails hanging out. Others they beheaded: they cut off their heads, or split their heads to pieces.

Some attempted to force their way out, but the Spaniards murdered them at the gates.

The blood of the warriors flowed like water and gathered into pools. The pools widened, and the stench of blood and entrails filled the air. The Spaniards ran into the communal houses to kill those who were hiding. They ran everywhere and searched everywhere; they invaded every room, hunting and killing.

GO ON TO THE NEXT PAGE.

Document 7

Source: Anonymous Aztec authors and artists, supervised by their teacher Spanish Franciscan friar Bernardino de Sahagún, *General History of the Things of New Spain*, also known as the *Florentine Codex*, 16th century C.E.

An epidemic broke out, a sickness of pustules. . . . [The disease] brought great desolation; a great many died of it. They could no longer walk about . . . no longer able to move or stir. . . . Starvation reigned, and no one took care of others any longer. . . . And when things were in this state, the Spaniards came.

END OF PART A

WORLD HISTORY
SECTION II

Part B
(Suggested planning and writing time—40 minutes)
Percent of Section II score—33 1/3

Directions: You are to answer the following question. You should spend 5 minutes organizing or outlining your essay.

Write an essay that:

+ Has a relevant thesis and supports that thesis with appropriate historical evidence.
+ Addresses all parts of the question.
+ Uses world historical context to show continuities and changes over time.
+ Analyzes the process of continuity and change over time.

2. Analyze the continuities and changes in labor systems in the global system between 1450 and 1750.

END OF PART B

WORLD HISTORY
SECTION II

Part C
(Suggested planning and writing time—40 minutes)
Percent of Section II score—33 1/3

Directions: You are to answer the following question. You should spend 5 minutes organizing or outlining your essay.

Write an essay that:

+ Has a relevant thesis and supports that thesis with appropriate historical evidence.
+ Addresses all parts of the question.
+ Makes direct, relevant comparisons.
+ Analyzes relevant reasons for similarities and differences.

3. Compare the process of political centralization that occurred in TWO of the following regions between 1450 and 1750.

+ East Asia
+ Russia
+ Middle East
+ Western Europe

STOP

END OF EXAM

Answer Key for Practice Exam 4

Answers for Section I:
Multiple-Choice Questions

1. A	19. C	37. A	55. B
2. D	20. A	38. D	56. D
3. C	21. D	39. B	57. A
4. A	22. C	40. C	58. C
5. C	23. A	41. A	59. B
6. B	24. A	42. D	60. C
7. C	25. C	43. A	61. A
8. D	26. B	44. D	62. D
9. B	27. D	45. B	63. C
10. A	28. B	46. C	64. B
11. C	29. D	47. C	65. A
12. D	30. A	48. A	66. C
13. B	31. A	49. D	67. D
14. A	32. C	50. B	68. B
15. C	33. B	51. C	69. A
16. A	34. D	52. A	70. C
17. B	35. A	53. C	
18. D	36. C	54. A	

Scoring the Multiple-Choice Section

Use the following formula to calculate your raw score on the multiple-choice section of the exam:

$$\underline{\hspace{3cm}} \times 0.8571 = \underline{\hspace{3cm}}$$

Number correct	**Weighted Section I score**
(out of 70)	**(do not round)**

The highest possible score for the multiple-choice section is seventy correct answers, for a score of 60.

Rationales:

1. Answer: A

    Explanation: The collapse of empires in the twentieth century, which became a global phenomenon in the second half of the century, gave imperialism a negative connotation. Views of Columbus reflected this change in attitude toward the notion of empire. Since his voyage to the Americas initiated the first stage of European imperialism, the reputation of Columbus by the late twentieth century was tarnished with the same brush.

    Page Reference: p. 559

KEY CONCEPT	THEME	SKILL
4.1.III.C	3: State-Building,	Argumentation
4.1.V.A	Expansion, and Conflict.	Continuity and Change

2. Answer: D

   Explanation: The second stage of European expansion was well underway by the late nineteenth century. The U.S. was a new participant in this phase, and the notion of "Manifest Destiny" was used to justify westward expansion as well as overseas expansion. For Americans at this time, Columbus's arrival in the Americas made possible the last four centuries of American achievements.

   Page Reference: p. 559

KEY CONCEPT	THEME	SKILL
4.1.III.C	3: State-Building, Expansion, and Conflict.	Interpretation

3. Answer: C

   Explanation: For the indigenous people of the Americas, Columbus's arrival destroyed their societies and cultures. The European presence in the Americas brought disease, destruction, death, and enslavement for many. Consequently, for many indigenous people today, Columbus's arrival was an invasion.

   Page Reference: p. 559

KEY CONCEPT	THEME	SKILL
4.1.V.A	3: State-Building, Expansion, and Conflict.	Interpretation

4. Answer: A

   Explanation: In contrast to the alternating monsoon winds of the Indian Ocean, the winds in the Atlantic Ocean blew in the same direction. Once European sailors understood the wind and current patterns, they could better navigate their ships across the Atlantic.

   Page Reference: p. 619

KEY CONCEPT	THEME	SKILL
4.1.III.C	1: Interaction Between Humans and the Environment.	Causation

5. Answer: C

   Explanation: Prior to 1492, the Americas and the Afro-Eurasian world had had absolutely no contact with one another for thousands of years. Europeans borrowed extensively from the classical civilizations around the Mediterranean and the Indian Ocean. China was also an important source of knowledge and inventions.

   Page Reference: p. 619

KEY CONCEPT	THEME	SKILL
4.1.II	2: Development and Interaction of Cultures.	Contextualization Synthesis

6. Answer: B

    Explanation: The centuries between 1450 and 1750, conventionally characterized as the "early modern era," was a period of expansion for both land and maritime empires. The Chinese, Russian, Ottoman, and Mughal empires represent land empires that grew in size during this period. The overseas colonies in the Americas of the European powers represent new maritime empires during this period.

    Page Reference: p. 618

KEY CONCEPT	THEME	SKILL
4.1.III.A-D 4.3.II.A-C	3: State-Building, Expansion, and Conflict.	Periodization

7. Answer: C

    Explanation: The fifteenth century in Ming dynasty China was a period of growth and expansion. The expeditions launched by the Ming emperor enabled China to control most of the commercial networks in the Indian Ocean, which stretched the entire width of the Indian Ocean basin. In this respect, the expeditions facilitated long-distance trade.

    Page Reference: pp. 567–68

KEY CONCEPT	THEME	SKILL
4.1.III.A	3: State-Building, Expansion, and Conflict.	Interpretation Contextualization

8. Answer: D

    Explanation: The Indian Ocean commercial networks were dominated by Muslim merchants by the fifteenth century. As Muslim merchant communities spread throughout the region, certain cities rose in importance. Malacca emerged as an important port at this time because of its strategic location at the nexus of trade routes.

    Page Reference: pp. 567, 580

KEY CONCEPT	THEME	SKILL
4.1.I 3.3.II.C	4: Creation, Expansion, and Interaction of Economic Systems.	Contextualization Causation

9. Answer: B

    Explanation: Timur, also known as Tamerlane, was a Turkic warrior who sought to restore the glory of the Mongol Empire. Timur and his armies expanded into Russia, Persia, and India. After the collapse of his empire by the end of the fifteenth century, no other empire headed by nomadic peoples emerged again.

    Page Reference: pp. 565, 567

KEY CONCEPT	THEME	SKILL
4.3.II.B	3: State-Building, Expansion, and Conflict.	Contextualization

10. Answer: A

Explanation: In contrast to the Middle East and India, where the spread of Islam was accompanied by military conquest, in West Africa and Southeast Asia, Islam arrived via merchants and missionaries. As Muslim merchant communities spread throughout each region, they introduced their religious beliefs. The activities of Sufi holy men contributed much to the spread of Islam in both regions.

Page Reference: p. 580

KEY CONCEPT	THEME	SKILL
3.1.III.A	2: Development and Interaction of Cultures.	Comparison

11. Answer: C

Explanation: Zheng He exemplifies the cosmopolitan features of Chinese civilization in the fifteenth century. Born a Muslim, Zheng He was also receptive to other religions. His construction of the trilingual tablet that paid homage to the major figures in Buddhism, Islam, and Hinduism reflect his tolerant and eclectic approach to religious and cultural difference.

Page Reference: p. 573

KEY CONCEPT	THEME	SKILL
4.1.III.A 4.1.VI.D	2: Development and Interaction of Cultures.	Evidence Contextualization

12. Answer: D

Explanation: The Islamic world played an important role in the preservation and transmission of the legacy of the ancient Greek and Roman civilizations. Living in Muslim Spain, Ibn Rushd's translations of Aristotle's work made available to Europeans the thought of Aristotle. The illuminated page acknowledges that intellectual debt to Islamic scholarship.

Page Reference: pp. 570, 604–06

KEY CONCEPT	THEME	SKILL
4.1.VII.B	2: Development and Interaction of Cultures.	Interpretation

13. Answer: B

Explanation: The Italian Renaissance in particular actively sought to recover the knowledge from ancient Greece and Rome. Since the Islamic world had been an important depository of that knowledge since the fall of the Roman Empire, Italian artists also looked to the Islamic world.

Page Reference: pp. 570, 604–06

KEY CONCEPT	THEME	SKILL
4.1.VII.B 3.1.III.D	2: Development and Interaction of Cultures.	Contextualization Synthesis

14.   Answer: A

Explanation: The small number of Spanish women who migrated to the Americas meant that the majority of Spanish male immigrants married indigenous women. Consequently, a mestizo population emerged. By the nineteenth century, people of mixed-race background constituted the majority of the population in Mexico.

Page Reference: pp. 628–29

KEY CONCEPT	THEME	SKILL
4.2.II.D 4.1.IV.D	1: Interaction Between Humans and the Environment. 5: Development and Transformation of Social Structures.	Causation

15.   Answer: C

Explanation: The factory system emerged with the Industrial Revolution. All the other choices represent various forms of coerced labor. The encomienda and repartimiento systems entitled certain Spanish settlers to the labor, gold, and harvest of the local population. In the hacienda system, low wages and high taxes pushed native workers into debt peonage.

Page Reference: p. 627

KEY CONCEPT	THEME	SKILL
4.2.I.D	4: Creation, Expansion, and Interaction of Economic Systems.	Comparison

16.   Answer: A

Explanation: The labor-intensive, large-scale production of sugar was the basis of the plantation economy in Brazil and the Caribbean. In contrast to Mexico and Peru, where sufficient numbers of the indigenous population survived to constitute the majority of the workforce, in the Caribbean, the demographic collapse was more devastating. In Brazil, many fled inland. Consequently, plantation owners turned to the Atlantic slave trade for a cheap source of labor.

Page Reference: p. 630

KEY CONCEPT	THEME	SKILL
4.2.I.C	4: Creation, Expansion, and Interaction of Economic Systems.	Comparison

17.   Answer: B

Explanation: Mulattoes were the products of unions between Portuguese men and African women. Mestizos were the mixed-race descendants of Spanish men and indigenous women. *Peninsulares* were Spanish-born, while creoles were Spaniards born in the Americas.

Page Reference: p. 632

KEY CONCEPT	THEME	SKILL
4.2.II.D 4.1.IV.D	5: Development and Transformation of Social Structures.	Contextualization

18.   Answer: D

Explanation: The formation of a modern state occurred at the same time that Russia was expanding into new territory. In the case of Western Europe, Spain, Britain, France, the Dutch Republic, and Portugal were already established as separate states before they established empires in the Americas. In the case of Russia, the contours of that state were shaped by imperial expansion from the outset.

Page Reference: p. 639

KEY CONCEPT	THEME	SKILL
4.3.II.B	3: State-Building, Expansion, and Conflict.	Comparison

19.   Answer: C

Explanation: The Silk Roads that spanned Eurasia had once connected distant parts of the continent. Increasingly, oceanic trade overtook land-based commerce. The Silk Roads were generally left neglected.

Page Reference: pp. 641–42

KEY CONCEPT	THEME	SKILL
4.1.I	4: Creation, Expansion, and Interaction of Economic Systems.	Contextualization

20.   Answer: A

Explanation: Louis XIV believed that public displays of the power of the monarchy were important for establishing political legitimacy. The grandeur of the spectacle impressed upon all observers the magnificence and majesty of the monarch. The choice of the sun as the symbol of the monarch was intended to drive home that point.

Page Reference: pp. 657–58

KEY CONCEPT	THEME	SKILL
4.3.I.A	3: State-Building, Expansion, and Conflict.	Interpretation

21.   Answer: D

Explanation: Louis XIV is sometimes referred to as the Sun King because he felt the sun was the most fitting symbol for the monarch. In his memoirs, he invoked the imagery of the sun to portray his rule as enlightening, relentless, steady, and evenhanded.

Page Reference: p. 658

KEY CONCEPT	THEME	SKILL
4.3.I.A	3: State-Building, Expansion, and Conflict.	Interpretation

22. Answer: C

Explanation: The largest silver mine in the world was in Potosí in the present-day country of Bolivia. Silver mining was the basis of the economy. On the map, Potosí is indicated as a point of origin in the arrow that connects the city to Lima.

Page Reference: p. 680

KEY CONCEPT	THEME	SKILL
4.1.IV.B	4: Creation, Expansion, and Interaction of Economic Systems.	Contextualization

23. Answer: A

Explanation: The mining of silver had detrimental effects on the environment. Forests were cleared, soil erosion destroyed the fertility of the land, and flooding became more frequent.

Page Reference: pp. 681–82

KEY CONCEPT	THEME	SKILL
4.1.V.E	1: Interaction Between Humans and the Environment.	Causation

24. Answer: A

Explanation: Both the Ottoman and Mughal empires were Islamic states that incorporated non-Muslim subjects into their administrative structures. The Ottoman did this through the practice of *devshirme* in which Christian boys from the Balkans were trained for the elite Janissary units. The Mughal ruler Akbar did this by allowing Hindus to serve in high positions in the government and military.

Page Reference: pp. 642, 646

KEY CONCEPT	THEME	SKILL
4.3.I.C 4.3.I.D	3: State-Building, Expansion, and Conflict.	Comparison

25. Answer: C

Explanation: The mass migration of Russian settlers to Siberia in the wake of Russian expansion transformed the landscape and demography of Siberia. Land that had been previously used for hunting and grazing was transformed into farms. The local population gave up their nomadic way of life and were absorbed into the Russian population.

Page Reference: p. 637

KEY CONCEPT	THEME	SKILL
4.2.I.A	3: State-Building, Expansion, and Conflict.	Causation

26. Answer: B

Explanation: Both movements emphasized rigorous techniques for ascertaining truth and produced works generally considered to be scientific. However, the *kaozheng* movement in China applied that approach to better understanding the past. The European Scientific Revolution used the new approach to understand the natural world.

Page Reference: p. 738

KEY CONCEPT	THEME	SKILL
5.3.I.A	2: Development and Interaction of Cultures.	Comparison

27. Answer: D

Explanation: The Qing dynasty wanted to preserve the "martial" character of the Central Asian peoples and thus restricted the migration of Chinese, who were viewed as "soft." In contrast, Russian conquest of Siberia was followed by the mass migration of Russian settlers who transformed the landscape and demography of the area. By the early eighteenth century, Russians comprised the majority of the population in Siberia.

Page Reference: pp. 637, 641

KEY CONCEPT	THEME	SKILL
4.3.II.B	3: State-Building, Expansion, and Conflict.	Comparison

28. Answer: B

Explanation: The Russian government and military were generally staffed by Russians. In contrast, the Qing dynasty, the Mughal Empire, and the Ottoman Empire incorporated conquered peoples into the bureaucracy and military.

Page Reference: pp. 637, 641, 642, 646

KEY CONCEPT	THEME	SKILL
4.3.I.D	3: State-Building, Expansion, and Conflict.	Comparison

29. Answer: D

Explanation: These empires encompassed people of different religions and ethnicities. The rulers in all three empires insisted on political loyalty and demanded obedience from their subjects; in this respect, they ruled as absolute monarchs. In cultural and religious matters, they had a more open policy, provided that cultural and religious freedom did not subvert the political order.

Page Reference: pp. 640, 642–43, 646

KEY CONCEPT	THEME	SKILL
4.3.I.C	3: State-Building, Expansion, and Conflict.	Comparison

30. Answer: A

Explanation: Japan never came under British rule, so the Japanese never paid tribute to the British Empire. In the pre-modern world, tribute collection was a primary source of funds for empire building. The Russians collected tribute from Siberians, the Spanish from the indigenous peoples in Latin America, and the Mongols from the Russian princes.

Page Reference: pp. 533, 629, 637

KEY CONCEPT	THEME	SKILL
4.3.I.E	3: State-Building, Expansion, and Conflict.	Comparison Continuity and Change

31.   Answer: A

Explanation: Creoles and *peninsulares* were both Spanish. Creoles were Spaniards born in the Americas. *Peninsulares* were Spaniards born in Spain. *Peninsulares* viewed themselves as superior to creoles, even though both formed the elite in Spanish America.

Page Reference: p. 628

KEY CONCEPT	THEME	SKILL
4.2.II.A	5: Development and Transformation of Social Structures.	Contextualization

32.   Answer: C

Explanation: Since the majority of enslaved Africans sent to the Americas were male, there were more women than men in African societies. The imbalance in the sex ratio enabled men to marry multiple wives. With most of the men gone, the labor demands on women increased. Slavery in Africa persisted, with female slaves now constituting the majority of slaves in Africa.

Page Reference: p. 694

KEY CONCEPT	THEME	SKILL
4.2.I.B 4.2.II.C	5: Development and Transformation of Social Structures.	Causation

33.   Answer: B

Explanation: European traders found it advantageous to marry local women in West Africa and North America because it gave them access to local commercial networks. In Spanish America, the scarcity of Spanish female immigrants contributed to the rise in interracial unions.

Page Reference: pp. 628–29, 685, 694–95

KEY CONCEPT	THEME	SKILL
4.2.II.C	5: Development and Transformation of Social Structures.	Comparison Contextualization

34.   Answer: D

Explanation: Early modern Europe and Tokugawa Japan both witnessed the emergence of stronger centralized governments at the expense of local powerholders. The monarchies in Britain, France, and Spain sought to check the power of the nobility with varying degrees of success and resistance. Similarly, the Tokugawa shogunate sought to control the daimyo through the alternate attendance system.

Both the European nobility and the Japanese daimyo enjoyed a great deal of autonomy in their estates outside the capital.

Page Reference: pp. 493, 569, 948

KEY CONCEPT	THEME	SKILL
4.2.II.B	3: State-Building, Expansion, and Conflict.	Comparison Contextualization

35. Answer: A

Explanation: Although their rituals were very different, both the Aztec Empire and the Chinese dynasties emphasized the importance of rituals in maintaining the correct relationship between heaven and earth. Failure to do so would inevitably bring disaster. Aztec kings and Chinese emperors both considered the regular performance of prescribed rituals as the basis of their political legitimacy.

Page Reference: pp. 136, 657

KEY CONCEPT	THEME	SKILL
4.3.I.B	3: State-Building, Expansion, and Conflict.	Comparison Contextualization

36. Answer: C

Explanation: The frequent conflicts between France and England over contested territory in France in the Hundred Years' War (1337–1453) is an example of the divisive and competitive nature of the European state system. The frequency of interstate conflicts contributed to the state-building process in Europe in the early modern era.

Page Reference: p. 569

KEY CONCEPT	THEME	SKILL
4.3.III	3: State-Building, Expansion, and Conflict.	Contextualization

37. Answer: A

Explanation: Machiavelli wrote *The Prince* in response to the political climate of Italy at the time. Political success in this competitive environment went to those who were willing to do anything to achieve their goals.

Page Reference: p. 571

KEY CONCEPT	THEME	SKILL
4.1.VII.B 4.3.III	3: State-Building, Expansion, and Conflict.	Evidence Contextualization

38. Answer: D

Explanation: Although almost four centuries separate the two writers, both women echo similar sentiments on women's status. Both invoked reason to contest conventional assumptions of female inferiority. They argued that women were just as capable as men and called for equal education for women.

Page Reference: pp. 571–72, 805

KEY CONCEPT	THEME	SKILL
4.1.VII.B	5: Development and Transformation of Social Structures.	Comparison Continuity and Change

39. Answer: B

Explanation: Zoroastrianism emerged during the Persian Empire and therefore pre-dates the birth of Christianity. Vodou, Santeria, and Macumba emerged as new religions in the Americas that represent Africanized versions of Christianity. African practices like divination, dream interpretation, visions, and spirit possession blended with Christian practices like church attendance and the use of candles and crucifixes.

Page Reference: pp. 734–35

KEY CONCEPT	THEME	SKILL
4.1.VI.B 4.1.VI.D	2: Development and Interaction of Cultures.	Comparison

40. Answer: C

Explanation: The Qing dynasty established the Court of Colonial Affairs to administer newly conquered areas in Central Asia. Local elites staffed many of the official posts. The Inca rulers also appointed local officials to posts in the lower levels of the bureaucracy.

Page Reference: pp. 584, 597–98, 641

KEY CONCEPT	THEME	SKILL
4.2.II.B	3: State-Building, Expansion, and Conflict.	Comparison

41. Answer: A

Explanation: Most of the world's supply of silver in the early modern era came from Spanish America or Japan. The wide circulation of the standard Spanish silver coin known as "piece of eight" among merchant communities in North America, Europe, India, Russia, West Africa, and southern China is evidence of the global circulation of silver from Spanish America.

Page Reference: p. 680

KEY CONCEPT	THEME	SKILL
4.1.IV.B	4: Creation, Expansion, and Interaction of Economic Systems.	Evidence Contextualization

42. Answer: D

Explanation: The Columbian exchange refers to the transfer of plants, animals, and diseases between the Americas and the Afro-Eurasian region. It was initiated by Columbus's voyage to the Americas and spread through European colonization of the Americas. The Columbian exchange marks a key turning point in world history, heralding a new era. Because of the Columbian exchange, Native American populations were exposed to deadly Afro-Eurasian diseases against which they had no immunity.

Page Reference: pp. 611, 622, 624–25

KEY CONCEPT	THEME	SKILL
4.1.V.A 4.1.V.C	1: Interaction Between Humans and the Environment. 4: Creation, Expansion, and Interaction of Economic Systems.	Causation Periodization

43.　Answer: A

Explanation: Commercial networks were the strongest within rather than between the Mesoamerican and Andean civilizations, which represented the two major regions in the Americas. The diffusion of goods between North and South America was a slow and indirect process. This was due in large part to the absence of long-distance trading networks linking the Mesoamerican and Andean civilizations.

Page Reference: pp. 340–41

KEY CONCEPT	THEME	SKILL
3.1.I.B	4: Creation, Expansion, and Interaction of Economic Systems.	Interpretation

44.　Answer: D

Explanation: Buddhism originated in India and began to take hold in China after the collapse of the Han dynasty in the third century. Buddhist concepts were translated using terms and ideas drawn from China's own cultural traditions, mainly Confucianism and Daoism. The "way" was a term used in both. The expectation of wifely obedience reflected the patriarchal assumptions of Confucianism. Filial piety was a Confucian notion.

Page Reference: pp. 389–90

KEY CONCEPT	THEME	SKILL
3.2.I.C	2: Development and Interaction of Cultures.	Continuity and Change

45.　Answer: B

Explanation: While Confucianism placed new restrictions on women's lives in China and Korea, it did not have the same effect on Japanese women. Even after the introduction of Confucianism into Japan, women continued to enjoy considerable freedom and rights, particularly in inheritance. They were not secluded in the home. After marriage, the husband usually moved into the wife's household or the couple lived apart. Widow remarriage was not frowned upon as it was in China and Korea.

Page Reference: p. 383

KEY CONCEPT	THEME	SKILL
3.3.III.B	5: Development and Transformation of Social Structures.	Comparison

46. Answer: C

Explanation: The division between Eastern Orthodoxy and Roman Catholicism hardened as a result of the Crusades. Crusaders traveling throughout the Islamic world found a wealth of luxury goods from Asia that Europeans now wanted. The plantation system was also introduced into Europe. After the fall of the Roman Empire, the heritage of Greek learning was preserved by Muslim scholars. Thus, exposure to Muslim scholarship also brought back the Greek tradition to Europe.

Page Reference: p. 488

KEY CONCEPT	THEME	SKILL
3.2.II	2: Development and Interaction of Cultures. 4: Creation, Expansion, and Interaction of Economic Systems.	Causation

47. Answer: C

Explanation: Sufi missionaries were able to win many converts due to their willingness to assimilate popular beliefs and customs into Islam. This resulted in a blended Islam that synthesized elements from both local and Islamic traditions.

Page Reference: p. 438

KEY CONCEPT	THEME	SKILL
3.1.III.A 4.1.VI.A	2: Development and Interaction of Cultures.	Comparison

48. Answer: A

Explanation: Life as a nun offered women an alternative to marriage and family. Since Buddhist and Christian convents were run by women, the convent offered women a haven from patriarchal authority. Some women were able to assume positions of authority within the convent but never within the male-dominated church hierarchy.

Page Reference: p. 483

KEY CONCEPT	THEME	SKILL
3.3.III.D	5: Development and Transformation of Social Structures.	Comparison

49. Answer: D

Explanation: The Arabs, Persians, and Turks all converted to Islam. Through their military conquests, they spread Islam. Many people within their empires converted to Islam.

Page Reference: pp. 519–20

KEY CONCEPT	THEME	SKILL
3.1.III.A	3: State-Building, Expansion, and Conflict.	Comparison Causation Contextualization

50. Answer: B

Explanation: Marco Polo traveled throughout much of the territory that had been conquered by the Mongols during the thirteenth century. His writings include a wealth of information that provides a rare glimpse of the Mongol Empire, including the infrastructure it established to facilitate communication. For instance, Marco Polo remarked on the extensive network of relay stations that connected various parts of the empire.

Page Reference: p. 526

KEY CONCEPT	THEME	SKILL
3.2.I.A	3: State-Building, Expansion, and Conflict.	Contextualization Evidence

51. Answer: C

Explanation: Merchants grew rich as a result of the commerce-friendly policies of Mongol rulers. Although the Mongols did not engage in trade themselves, they provided many incentives in order to encourage commerce. The Mongols were then able to extract wealth by taxing the trade.

Page Reference: pp. 526, 540

KEY CONCEPT	THEME	SKILL
3.1.I.E	4: Creation, Expansion, and Interaction of Economic Systems.	Interpretation Evidence Synthesis

52. Answer: A

Explanation: The Mongol conquerors rewarded those who cooperated and punished those who resisted. The city of Moscow collaborated with the Mongols, becoming the main tribute collector for the Mongols. As a result, they were left largely alone and were in a better position to create a new Russian state after the Mongols left than those cities that had resisted.

Page Reference: p. 533

KEY CONCEPT	THEME	SKILL
3.3.II.C	3: State-Building, Expansion, and Conflict.	Causation

53. Answer: C

Explanation: Nomadic pastoralism relied on large domesticated animals like horses, camels, goats, sheep, cattle, yaks, and reindeer. These animals were used for transportation, food, and building materials. In the Americas, the absence of animals that could be domesticated prevented nomadic pastoralism from taking root.

Page Reference: p. 514

KEY CONCEPT	THEME	SKILL
3.3.III.A	4: Creation, Expansion, and Interaction of Economic Systems.	Comparison Causation

54. Answer: A

Explanation: Although both China and European countries launched maritime expeditions in the fifteenth century, they had different motivations. China saw the expeditions led by Zheng He as a means to expand the tribute system. Portugal and Spain, on the other hand, had religious and commercial motives.

Page Reference: p. 575

KEY CONCEPT	THEME	SKILL
4.1.III.A-C	3: State-Building, Expansion, and Conflict. 4: Creation, Expansion, and Interaction of Economic Systems.	Comparison

55. Answer: B

Explanation: The Safavid Empire imposed the Shia version of Islam on its people, making it the official religion of the state. Although to different extents, the Ottoman, Songhay, and Mughal empires accommodated the different religions of the people they governed. Non-Muslims were sometimes given access to official positions.

Page Reference: pp. 578–79

KEY CONCEPT	THEME	SKILL
4.3.I.C	3: State-Building, Expansion, and Conflict.	Comparison

56. Answer: D

Explanation: Although not egalitarian, the gender parallelism characteristic of Inca and Aztec society granted men and women power and influence in their respective spheres. There were separate religious cults for each sex. Parallel political hierarchies were staffed by men and women.

Page Reference: p. 586

KEY CONCEPT	THEME	SKILL
3.3.III.B	5: Development and Transformation of Social Structures.	Comparison Interpretation

57. Answer: A

Explanation: The view of the Aryan invasion as sudden and destructive reinforces rather than overturns past views that credit the Aryan invaders for creating a new civilization that replaced the Indus Valley civilization. Recent scholars have proposed alternative views. Some dismiss the Aryan invasion thesis and argue that Aryans were already living in the Indus Valley. Others contend that the civilization that emerged evolved from the gradual assimilation of Aryan migrants (not invaders) into the local population. Still others maintain that the new civilization attributed to the Aryans was actually shaped by the earlier Indus Valley civilization.

Page Reference: p. 141

KEY CONCEPT	THEME	SKILL
2.2.I 1.3.III.E	3: State-Building, Expansion, and Conflict.	Argumentation

58. Answer: C

Explanation: After the bloody battle against Kalinga, Ashoka converted to Buddhism and adopted a more moralistic approach to imperial governance. He issued a number of edicts to publicize his intentions to rule more benevolently and justly. Many of these edicts were carved on pillars and stones throughout his empire.

Page Reference: pp. 142, 152–54

KEY CONCEPT	THEME	SKILL
2.2.I	3: State-Building, Expansion, and Conflict.	Evidence

59. Answer: B

Explanation: Islam did not emerge until the seventh century, during the third wave of civilizations (c. 500–1500). Both the Persian and Chinese empires ruled through a bureaucracy that enabled the imperial center to effectively rule distant parts of the empire. They built roads and canals to promote political and economic integration. They standardized currency and coinage to facilitate commerce within the empire.

Page Reference: pp. 121–22, 135, 138

KEY CONCEPT	THEME	SKILL
2.2.II.A-C	3: State-Building, Expansion, and Conflict.	Comparison

60. Answer: C

Explanation: Beginning with the Han dynasty, Confucianism became the official ideology, and a civil service examination system began to take shape. Confucius emphasized the importance of having morally virtuous men in power. While laws had their place, they were useless in the absence of good men to interpret and apply them. Thus, the Chinese imperial tradition emphasized the importance of good men over good laws.

Page Reference: p. 138

KEY CONCEPT	THEME	SKILL
2.2.II.A	3: State-Building, Expansion, and Conflict.	Comparison

61. Answer: A

Explanation: Renaissance artists saw themselves as "returning to the sources." They found inspiration in the art and literature of ancient Greece and Rome. The architectural style of the Parthenon represents the style of ancient Greece that influenced Renaissance artists.

Page Reference: pp. 126, 570

KEY CONCEPT	THEME	SKILL
2.1.V.B	2: Development and Interaction of Cultures.	Continuity and Change

62. Answer: D

Explanation: Ashoka promoted a policy of tolerance and harmony in religious matters. His support of Buddhism did not lead him to ban other religions in India. In contrast, state support of Christianity in the Roman Empire led to policies aimed at making Christianity the only religion.

Page Reference: p. 192

KEY CONCEPT	THEME	SKILL
2.1.II.A 2.1.II.D	2: Development and Interaction of Cultures. 3: State-Building, Expansion, and Conflict.	Comparison

63. Answer: C

Explanation: Dreamtime refers to the world outlook of the earliest human communities in Australia. Patriarchy had not yet emerged as a distinctive system that shaped gender relations. The Hindu, Confucian, and Christian traditions all reinforced patriarchy by justifying, in various ways, the subordinate status of women.

Page Reference: pp. 171, 175–76, 189

KEY CONCEPT	THEME	SKILL
2.1.III	5: Development and Transformation of Social Structures.	Comparison

64. Answer: B

Explanation: In China, slaves constituted about 1 percent of the population. In Athens, slaves represented about a third of the population. Slavery was even more widespread in the Roman Empire, with almost 40 percent of the population enslaved. In Sparta, helots represented a status group defined by permanent servitude; they outnumbered the free citizens of Sparta.

Page Reference: pp. 229–32, 238

KEY CONCEPT	THEME	SKILL
2.2.III.B-C	4: Creation, Expansion, and Interaction of Economic Systems.	Comparison

65. Answer: A

Explanation: Elite status in China was attached to the civil service examination system. The exams tested mastery of the Confucian classics; in this way, elite status was associated with education. Successful candidates on the exam were entitled to privileges and were eligible for official posts.

Page Reference: pp. 219–20

KEY CONCEPT	THEME	SKILL
2.2.III.B	5: Development and Transformation of Social Structures.	Contextualization

66.   Answer: C

Explanation: The Bantu migrants were a group of people loosely unified by a common language. Their migration throughout the southern half of Africa was gradual and driven by individual families rather than powerful states.

Page Reference: p. 283

KEY CONCEPT	THEME	SKILL
3.1.II.B	1: Interaction Between Humans and the Environment.	Causation

67.   Answer: D

Explanation: China had an imperial system with the emperor ruling over the entire country. In classical Greece, ancient Mesopotamia, and Maya civilization, the city-state represented the dominant political form. In none of these civilizations did an empire emerge that brought the entire area under one ruler.

Page Reference: p. 274

KEY CONCEPT	THEME	SKILL
2.2.III.A	3: State-Building, Expansion, and Conflict.	Comparison

68.   Answer: B

Explanation: Human mastery of fire occurred during the Paleolithic era. The Neolithic Revolution refers to the transition to agriculture. This involved the deliberate cultivation of plants, domestication of animals, and intensification of agriculture.

Page Reference: pp. 26–27

KEY CONCEPT	THEME	SKILL
1.2.I.A	4: Creation, Expansion, and Interaction of Economic Systems.	Continuity and Change

69.   Answer: A

Explanation: Rulers in the First Civilizations invariably invoked the sacred to legitimize their authority. In China, the emperor was the Son of Heaven. In Mesopotamia, royal symbols were reputed to be of divine origin. In Egypt, the pharaoh was believed to possess divine qualities.

Page Reference: p. 77

KEY CONCEPT	THEME	SKILL
1.3.II.A	3: State-Building, Expansion, and Conflict.	Comparison

70.   Answer: C

> **Explanation:** The earliest use of writing served an accounting function. States in the First Civilizations used writing for record-keeping purposes. Scribes kept track of taxes, debts, and wages.

> **Page Reference:** p. 78

KEY CONCEPT	THEME	SKILL
1.3.III.C	2: Development and Interaction of Cultures.	Causation

Answer Guide for Section II:
Part A

General Guidelines for Answering a Document-Based Question (DBQ):

1.   Pre-Write. Create a brief outline before you start writing.
2.   Write your DBQ in a multiple-paragraph structure. In your first paragraph, write an introduction that clearly states your thesis.
3.   Present your arguments in body paragraphs. Body paragraphs should integrate groupings of documents, demonstrate understanding of documents, support the thesis using documents as evidence, analyze point of view, and possibly include additional relevant historical content. Present your arguments in body paragraphs that focus on a grouping of documents and that put forth a single argument centered on answering the prompt.
4.   In your final paragraph, write a conclusion that includes a reworded restatement of your thesis.

AP World History DBQ essays are scored using a core scoring method with a maximum score of nine. In the basic core, you may earn the following seven points:

- ✦ one point for a thesis
- ✦ one point for addressing and understanding the documents
- ✦ up to two points for using the documents as evidence to answer the prompt
- ✦ one point for grouping the documents
- ✦ one point for analyzing Point of View (POV)
- ✦ one point for identifying and explaining the need for an additional document

If you earn ALL seven basic core points you have the chance to earn up to two additional points in what is called expanded core. Expanded core points may be granted for the following features:

- ✦ an excellent, sophisticated, and comprehensive thesis
- ✦ insightful document analysis
- ✦ analyzing POV in all or most documents
- ✦ including extra document groupings or additional documents
- ✦ incorporating relevant historical content not found in the documents

Below is a detailed description of what you will need to do in your answer to earn each basic core point for this essay.

Thesis (1 point): To earn a point in this category, you must write a thesis that responds to the entire prompt and outlines the specific arguments you will make based on a correct usage of the documents. You will need to mention the arguments you plan on making in your answer, and you will need to avoid generalizations that do not reflect reasonable interpretations of the documents. Thesis statements will only earn a point if they appear in the first or last paragraph of the essay. Common errors in thesis writing include merely rewriting the prompt or presenting an answer to only some parts of the prompt, so make sure you address the entire prompt and briefly present the specific arguments that you will use in your answer based on the documents.

> **Prompt:** Using the following documents, evaluate the factors that contributed to the success of the Spanish conquest of the Aztec Empire in the early 1500s. Identify an additional type of document and explain how it would help your evaluation of the Spanish conquest.

Examples:

> Example Thesis: "In the early 1500s C.E., the Spanish conquered the Aztecs due to factors including the harsh rule of the Aztecs, which created enemies that the Spanish turned into allies; the preexisting Aztec hierarchy and system of government, which made the Spanish imperial conquest easier; Spanish technological advantages; the use of native Doña Marina as a cultural mediator and interpreter; the brutality of the Spanish; and the impact of diseases on the Aztecs."

> ✦ This thesis earns the point by identifying the specific arguments based on the documents that the student will use to answer the prompt. It presents many factors contributing to the Spanish conquest of the Aztecs. It answers the entire prompt.

> Unacceptable Example: "The Spanish succeeded in their conquest of the Aztecs in the early 1500s due to a whole host of factors."

> ✦ This thesis does little other than state the obvious given the prompt.

Addressing and Understanding Documents (1 point): To earn this point, you must address ALL of the documents and demonstrate understanding of "all but one." This means that throughout your answer, you must show understanding of at least six of the seven documents.

Using Documents as Evidence (2 points): To earn two points, you must correctly incorporate at least six documents (although seven would be better) into arguments that answer the prompt. You will earn only one point if you use five of the seven documents in your arguments. If you use four or fewer documents in your essay, you will receive a zero in this category.

Grouping the Documents (1 point): Documents should be grouped in at least three ways in order to earn a point in this category. You can group documents by matching two or more documents that hold some relevant feature in common. Each example grouping below represents documents that, when used together, can make up an argument that answers the prompt.

Harsh Aztec Rule	Docs 1, 2
Preexisting Aztec Gov't with Hierarchy	Docs 1, 4, 5, 6
Aztec Enemies	Docs 2, 4
Spanish Technology	Docs 3, 4, 6
Spanish Violence/Brutality	Docs 3, 6
Spanish Treachery	Docs 4, 6
Doña Marina as Cultural Translator/Mediator	Docs 4, 5, 6
Aztec Mistakes in Hospitality/Not Seeing Danger	Docs 4, 5, 6
Diseases Brought by Spanish	Doc 7

Analyzing Point of View (1 Point): Many students find it challenging to earn the point in this category. The best way to earn the Point of View (POV) point is to go beyond the basic identity of the source author and the source itself, as described in the document source line. In order to write a successful POV statement, you should try to establish a better understanding of the identity of the author; you can do this by asking yourself questions about the author and the source. What is the author's gender or social class? What religion does the author follow? What is the author's profession? Does the author have an identifiable ethnicity, nationality, or other allegiance to a particular group? Is the source from a poem, essay, or novel? What was the source used for? Once you've asked these questions, go further and explain how some of these factors may have influenced the content of the source. Your complete POV statement should both identify the influences that may have shaped the author or source and explain how those particular influences have specifically affected the content of the document. Below are some examples of POV statements based on the documents from this question.

Examples of POV Statements:

Document 1: "Source: King Moctezuma I, Aztec emperor, *Laws, Ordinances, and Regulations*, c. 1450 C.E."

✦ The laws issued by King Moctezuma represent his position as king. He issued laws as the supreme governor of the Aztec Empire, and the purpose of laws of empire are typically to support and reinforce the legitimacy of the current government and to create an orderly society. Moctezuma I issued these laws as king in part to solidify his own rule, and as such, they reinforce his status as ruler.

Document 2: "Source: Diego Durán, Dominican friar fluent in the Aztec language Nahautl, *Book of the Gods and Rites*, 1574–1576 C.E."

✦ Diego Durán was a Catholic Christian monk. As a devout Catholic priest, he would be likely to emphasize and document the brutal aspects of the Aztecs' religion, and he would have wanted to justify replacing it with Catholicism.

Document 5: "Source: Anonymous Tlaxcalan artists, mural in the royal house of Tlaxcalans depicting a meeting between Moctezuma, Cortés, and Doña Marina, *Lienzo de Tlaxcala*, 1560 C.E."

✦ As ethnic Tlaxcalans, whose leaders allied with the Spanish in conquest of the Aztecs, these muralists might be highlighting the role of Doña Marina to bring attention to the role the Tlaxcalans played in the defeat of the Aztecs. This choice of subject may be useful to Tlaxcalans in reminding the Spanish of their help and in maintaining a special status under Spanish rule. It may also reflect Tlaxcalan pride in playing a role in overthrowing Moctezuma.

You should write as many POV statements as you are able to produce. You can earn the POV point with as few as two correct POV statements; however, it's not uncommon to make errors in writing POV statements. For that reason, it's safer to provide more than just two in order to make up for any errors. Additionally, if you earn all of the basic core points, an extra POV statement can earn you an expanded core point.

Additional Document Statement (1 Point): A good additional document statement identifies a missing document that, if added to the provided documents, would help make a better answer to the question. You are only required to make a single additional document statement to earn a point, but you should aim to identify a minimum of three additional documents. This allows room for mistakes, and after the first correct additional document statement, any extras can earn you bonus points in the expanded core if you earn all seven points in the basic core. You should be careful to avoid the common mistake of asking for a type of document that is already provided. Additional document statements must meet three standards to be considered successful:

✦ The document suggested must be historically plausible.

✦ The statement must include an explanation of **why** the additional document would be useful in answering the prompt.

✦ The analysis of **why** must speculate about the particulars of what the missing document might include. In other words, a successful additional document suggestion is historically possible given the time and place, includes an explanation of how the new source would help answer the prompt, and goes as far as speculating on arguments that the suggested source might support.

Document Analysis

Document 1: "Source: King Moctezuma I, Aztec emperor, *Laws, Ordinances, and Regulations*, c. 1450 C.E." This document is likely one of the more difficult documents to incorporate. It reveals the harsh rule of the Aztecs and also the fact that the Aztecs ruled as an empire with laws and hierarchy. It can be used simply to show that the harshness of Aztec government may have made it easier for the Spanish to make alliances with people ruled by Aztecs. Or it may be used to make a more difficult argument that the Spanish found it easier to conquer and rule because they were imposing a Spanish empire over a preexisting empire. The Spanish did not need to "teach" the people they conquered how to pay tribute or what symbols of status and hierarchy meant. These notions already existed in Central America under Aztec rule, so there was less difficulty in taking over a preexisting set of imperial relations than there may have been in creating the empire where one did not previously exist.

Document 2: "Source: Diego Durán, Dominican friar fluent in the Aztec language Nahautl, *Book of the Gods and Rites*, 1574–1576 C.E." Durán exposes the harsh Aztec rule in the form of making human sacrifices. The harsh rule grouping would then be of Documents 1 and 2. It also shows that the Aztecs had enemies since it describes the sacrifices as captured prisoners, so this document could be grouped with Document 4 to show that the Aztecs fought in wars against enemies. (Document 5 could also be used in this grouping if you remember the connection of Doña Marina to the Tlaxcalans, although this use is not required or necessary.)

Document 3: "Source: Manuscript images depicting Spanish forces on the left and Aztecs on the right by anonymous Aztec authors and artists, supervised by friar Bernardino de Sahagún, *General History of the Things of New Spain*, also known as the *Florentine Codex*, 16th century C.E." This document shows the Spanish advantage in technology and also the brutality of the Spanish conquest in turning cannons on people lacking gunpowder or guns. Spanish technological advantages included ships, cannons, guns, steel weapons, and the use of crossbows. The image shows Aztecs using bows. Additionally, the image shows the Spanish on horses, which was another of their military advantages.

Document 4: "Source: Bernal Diaz del Castillo, Spanish soldier, conquistador, and one of Cortés's officers, *The Conquest of New Spain*, 16th century C.E." Diaz tells of events similar to those found in Document 6, and his version shows a number of factors that aided the Spanish conquest. He describes Moctezuma's reception of the Spanish as respected foreign diplomats, which makes the Spanish attack more impactful and treacherous, and he mentions technological advantages such as guns. Diaz portrays the helpful role played by Doña Marina as a cultural mediator and translator. He wrote about the Aztec enemies the Tlaxcalans who allied with the Spanish and shows mistakes made by Moctezuma such as welcoming the Spanish into his capital and dismissing the stories of Aztec powers as mythological foolishness.

Document 5: "Source: Anonymous Tlaxcalan artists, mural in the royal house of Tlaxcalans depicting a meeting between Moctezuma, Cortés, and Doña Marina, *Lienzo de Tlaxcala*, 1560 C.E." This document is best used to show the role played by Doña Marina as a cultural mediator and translator and the Aztec use of allies in the conquest.

Document 6: "Source: Anonymous Aztec illustrated histories translated from the Nahuatl language, *The Broken Spears: The Aztec Account of the Conquest of Mexico*, 1500s C.E." The beginning of this document reflects similar themes as those in Diaz's account in Document 4. It can be used to argue that the Aztecs ruled as an empire with hierarchy to show the impact of Spanish weapons technology and the violence or brutality the Spanish were willing to employ in the conquest. It echoes Diaz's portrayal of Doña Marina's role and also reveals Moctezuma's mistakes in receiving the Spanish and underestimating their capabilities.

Document 7: "Source: Anonymous Aztec authors and artists, supervised by their teacher Spanish Franciscan friar Bernardino de Sahagún, *General History of the Things of New Spain*, also known as the *Florentine Codex*, 16th century C.E." This document reveals the impact of disease. It does not fit well into a group with other documents, but it does represent an important factor in the conquest and can be used to answer the prompt, but not in an obvious intuitive way as a part of a document grouping.

Answer Guide for Section II: Part B

2. Analyze the continuities and changes in labor systems between 1450 and 1750.

What Does the Question Ask?

This question deals with the systems that organized how people worked during a period of tremendous global interactions. The question is open ended. You can choose to write about the region or regions of the world that you know the best.

Listed below is the scoring system used to grade continuity and change-over-time essays; also included are guidelines and examples for how to earn each point for this question.

Has Acceptable Thesis (1 point)

+ The thesis needs to correctly address both continuity and change in labor systems between 1450 and 1750.
+ The thesis should appear in the first paragraph (although it may also count if it is in the conclusion).
+ The thesis can be one sentence or multiple sentences.

Examples:

+ Example One: During the period from 1450 to 1750, slavery continued to be an important system of labor. The institution of slavery, however, expanded dramatically across the Atlantic Ocean as African slaves were brought over to the New World.

✦ Example Two: Most of the world's population still worked in agriculture during the time span from 1450 to 1750. An increasing number of people during this time were involved in making trade items and small-scale manufacturing.

✦ Example Three: When Europeans came into the New World, they continued some of the forced labor systems that the Native Americans had used. They also introduced new forced labor systems from 1450 to 1750.

✦ Unacceptable Example: During the period from 1450 to 1750, large factories developed in Britain and throughout Europe that employed thousands of people working in the same place. These factories used coal for energy, leading to more people working in coal mines and enduring horrible working conditions.

   • This is an unacceptable thesis because the information about industrialization applies to the time period after 1750. Additionally, this example does not address continuity.

Addresses All Parts of the Question (2 points)

✦ The essay accurately addresses both a continuity (1 point) and a change (1 point).

✦ The statements of continuity and change may not appear in the thesis.

Examples:

✦ Example One: Slavery had existed long before 1450 and lasted long after 1750. Soon after Europeans created colonies in the Americas, they brought over slaves from Africa to work the plantation fields.

   • The first statement in the example above addresses continuity, while the second statement addresses change.

✦ Example Two: In all parts of the world, people continued to work the land as peasant farmers. In addition to farming, many people in Asia were increasingly involved with small-scale manufacturing of items for trade.

   • The first statement in the example above addresses continuity, while the second statement addresses change.

✦ Example Three: Several of the labor systems that Native Americans used were adapted by the Europeans and continued into the eighteenth century. The Europeans who settled the Americas also established new ways of exploiting the native labor, such as the *encomienda* system.

   • The first statement in the example above addresses continuity, while the second statement addresses change.

Substantiates Thesis with Appropriate Historical Evidence (2 points)

✦ A piece of historical evidence is a fact that is correct and relevant to the time period.

✦ To earn the full two points in this category, an essay should have five or more pieces of evidence.

✦ To earn only one point in this category, an essay needs three or four pieces of evidence.

✦ Points for evidence can be earned even if the thesis point is not earned.

Examples:

✦ Example One: Slavery existed in Africa, Asia, the Middle East, and other regions of the world throughout this period. The trade of slaves in the Mediterranean and Black Sea areas by Islamic merchants also continued. Europeans, who were looking for a large labor supply, started a transatlantic slave trade. About ten million Africans were shipped by the Middle Passage into the Caribbean and Latin

America. These slaves worked on plantations growing sugarcane and cash crops. In Africa, the slave trade transformed politics by creating powerful new elites who were linked to the traffic in slaves.

✦ Example Two: Peasants farmed fields in Europe for landlords who would take a portion of the crop. In China, India, and the Middle East, farmers also tended to work for larger landowners. Russian farmers were often serfs who were forced to work much like slaves. Some peasants made textiles in addition to working in the fields. In China, people made silk from the threads of silkworms. In India, cotton textile work intensified. In Europe, peasants continued to make linen and woolen cloth.

✦ Example Three: The Aztecs used slave labor for a variety of purposes including human sacrifice. Slaves were sold in the open marketplace by the Aztecs. The Spanish also practiced slavery by forcing Native Americans into working on building projects, in mines, and in the fields. The Spanish also continued to use the Inca system of *mita*, a forced labor tax, on villages in South America. The vast scale of new plantations required a new type of labor supply, so the Spanish and other Europeans introduced African slaves in order to meet demand.

Uses Relevant Historical Context (1 point)

✦ Historical context places the issue discussed in the essay into a broader global perspective.

Examples:

✦ Example One: The trade in slaves for the Middle East involved a large system that captured non-Muslim people in parts of southern Europe and in Africa and brought them to the cities of the Middle East for a wide variety of purposes.

✦ Example Two: The increase in global trade in the Indian Ocean and with Europe led to increased textile production in Asia. (Note that this statement could count as either analysis or historical context.)

✦ Example Three: As part of the process of colonization, the Spanish and the Portuguese came to the Americas, captured large number of natives, and enslaved them to work in mines and on plantations.

Analyzes the Process of Continuity or Change (1 point)

✦ Analysis explains why the continuity or change occurred.

Examples:

✦ Example One: Because Native Americans died of diseases so quickly after the Europeans enslaved them, African slaves became the largest factor in plantation agriculture.

✦ Example Two: In every region of the world, people continued to work in agriculture because improved farming techniques had not yet increased productivity enough to allow a majority of people to leave farming.

✦ Example Three: The Spanish used the *encomienda* system because it resembled the system of feudalism that was practiced in Europe.

Expanded Core

You must earn all seven points in the basic core before earning any points in the expanded core. Points awarded in the expanded core reflect the general excellence of the essay. Any one aspect of your essay, such as the thesis or evidence, might be particularly insightful and earn a point in the expanded core. Essays that have a high degree of analysis and historical context often earn expanded core points if they have earned all of the other basic core points. Clarity of organization, strong cause-effect analysis, and particularly insightful ideas can make your essay stand out as excellent.

Examples:

- ✦ Example One: A sophisticated discussion of how the system of slavery transformed in different time periods within the 1450–1750 time frame could earn points in the expanded core.
- ✦ Example Two: A structured analysis of different types of peasant agriculture and small-scale manufacturing with examples from different geographic regions could earn points in the expanded core.
- ✦ Example Three: A detailed set of evidence about Native American and European forced labor systems in Latin America and the Caribbean could earn points in the expanded core.

Answer Guide for Section II: Part C

3. Compare the process of political centralization that occurred in TWO of the following regions between 1450 and 1750.

- ✦ East Asia
- ✦ Russia
- ✦ Middle East
- ✦ Western Europe

What Does the Question Ask? This question deals with the methods in which political states consolidated their power. Although this is a political question, you can write about aspects of religion, economics, and even architecture if the evidence is linked to the topic of political centralization.

Listed below is the scoring system used to grade comparative essays; also included are guidelines and examples for how to earn each point for this question.

Has Acceptable Thesis (1 point)

- ✦ The thesis needs to correctly address the process of political centralization in two of the four regions.
- ✦ The thesis should appear in the first paragraph (although it may also count if it is in the conclusion).
- ✦ The thesis can be one sentence or multiple sentences.

Examples:

- ✦ Example One: In Japan and in Russia, the rulers weakened the role of the nobility in order to centralize their power. They pursued opposite policies, however, on their outreach to the rest of the world.
- ✦ Example Two: Western European countries and Middle Eastern countries gained a great deal of power by expanding dramatically in size. Each region centralized its military in different ways.
- ✦ Example Three: China and France both politically centralized under the rule of all-powerful monarchs. Different approaches to how religion influenced politics emerged in each country.

+ Unacceptable Example: Political centralization occurred in both the Middle East and Japan. The process of centralization, however, differed greatly.
  - This is an unacceptable thesis because the student did not mention much beyond the terms of the question itself. More specificity is required.

Addresses All Parts of the Question (2 points)

+ The essay accurately addresses both a valid similarity (1 point) and a valid difference (1 point).
+ The statements of comparison may not appear in the thesis.

Examples:

+ Example One: Both Peter the Great and Tokugawa Ieyasu moved their countries from weak and fragmented to powerful nation-states. Tsar Peter opened Russia to Westernization, while Ieyasu closed Japan to outside influence.
  - The first statement in the example above addresses similarities, while the second statement addresses difference.

+ Example Two: The Ottoman Empire gained more power by spreading its influence in the Mediterranean area. Spain also became more centralized through expanding its empire, but it expanded mostly to the Western Hemisphere.
  - The first statement in the second sentence above addresses similarity, while the second statement addresses difference.

+ Example Three: Louis XIV of France and the emperors of China built incredible palaces that served as showcases of their central power. Louis used Christianity as a way of consolidating power. The empires of China, on the other hand, used Confucianism.
  - The first statement in the example above addresses similarity, while the second statement addresses difference.

Substantiates Thesis with Appropriate Historical Evidence (2 points)

+ A piece of historical evidence is a fact that is correct and relevant to the time period.
+ To earn the full two points in this category, an essay should have five or more pieces of evidence.
+ To earn only one point in this category, an essay needs three or four pieces of evidence.
+ Points for evidence can be earned even if the thesis point is not earned.

Examples:

+ Example One: In order to understand the rest of the world better, Peter the Great traveled to other countries. He wanted to transform Russia into a modern country with up-to-date Western technologies and culture. He built a new capital of St. Petersburg as a window to the rest of the world. The Japanese shoguns brought different daimyos under their control and forced their obedience. Christians were persecuted as a means of increasing the power of the central government, and the shoguns closed off Japan from contact with the rest of the world.
+ Example Two: Ferdinand and Isabella consolidated their separate kingdoms into one united Spain. They forced out anyone in the country who wasn't Roman Catholic. After the discoveries of Columbus, they spread their influence broadly to the New World and as a result gained more power. The Ottoman sultans used an elite set of soldiers who were recruited from non-Muslim families. These soldiers were used by the sultans in military campaigns, as bodyguards and as advisors, in order to maintain political control.

✦ Example Three: Chinese emperors had a bureaucratic elite of civil servants who had studied Confucianism in depth. The emperors performed public rituals in temples in order to show their connection to religious values. The Forbidden Palace in Beijing displayed the central authority of the emperor. Similarly, Louis the XIV used the palace of Versailles to display his authority. He saw himself as the "Sun King," in other words, the center of the universe, and he used the French military and royal officials to centralize his political control.

Makes a Direct, Relevant Comparison (1 point)

✦ A direct comparison is an explicit, concrete, and factually correct statement of either similarity or difference.

Examples:

✦ Example One: Peter the Great and Tokugawa Ieyasu created new capitals in order to better consolidate their rules.
✦ Example Two: The rulers of both Spain and the Ottoman empires used militarism in order to keep control over their far-flung empires.
✦ Example Three: Both the Chinese emperors and French kings ruled through divine right. The people viewed their authority as coming from heaven.

Analyzes at Least One Reason for a Similarity or Difference (1 point)

✦ Analysis explains a reason for the similarity or difference.

Examples:

✦ Example One: The new capitals of St. Petersburg and Edo (Tokyo) helped the rulers control the noble class because each noble had to spend time in the capital city serving the interests of the state.
✦ Example Two: Expanding military powers, such as the Ottomans and the Spanish, brought in great wealth in the form of tributes, taxes, and spoils of war. This kind of wealth helped to centralize the political power of the ruling elite.
✦ Example Three: Both the Chinese emperors and Louis XIV used enormous palaces and elaborate court rituals to convince people both inside and outside of their countries of their importance and power.

Expanded Core

You must earn all seven points in the basic core before earning any points in the expanded core. Points awarded in the expanded core reflect the general excellence of the essay. Any one aspect of your essay, such as the thesis or evidence, might be particularly insightful and earn a point in the expanded core. Essays that have a high degree of analysis and historical context often earn expanded core points if they have all of the other basic core points. Clarity of organization, strong cause-effect analysis, and particularly insightful ideas can make your essay stand out as excellent.

Examples:

✦ Example One: Multiple comparisons between the Japanese and Russian approaches to political centralization could earn points in the expanded core.
✦ Example Two: A detailed explanation of the military systems of both Spain and the Ottoman Empire could earn points in the expanded core.
✦ Example Three: A thorough analysis of how the ruling styles of both China and France led to increasing political power could earn points in the expanded core.

PERIOD FIVE
Industrialization and Global Integration, c. 1750 to c. 1900

PART FIVE
The European Moment in World History, 1750–1914

AP World History Key Concepts

5.1: Industrialization and Global Capitalism

5.2: Imperialism and Nation-State Formation

5.3: Nationalism, Revolution, and Reform

5.4: Global Migration

The Big Picture: European Centrality and the Problem of Eurocentrism

The "long nineteenth century" has also been called the European century because of the dominance of Europe on the world stage. Chapters 16 and 17 explore the theme of modernity—the creation of a new form of human society following the Scientific, French, and Industrial revolutions—that envisioned social and gender equality, an end to slavery, and participation by common people in government. At the same time, through industrialization, European societies reshaped the planet in a manner paralleled only by the Agricultural Revolution. Chapters 18 and 19 explore how these modern European societies exercised their power either directly in empires or indirectly through economic penetration, missionary activity, and military intervention.

By making the prime meridian run through Greenwich, England, Europeans reformulated geography to place themselves literally at the center of the map. In addition, textbooks and historians were also Europe-centered, downplaying the contributions of other civilizations and emphasizing the role of Europe in the race for progress and modernization. With the development of the discipline of world history after World War II, the key question became: "How can we avoid an inappropriate Eurocentrism when dealing with a phase of world history in which Europeans were in fact central?" World history places the European moment, without denying its importance, in the context of continuing patterns of historical development.

✦ The European moment in world history has been both recent and brief, and other societies have had long periods of regional influence, such as the Greeks, Arabs, Chinese, Mongols, Incas, and Aztecs. While Europeans were the first to exercise this influence on a global scale, events at the end of the twentieth and the beginning of the twenty-first centuries indicate an erosion of European power.

✦ Europe's rise occurred in a global context: the Chinese withdrew their fleet from the Indian Ocean; Native Americans lacked immunity to Eurasian diseases and were weakened by internal strife; and the Industrial Revolution was stimulated by Asian superiority in textile and pottery production and relied on New World resources and markets and the cooperation of local elites.

✦ Europeans faced resistance to their global dominance and were forced to modify their policies in Africa and South Asia.

✦ People around the world adapted European ideas and practices to local circumstances and used these ideas and practices to benefit themselves. For example, the Haitian Revolution used French ideas about the "rights of man"; European ideas of nationalism were used in anti-European, anticolonial movements in Africa and Asia. Hindus used British-introduced railroads to go on pilgrimages; and the industrial development of Japan and Russia followed a different pattern from industrial development in England.

✦ The rise of Europe was not the only thing happening on the world stage during the long nineteenth century. China was absorbing a huge population increase and suffered through peasant rebellions. Muslim and Hindu cultures continued to evolve in India under British rule. And African societies experienced religious wars and wars of state formation.

CHAPTER SIXTEEN

Atlantic Revolutions, Global Echoes, 1750–1914

AP World History Key Concepts

5.1: Industrialization and Global Capitalism

See Chapter 17 for more complete discussion of this key concept.

5.2: Imperialism and Nation-State Formation

II. Imperialism influenced State formation and contraction around the world.

The development and spread of nationalism as an ideology fostered new communal identities. For example, nationalism inspired the unification of Germany and Italy. Nationalism also inspired anti-imperial resistance, which led to the contraction of the Ottoman Empire as Greece and Serbia gained independence. Nationalism also encouraged the "Egypt for Egyptians" movement, which protested British and French intrusion in Egypt. As an ideology, nationalism proved quite flexible and inspired ethnic groups to revolt against the Ottoman, Austrian, and Russian empires. *See Chapters 17 through 19 for more complete discussion of this key concept.*

5.3: Nationalism, Revolution, and Reform

I. The rise and diffusion of Enlightenment thought that questioned established traditions in all areas of life often preceded the revolutions and rebellions against existing governments.

II. Beginning in the eighteenth century, peoples around the world developed a new sense of commonality based on language, religion, social customs, and territory. These newly imagined national communities linked this identity with the borders of the state, while governments used this idea to unite diverse populations.

III. Increasing discontent with imperial rule propelled reformist and revolutionary movements.

IV. The global spread of European political and social thought and the increasing number of rebellions stimulated new transnational ideologies and solidarities.

Enlightenment ideals of progress and perfectibility—the notion that society and government could be improved by rational human efforts—led to the idea of natural rights such as liberty, equality before the law, free trade, religious toleration, and republicanism. Further, Enlightenment thinkers challenged established beliefs in the divine right of kings, mercantilism, aristocratic privilege, and church authority. These ideals spread rapidly through newspapers, pamphlets, and books, not only across the Atlantic to colonies of France, Spain, Britain, and Portugal, but also to areas outside of the Atlantic world. Colonial rebellions occurred in British North America and Spain's American colonies. France went through a revolution that had far-reaching implications; not only did their revolution create a more radical society than those in the Americas, but France, through its conquering armies under Napoleon, spread its revolutionary ideals to Eastern Europe and Russia. Haiti, France's lucrative Caribbean colony, rose up in the only successful slave rebellion in history, partly basing the rebellion on Enlightenment ideas.

Other consequences of the Atlantic revolutions and Enlightenment ideals included other liberation movements, like abolition and feminism. An unintended consequence of Napoleon's conquering armies was the spread of French ideals of liberty, equality, and fraternity and the rise of nationalism in Eastern Europe in opposition to French occupation. Nationalism involved the redirecting of individual loyalties from family, clan, and village to loyalty to a nation-state, reinforced by the government through schools, public rituals, mass media, compulsory military service, and official state languages. Ethnic nationalism became a potent force that threatened diverse empires such as the Ottoman, Russian, Austrian, and Chinese.

5.4: Global Migration

II. Migrants relocated for a variety of reasons.

Europeans continued to migrate for economic reasons to colonies or to industrializing urban centers in Europe. Following rebellions in the Americas, some people (usually elites who had "lost" in the rebellion) either migrated back to the mother country or went into exile. Indentured laborers were imported from Asia to take over work formerly performed by slaves. *See Chapters 18 through 19 for more complete discussion of this key concept.*

Theme 1: Interaction Between Humans and the Environment

Political revolutions in the Atlantic world and Enlightenment ideals had environmental ramifications. The Haitian Revolution, the only successful slave rebellion, led to the destruction of large plantations and the division of the land into small farms for freed slaves. Instead of producing export crops such as sugar or coffee, these small farms now produced food for local consumption. In addition, the end of slavery in the Americas led to indentured servitude to supply labor for mines, construction, and plantations in the Caribbean, Peru, South Africa, Hawaii, and Malaysia. *See Chapter 17 for discussion of the consequences of the Industrial Revolution on the environment.*

Theme 2: Development and Interaction of Cultures

The French Revolution had far-reaching effects on all parts of French society and culture. In a foment of anti-clericalism, the new revolutionary government made priests employees of the state and temporarily turned the Cathedral of Notre Dame into the Temple of Reason. Control of education shifted from church to state in order to better inculcate nationalist and revolutionary ideals. Romantic poets such as William Wordsworth (an Englishman) wrote sonnets praising the Revolution as a new beginning for humanity. Newly-awakened nationalist groups often built a sense of cultural and ethnic identity by appealing to their shared linguistic and cultural past through folktales, music, dances, and traditions (the famous Grimm's collection of fairytales are an example). Artists and writers also supported liberal social movements. Henrik Ibsen's play *A Doll's House*, for example, generated discussion on the role of women in society. *See Chapters 18 and 19 for detailed discussion of cultural interaction in this period.*

Theme 3: State-Building, Expansion, and Conflict

The Atlantic revolutions took place in a global context, including the collapse of the Safavid dynasty in Persia, the fragmentation of the Mughal Empire, peasant revolts in Russia and China, Islamic revolutions in West Africa, and the *mfecane* movement (a series of wars and migrations) in southern Africa. However, the Atlantic revolutions were distinctive in that the wars were global rather than regional and were connected to each other, both philosophically (they were based on Enlightenment ideals like the possibility of creating a better government based on liberty, religious tolerance, equality, popular sovereignty, and free trade) and directly, through correspondence between revolutionary leaders and financial and military aid. John Locke articulated his belief that a social contract existed between the ruler and the ruled, and that if the government no longer protected the natural rights of the people, they had the right to change the government. The Atlantic Revolutions also had global impact, carrying ideas about equality, abolition of slavery, extension of the franchise, constitutional government, and nationalism around the world.

There were, however, differences in the revolutions, based on the specific circumstances of each region. The American Revolution was the first, ending in a constitution and a federal government that expanded participation to many white males and a Bill of Rights designed to protect individual rights against the power of a strong state. The Americans had benefitted from a period of benign neglect while England pursued its political affairs on the Continent; they developed a series of local assemblies dominated by local property owners and merchants and came to consider this autonomy to be part of their rights as Englishmen. With a lack of entrenched nobility and established church and with more economic opportunity and readily available land, Americans had less poverty and more social mobility than most other regions. Rebellion grew out of the sudden effort of the British to reestablish political control over the colonies and to raise revenue to pay for its struggle with France. Using Enlightenment ideas such as popular sovereignty, natural rights, and consent of the governed, the Americans rebelled. There was no major social reformation; government remained in the hands of the existing elite with a widening of the franchise to many white men, slavery was not abolished, and voting rights were not extended to women and people of color. One of the most important and globally influential aspects of the revolution was stated in the Declaration of Independence; the right of people to resort to revolution to protect natural rights. That pronouncement, along with the model of the Constitution and Bill of Rights (which set forth separation of church and state, republican government, protection of individual rights, and checks and balances) showed that Enlightenment ideals could be the basis of government.

The French Revolution a few years later was in part caused by the fiscal crisis precipitated by French support for the American rebels against England. French soldiers returned from North America filled with revolutionary ideals. When the king attempted to deal with the fiscal crisis by calling the Estates General into session, the Third Estate quickly took control and reconstituted itself as a National Assembly, which drew up the Declaration of the Rights of Man and Citizen, based on ideas from Enlightenment thinkers and the example of the Americans. This revolution was more "personal" than the Americans' rebellion against a monarch across the ocean; French nobles and the clergy had prerogatives and feudal rights that prevented the rising middle class or rural peasants from prospering, and urban workers suffered from a drop in income and rising prices for bread. The conflict between classes led to a more violent revolution and one that had profound social implications. Those representing the *ancien régime* (the old order) were overthrown or executed, including the king and queen. Church lands were confiscated and sold, priests were placed under the control of the state, and education was secularized to indoctrinate children with revolutionary ideals. French revolutionaries did not seek to restore their rights, as had the Americans, but rather to demolish the old order and create something new. They created a republic, reformed administrative structures, declared freedom of worship for Jews and Protestants, created a standing army based on universal draft, and abolished all remaining feudal obligations and social distinctions. The revolution faced military opposition from other European countries, who feared that the notion of beheading a king might catch on elsewhere. Within France, fear of antirevolutionary movements led to the Reign of Terror. As much as French men benefitted, they failed to make significant changes for women despite women's enthusiastic support for the revolution. The ideals of the revolution—liberty, equality, and fraternity—were spread by Napoleon and the French army throughout most of Europe. The society that emerged under the leadership of the Emperor Napoleon preserved civil equality, the secular legal system, and religious freedom but under a military dictatorship. Resentment of French domination created a sense of nationalism in subjected countries (such as the German states in the Austrian Empire), while military resistance from Britain and Russia ultimately led to Napoleon's defeat.

Revolutionary ideology spread to French colonies: Saint Domingue (later Haiti) was a rich sugar colony that was controlled by a small number of white planters (*grands blancs*) who wanted freedom from French control, less affluent white men (*petits blancs*) who wanted legal equality with the *grands blancs*, freedmen who wanted equality with white Haitians, and a large number of slaves, subjected to extremely brutal conditions, who wanted slavery abolished. Slaves burned plantations and killed white landowners and mixed-race people. A former slave, Toussaint Louverture, took control and resisted both the French and the landowners. The Haitian Revolution thus became the only successful slave rebellion in history. The new government became the second independent republic in the Americas and leant its support to the rebellions in the Spanish colonies on the condition that newly established governments free all slaves. All Haitians were declared equal before the law and defined as "black." Haiti's example led to the fear of other slave revolts, leading to a socially conservative elite in Latin America.

Rebellions in mainland Latin America were led primarily by elite creoles (people of pure European ancestry, born in the Americas) who resented Spain's attempts to dominate its colonies and increase revenue through high taxes and tariffs. Creole intellectuals had absorbed Enlightenment ideas of popular sovereignty, personal liberty, and republican government, but geographical obstacles and regionalism prevented the scattered rebellions from joining forces as had the thirteen North American colonies. Latin American revolutions were also more conservative because Spanish rule had been more authoritarian than British rule, class divisions were more pronounced, and white settlers were vastly outnumbered by Native Americans, African descendants, and mestizos (people of mixed Native American and European ancestry). With the conquest of Spain and Portugal by Napoleon, however, creole elites were forced into action. Latin American revolutions also included internal class struggles and were not simply rebellions against colonial rule. An alliance of the military and church with the elites provided some assurance that a social rebellion would not prevail. Nationalism was used by leaders such as Simón Bolivar as a means of getting the support of lower classes in the rebellion against Spanish rule—and many of the leaders were actually liberals with Enlightenment leanings—but little social reform actually resulted from these independence movements. *Also see Chapters 17 through 19 for discussion of imperial expansion and conflict.*

Theme 4: Creation, Expansion, and Interaction of Economic Systems

See Chapter 17 for discussion of the Industrial Revolution and its consequences.

Theme 5: Development and Transformation of Social Structures

The various revolutions in this period had different effects on social structures, depending in part on the causes and on the leaders of the revolution. The Haitian Revolution was the most racially and socially radical; slaves and freedmen violently overthrew French colonial rule and killed many of the detested plantation owners, all of the citizens of the new Haiti were declared to be black (even if they were of mixed European and African ancestry), and legal equality was enforced. From a nation of social and racial extremes, Haiti became a nation of small, often-impoverished farmers.

The least radical revolution socially was that of the British North American colonists. Due to long neglect by the British crown (which was more involved in its more lucrative Caribbean colonies and conflict with France), American colonists had developed a society based on "the rights of Englishmen," with a large amount of local self-government. While wealthy men such as Washington or Adams were the leaders of the rebellion, the absence of entrenched nobility or an established church and the availability of "free" land led to a society that had fewer distinctions than most others in the world at the time—for free white men, that is. When the Americans rebelled, it was not against social inequality within the Americas, but against the crown's attempt to reimpose direct rule and raise taxes. The social structure changed little because of the rebellion, only gradually widening participation in government to include all white males. Slavery remained intact in southern states, and women were not given political rights under the new Constitution. The abolition movement, both in England and the northern states, gradually gained momentum, but the actual freeing of slaves awaited the Civil War.

The rebellions of Spanish creoles against Spanish rule also had little effect on their societies; creoles simply replaced the *peninsulares* (people of European ancestry born in

Spain) at the top of the social structure as the owners of land and wealth. Slaves were freed, but people of color retained their place at the bottom of the social scale.

The French Revolution was truly a revolution of social classes; the Third Estate revolted against the dual "oppressors" of the clergy and nobility. The first liberal phase of the revolution was led by the middle class (such as doctors, judges, lawyers, merchants, and bureaucrats) with some allies from the lower nobility and clergy. It was based on Enlightenment ideals and moved toward equality before the law and a society where merit determined social rank. The revolution quickly became more radical with power shifting to urban "mobs" and peasant revolts. This more radical phase of the revolution ended special taxes and feudal prerogatives and work obligations of the peasantry, confiscated and sold church land, granted toleration to Jews and Protestants, executed the king and queen, set up universal male suffrage and a republican government, and then turned to devour itself under the Reign of Terror. Napoleon took control and retained the ideal of social equality but left little individual freedom under his military rule.

Russia, inspired both by Enlightenment ideals and the desire to modernize, freed its serfs and gave them portions of the nobles' land. Most peasants, however, remained impoverished, due to the growth in rural population and the imposition of new taxes and duties. This burden added to the social unrest in late nineteenth- and early twentieth-century Russia.

While some Enlightenment thinkers favored equality for women, none of the revolutions improved women's social and legal status. In the Americas, women did not receive voting rights or the right to participate in the new governments, even though they often helped raise money and supported the revolutionary movements. The French Revolution saw profound participation by urban women—from the storming of the Bastille, to the march of women on Versailles to obtain bread for their children, to the revolutionary activities of women such as Olympe de Gouges (who proposed that women should have the same political rights as men). However, even radical revolutionaries declared that women should remain under the control of men and out of the political world. Englishwoman Mary Wollstonecraft responded with *Vindication of the Rights of Woman*, an early expression of feminist sentiment. Though the new governments did not include equality for women, the movement for equal rights grew. The Seneca Falls Conference in New York in 1848 demanded legal equality and suffrage for women, as well as equal access to schools and universities. By 1900, some women had been admitted to universities and the learned professions, but suffrage was delayed in most countries until after World War I.

CHAPTER SEVENTEEN

Revolutions of Industrialization, 1750–1914

AP World History Key Concepts

5.1: Industrialization and Global Capitalism

I. Industrialization fundamentally changed how goods were produced.

II. New patterns of global trade and production developed and further integrated the global economy as industrialists sought raw materials and new markets for the increasing amount and array of goods produced in their factories.

III. To facilitate investments at all levels of industrial production, financiers developed and expanded various financial institutions.

IV. There were major developments in transportation and communication.

V. The development and spread of global capitalism led to a variety of responses.

VI. The ways in which people organized themselves into societies also underwent significant transformations in industrialized states due to the fundamental restructuring of the global economy.

The Industrial Revolution, the most significant change in how humans live since the beginning of agriculture, involved the switching of energy sources from wind, water, and muscle power to machines powered by steam and later electricity. Beginning with the production of machine-made textiles in Britain, factories produced large amounts of goods more cheaply than could be done by individual craftsmen. Innovation piled on innovation, rapidly changing all facets of manufacturing and also changing the way people lived.

The development of the steam engine provided new sources of power for factories and led to new methods of transportation like the steamship or railroad. These new methods of transportation allowed access to raw materials and markets around the world. Global trade fed cash crops and raw materials to the factories of Europe and North America, where manufactured goods were produced to be sold at a profit on the world market as well as to internal markets to consumers who now had more income as industrial workers, and, after an initial drop, the standard of living in industrial countries rose.

Nations pursued different paths to industrialize: Western Europe, especially Britain, had governments and legal systems largely responsive to the interests of financiers and commercial classes, growing populations, available capital (largely from overseas enterprises), raw materials, and a respect for science and technology. The United States created the most favorable climate for large corporations to emerge with little government regulation, while Russian industrialization came at the direction of an autocratic ruler. All industrializing countries saw major social reorganization—some with turmoil that was moderated with the gradual inclusion of workers' interests in government, and some with violent revolution when no such accommodation was made.

5.2 Imperialism and Nation-State Formation

See Chapters 16, 18, and 19 for discussion of this key concept.

5.3 Nationalism, Revolution, and Reform

See Chapter 16 for discussion of this key concept.

5.4: Global Migration

I. Migration in many cases was influenced by changes in demography in both industrialized and unindustrialized societies that presented challenges to existing patterns of living.

II. Migrants relocated for a variety of reasons.

III. The large-scale nature of migration, especially in the nineteenth century, produced a variety of consequences and reactions to the increasingly diverse societies on the part of migrants and the existing populations.

The global age saw global migration. Industrial states saw internal migration of displaced agricultural labor to cities, where people looked for jobs in new industries or as domestic servants. In addition, population growth in Europe led to migration to colonies, some of which became settler colonies such as Australia, New Zealand, and North America. Some Europeans also migrated to newly acquired empires (such as India or South Africa). Thriving industrial countries such as the United States, which also had vast amounts of sparsely occupied land, encouraged immigration of Europeans as well as indentured labor from Asia. Latin American countries, such as Argentina and Brazil, encouraged migration of Europeans, mostly from Spain, Portugal, and Italy. Not all of these migrants remained in the New World, and many returned to their homelands after a few years.

Theme 1: Interaction Between Humans and the Environment

The Industrial Revolution that began in Europe, specifically in England, had such an impact on the environment that some scientists call the last 250 years the Anthropocene Age or the Age of Man. For the first time in human history, energy was not created by muscle power or renewable resources such as wood, wind, and water. On the positive side, technological innovation increased rapidly, partly spurred by population pressure and the subsequent depletion of wood as a fuel, and partly by stimulation from technological innovations such as textiles from China and India. New methods in agriculture (such as crop rotation, selective breeding of animals, higher-yield seeds, and lighter plows) and technology (such as chemical fertilizers, pesticides, mechanical reapers, and refrigeration) also helped increase the food supply while decreasing the need for rural labor. On the negative side, the extraction of nonrenewable raw materials (such as coal, iron, petroleum, copper, and tin) altered the landscape. Increased urban density, the use of fossil fuels (such as coal for steam engines and heating) and industrial waste led to water and air pollution, which in turn increased human diseases such as respiratory illness, typhoid, and dysentery.

The Industrial Revolution also contributed to population movement. Internal migration continued as displaced rural workers moved to urban areas where they hoped to find work. Western Europeans also migrated to North and South America, Australia and New Zealand, and South Africa. European Russians migrated to Siberia, largely replacing native Siberians. These migrations were caused by population pressure, poverty, the displacement of peasant farmers, the need for labor overseas, the availability of land (especially in North America), and declining costs and time involved in transportation by railroad or steamship.

Theme 2: Development and Interaction of Cultures

See Chapters 16, 18, and 19 for discussion of this theme.

Theme 3: State-Building, Expansion, and Conflict

Western European states, unlike Asian empires, were relatively small and decentralized. They engaged in hefty competition, both in dynastic wars within Europe and in colonial enterprises outside of Europe. Western European monarchs, especially the British, circumvented resistant land-based aristocrats and the church and instead forged ties with the commercial middle class to more efficiently obtain power and income for the costs of keeping a standing army and supplying the basic needs of government.

The government of Great Britain especially came under the control of and was favorable to the commercial class, sidelining the traditional aristocracy, although British nobles were far more likely than those in other countries to invest in lands and commerce, and later in industry. The English crown granted charters not only to cities but also to companies and corporations in exchange for much-needed cash. The government also protected inventions, sponsored scientific societies and "practical" universities where new discoveries could be shared, suppressed labor unions and strikes, set tariffs to benefit local industry or landowners, provided support for shipping by improving ports and creating a powerful navy, passed laws and regulations favorable to industry and trade, and promoted immigration of skilled craftsmen regardless of religion.

Countries such as the United States also supported the creators of industry with tax breaks, grants of land to railroads, laws favoring the formation of corporations, and patents to protect innovation. No major political party emerged in the United States to support workers, unlike in Britain and Germany where socialist and labor parties reflected the interests of the newly enfranchised working class.

Russia was the only country in Europe to be ruled by an absolute monarch. The tsars ordered creation of railroads and heavy industry but did not allow the workers to have any voice in working conditions or government. There were no legal political parties, so no labor or socialist parties could form to represent workers. Large-scale strikes erupted along with an uprising in 1905 involving workers, peasants, intellectuals, students, and the military. The revolution was suppressed. In the aftermath, a few reforms were instituted, but they were not enough to relieve the growing social unrest that led to the Russian Revolution in 1917. Russia was the only society that had a violent revolution as part of its process of industrialization.

Latin American countries were beset by internal revolts and conflicts. Conservatives, mostly large landowners allied with military officers and the church, favored centralized authority, military support, and maintenance of the status quo socially and economically. Liberals preferred federalism, attacked the power of the church, and wanted limited social reforms. Conflicts often led to military rule under *caudillos* to restore order. Constitutions were written and then discarded, only to be rewritten again. Creoles remained in charge and benefitted economically, largely from the sale of cash crops and ore. Governments protected the interests of foreign owners, such as the United Fruit Company, and became known as "banana republics." This dependency on foreign markets and investors was seen as a new form of economic colonialism. Europeans, largely displaced peasants, were also encouraged to immigrate to work the *haciendas* (plantations and ranches). Mexico endured years of dictatorial rule with violent revolts that erupted into a revolution in the early twentieth century: middle class liberals joined with workers and peasants to overthrow the dictator, Porfirio Díaz. Their new constitution created universal male suffrage, instituted land reform, limited foreign ownership, and curtailed the role of the church by removing education from its control. *See Chapters 18 and 19 for discussion of imperialism in Africa and Asia.*

Theme 4: Creation, Expansion, and Interaction of Economic Systems

The combination of scientific and technological advances that led to the Industrial Revolution began in Great Britain and rapidly spread to Western Europe, North America, and beyond. Factors that contributed to Britain's economic development included the following:

- ✦ access to wealth from colonies in the Caribbean, North America, and India
- ✦ a highly commercialized economy favoring innovation
- ✦ a growing population
- ✦ an aristocratic class that was willing to invest in commerce and industry
- ✦ a large merchant fleet protected by the powerful British navy
- ✦ a political system that was favorable to and encouraged economic innovation, including patent laws, control of Parliament by commercial interests, checks on the power of the king, and willingness to impose protective tariffs and suppress workers' strikes
- ✦ a legal system that made it easy to form corporations
- ✦ existing infrastructure such as roads and canals
- ✦ science and learned societies that sponsored practical discoveries and "useful knowledge"
- ✦ a geographical location as an island on the Atlantic coast of Europe that protected Britain from continental wars
- ✦ possession of natural resources, especially coal and iron
- ✦ a relatively fluid social structure

The Industrial Revolution first manifested itself in the textile industry, then moved to the large-scale production of steel and steam-powered engines, including turbines, to run machines in factories as well as locomotives and steamships. The second phase of the Industrial Revolution centered on electricity as a power source, chemicals, and inventions in communication such as the telegraph and telephone. Overseas colonies were exploited for raw materials and used as markets for new manufactured goods.

Other countries followed Britain in industrializing, but each developed its own pattern. In the United States, the textile mills of New England were the first to develop, but the pace of industrial development increased rapidly following the Civil War and the development of the transcontinental railroad system. By 1914, the United States—because of its vast internal market, availability of raw materials and foreign capital, and sympathetic government regulations which allowed huge corporations such as U.S. Steel to dominate the market—produced a volume of manufactured goods equal to that of Britain, Germany, and France combined. The U.S. made its own contributions to industrialization such as mass production (using assembly lines and interchangeable parts), scientific management, and advertising.

After losses in the Crimean War, autocratic Russia sought economic improvement through top-down measures. The Russian tsar freed the serfs, supported heavy industry, invested in building railroads, and encouraged foreign capital and technological expertise.

Latin America did not undergo significant industrialization in the nineteenth century. Instead, conservative landowning elites provided raw materials and cash crops to the world market. Economic growth in Latin America was financed by foreign capital and depended on decisions made in Europe and North America, a form of economic colonialism.

Theme 5: Development and Transformation of Social Structures

Industrialization radically changed the social structure of countries; it was the first major change of social structures since the First Civilizations developed agriculture and a stratified society based on the ownership of land. Britain was the first industrialized nation, and its class system changed with some internal turmoil, but without a revolution. The landowning aristocracy continued to control much of the land, leased to tenant farmers, and profited from the rapidly growing population's need for food. The aristocracy slowly declined, however, as wealthy urban dwellers (bankers, financiers, manufacturers, and business owners) became more dominant. By the end of the nineteenth century, business held control of the government, but aristocrats still retained high social prestige.

The middle class grew not only in numbers but in importance. It was composed of those in many professions that did not exist in prior centuries as well as more traditional university-educated men (and much later women). The upper middle class—bankers, factory and mine owners, and merchants—often assimilated or married into the aristocracy. The wealthier middle classes also often held political office and sent their sons to prestigious universities, such as Oxford or Cambridge. The more numerous "middle" middle class was made up of educated professionals, such as doctors, lawyers, engineers, scientists, teachers, journalists, and smaller business owners. Members of the middle classes often supported liberalism, characterized by support for constitutional government, private property, free trade, and moderate social reform. They also championed respectability, combining notions of social class, virtuous behavior, thrift, and hard work. Many came to believe that they prospered because of their enterprising spirit and that the poverty that others suffered was caused by laziness, intemperance, or misconduct.

Wealthier middle-class women moved almost exclusively into domestic roles and became the primary arbiters of family consumption. They managed households run by servants, supervised childrearing, engaged in charitable activities, and pursued "refined" tasks such as music, embroidery, or drawing.

Lower middle-class families distinguished themselves from the laboring classes by working in service sector jobs. Many of these jobs (such as telephone operator or secretary) became the exclusive domain of women and were paid lower and had less prestige than jobs held by men. Lower middle-class women often left the workforce after marriage and certainly after having children.

The working class varied greatly, from highly skilled craftsmen at the top to unskilled laborers at the bottom. Their lives were often confined to urban slums which were overcrowded, filthy, polluted, and disease ridden. One of the major public works undertaken during the nineteenth century was the creation of sewers and clean, piped water in London. The pace and conditions of labor changed drastically for people who moved from rural areas into factories; machines set the pace, breaks were few, hours were long, working conditions hazardous, and discipline was strictly enforced by managers.

Women and children were among the first factory workers in textile mills and in the coal mines. Women were not permitted in supervisory positions, nor were they welcome in labor organizations. Those who did not work in factories often found jobs as domestic servants. Upon marriage, a working-class husband expected his wife to remain at home, but she continued to contribute to the family income by doing laundry, sewing, or taking in borders in addition to the domestic tasks she performed for her family.

Because of often intolerable working conditions, workers (especially skilled workers) sometimes responded by organizing associations or labor unions, pushing for political reform and voting rights. There were also occasional strikes and protests that at times included destroying the machines. Government forces put down strikes and violence. Reformers called for better treatment; Robert Owen created a model factory town for his workers in New Lanark, Scotland, while more radical socialists such as Karl Marx believed that a class revolt, in which workers would seize control of society from the "capitalists" who oppressed them, was imminent. The rise of labor parties and broadening of the right to vote diffused revolutionary movements among workers in Western Europe, as did improving working conditions and a higher standard of living.

Nationalism also helped diffuse class tensions by encouraging laborers to identify as German, French, or English and not as members of an international class of workers. Social equality eroded in the United States after industrialization, and some people saw the inequalities as an example of "survival of the fittest." Only in Russia did actual class revolution take place (see Chapter 21).

CHAPTER EIGHTEEN

Colonial Encounters in Asia and Africa, 1750–1950

AP World History Key Concepts

5.1: Industrialization and Global Capitalism

I. Industrialization fundamentally changed how goods were produced.

II. New patterns of global trade and production developed and further integrated the global economy as industrialists sought raw materials and new markets for the increasing amount and array of goods produced in their factories.

III. To facilitate investments at all levels of industrial production, financiers developed and expanded various financial institutions.

IV. There were major developments in transportation and communication.

V. The development and spread of global capitalism led to a variety of responses.

VI. The ways in which people organized themselves into societies also underwent significant transformations in industrialized states due to the fundamental restructuring of the global economy.

The "new imperialism" brought much of the world into global trade networks in the nineteenth century, either through direct colonial rule or through economic colonialism. New methods of transportation such as steamships, canals, and railroads greatly reduced the amount of time needed to move goods from the far corners of the earth back to the industrialized nations. Refrigeration allowed food crops to be moved long distances as well. The undersea telegraph cable allowed far-flung economic and governmental institutions to have almost instantaneous access to information.

Newly industrialized countries of Europe, Japan, and the United States sought new sources of raw materials and markets for their manufactured goods. European countries used their surplus capital to invest in building infrastructure such as railroads and canals in their colonies and in "little Europes," regions such as Argentina or the United States where native people had largely been replaced with those of European stock. Some regions, such as the African Congo under King Leopold II of Belgium, forced villagers to go into the forest to collect rubber instead of growing food crops. In Dutch-controlled Indonesia, the culture system—an economic system where landowners could require local farmers to grow export crops as a means to pay their taxes—limited people's ability to grow enough food and led to famine. The demand for cash crops spurred the growth of plantation agriculture in many colonies, displacing small subsistence farms and forcing the local people to work for low wages on these large farms. Some regions, such as British South Africa, also moved native men into mining camps to extract mineral resources under harsh conditions. Often, native people were forced onto marginal "homelands," such as Bantustans in South Africa or reservations in the United States, and were subject to restrictions on movement and limitations of rights. In South Africa, the large but still minority white population set up strict legal separation between races known as apartheid.

5.2: Imperialism and Nation-State Formation

I. Industrializing powers established transoceanic empires.

II. Imperialism influenced state formation and contraction around the world.

III. New racial ideologies, especially Social Darwinism, facilitated and justified imperialism.

Competition between industrialized nations for sources of raw materials, markets for manufactured goods, and places to invest capital brought most of Africa, India, Oceania, and parts of Southeast Asia under direct rule. Often, colonization followed trading companies such as the British East India or Dutch East India companies. New, supposedly scientific racial theories, including social Darwinism, were used to justify subjugating less technologically advanced regions as was the stated desire to spread what Europeans viewed as their superior civilization and religion. The already-weakened Mughal Empire lost control of most of India to the British. In South Africa, both the Boers, who were descendants of Dutch cape-colony farmers, and the Zulus were defeated by the British, who also established settler colonies in Australia and New Zealand. An industrializing and modernizing Japan staked out its claim to imperial status by colonizing Korea and Taiwan. Southeast Asian kingdoms, including Vietnam, lost sovereignty to the French, who also conquered large expanses of land in northern Africa. Russia and the United States continued their transcontinental territorial expansion as well, replacing and isolating indigenous people.

5.3: Nationalism, Revolution, and Reform

I. The rise and diffusion of Enlightenment thought that questioned established traditions in all areas of life often preceded the revolutions and rebellions against existing governments.

See Chapter 16 for further discussion of this key concept.

II. Beginning in the eighteenth century, peoples around the world developed a new sense of commonality based on language, religion, social customs, and territory. These newly imagined national communities linked this identity with the borders of the state, while governments used this idea to unite diverse populations.

See Chapters 16, 17, and 19 for further discussion of this key concept.

III. Increasing discontent with imperial rule propelled reformist and revolutionary movements.

See Chapter 16 for further discussion of this key concept.

IV. The global spread of European political and social thought and the increasing number of rebellions stimulated new transnational ideologies and solidarities.

Just as Napoleon's advancing French armies spurred the rise of nationalism in conquered territories of Eastern Europe, so too did New Imperialism spread reactions that ultimately led to anticolonial movements. Some local elites found that cooperation with European rulers allowed them to maintain their elite status and gave them limited autonomy. Other groups, such as the Zulu, Shona, or Ethiopians, fought colonial takeover or rebelled against colonial rule. See Map 18.1, page 886, for Asian colonies and rebellions, and Map 18.2, page 887, for African colonies and rebellions. European-educated colonial men also learned about the ideals of self-determination, constitutional government, and protection of individual rights, which led them to question why those rights did not apply to people in colonies. They later formed a cadre of liberal voices seeking independence and nationhood. Europeans often created new ethnic identities in the regions they conquered to facilitate governing, such as creating tribal units in Africa based on linguistic groups. These ethnic identities often later formed the basis of anticolonial resistance or even attempted new definitions such as pan-Africanism. *See Chapters 16, 17, and 19 for further discussion of this key concept.*

5.4: Global Migration

I. Migration in many cases was influenced by changes in demography in both industrialized and unindustrialized societies that presented challenges to existing patterns of living.

II. Migrants relocated for a variety of reasons.

III. The large-scale nature of migration, especially in the nineteenth century, produced a variety of consequences and reactions to the increasingly diverse societies on the part of migrants and the existing populations.

Several types of migration took place during the nineteenth century. The growth of cities accelerated, whether by displaced rural workers seeking employment in industry or by the migration of displaced people to colonial capitals such as Lagos, Batavia, Calcutta, or Singapore. The colonial creation of a cash economy required local people to work for wages, often living in barracks-like arrangements far from home villages to be near plantations or mines; this arrangement was especially common in South Africa. Empires also encouraged long-distance movements of people to other colonies in order to meet labor needs; for example, some Indians and Chinese were transported by the British to work in plantations in the Caribbean or Southeast Asia, sometimes replacing the labor of freed slaves. Since many of the migrants were young, able-bodied men, gender and family life in home villages was disrupted. Women often maintained traditional female tasks while also taking on previously male tasks, and polygyny (the practice of having more than one wife) increased in some regions.

Europeans also migrated to colonies whether as administrators or (to improve their standard of living) as plantation owners. Some Europeans came to settler colonies, such as Australia, New Zealand, North America, and Argentina, and largely replaced local peoples. Displaced rural peasants from countries such as Italy were invited to migrate to Latin American countries to work in agriculture; often they remained for a while and then returned to Europe. Not all migrants were welcomed by existing residents who saw this new labor source as a threat. Anti-immigrant movements formed and some governments enforced limitations on immigration from certain countries, as the United States did when it limited the number of Chinese immigrants.

Theme 1: Interaction Between Humans and the Environment

The need of industrialized nations for raw materials and cash crops led to environmental degradation in both Africa and Asia. In the Irrawaddy and Mekong River deltas of Southeast Asia, British and French colonizers encouraged massive rice production by improving irrigation and transportation and by enacting legislation that favored small farmers. Rice production soared, providing exports to feed people in other areas, but at great environmental cost: mangrove forests and swamps were destroyed, as well as the fish they sheltered, which also cut off a source of food for local people; dikes and canals stopped the flow of nutrient-rich silt into the delta, depleting the soil; and large amounts of methane gas (linked to global warming) was released. In Africa, rich farmlands were taken over by white farmers for plantations, and Africans were often removed to less-desirable land, such as the Bantustans in South Africa. The Bantustans were overcrowded, soil fertility declined, and forests were cut from hillsides, leading to erosion.

Another environmental consequence was the massive movement of people, sometimes in search of improving their financial situation and sometimes at the behest of colonial powers. Colonial administrations demanded cash to pay taxes and fees, while at the same time, native people were removed from the richest farmland. Millions of these displaced people sought work in European-owned plantations and mines, dividing families and upsetting gender balances and roles. Sometimes workers were transported overseas; millions of Indians, Chinese, and Japanese migrated to Southeast Asia to work on plantations growing sugarcane, tea, rubber, tobacco, and sisal (used to make rope). Life was harsh, and pay was low; poverty and disease led to high death rates. British authorities also moved South Asians to the West Indies (Trinidad and Jamaica) where their labor often replaced that of freed slaves. Impoverished Chinese workers went to tin mines in Malaysia and gold mines in Australia, Peru, and California. These migrants were often subjected to discrimination. African and Asian migrants also moved to large, racially segregated cities in the colonial world, hoping to find employment and upward mobility. *See Chapter 17 for discussion of the environmental consequences of the Industrial Revolution.*

Theme 2: Development and Interaction of Cultures

The dominance of Europeans led to cultural changes as groups absorbed European educations, responded to European missionaries, and created new identities. European education was offered in colonies, often at the hands of Christian missionaries, and was seen as a way for native people to modernize and achieve better positions in colonial society. More rarely, young men were sent to Europe for university educations and returned to form the core of doctors, lawyers, and lower-level bureaucrats in their home countries. Europeans viewed this process as a way to "civilize" the natives, bring the fruits of superior European culture, and prepare the way for "progress."

Some people in Asia or Africa embraced European culture, speaking French or English, wearing European clothes, learning about European literature, and seeing themselves as a modernizing vanguard for their societies and potentially as equal partners with Europeans. However, European racism usually prevented true upward mobility for educated colonial subjects, leading to frustration, resentment, and ultimately to anticolonial movements in the twentieth century. In India, western education led to religious reforms, revisiting and reinterpreting Brahmin texts to create a more uniform form of Hinduism out of numerous local beliefs and rituals.

Many colonial subjects received their educations, as well as health care, through missionaries spreading Christianity. Christianity was thus widely associated with modernization and education. Missionaries did create some cultural and social conflicts over gender and sexual activity as they attempted to enforce Western ideas about appropriate behavior. Christianity in Africa became Africanized, which often led missionaries to protest against "backsliding." The newly defined view of Hinduism was offered to the materialistic West as a form of spiritual renewal by Swami Vivekananda, who attended the Parliament of World Religions in 1893. In India, the British supported the Hindu renewal process, which set up future divisions in the subcontinent by Muslims who were thus seen as a separate community.

Perhaps the most profound impact of Western culture was its conception of ethnicity, begun in Europe as a form of nationalism following the revolutionary period, and a newly defined "scientific" view of race. Europeans began to define cultures in Africa and Asia by language and ethnic group, sometimes introducing those concepts for the first time to local people. It was to Europeans' advantage to denigrate African kings by calling them "chiefs" and their kingdoms as "tribes" because tribal culture was seen as less civilized and helped justify European racism and conquest. Later, Africans themselves adopted some of the new linguistic and ethnic identities. *See Chapters 16 and 19 for additional discussion of this theme.*

Theme 3: State-Building, Expansion, and Conflict

The Industrial Revolution and the rise of nationalism sparked a new wave of European expansion known as "new imperialism." Superior factory-made weapons (such as repeating rifles and machine guns), new methods of transportation (such as steamships and railroads), new methods of communication (such as the telegraph), and new medical advances (such as quinine to treat tropical diseases) allowed European empires to acquire most of Africa and much of Asia. In addition, the nationalistic competition between European nations played itself out in the scramble to acquire colonies that might provide raw materials or markets for manufactured goods. European leaders also felt that new markets were needed to keep manufacturing and employment at a high level in order to prevent social upheavals or revolutions.

Imperial powers justified their conquests by claiming they brought progress and the benefits of civilization to lesser peoples and developed a new kind of supposedly scientific racism to further justify their claims to superiority: social Darwinism. Social Darwinism, which was not part of Darwin's theories of evolution, claimed that human cultures operated under the concept of "survival of the fittest," which implied that when technologically superior European nations took over control of other cultures, those cultures were less fit or even racially inferior. It thus became an obligation for Europeans to spread civilization to inferior peoples.

In general, Europeans preferred informal control through economic penetration rather than through direct military conquest, but the threat of European military intervention was always present. In India and Indonesia, for example, the British East India and Dutch East India companies initially took advantage of fragmented local rule to make economically advantageous agreements, only later to be followed up with direct colonial rule as needed to enforce European "rights." Some regions were colonized with little overt conflict among European powers, such as the "scramble for Africa," where

European leaders agreed on which areas of the continent would be open to each country. Although resistance was strong (for example, from the Zulus and Boers), Ethiopia and Liberia were the only African countries to escape colonization. In Southeast Asia, only Siam (now Thailand) managed to retain its independence.

Certain groups perceived benefits in cooperation with colonial powers, including those who wanted to join European military forces or colonial administrations. In addition, in many areas, colonial rulers relied on local intermediaries such as Indian princes, Muslim emirs, or African rulers. Some people rebelled against colonial rule, as in the famous Indian Rebellion of 1857–1858, sometimes known as the Sepoy Mutiny. (See Map 18.1 and Map 18.2 on pp. 886–87 for examples of rebellions in Africa and Asia.)

Australia and New Zealand became British settler colonies like North America. As in North America, the native populations of Australia and New Zealand had been isolated from European diseases and so died at an alarming rate following contact, providing an opportunity for European settlers to replace them. The United States continued its imperial expansion to the west, sometimes exterminating Native Americans or moving them to reservations. Further, wars with Spain and Mexico also increased U.S. land holdings in the west and the Philippine Islands. Some freed American slaves moved to a West African territory they called Liberia and there became a colonial elite. Following European examples, Japan also became an imperial nation after undergoing its own industrialization by taking over Korea and Taiwan. Russia continued its territorial expansion in Central Asia. *See Chapters 17 and 19 for additional discussion of this theme.*

Theme 4: Creation, Expansion, and Interaction of Economic Systems

The New Imperialism brought more regions of the world into the global economy. The search for the raw materials (such as rubber, tin, copper, sisal, cotton, cocoa, and palm oils) needed for industrial development as well as other items that had value in global markets (such as coffee, tea, cacao, sugar, gold, and diamonds) led to colonial expansion. Further, since new sources of food were needed to supply workers in colonial plantations and mines, intensive cultivation of rice and other food crops were encouraged in some regions such as Southeast Asia. Many colonial economies involved forced labor on plantations or in mines or on state projects such as road and railroad building, constructing government buildings, or transporting goods. King Leopold II's Congo colony forced locals to collect rubber under such cruel and brutal conditions that other European states objected and forced Leopold to cede the colony to Belgium. The colonial government of the Dutch-controlled East Indies (now Indonesia) required peasants to cultivate 20 percent of their land in cash crops such as sugar or coffee to pay their taxes to the state, which then sold the products at a great profit on the open market. This cultivation system contributed to famines among the peasants. In German East Africa, peasant sabotage ended the attempt to force local peoples to grow of cotton. *See Chapters 17 and 19 for additional discussion of this theme.*

Theme 5: Development and Transformation of Social Structures

Turning colonies into cash economies as well as using coerced labor or low-paid labor in plantations and mines led to massive upheaval in social and gender roles in Africa. In mining regions, men were brought in for months or years, living apart from their families in barracks. In plantation economies, men were used in the cultivation of cash crops. This left women to assume what had been traditionally male economic roles, such as herding, clearing land, or growing some types of crops, while also maintaining traditional female roles such as childrearing, food preparation, planting, weeding, and harvesting kitchen crops. In some areas, as many as 40 to 50 percent of able-bodied males were absent from rural villages because they were working in mines or on plantations. In some regions, women used this gender imbalance to their advantage, moving into small-scale trade and marketing or growing crops that had cash value and marketing them.

Men educated in Western schools, which were often church-run, formed a new group in colonized countries. Some became colonial civil servants or enlisted in the military or police; others went to Europe to obtain university educations and returned as professionals or journalists, often forming the elite in post-colonial societies. *See Chapters 17 and 19 for additional discussion of this theme.*

CHAPTER NINETEEN
Empires in Collision: Europe, the Middle East, and East Asia, 1800–1914

AP World History Key Concepts

5.1: Industrialization and Global Capitalism

II. New patterns of global trade and production developed and further integrated the global economy as industrialists sought raw materials and new markets for the increasing amount and array of goods produced in their factories.

V. The development and spread of global capitalism led to a variety of responses.

Industrialization and the aggressive expansion of European states changed the Eurasian trading networks. Industrial states sought entry into the large Asia markets for their manufactured goods. At first, China, India, Japan, and the Ottoman Empire resisted these incursions. China especially refused to accept what they viewed as inferior goods in trade for traditional Chinese exports such as silk, tea, and porcelain. In the eighteenth century, China was able to forbid European merchants from entering the interior and limited their contact to a few ports along the coast. In the nineteenth century, however, following a series of rebellions and the Opium Wars, China had to submit to increasing European control of their markets.

Other Asian countries had to compete with European factory-made goods, which drove out local artisans whose work could not compete in price. By using a combination of military might and even smuggling, Europeans were able to force large Asian populations to become markets for factory-made goods and revert to becoming suppliers of raw materials to the factories of the West. While the Ottomans, Chinese, and Mughals attempted to reject, at one level or another, European control of worldwide trade networks, Japan chose to invest massively in creating its own industrial revolution and soon joined the West as a major producer and imperial power.

5.2: Imperialism and Nation-State Formation

I. Industrializing powers established transoceanic empires.

II. Imperialism influenced state formation and contraction around the world.

Asian empires, with the exception of the already fragmented Mughal Empire, did not succumb to direct colonization by Western industrial powers. Instead, they became "economic colonies" whose governments were unable to protect their people from economic exploitation. Forced to submit to unequal treaties requiring favorable trade concessions, the Qing dynasty and the Ottoman Empire were further weakened politically. Newly emerging ethnic nationalism led sections of the Ottoman Empire to revolt and break away. Japan, faced with similar threats from industrialized Western states, underwent radical political, economic, and social modernization and became an imperial state in its own right.

5.3: Nationalism, Revolution and Reform

III. Increasing discontent with imperial rule propelled reformist and revolutionary movements.

IV. The global spread of European political and social thought and the increasing number of rebellions stimulated new transnational ideologies and solidarities.

At the same time that they faced threats from Western powers, the Ottoman Empire and the Qing dynasty in China faced internal challenges as well. The Ottomans faced rebellion from ethnic nationalist groups within the empire, especially in the Balkans and Egypt, while the Qing dynasty was opposed by both peasant revolts and ethnic Chinese who saw the Qing as foreign rulers. The Japanese faced a short-lived regional revolt, but from conservative samurai and not from an ethnic nationalist movement. All three nations, when confronted with aggressive and militarily superior Western states, had to decide the extent to which they would modernize or Westernize their governments and economies. China did not respond until the nineteenth century with a self-strengthening movement, which borrowed "cautiously" from the West, but this movement was diverted by conservative landowning gentry. After the Boxer Uprising, reformists wanted to turn to Western political systems as a model, seeking limited constitutional rule and wider involvement by the people. Chinese nationalism rejected not only Western imperialism but also the foreign Qing dynasty which was overthrown in 1911.

The Ottomans also faced conservative forces such as the Janissaries and *ulama* who were opposed to Westernization and modernization. Reform-minded groups such as the Young Ottomans and the Young Turks believed that Islam was compatible with modernization. The Tanzimat reforms attempted to establish European-style secular courts and legal systems, but the sultan soon returned to autocratic rule. After a military coup, the Young Turks pushed forward with reforms along Western lines: schools and courts were secularized and political parties and elections were introduced. However, the reformers also promoted a national identity based on Turkish language and culture, which further alienated other ethnic groups outside of the Anatolian homeland.

Intense nationalism was also the source of reform in Japan when confronted with Western powers. After succumbing at first to unequal treaties, a group of samurai deposed the shogun and returned the country to rule by the young, reform-minded emperor Meiji. To achieve national unity, the role of the emperor was elevated, and the daimyo and samurai renounced their status and special privileges. A constitution was written in 1889; it was modeled on Germany's constitution, with an elected parliament that was advisory only, political parties, and democratic ideals but with power vested in the military-supported emperor and members of the oligarchy, a select group of men who controlled most decisions.

5.4: Global Migration

See Chapters 17 and 18 for discussion of global migration.

Theme 1: Interaction Between Humans and the Environment

China's population quadrupled between 1650 and 1850 without corresponding gains in agricultural production, leading to ever-smaller peasant farms as well as famine and a series of peasant uprisings. Japan, like other industrial powers, needed increased access to raw materials that could not be supplied in their tiny island nation; as a result, it colonized parts of Manchuria, Korea, and Taiwan. *See Chapters 17 and 18 for a detailed discussion of the impact of the Industrial Revolution and imperialism on this theme.*

Theme 2: Development and Interaction of Cultures

Chinese culture, long centered on Confucian values and the conservative nature of the landed gentry, did not easily adapt to Western intrusions. As Qing society became weaker in the nineteenth century, some argued for a return to traditional Han Chinese culture (in opposition to the Qing dynasty's Manchu culture or borrowing from the West). The charismatic leader Hong Xiuquan, who believed that he was the younger brother of Jesus and supported revolutionary changes in society along with millenarian beliefs, led the Taiping Uprising (1850–1864), rejected Confucian, Daoist, and Buddhist beliefs, and called for a very different society instead of a return to an idealized past.

The Ottoman Empire also rejected much of Western culture, which it felt was inferior to Islamic culture. Both the conservative *ulama* (religious scholars) and the Janissaries rejected reforms, believing that to support modernization meant Westernization, including materialism and Christianity. The Tanzimat reforms, however, included new elementary and secondary schools that were based on European models and a more secular and less Islamic character of the state. Progressive women held salons, similar to those of Enlightenment France, where both male and female intellectuals discussed the future. In Japan, Meiji reformers did not see the need to reject core beliefs in order to embrace modernization, as had many reformers in China and the Ottoman Empire.

Japan selectively adopted Western culture and embraced its educational system, its dances and music, its movies and newspapers, and its dress and hairstyles. Shinto became an official state religion, with the Emperor, who was still viewed as the direct descendent of the sun goddess Amaterasu, at its head.

Theme 3: State-Building, Expansion, and Conflict

Both the Qing dynasty and the Ottoman Empire in the nineteenth century endured contraction, fragmentation, and rebellion in addition to economic and political encroachment by Western industrial and imperial powers, but they maintained formal independence until the twentieth century. Japan, on the other hand, became an imperializing and industrialized nation. All of these states (as well as Persia, Ethiopia, and Siam) had to deal with European military power and the political competition between states; became intertwined with the global networks of capitalism, trade, investment, and migration set up by Western industrial powers; had to adapt to or resist Western culture and languages; and had to determine to what extent they wanted to modernize.

China, under the control of the Qing dynasty (a foreign occupying power from Manchuria), underwent an internal crisis in the nineteenth century. Centralized government gave way to control by local landowners who created their own armies to try to extract more revenue from already destitute peasants. The imperial administration showed the classic signs of a declining dynasty: failure to put down rebellions or protect from foreign incursions plus the inability to collect revenue, prevent floods, prevent corruption, protect internal trade, or ensure that enough food was grown. Peasant revolts such as the Taiping or the Boxer uprisings devastated the country, passed more power to the gentry, and were only put down with the support of Western militaries. The Opium Wars further weakened imperial rule, leading to unequal treaties that also granted territorial and trade concessions to Western powers. China was being dismembered (see Map 19.1, p. 938) and no longer controlled its own destiny.

The Ottoman Empire was similarly in decline and became known as the "sick man of Europe." Ottoman power and territory was diminished by Russian, British, Austrian, and French aggression (See Map 19.2, p. 943), but the Turks managed to avoid direct colonial rule. The Ottoman Empire also suffered from the inability to collect revenue, a loss of control to provincial warlords, and a loss of their military might. However, unlike China, the Ottoman rulers were not seen as foreigners; they were Turkic and Muslim like the core of their empire. There were several attempts to reform the empire. In the late eighteenth century, Sultan Selim III brought in European advisers and techniques to begin reforming the military, but opposition from the *ulama* and the Janissaries led to his murder. The Tanzimat reforms of the nineteenth century attempted to create a stronger, centralized state by encouraging factories, conducting land reform, creating telegraphs, steamships, and railroads, and creating new Western-style secular law codes, courts, and educational system. Further, the reforms created a new national identity, one that was not based on ethnicity or religious group, by removing distinctions between Muslims and non-Muslims. The intelligentsia, lower-level government officials, and military officers, most of whom had Western educations, were called the "Young Ottomans." They supported a democratic, constitutional government to strengthen the state from European aggression and felt that Islam could accommodate Western scientific knowledge while escaping its materialism. By the end of the century, the government had reverted to autocratic rule but was opposed by the "Young Turks," drawn from the same groups that formed the Young Ottomans. A military coup brought them to power in 1908, and they pushed for secular education, secular courts and legal system, political parties, Turkish as the official language (instead of Arabic), and the same laws regardless of religion. Turkish nationalism led to increased nationalism from other ethnic groups in the empire and led to its dismemberment after World War I.

Japan embraced modernization and Westernization. After Commodore Perry arrived with his black fleet of ships armed with cannon, the Tokugawa shogunate was forced into unequal treaties, which ended Japan's policy of isolation. The Meiji restoration, led by young, progressive samurai, restored power to the emperor in order to save Japan from foreign domination by radically transforming and Westernizing Japanese government and society. To achieve national unity, the daimyo (landowning nobility) were replaced by regional governors, and the samurai warrior class was abolished. The army was built by conscripting all social classes. All Japanese were legally commoners and equal as subjects of the emperor. "Civilization and Enlightenment" was the motto that governed far-reaching reforms; a constitution, based on Germany's constitution, was drafted with a parliament in an advisory role and ultimate power in the hands of the emperor, who was supported by the military and an oligarchy. After undergoing similar economic reforms, Japan emerged as an industrial, imperial state; it captured colonies in Korea, Manchuria, and Taiwan as well as other islands nearby. Japan's defeat of Russia in 1905 sparked rebellion in Russia and nationalistic hope in regions controlled or threatened by Europeans, such as Egypt, Aceh (Indonesia), and the Ottoman Empire. *See Chapters 16, 17, and 18 for additional discussion of this theme.*

Theme 4: Creation, Expansion, and Interaction of Economic Systems

Backed by wealth generated by the Industrial Revolution, Western powers were aggressively seeking control of trade systems, new markets for manufactured goods, and new supplies of raw materials. At the same time, smaller or more fragmented states (such as Mughal India, the East Indies, and most of Africa) were taken over and colonized. Asian states such as the Ottoman Empire, Qing dynasty China, and Japan were faced with similar problems—how to modernize their economies and states in order to prevent European domination.

China responded slowly to the changing economic system that no longer placed it in the center and in control. As government control weakened, the ability to collect taxes also dwindled. The country was wracked by rebellion, which also disrupted the economy. The introduction of smuggled opium by the British into China not only created millions of addicts but also drained silver from the economy and created a huge trade imbalance, which was something new for the Middle Kingdom (see Snapshot: Chinese/British Trade at Canton, p. 936). The subsequent Opium Wars left Europeans in control of the economy, able to extract raw materials, enter into inland trade, and build railroads to export goods to the coast. Foreign goods and investments flooded into China, destroying the livelihoods of local craftsmen and preventing businessmen developing capital to fund an industrial revolution. The "self-strengthening" movement attempted modest reforms, such as repairing dikes and irrigation canals, expanding coal mining, creating a telegraph system, creating factories to make steel and textiles, and building modern arsenals and shipyards. Conservative landowning gentry feared even this limited economic progress, and much of the capital, machinery, and expertise for economic reform came from foreigners.

The Ottoman Empire, in closer contact with Europe, also launched "defensive modernization" in response to growing European economic power. As portions of the empire fell away, revenue became a problem, exacerbated by loss of control of the lucrative Afro-Eurasian commerce as Europeans used direct sea routes to East Asia. Further, Ottoman artisans were hard-hit by competition from cheap European manufactured goods. In debt, the Empire had to rely on foreign investment for any economic development, which led to foreign control of much of Ottoman revenue generation. The Tanzimat reforms encouraged infrastructure growth (such as railroads and telegraphs), steamships, a postal service, and resettlement of agricultural land. War with Russia led to reversion to older forms, and the Ottomans, like the Chinese, were unable to create an industrial economy.

Japan used state support to create a modern industrial economy—the only country outside of the West to do so in the nineteenth century. New Meiji governors replaced the daimyo and collected taxes for the state. Travel and trade were opened up again, ending Tokugawa restrictions. Studying Western science and technology was encouraged, both by sending Japanese for schooling abroad and by encouraging foreign experts to come to Japan. The government established factories (especially textiles), which it later sold to investors, created railroads, a postal system, a national currency and banking. Large firms called *zaibatsu* led in the manufacture of textiles, munitions, and industrial goods—all done without the massive foreign debt incurred by the Ottomans. By 1905, Japan's military reform and new armaments allowed it to defeat Russia in the Russo-Japanese War. *See Chapters 17 and 18 for additional discussion of this theme.*

Theme 5: Development and Transformation of Social Structures

Rapid population growth left China with an impoverished, over-taxed, and starving peasant class, which led to several rebellions, including the Taiping and the Boxer rebellions. The landed gentry was extremely conservative and prevented radical urbanizing or industrializing reforms, but the "self-strengthening" movement was able to restore social order in the countryside by supporting landlords in their repair of irrigation systems. Educated Chinese felt as though no change was possible under the empire, so they joined clubs, formed study groups, and read newspapers in an attempt to decide what reforms would help China. While traditional gender roles were maintained during this time period, some revolutionary groups such as the Taiping Rebellion allowed women to fight. Some educated women rejected traditional gender roles as part of the rejection of the Qing dynasty and the failure of traditional Chinese government and society to stand up to foreign imperialism.

Ottoman society underwent more social changes than Chinese society. As Turkish ethnic nationalism became more important to the Ottoman state, regions of the empire such as Greece, the Balkans, and North Africa redefined their own ethnic identity in opposition and began independence movements that further weakened the empire. A core issue for Ottoman modernization and Westernization became whether these reforms were compatible with the majority religion of Islam. Conservative forces within the empire, such as the *ulama* and the Janissaries, held to traditional views of the state as fundamentally Islamic and opposed secularization. Reformers such as the Young Ottomans argued that Muslim society could accept economic, social, and political reforms in a modern Islamic framework. The Young Turks restricted polygamy and permitted women to attend university, wear Western clothing, and obtain divorces.

Japanese society underwent a profound restructuring after the Meiji Restoration. The old Confucian-based social order ended. The daimyo and samurai surrendered their positions and became common citizens equal under law with all others, including the previously scorned merchant class. Many former samurai found themselves new roles in the army, government bureaucracy, or industry. All classes were conscripted into the emperor's new army. A conservative group of samurai did rebel in 1877 (also called the Satsuma Rebellion) but did little to hold back the winds of change sweeping through the country. However, rural peasants did not benefit as much from the modernization program, leading to violence in 1883–1884. Partly as a result of this rural poverty, many farmers sold or sent their daughters to work in the new textile mills under harsh conditions and low wages. Rates of rural female infanticide also grew. Women were still excluded from politics, although education was becoming even more common. *See Chapters 17 and 18 for additional discussion of this theme.*

PRACTICE EXAM 5

WORLD HISTORY
SECTION I

Note: This exam uses the chronological designations B.C.E. (before the common era) and C.E. (common era). These labels correspond to B.C. (before Christ) and A.D. (anno Domini), which are used in some world history textbooks.

TIME — 55 Minutes
70 Questions

Directions: Each of the questions or incomplete statements below is followed by four suggested answers or completions. Select the one that is best in each case.

1. How did the Industrial Revolution solve an emerging energy crisis in the eighteenth century?
   (A) It emphasized intensive use of the renewable energy sources of wind and water.
   (B) It introduced the use of coal, oil, and natural gas as sources of fuel.
   (C) It facilitated the migration of the rural population to towns and cities.
   (D) It encouraged the global trend toward economic protectionism.

2. Which group would agree with the view of the capitalist system offered by the poster?
   (A) Pacifists
   (B) Nationalists
   (C) Socialists
   (D) Bourgeoisie

GO ON TO THE NEXT PAGE.

3. All of the following represent responses of Asian or African societies to the European presence in the nineteenth and early twentieth centuries EXCEPT the

 (A) Indian Rebellion
 (B) Boxer Rebellion
 (C) Maji Maji Uprising
 (D) Bolshevik Revolution

4. In what respect were Qing China and the Ottoman Empire similar in the nineteenth century?

 (A) Both created industrial economies that enabled them to compete with Europe on an equal footing.
 (B) Both successfully strengthened and centralized their states to defend their territory from European intrusion.
 (C) Both lost their independence to Japan in the late nineteenth century.
 (D) Both launched programs of defensive modernization to achieve parity with the West.

5. The map above shows Europe around

 (A) 1790
 (B) 1820
 (C) 1850
 (D) 1880

GO ON TO THE NEXT PAGE.

6. All of the following established empires in the Asia and/or the Pacific in the nineteenth century EXCEPT
   (A) Spain
   (B) France
   (C) the United States
   (D) Japan

7. Which of the following resulted from the employment of colonial subjects in European-owned plantations, mines, construction projects, and businesses?
   (A) Migration of colonial subjects to work sites overseas
   (B) Resurgence of the slave trade in Africa and Asia
   (C) Decrease in racial discrimination
   (D) Normalcy and stability for colonial subjects

8. How did Britain's geography affect its Industrial Revolution?
   (A) Proximity to France made it vulnerable to invasions during the reign of Napoleon.
   (B) Its northern location minimized the effects of the Little Ice Age.
   (C) Coal and iron ore deposits were abundant and close to each other.
   (D) Trees covered most of the country, providing a renewable source of energy.

9. Which of the following groups benefitted the most from the Industrial Revolution in nineteenth-century Britain?
   (A) The aristocracy
   (B) The middle classes
   (C) The laboring classes
   (D) Women

10. A consequence of European imperialism in the nineteenth century was the
    (A) rise of nationalism in the countries that felt victimized by imperialism
    (B) triumph of agricultural societies over industrial societies
    (C) wholesale rejection of industrialization and socialism
    (D) rejection of global capitalism in favor of communist revolution

11. "Everyone who knows a little about aboriginal races is aware that those races which are of a low type mentally and who are at the same time weak in constitution rapidly die out when their country comes to be occupied by a different race much more rigorous, robust, and pushing than themselves."

    Reverend Bishop Hale, late 19th century

    The perspective expressed in the above quotation was used by Europeans to justify which of the following in the nineteenth century?
    (A) Communism
    (B) Imperialism
    (C) The Great Dying
    (D) The Crusades

GO ON TO THE NEXT PAGE.

12. Which of the following reflects a new element in European views of non-Europeans in the nineteenth century?

   (A) The idea that non-Europeans could assimilate into European society by Westernizing
   (B) The belief that the racial inferiority of non-Europeans could be scientifically proven
   (C) The portrayal of less technologically developed people as "noble savages"
   (D) The view of non-Christians as "heathen"

13. Which of the following describes how the movement toward industrialization in the nineteenth century affected Latin America?

   (A) A large market for manufactured goods developed in Latin America.
   (B) Latin America provided cheap labor for foreign-owned manufacturing industries.
   (C) Latin America exported textiles, machinery, tools, weapons, and luxury goods to the United States and Europe.
   (D) Latin America provided the food products, raw materials, and markets for industrializing countries.

14. After the Meiji restoration, how did Japan seek to remain free of foreign domination?

   (A) By closing off the country to all Western influence.
   (B) By drawing on examples of Western modernization to transform Japanese society.
   (C) By allying itself with China to collectively resist Western influence.
   (D) By embracing universal suffrage and equality for women.

15. In what respect were Ethiopia's and Siam's encounters with European imperialism in the nineteenth century similar?

   (A) Both avoided the colonization to which their neighbors succumbed.
   (B) Both negotiated an agreement with the U.S. to guarantee their independence.
   (C) Both became settler colonies.
   (D) Both became "neo-European" societies.

16. "In place of the old bourgeois society, with its classes and class antagonisms, we shall have an association in which the free development of each is the condition for the free development of all."

   Karl Marx and Friedrich Engels, The Communist Manifesto, *1848*

   The society envisioned in the quote above can be described as one

   (A) controlled by a totalitarian state
   (B) made up only of the middle class
   (C) without classes and inequality
   (D) run by the captains of industry

GO ON TO THE NEXT PAGE.

17. In contrast to the sixteenth century, China during the nineteenth century
    - (A) declined in international prominence and power
    - (B) became a leading industrial power
    - (C) became a colonial power that rivaled European powers in the Indian Ocean
    - (D) absorbed Korea and Japan into its tribute system

18. "... a class of laborers, who live only so long as they find work, and who find work only so long as their labor increases capital. These laborers, who must sell themselves piece-meal, are a commodity, like every other article of commerce, and are consequently exposed to all the vicissitudes of competition, to all the fluctuations of the market."

    Karl Marx and Friedrich Engels, The Communist Manifesto, *1848*

    "... the skilled workman, unless trained in good habits, may exhibit no higher a life than that of the mere animal; and the earning of increased wages will only furnish him with increased means for indulging in the gratification of his grosser appetites. ... This habitual improvidence ... is the real cause of the social degradation of the artisan."

    Samuel Smiles, Thrift, *1875*

    Which of the following statements captures the explanations for the poverty of the working class offered by the writers above?
    - (A) The first passage blames the capitalist system, while the second passage blames the workers' habits.
    - (B) The first passage blames increasing demand for unskilled labor, while the second passage blames declining wages.
    - (C) Both agree that industrial capitalism will ultimately improve the lives of the working class.
    - (D) Both agree that the government should establish a minimum wage for workers.

19. "... a class of laborers, who live only so long as they find work, and who find work only so long as their labor increases capital. These laborers, who must sell themselves piece-meal, are a commodity, like every other article of commerce, and are consequently exposed to all the vicissitudes of competition, to all the fluctuations of the market."

    Karl Marx and Friedrich Engels, The Communist Manifesto, *1848*

    The class of laborers described in the quote above emerged as a result of the
    - (A) French Revolution
    - (B) Agricultural Revolution
    - (C) Industrial Revolution
    - (D) Scientific Revolution

20. Which of the following was the only country outside of Europe and North America that successfully industrialized by the late nineteenth century?
    - (A) Qing China
    - (B) Meiji Japan
    - (C) Mughal India
    - (D) Ottoman Empire

GO ON TO THE NEXT PAGE.

21. The second wave of European conquests that occurred between 1750 and 1914 differed from the first phase in all of the following ways EXCEPT

   (A) the rise of Germany, Italy, Belgium, the U.S., and Japan as new colonial powers
   (B) the greater reliance on economic penetration
   (C) the focus on Asia and Africa
   (D) the dominant role played by Spain and Portugal

22. Which of the following benefitted from the U.S. military interventions depicted in Map 17.5?

   (A) United Fruit Company
   (B) Standard Oil Company
   (C) General Motors
   (D) League of Nations

GO ON TO THE NEXT PAGE.

23. What did the Atlantic revolutions in the U.S., France, Haiti, and Latin America share in common?

    (A) A militant commitment to the abolition of slavery
    (B) A widespread tolerance of all religions
    (C) A political vocabulary inspired by the Enlightenment
    (D) A racial divide that expressed itself in civil war

24. ". . . the race to which we belong, the Aryan, has always played the leading part in the great drama of the world's progress."

    William O. Swinton, An Outline of the World's History, *1874*

    Which of the following offers a counterargument to the view of world history presented above?

    (A) Western culture is the most widely imitated of the world's cultures.
    (B) European domination of the world reflects the will of Providence.
    (C) Christianity is uniquely suited to modernization and innovation.
    (D) The Arabs, Chinese, and Mongols have each dominated the world stage.

25. Which of the following would be the most useful source of evidence for researching the new working conditions created by the Industrial Revolution?

    (A) Tax records of skilled and unskilled workers
    (B) Birth certificates with no father's name identified
    (C) City maps showing the major transportation points
    (D) Company manuals listing rules for factory workers

26. "We hold these truths to be self-evident, that all men and women are created equal."

    Elizabeth Cady Stanton, 1848

    The statement above reflects all of the following EXCEPT the

    (A) influence of the American Declaration of Independence
    (B) use of Enlightenment ideals to improve women's status
    (C) dependence on Marxist historical analysis to argue for women's emancipation
    (D) expression of a feminist consciousness reflected in the women's suffrage movement

GO ON TO THE NEXT PAGE.

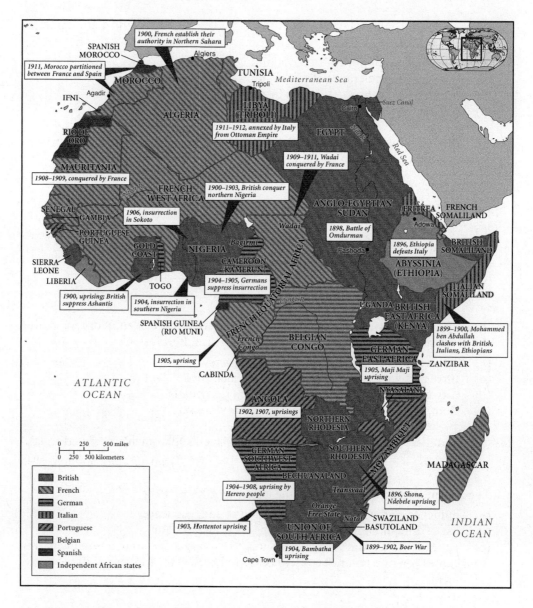

27. The map above reflects the outcome of which of the following?

    (A) The scramble for Africa
    (B) The great dying
    (C) The Middle Passage
    (D) The African National Congress

28. In the late nineteenth century, the governments of Canada, Australia, New Zealand, and the United States all responded to Chinese immigration by

    (A) promoting values of multiculturalism and celebrating ethnic diversity
    (B) implementing policies that made it easier for Chinese immigrants to acquire citizenship
    (C) passing legislation to curb the flow of Chinese immigrants into their country
    (D) concluding treaties with China guaranteeing a fixed quota of Chinese immigrants

GO ON TO THE NEXT PAGE.

29. What made Martin Luther's Ninety-five Theses revolutionary?

    (A) The condemnation of the Church's selling of indulgences
    (B) The idea that an individual could find salvation by faith alone
    (C) The proposal that knowledge should be based on observations and experiments
    (D) The theory that the sun was the center of the universe

30. "Having bought my compliment of 700 slaves . . . I set sail. . . . I deliver'd alive at Barbados . . . 372, which being sold, came out at about 19 pounds per head."

    Thomas Phillips, English merchant, 1694

    "The closeness of the place, and the heat of the climate, added to the number in the ship . . . almost suffocated us. This produced copious perspirations . . . and brought on a sickness among the slaves, of which many died, thus falling victims to the improvident avarice . . . of their purchasers."

    Olaudah Equiano, former slave, 1789

    Despite their very different roles, both writers provide evidence based on their personal experiences in the slave trade that

    (A) European merchants reaped tremendous profits with minimal loss
    (B) prices of slaves had to be negotiated at the point of embarkation
    (C) the volume in the slave trade declined during the eighteenth century
    (D) many slaves died on board the slave ships headed to the Americas

31. All of the following reflect the new approach to knowledge that began with the Scientific Revolution in Europe and influenced Enlightenment thinkers EXCEPT

    (A) faith
    (B) reason
    (C) empiricism
    (D) secularism

32. Which describes the role Europeans played in the economy of the early modern era?

    (A) They controlled the markets of the East to work to their advantage.
    (B) They operated as middlemen, transporting American silver to Asia.
    (C) They established and enforced a new international system of trade.
    (D) They dominated the global trade in textiles, tea, and spices.

33. Which of the following represents a new political concept introduced by Enlightenment thinkers?

    (A) Mercantilism
    (B) Totalitarianism
    (C) The social contract
    (D) Divine right of kings

GO ON TO THE NEXT PAGE.

34. Which of the following describes the role of the silver trade in the early modern world?

 (A) It contributed to the decline of Spanish power and influence in Europe and the Americas.
 (B) It established the first direct and sustained commercial link between the Americas and Asia.
 (C) It shifted the global balance of trade permanently in favor of European countries.
 (D) It crippled the once-thriving trading networks in the Indian Ocean basin.

35. Which of the following describes how the printing press contributed to the spread of the Protestant Reformation in Europe?

 (A) It fostered mutual understanding and consensus between Catholics and Protestants.
 (B) It enabled the printing of various translations of the Bible in vernacular languages.
 (C) It was used by the Catholic Church to print and disseminate its findings from the Council of Trent.
 (D) It led to the creation of the Society of Jesus and ended missionary activities abroad.

36. How did slavery in the Americas differ from past practices of slavery elsewhere in the world?

 (A) Only men were enslaved and sent to the Americas.
 (B) Only criminals were shipped off as slaves to the Americas.
 (C) Slavery in the Americas was more humane than all past instances of slavery in the world.
 (D) Slavery in the Americas was associated with race and the plantation economy.

37. Which of the following explains why Portugal, Spain, France, and Britain were the first to expand into the New World?

 (A) They had a long tradition of overseas exploration.
 (B) They were located on the Atlantic coast and therefore closer to the Americas.
 (C) They needed new markets to export surplus goods.
 (D) They sought coal and iron to fuel their industrial revolutions.

38. Which of the following policies reflects the mercantilist thinking shared by all European rulers in the early modern era?

 (A) Promoting capital investments
 (B) Encouraging free trade
 (C) Guaranteeing religious freedom
 (D) Accumulating gold and silver

39. Which of the following offers evidence of how indigenous peoples in Mesoamerica blended local customs with Catholic beliefs and practices?

 (A) Sufi mysticism
 (B) The Virgin of Guadalupe
 (C) The bhakti movement
 (D) Movements of "extirpation"

GO ON TO THE NEXT PAGE.

40. What did the Ottoman practice of *devshirme* and the Chinese examination system during the Qing dynasty share in common?

    (A) Both fostered hostility toward the state and contributed to the collapse of the Ottoman and Chinese empires.

    (B) Both created a hereditary status group whose task was to create the educational curriculum of religious schools.

    (C) Both were means by which the state recruited political and military talent from conquered subjects.

    (D) Both represent the earliest prototypes of a public education system that was open to boys and girls.

41. How did Chinese and Russian expansion into Central Asia affect the nomadic peoples inhabiting the steppe lands?

    (A) They lost their political independence and economic prosperity.

    (B) They regained their status as the cosmopolitan crossroads of Eurasia.

    (C) They abandoned their nomadic lifestyles and assimilated into Chinese and Russian society.

    (D) They formed a military confederation and successfully fought for their independence.

42. Which of the following features distinguished the Atlantic slave trade in the early modern period from slavery in the pre-modern Islamic world?

    (A) The slave population was predominantly male.

    (B) Some slaves gained positions in the military and government.

    (C) Most slaves worked in large-scale agricultural enterprises.

    (D) Slave status was limited to prisoners of war and criminals.

43. Which of the following describes a similarity between the spread of Islam from the seventh to tenth centuries and the spread of Christianity in the sixteenth century?

    (A) Religious conversion occurred more frequently in societies that were centered on a literate religion.

    (B) Missionaries faced the most resistance to conversion among people who practiced orally based religions.

    (C) Widespread conversion occurred as military conquest led people to question the power of local gods.

    (D) Forced conversions were common as people saw no benefit to converting to Islam or Christianity.

44. Which of the following provides evidence of the "Indianization" of Southeast Asia?

    (A) The use of Angkor Wat as a Hindu, and later, Buddhist temple

    (B) The use of Arabic script to write the Swahili language

    (C) A bronze African lion with Indian designs

    (D) The adoption of Islam as the state religion in Champa

45. The form of governance that characterized Swahili civilization from 1000 to 1500 was most similar to the

    (A) empires of ancient Rome and China

    (B) khanates of the Mongol Empire

    (C) complex societies of the eastern woodlands in North America

    (D) competitive and independent city-states of ancient Greece

GO ON TO THE NEXT PAGE.

46. Which of the following innovations facilitated trade along the Silk Roads of Central Asia and the Sand Roads across the Sahara between the fourth and sixteenth centuries?

    (A) Lateen sails
    (B) Camel saddles
    (C) Monsoon winds
    (D) Hacienda system

47. Which of the following played an important role in the growth of Venice, Jenne-jeno, and Cahokia in the tenth century?

    (A) War
    (B) Religion
    (C) Commerce
    (D) Diplomacy

48. Which of the following describes an effect of commerce on women living in regions engaged in long-distance trade?

    (A) Weaving of textiles came to be considered women's work.
    (B) Women had more opportunities to travel and trade.
    (C) The sale of women as concubines and slaves became internationalized.
    (D) Patriarchy weakened as women's contribution to the household economy was recognized.

49. Which of the following state policies contributed to China's economic revolution around the tenth century?

    (A) Suppression of internal trade in order to increase long-distance trade
    (B) Reliance on warfare to procure slaves to work in agriculture and industry
    (C) Relaxation of border controls to encourage large-scale immigration of Japanese workers
    (D) Construction of a network of internal waterways that provided cheap transportation

50. Which of the following best describes China's relationship with the Xiongnu, Uighurs, Khitan, and Jurchen from the Han dynasty to the Song dynasty?

    (A) All four accepted their subordinate position and paid annual tribute to China.
    (B) All four were ultimately conquered by China and assimilated into the Chinese population.
    (C) The rulers of the Chinese dynasties were ethnically Xiongnu, Uighur, Khitan, or Jurchen.
    (D) China appeased them by sending them valuable goods in return for not attacking.

51. Which of the following describes an effect of Confucianism on women in China and Korea from the tenth to the fourteenth century?

    (A) The greater mobility enjoyed by elite women
    (B) The tightening of patriarchal controls on women
    (C) The emphasis on matrilineal succession
    (D) The decline in practices of concubinage

GO ON TO THE NEXT PAGE.

52. This question is based on the Snapshot feature on Chinese technological achievements on page 386. Which of the following explains the lag between the time each innovation was developed in China and the time it appeared in Europe?

    (A) Long periods of disunity in China
    (B) China's policy of isolationism
    (C) Europe's distance from China
    (D) Europe's control of the Silk Roads

53. Scholars point to all of the following as evidence of the influence of Central Asian local traditions on the Islamic Ottoman Empire EXCEPT the

    (A) strict adherence to the sharia
    (B) predominance of the Turkish language
    (C) ecstatic turning dances of Sufi practices
    (D) relative freedom women enjoyed

54. Which of the following is an example of how the Germanic kingdoms that emerged in medieval Europe drew from traditional sources to legitimize their power?

    (A) Rulers invoked the Mandate of Heaven.
    (B) Rulers claimed the divine right of kings.
    (C) Rulers signed a social contract.
    (D) Rulers had the pope crown them emperor.

55. Recent reinterpretations of the role of pastoral peoples in world history have highlighted all of the following EXCEPT their

    (A) adaptation to inhospitable environments
    (B) innovations in technology and state building
    (C) role in promoting cross-cultural exchange
    (D) development of an elite literary culture

56. In the fifteenth century, what did the Igbo people in West Africa have in common with the Iroquois people in North America?

    (A) Centralized kingdoms and stratified societies
    (B) Plantation economies dependent on slave labor
    (C) Institutions for resolving conflict in the absence of a centralized state
    (D) Seclusion of women based on deeply embedded cultural beliefs

57. Which of the following features of the Qin dynasty did the later Han dynasty retain?

    (A) Standardization of weights, measures, and currency
    (B) Adoption of Legalism as the official political ideology
    (C) Use of a civil service examination system to recruit officials
    (D) Incorporation of democratic features that gave people a voice

58. The Roman and Chinese empires of second-wave civilizations shared all of the following features EXCEPT a

    (A) universalistic view of their empire
    (B) secular definition of political power
    (C) heavy investment in public works
    (D) divine justification for imperial rule

GO ON TO THE NEXT PAGE.

59. How did the Roman and Chinese empires of second-wave civilizations differ in their treatment of the people they conquered?

    (A) The Romans demanded cultural uniformity, while the Chinese imposed religious conformity.

    (B) The Romans enslaved subject populations, while the Chinese conscripted them into the military.

    (C) The Romans encouraged intermarriage, while the Chinese created segregated communities.

    (D) The Romans focused on political integration, while the Chinese emphasized cultural assimilation.

60. India's political history during the age of second-wave civilizations most resembled that of

    (A) Western Europe after the fall of the Roman Empire
    (B) inner and outer Eurasia under Mongol rule
    (C) China from the Han dynasty to the Song dynasty
    (D) Arabia since the birth of Islam

61. Which of the following reflects the same amoral, political philosophy expressed in the *Arthashastra (The Science of Worldly Wealth)* used by rulers of the Mauryan Empire?

    (A) Adam Smith's *The Wealth of Nations*
    (B) Galileo's *The Starry Messenger*
    (C) Niccolò Machiavelli's *The Prince*
    (D) Karl Marx's *The Communist Manifesto*

62. Which of the following illustrates the role of historical interpretation in shaping the contemporary notion in the West of an East/West divide?

    (A) The attribution of the Mauryan ruler Ashoka's conversion to Buddhism to the military campaign against Kalinga

    (B) The view of the Greek defeat of the Persian Empire as the victory of Greek freedoms over Persian despotism

    (C) The synthesis of Legalism and Confucianism in the Chinese imperial tradition since the Han dynasty

    (D) The interpretation that Aryan invaders from Central Asia destroyed the Indus River civilization in India

63. Which of the following texts is associated with a new kind of popular Hinduism that emerged in the centuries following the birth of Buddhism?

    (A) *Epic of Gilgamesh*
    (B) *Analects*
    (C) *The Republic*
    (D) *Ramayana*

64. By the fourth century, Christianity was adopted as the state religion in all of the following regions EXCEPT

    (A) the Persian Empire
    (B) Armenia
    (C) Axum
    (D) the Roman Empire

GO ON TO THE NEXT PAGE.

65. Later generations of Europeans would claim all of the following features of the classical Greek intellectual tradition as the basis of an emerging "Western" civilization EXCEPT the

 (A) nonreligious explanation of the material world
 (B) constant questioning of conventional wisdom
 (C) categorical rejection of logic and argumentation
 (D) absolute confidence in human reason

66. All of the following contributed to the weakening of patriarchy in China from the third century to the tenth century EXCEPT the

 (A) discrediting of Confucianism
 (B) influence of nomadic cultures
 (C) popularity of Daoism
 (D) creation of the civil service

67. By the first century C.E., the languages spoken by most people living in the southern half of Africa were linguistically similar. Which of the following contributed to this linguistic similarity?

 (A) The Arab conquest
 (B) The Bantu migration
 (C) The Middle Passage
 (D) The Columbian exchange

68. Which of the following is the term used to refer to the period during which humans spread from Africa, using stone tools to adapt to the different environments they encountered?

 (A) Paleolithic
 (B) Neolithic
 (C) "Secondary products revolution"
 (D) "The original affluent society"

69. The absence of large animals that could be domesticated in the Americas distinguished the Agricultural Revolution in the Americas from similar processes in the Afro-Eurasian world in all of the following ways EXCEPT the

 (A) lack of manure to fertilize the soil led to lower agricultural yields
 (B) absence of labor-saving mechanisms like the plow and pull carts
 (C) simultaneous transition to agriculture in both North and South America
 (D) transition to agriculture was accompanied by a continued reliance on hunting and fishing

70. Regarded as the "mother civilization" of Mesoamerica, the Olmecs left a cultural legacy that is manifested in all of the following features of later civilizations in the Americas EXCEPT

 (A) mound building
 (B) ritual sacrifice
 (C) bloodletting by rulers
 (D) religious monotheism

STOP

END OF SECTION I

WORLD HISTORY
SECTION II

Part A
(Suggested writing time — 40 minutes)
Percent of Section II score — 33 1/3

Directions: The following question is based on the accompanying Documents 1–7. (The documents have been edited for the purpose of this exercise.)

This question is designed to test your ability to work with and understand historical documents.

Write an essay that:

+ Has a relevant thesis and supports that thesis with evidence from the documents.
+ Uses all of the documents.
+ Analyzes the documents by grouping them in as many appropriate ways as possible. Does not simply summarize the documents individually.
+ Takes into account the sources of the documents and analyzes the authors' points of view.
+ Identifies and explains the need for at least one additional type of document.

You may refer to relevant historical information not mentioned in the documents.

1. Using the following documents, analyze Chinese imperial government responses to British trade and the long-term effects of British trade on Qing dynasty China from 1750 c.e. to 1900 c.e. Identify an additional type of document and explain how it would help your analysis of Chinese government responses to and long-term effects of British trade.

GO ON TO THE NEXT PAGE.

Document 1

Source: Chinese Qing dynasty Emperor Qianlong, "Message to King George III," a letter to the British monarch, 1793.

You, O King, from afar have yearned after the blessings of our civilization . . . have sent an Embassy across the sea. . . . I have already taken note of your respectful spirit of submission, have treated your mission with extreme favor and loaded it with gifts. . . . Thus has my indulgence been manifested.

Hitherto, all European nations, including your own country's barbarian merchants, have carried on their trade with our Celestial Empire at Canton. Such has been the procedure for many years, although our Celestial Empire possesses all things in prolific abundance and lacks no product within its own borders. There was therefore no need to import the manufactures of outside barbarians in exchange for our own produce. But as the tea, silk, and porcelain which the Celestial Empire produces are absolute necessities to European nations and to yourselves, we have permitted, as a signal mark of favor, that . . . [approved Chinese trading firms] should be established at Canton, so that your wants might be supplied and your country thus participate in our beneficence.

Your request for a small island . . . where your merchants may reside and goods be warehoused, arises from your desire to develop trade. . . . Consider, moreover, that England is not the only barbarian land which wishes to establish relations with our civilization and trade with our Empire: supposing that other nations were all to imitate your evil example and beseech me to present them each and all with a site for trading purposes, how could I possibly comply? This also is a flagrant infringement of the usage of my Empire and cannot possibly be entertained. . . .

If, after the receipt of this explicit decree, you . . . allow your barbarian merchants to proceed to Zhejiang and Tianjin, with the object of landing and trading there, the ordinances of my Celestial Empire are strict in the extreme, and the local officials, both civil and military, are bound reverently to obey the law of the land. Should your vessels touch the shore, your merchants . . . will be subject to instant expulsion. In that event your barbarian merchants will have had a long journey for nothing. Do not say that you were not warned in due time! Tremblingly obey and show no negligence!

GO ON TO THE NEXT PAGE.

Document 2

Source: Xu Naiji, a senior official and advisor to Qing Emperor Daoguang, "An Argument for Legalization," 1836.

Formerly, the barbarian merchants brought foreign money to China; which being paid in exchange for goods, was a source of pecuniary advantage to the people of all the sea-board provinces. But lately, the barbarian merchants have clandestinely sold opium for money, which has rendered it unnecessary for them to import foreign silver. Thus foreign money has been going out of the country, while none comes into it.

It is proposed entirely to cut off the foreign trade, thus to remove the root, to dam up the source of the evil. The Celestial Dynasty would not, indeed, hesitate to relinquish the few millions of duties arising therefrom. But all the nations of the West have had a general market open to their ships for upward of a thousand years, while the dealers in opium are the English alone; it would be wrong, for the sake of cutting off the English trade, to cut off that of all the other nations. Besides, the hundreds of thousands of people living on the sea-coast depend wholly on trade for their livelihood, and how are they to be disposed of? Moreover, the barbarian ships, being on the high seas, can repair to any island that may be selected as an entre-pôt, and the native sea-going vessels can meet them there; it is then impossible to cut off the trade . . . Thus it appears that, though the commerce of Canton should be cut off, yet it will not be possible to prevent the clandestine introduction of merchandise.

Since then, it will not answer to close our ports against [all trades], and since the laws issued against opium are quite inoperative, the only method left is to revert to the former system, to permit the barbarian merchants to import opium paying duty thereon as a medicine, and to require that, after having passed the Custom-House, it shall be delivered to the . . . [approved Chinese trading firms] only in exchange for merchandise, and that no money be paid for it.

It becomes my duty, then, to request that it be enacted, that any officer, scholar, or soldier, found guilty of secretly smoking opium, shall be immediately dismissed from public employ, without being made liable to any other penalty. . . .

Lastly, that no regard be paid to the purchase and use of opium on the part of the people generally. . . .

Besides, the removal of the prohibitions refers only to the vulgar and common people, those who have no official duties to perform. So long as the officers of the Government, the scholars, and the military are not included, I see no detriment to the dignity of the Government. And by allowing the proposed importation and exchange of the drug for other commodities, more than ten millions of money will annually be prevented from flowing out of the Central land.

GO ON TO THE NEXT PAGE.

Document 3

Source: British company records, 1835–1836.

Chinese/British Trade at Canton, 1835–1836 (values in Spanish dollars)			
BRITISH EXPORTS TO CANTON		**BRITISH IMPORTS FROM CANTON**	
Opium	17,904,248	Tea	13,412,243
Cotton	8,357,394	Raw silk	3,764,115
All other items	6,164,981	All other items	6, 676,541
Total:	32,426,623	Total:	23,852,899

Document 4

Source: Lin Zexu, a senior official sent by Qing Emperor Daoguang to suppress the illegal opium trade, "A Moral Appeal to Queen Victoria," 1839.

We find . . . your country . . . [distant] from China. Yet there are barbarian ships that strive to come here for trade for the purpose of making a great profit. The wealth of China is used to profit the barbarians. . . . By what right do they . . . use this poisonous drug to injure the Chinese people? . . .

Let us ask, where is your conscience? I have heard that the smoking of opium is very strictly forbidden by your country; that is because the harm caused by opium is clearly understood. Since it is not permitted to do harm to your country, then even less should you let it be passed on to the harm of other countries—how much less to China! Of all that China exports to foreign countries, there is not a single thing which is not beneficial to people: they are of benefit when eaten, or of benefit when used, or of benefit when resold: all are beneficial. Is there a single article from China which has done any harm to foreign countries? . . . [O]ur Celestial Court lets tea, silk, and other goods be shipped without limit and circulated everywhere without begrudging it in the slightest. This is for no other reason but to share the benefit with the people of the whole world . . .

We have heard heretofore that your honorable ruler is kind and benevolent. Naturally you would not wish to give unto others what you yourself do not want . . .

Therefore in the new regulations, in regard to those barbarians who bring opium to China, the penalty is fixed at decapitation or strangulation. This is what is called getting rid of a harmful thing on behalf of mankind . . .

After receiving this dispatch will you immediately give us a prompt reply regarding the details and circumstances of your cutting off the opium traffic? Be sure not to put this off.

GO ON TO THE NEXT PAGE.

Document 5

Source: *The Treaty of Nanjing,* ending the First Opium War between Britain and China, 1842.

I.

There shall henceforward be peace and friendship between Her Majesty the Queen of the United Kingdom of Great Britain and Ireland and His Majesty the Emperor of China. . . .

II.

His Majesty the Emperor of China agrees, that British subjects, with their families and establishments, shall be allowed to reside, for the purposes of carrying on their mercantile pursuits, without molestation or restraint, at the cities and towns of Canton, Amoy, Foochowfoo, Ningpo, and Shanghai. . . .

III.

It being obviously necessary and desirable that British subjects should have some port whereat they may [maintain] and refit their ships when required, and keep stores for that purpose, His Majesty the Emperor of China cedes to Her Majesty the Queen of Great Britain, &c., the Island of Hong-Kong. . . .

IV.

The Emperor of China agrees to pay the sum of 6,000,000 of dollars, as the value of the opium which was delivered up at Canton in the month of March, 1839, as a ransom for the lives of Her Britannic Majesty's Superintendent and subjects, who had been imprisoned and threatened with death by the Chinese High Officers. . . .

V.

. . . His Imperial Majesty further agrees to pay to the British Government the sum of 3,000,000 of dollars, on account of debts due to British subjects by some of the . . . [Chinese trading firms] who owe very large sums of money to subjects of Her Britannic Majesty.

VI.

The Government of Her Britannic Majesty having been obliged to send out an expedition to demand and obtain redress for the violent and unjust proceedings of the Chinese High Authorities towards Her Britannic Majesty's officer and subjects, the Emperor of China agrees to pay the sum of 12,000,000 of dollars, on account of the expenses incurred. . . .

XII.

On the assent of the Emperor of China to this Treaty being received, and the discharge of the first installment of money, Her Britannic Majesty's forces will retire from Nanking and the Grand Canal, and will no longer molest or stop the trade of China. . . .

GO ON TO THE NEXT PAGE.

Document 6

Source: French cartoon, "Carving Up the Pie of China," late 1890s.

END OF PART A

WORLD HISTORY
SECTION II

Part B
(Suggested planning and writing time — 40 minutes)
Percent of Section II score — 33 1/3

Directions: You are to answer the following question. You should spend 5 minutes organizing or outlining your essay.

Write an essay that:

- ✦ Has a relevant thesis and supports that thesis with appropriate historical evidence.
- ✦ Addresses all parts of the question.
- ✦ Uses world historical context to show continuities and changes over time.
- ✦ Analyzes the process of continuity and change over time.

2. Analyze the continuities and changes in the global process of industrial development during the period from 1750 to 1900.

END OF PART B

WORLD HISTORY
SECTION II

Part C
(Suggested planning and writing time—40 minutes)
Percent of Section II score—33 1/3

Directions: You are to answer the following question. You should spend 5 minutes organizing or outlining your essay.

Write an essay that:

- ✦ Has a relevant thesis and supports that thesis with appropriate historical evidence.
- ✦ Addresses all parts of the question.
- ✦ Makes direct, relevant comparisons.
- ✦ Analyzes relevant reasons for similarities and differences.

3. Compare the revolutionary process in France (1789–1801) with the revolutionary process in St. Domingue/Haiti (1791–1804).

STOP

END OF EXAM

Answer Key for Practice Exam 5

Answers for Section I: Multiple-Choice Questions

1. B	19. C	37. B	55. D
2. C	20. B	38. D	56. C
3. D	21. D	39. B	57. A
4. D	22. A	40. C	58. B
5. D	23. C	41. A	59. D
6. A	24. D	42. A	60. A
7. A	25. D	43. C	61. C
8. C	26. C	44. A	62. B
9. B	27. A	45. D	63. D
10. A	28. C	46. B	64. A
11. B	29. B	47. C	65. C
12. B	30. D	48. A	66. D
13. D	31. A	49. D	67. B
14. B	32. B	50. D	68. A
15. A	33. C	51. B	69. C
16. C	34. B	52. C	70. D
17. A	35. B	53. A	
18. A	36. D	54. D	

Scoring the Multiple-Choice Section

Use the following formula to calculate your raw score on the multiple-choice section of the exam:

$$\underline{\hspace{3cm}} \times 0.8571 = \underline{\hspace{3cm}}$$

Number correct (out of 70)   **Weighted Section I score (do not round)**

The highest possible score for the multiple-choice section is seventy correct answers, for a score of 60.

Rationales:

1. Answer: B

   Explanation: Population growth increased worldwide. As a result, existing sources of fuel, principally wood and charcoal, were dwindling. The ability to tap the energy potential of fossil fuels such as coal, oil, and natural gas offered greater quantities of energy for human use.

   Page Reference: p. 828

KEY CONCEPT	THEME	SKILL
5.1.I.B	1: Interaction Between Humans and the Environment.	Causation

2. Answer: C

   Explanation: Although their methods varied, socialists shared in common the belief that capitalism exploited the working class. Those inspired by the revolutionary idealism of Marxism insisted on a violent overthrow of the entire capitalist system. More moderate socialists advocated using democratic political processes to work for reform that would benefit the working class.

   Page Reference: p. 843

KEY CONCEPT	THEME	SKILL
5.1.V.A	2: Development and Interaction of Cultures.	Interpretation

3. Answer: D

   Explanation: The Bolshevik Revolution toppled the provisional government in Russia and established the Soviet Union under the leadership of the communist Bolshevik Party. The Indian Rebellion began as a mutiny of Indian soldiers but soon spread throughout much of India, enflamed by resentment of British rule. The Boxer Rebellion opposed the foreign presence in China, especially the spread of Christianity. The Maji Maji uprising in German East Africa in 1905 was one of many examples of violent resistance to the European conquest of Africa.

   Page Reference: pp. 887, 890, 939, 958

KEY CONCEPT	THEME	SKILL
5.3.III.D	3: State-Building, Expansion, and Conflict.	Comparison Causation

4. Answer: D

   Explanation: Qing China launched the self-strengthening movement, which sought to borrow Western technology to build up China's military and industries. In the Ottoman Empire, the Tanzimat reforms also borrowed from the West to modernize its economy and social and legal institutions. Both aimed to strengthen the state in the face of Western incursions into their territories.

   Page Reference: pp. 939, 944, 946

KEY CONCEPT	THEME	SKILL
5.3.III.F	3: State-Building, Expansion, and Conflict.	Comparison

5. Answer: D

   Explanation: The map shows Germany and Italy as new states in the late nineteenth century. The spread of nationalism, especially in the nineteenth century, led to political unification in Germany and Italy. By the early 1870s, both emerged for the first time as sovereign nation-states.

   Page Reference: p. 803

KEY CONCEPT	THEME	SKILL
5.3.II	3: State-Building, Expansion, and Conflict.	Contextualization

6. Answer: A

Explanation: The role of Spain, along with Portugal, diminished in this second phase of European expansion. France colonized Indochina (Southeast Asia). Japan colonized Taiwan and Korea. The United States controlled the Philippines after defeating the Spanish.

Page Reference: pp. 881, 937–38, 954

KEY CONCEPT	THEME	SKILL
5.2.I.B	3: State-Building, Expansion, and Conflict.	Comparison Contextualization

7. Answer: A

Explanation: Many colonial subjects worked for Europeans and received wages. Some sought better opportunities; a few were ordered to migrate to new sites to work by their colonial rulers. Since most of the work was abroad, many migrated overseas.

Page Reference: p. 896

KEY CONCEPT	THEME	SKILL
5.4.II.A	1: Interaction Between Humans and the Environment.	Causation

8. Answer: C

Explanation: Nature had endowed Britain with ample supplies of coal and iron ore. Deposits were concentrated in certain areas and easily accessible, making the extraction of the deposits relatively inexpensive. Coal and iron ore were the new sources of energy that jumpstarted Britain's Industrial Revolution.

Page Reference: p. 835

KEY CONCEPT	THEME	SKILL
5.1.I.A	1: Interaction Between Humans and the Environment.	Causation

9. Answer: B

Explanation: Those who reaped tremendous profits from industrialization—factory and mine owners, bankers, and merchants—formed the upper ranks of the middle class. Professionals like doctors, lawyers, engineers, scientists, teachers, and journalists also found new opportunities for upward mobility in the industrial economy.

Page Reference: p. 837

KEY CONCEPT	THEME	SKILL
5.1.VI.A	5: Development and Transformation of Social Structures.	Causation

10. Answer: A

    Explanation: Those countries facing the threat of colonial rule generally defined nationalism in terms of anti-imperialism. In Japan, resentment of Western incursions fostered an aggressive nationalism. In response to British and French interference, an "Egypt for the Egyptians" movement gained momentum.

    Page Reference: p. 805

KEY CONCEPT	THEME	SKILL
5.3.III.D	3: State-Building, Expansion, and Conflict.	Causation

11. Answer: B

    Explanation: In the nineteenth century, social Darwinism was used to justify European imperialism in Asia and Africa. Europeans considered themselves to be the superior race, characterized by their rigor, strength, and aggression. Other races were deemed intellectually and physically inferior, doomed to extinction by their natural weakness.

    Page Reference: p. 884

KEY CONCEPT	THEME	SKILL
5.2.III	2: Development and Interaction of Cultures.	Interpretation Causation

12. Answer: B

    Explanation: In the nineteenth century, racial stereotypes were given scientific validity by Europeans who believed that race and civilization were inextricably linked. In social Darwinism, Charles Darwin's theory of evolution was used to distinguish between "strong" and "weak" states and to rank human societies along racially defined lines.

    Page Reference: pp. 882–84

KEY CONCEPT	THEME	SKILL
5.2.III	2: Development and Interaction of Cultures.	Continuity and Change

13. Answer: D

    Explanation: Latin America's place in the global economy was to supply raw materials and agricultural products to the industrialized world. Countries specialized in one or two exports: copper and nitrates from Chile, tin from Bolivia, guano from Peru, sisal from Mexico, beef from Argentina, cacao from Ecuador, coffee from Brazil and Guatemala, sugar from Cuba, and bananas from Central America. In return, industrialized countries sold manufactured goods such as textiles, machines, tools, weapons, and luxury items to Latin American countries.

    Page Reference: p. 854

KEY CONCEPT	THEME	SKILL
5.1.II.A	4: Creation, Expansion, and Interaction of Economic Systems.	Causation

14. Answer: B

     Explanation: In 1853, the U.S. sent a naval fleet headed by Commodore Matthew Perry to Japan with a list of demands that would have opened Japan up to foreign commerce and exchange. The image portrays Perry and his second-in-command in a negative light, reflecting the xenophobia of many in Japanese society. The Tokugawa shogunate's acceptance of the U.S. terms contributed to its collapse in the Meiji Restoration.

     Page Reference: pp. 949–50

KEY CONCEPT	THEME	SKILL
5.2.II.A	3: State-Building, Expansion, and Conflict.	Contextualization

15. Answer: A

     Explanation: With the exception of Ethiopia and Liberia, the entire continent of Africa was brought under European colonial rule. Similarly, while Indochina came under French rule, South Asia under British rule, the East Indies under Dutch rule, the Philippines under Spanish and later American rule, the kingdom of Siam was able to retain its independence.

     Page Reference: p. 888

KEY CONCEPT	THEME	SKILL
5.2.III.D	3: State-Building, Expansion, and Conflict.	Comparison

16. Answer: C

     Explanation: Marx and Engels condemned the class conflict and inequalities generated by industrial capitalism. They called for a proletarian revolution to overthrow the capitalist system and the bourgeois state that maintained it. Only then could a socialist society be created, one in which everyone shared equally in the fruits of labor.

     Page Reference: pp. 842, 870

KEY CONCEPT	THEME	SKILL
5.1.V.A	2: Development and Interaction of Cultures.	Interpretation

17. Answer: A

     Explanation: In the nineteenth century, the Qing dynasty in China faced both internal and external threats. The first Opium War initiated a pattern of defeats at the hands of imperial powers. From within, a wave of peasant rebellions crippled the Qing state's ability to maintain order. Where China had been able to maintain its position as the "Middle Kingdom" in the sixteenth century, by the nineteenth century, China was forced to accept its subordinate position in the industrialized world.

     Page Reference: pp. 936–38

KEY CONCEPT	THEME	SKILL
5.3.III.A 5.2.I.E	3: State-Building, Expansion, and Conflict.	Continuity and Change

18. Answer: A

Explanation: Reflecting socialist theory, Marx and Engels attributed the immiseration of the working class to the competitive nature of the capitalist system, which exploited the working class. Samuel Smiles, reflecting the view of many in the middle class, attributed the poverty of the working class to its members own individual failings, in particular, a tendency to spend all their wages rather than save and invest their money for the future.

Page Reference: pp. 837, 842, 866–70

KEY CONCEPT	THEME	SKILL
5.1.V.A 5.1.VI.A	5: Development and Transformation of Social Structures.	Interpretation

19. Answer: C

Explanation: In *The Communist Manifesto,* Karl Marx and Friedrich Engels argued that industrial capitalism created two polarized classes: the bourgeoisie and the proletariat. They defined the proletariat as the modern working class, a product of the capitalist system.

Page Reference: pp. 839, 867–70

KEY CONCEPT	THEME	SKILL
5.1.VI.A	5: Development and Transformation of Social Structures.	Causation

20. Answer: B

Explanation: The state that emerged after the Meiji Restoration in 1868 launched an intensive program of industrialization that by the century's end transformed Japan into a modern industrial nation. By the time Japan began industrializing, knowledge and methods of industrial production were easily accessible. Borrowing selectively from the West, Japan was able to complete in about three decades what had taken Britain, for instance, a century to complete.

Page Reference: pp. 952–53

KEY CONCEPT	THEME	SKILL
5.1.I.D 5.1.V.C	4: Creation, Expansion, and Interaction of Economic Systems.	Comparison

21. Answer: D

Explanation: In the first phase of European conquests, Spain and Portugal led the way, with Spain emerging as the dominant player. In the second phase, Spain and Portugal played only minor roles. Spain lost the Philippines to the U.S., and Portugal only held a few colonies.

Page Reference: p. 884

KEY CONCEPT	THEME	SKILL
5.2.I.B	3: State-Building, Expansion, and Conflict.	Periodization Continuity and Change

22. Answer: A

Explanation: The U.S. government authorized military intervention in Central America in order to support American corporate interests. The United Fruit Company was a U.S.-owned company based in Central America.

Page Reference: p. 859

KEY CONCEPT	THEME	SKILL
5.2.I.E 5.1.III.C	4: Creation, Expansion, and Interaction of Economic Systems.	Interpretation Contextualization

23. Answer: C

Explanation: Revolutionaries in the Atlantic revolutions drew from the discourse of the Enlightenment to justify their rebellion. The Enlightenment ideals of freedom and equality were invoked to overthrow arbitrary governments and, in the case of Haiti, also to abolish slavery.

Page Reference: p. 784

KEY CONCEPT	THEME	SKILL
5.3.III.A 5.3.I.D	2: Development and Interaction of Cultures.	Comparison

24. Answer: D

Explanation: The quote reflects the Eurocentrism of the time, when European power and influence was at its peak. Recent views of world history have sought to offer a more balanced view by emphasizing how recent European global domination is, pointing to earlier periods of domination under previous civilizations such as the Arabs, Chinese, and Mongols.

Page Reference: pp. 775–77

KEY CONCEPT	THEME	SKILL
5.2.III	2: Development and Interaction of Cultures.	Argumentation

25. Answer: D

Explanation: The factory system required a disciplined and focused workforce to increase productivity. To that end, many factories issued rules aimed at curbing worker behavior that contributed to lower productivity. Heavy fines were often imposed for infractions, however minor.

Page Reference: p. 840

KEY CONCEPT	THEME	SKILL
5.1. I.C	4: Creation, Expansion, and Interaction of Economic Systems.	Evidence

26. Answer: C

Explanation: Stanton's statement does not reflect the class concerns articulated in Marxism. Stanton inserted "women" into the opening lines of the American

Declaration of Independence to argue that the founding principles of the nation should include women. She also invoked the Enlightenment ideal of equality to argue for equal rights for women. Stanton made this statement at the Seneca Falls Conference, which was a key event in the women's suffrage movement.

Page Reference: p. 806

KEY CONCEPT	THEME	SKILL
5.3.I.E 5.3.IV.B 5.3.I.D	5: Development and Transformation of Social Structures.	Interpretation Synthesis

27. Answer: A

Explanation: "The "scramble for Africa" refers to the partitioning of most of the African continent amongst the European powers. This began in the last quarter of the nineteenth century and ended in the early twentieth century. As the map shows, the European conquest of Africa was violently resisted throughout Africa.

Page Reference: pp. 885–87

KEY CONCEPT	THEME	SKILL
5.2.I.C	3: State-Building, Expansion, and Conflict.	Contextualization

28. Answer: C

Explanation: In the late nineteenth century, shrinking opportunities and widespread poverty in China made emigration an attractive option for many Chinese men. The gold rushes in the U.S., Canada, New Zealand, and Australia attracted many Chinese immigrants. In response to the influx of immigrants, Canada, New Zealand, and Australia all imposed a head tax on Chinese immigrants. As part of the White Australia Policy, Australia passed its first Chinese Exclusion Act in 1855. The U.S. passed the Chinese Exclusion Act in 1882. Canada passed the Chinese Exclusion Act in 1923.

Page Reference: p. 898

KEY CONCEPT	THEME	SKILL
5.4.III.C	1: Interaction Between Humans and the Environment.	Comparison Contextualization

29. Answer: B

Explanation: Luther's argument that salvation was a matter of individual faith challenged the role of the Catholic Church in mediating people's relationship with God. He arguedthat people should be able to read the Bible and interpret its teachings for themselves. Luther's idea of justification by faith alone sparked irreconcilable differences in doctrinal interpretations that expressed themselves in the Protestant Reformation.

Page Reference: p. 722

KEY CONCEPT	THEME	SKILL
4.1.VI.B	2: Development and Interaction of Cultures.	Continuity and Change

30. Answer: D

    Explanation: The plantation-based economy in the Americas, concentrated in the Caribbean and Brazil, depended almost exclusively on African slave labor. For African slaves, the transatlantic journey from West Africa to the Americas, referred to as the Middle Passage, was a horrific experience. From 1500 to 1866, an estimated 12.5 million Africans were enslaved, but about 10.7 million made it alive to the Americas. The mortality rate was estimated at 14 percent.

    Page Reference: pp. 687, 693

KEY CONCEPT	THEME	SKILL
4.2.I.C	4: Creation, Expansion, and Interaction of Economic Systems.	Evidence Interpretation

31. Answer: A

    Explanation: The Scientific Revolution rejected faith-based approaches to knowledge, proposing instead new methods for ascertaining truth. They emphasized reason, empiricism, experimentation, and observation. Enlightenment thinkers would apply the same methodology in their investigations of political, economic, cultural, and social institutions.

    Page Reference: pp. 744–45

KEY CONCEPT	THEME	SKILL
5.3.I.A 5.3.I.B	2: Development and Interaction of Cultures.	Continuity and Change

32. Answer: B

    Explanation: Although Europeans had established themselves in the new global economy of the early modern period, they did not dominate the world economy. Asia in general and China in particular played a more central role in the early modern economy. Europeans competed with one another for a share of the market in Asia.

    Page Reference: p. 682

KEY CONCEPT	THEME	SKILL
4.1.IV.A	4: Creation, Expansion, and Interaction of Economic Systems.	Periodization

33. Answer: C

    Explanation: Enlightenment thinkers like John Locke and Jean-Jacques Rousseau invoked the concept of the social contract to describe a new relationship between the people and the state. The idea of the social contract emphasized the consent of the governed and promoted forms of government in which protection of the people's rights was central to the task of the state.

    Page Reference: pp. 745–46

KEY CONCEPT	THEME	SKILL
5.3.I.C	2: Development and Interaction of Cultures.	Continuity and Change

34. Answer: B

    Explanation: Rich silver deposits in South America and Japan fueled and linked the global economy during the early modern period. Europeans used the silver from the Americas to purchase goods in Asia. Spain played a vital role in the global flow of silver, shipping the silver from its mines in Bolivia to Acapulco in Mexico, and then across the Pacific to the Philippines.

    Page Reference: pp. 679–80

KEY CONCEPT	THEME	SKILL
4.1.IV.B	4: Creation, Expansion, and Interaction of Economic Systems.	Causation

35. Answer: B

    Explanation: Despite the different sects that emerged from the Protestant Reformation, they all shared in common the belief that individuals should be able to read and interpret the Bible for themselves. The printing press facilitated this process as the Bible became the most widely printed text. The Bible was translated into the languages that people spoke.

    Page Reference: p. 723

KEY CONCEPT	THEME	SKILL
4.1.VI.B	2: Development and Interaction of Cultures.	Causation

36. Answer: D

    Explanation: The Atlantic slave trade drew exclusively from Africa. Consequently, slave status became associated with "blackness." Slavery in the Americas was also associated with the plantation economy. The cultivation of labor-intensive cash crops like sugar, tobacco, and cotton was dependent on slave labor.

    Page Reference: pp. 688–89

KEY CONCEPT	THEME	SKILL
4.2.I.C	4: Creation, Expansion, and Interaction of Economic Systems.	Continuity and Change Comparison

37. Answer: B

    Explanation: In the early modern period, these European countries had the political will, financial resources, and technological capabilities to launch voyages across the Atlantic. Their geographic location on the Atlantic rim placed them closer to the Americas than any potential competitors from Eurasia.

    Page Reference: p. 619

KEY CONCEPT	THEME	SKILL
4.1.III.B-D	3: State-Building, Expansion, and Conflict.	Comparison

38. Answer: D

    Explanation: The dominant economic doctrine in early modern Europe was mercantilism. Mercantilist policies emphasized exports and the stockpiling of precious metals, especially gold and silver. States favored mercantilist policies because such policies increased state wealth.

    Page Reference: p. 626

KEY CONCEPT	THEME	SKILL
4.1.IV.C	4: Creation, Expansion, and Interaction of Economic Systems.	Comparison Contextualization

39. Answer: B

    Explanation: In Mexico, Mesoamerican and Spanish conceptions of divine motherhood merged in the cult of the Virgin of Guadalupe. Legend holds that a dark-skinned Virgin Mary appeared to a Mexican peasant in 1531. From this, the cult of the Virgin of Guadalupe emerged, a hybrid product of Catholic and indigenous culture.

    Page Reference: pp. 719, 732

KEY CONCEPT	THEME	SKILL
4.1.VI.B 4.1.VI.D	2: Development and Interaction of Cultures.	Evidence

40. Answer: C

    Explanation: Both the Ottoman practice of *devshirme* and the Chinese examination system were means by which the state recruited the personnel for its bureaucracy and military. In *devshirme*, young boys were recruited from the Christian communities in the Balkans and trained for the elite Janissary units. In the civil service examination system, Chinese men who passed the exams were eligible for official posts in the government.

    Page Reference: pp. 646, 651

KEY CONCEPT	THEME	SKILL
4.3.I.D	3: State-Building, Expansion, and Conflict.	Comparison

41. Answer: A

    Explanation: With the incorporation of portions of Central Asia into the Chinese or Russian empires, the pastoral societies that dominated the region began an irreversible decline. Pastoral peoples no longer had open land for their animals to graze. As a result, many left the nomadic life, with a great many reduced to poverty. In Mongolia, the nobility found themselves falling into debt to Chinese merchants.

    Page Reference: pp. 641–42

KEY CONCEPT	THEME	SKILL
4.3.II.B	3: State-Building, Expansion, and Conflict.	Comparison Causation

42. Answer: A

    Explanation: In the pre-modern Islamic world, female slaves were preferred. In contrast, the Atlantic slave trade drew mostly male labor from Africa. Since slave labor was needed to work the plantations in the Americas, the preference was for male workers.

    Page Reference: pp. 688–89

KEY CONCEPT	THEME	SKILL
4.2.I.C	4: Creation, Expansion, and Interaction of Economic Systems.	Continuity and Change Periodization

43. Answer: C

    Explanation: The first phase of Islamic expansion was largely through military conquest. Similarly, the first stage of European expansion occurred through military conquest. Defeat convinced many among the conquered populations that traditional gods had been too weak to protect them and that the religion of their conquerors was superior to their own. Many were receptive to religious conversion.

    Page Reference: pp. 421, 728

KEY CONCEPT	THEME	SKILL
3.1.III.A	2: Development and Interaction of Cultures. 3: State-Building, Expansion, and Conflict.	Comparison

44. Answer: A

    Explanation: Hinduism and Buddhism were religions that originated in India and spread throughout Asia. The temple complex at Angkor Wat in Southeast Asia was originally constructed by the state as a Hindu temple. Beginning in the late thirteenth century, it became a religious site for Buddhists.

    Page Reference: p. 331

KEY CONCEPT	THEME	SKILL
3.1.III.D	2: Development and Interaction of Cultures.	Contextualization Evidence

45. Answer: D

    Explanation: Swahili civilization was composed of a number of independent city-states ruled by their own king. They competed with one another in Indian Ocean commerce. They resembled the city-states of ancient Greece.

    Page Reference: p. 333

KEY CONCEPT	THEME	SKILL
3.2.I.B	3: State-Building, Expansion, and Conflict.	Comparison

46. Answer: B

Explanation: Long-distance trade along both routes relied heavily on the use of domesticated pack animals like camels, horses, and oxen. The development of saddles, along with yokes and stirrups, made it easier to use such animals to cross the vast expanse of Eurasia and the Sahara.

Page Reference: pp. 319, 335

KEY CONCEPT	THEME	SKILL
2.3.II.A 3.1.I.C	4: Creation, Expansion, and Interaction of Economic Systems.	Comparison Contextualization

47. Answer: C

Explanation: Venice emerged by the tenth century as an important center of the commercial networks connecting the Mediterranean to the Black Sea and the Atlantic coastline. Jenne-jeno was the most well-known of the city-states that comprised the Niger Valley civilization, which began to decline in the tenth century. Its location at a transfer point along the Niger River contributed to its rise. In North America, Cahokia's location at the intersection of the Mississippi, Illinois, and Missouri rivers made it an important hub for regional trade from the tenth to the thirteenth century.

Page Reference: pp. 325, 335, 340

KEY CONCEPT	THEME	SKILL
3.1.I.A-B	4: Creation, Expansion, and Interaction of Economic Systems.	Comparison Causation Contextualization

48. Answer: A

Explanation: Since textile weaving was done at home, it was associated with women. As the demand for textiles increased, textile production came to be identified as women's work. In China, for instance, the demand for silk resulted in the feminization of the silk industry.

Page Reference: pp. 320, 336

KEY CONCEPT	THEME	SKILL
3.3.I.C 3.3.III.B	4: Creation, Expansion, and Interaction of Economic Systems. 5: Development and Transformation of Social Structures.	Causation Comparison

49. Answer: D

Explanation: The increase in commercial activity was facilitated by the state's construction of an infrastructure that encouraged regional trade. The Tang and Song states created a dense network of internal waterways that stretched an estimated 30,000 miles. These waterways connected the different parts of the empire and reduced transportation costs, thereby facilitating trade.

Page Reference: pp. 368–69

KEY CONCEPT	THEME	SKILL
3.1.I.D	4: Creation, Expansion, and Interaction of Economic Systems.	Causation

50. Answer: D

Explanation: In contrast to the rhetoric of the tribute system, which placed China in a superior position, China's relations with the nomadic peoples of the northern steppes was on an equal basis. The Xiongnu, Uighurs, Khitan, and Jurchen in particular posed a constant threat to the Chinese state. To placate them, successive Chinese dynasties sent them goods.

Page Reference: pp. 374–76

KEY CONCEPT	THEME	SKILL
2.2.IV.B 3.3.II.A	3: State-Building, Expansion, and Conflict.	Continuity and Change Comparison

51. Answer: B

Explanation: The Confucian revival in the Song dynasty, referred to as Neo-Confucianism, emphasized the subordination of women to men and the separation of the sexes. Submission and passivity were extolled as female virtues. The spread of this strand of Confucianism into the Korean peninsula, particularly after the fourteenth century, placed new restrictions on women.

Page Reference: pp. 367, 371, 378–79

KEY CONCEPT	THEME	SKILL
3.3.III.D	5: Development and Transformation of Social Structures.	Comparison Continuity and Change

52. Answer: C

Explanation: Europe's location on the western extreme of the Eurasian continent meant that technological innovations originating in China, which was on the eastern end, had to travel great distances. Since the transfer of technology often occurred along trade routes, Europe's marginalized position in the commercial networks of Eurasia also placed Europe at a disadvantage.

Page Reference: pp. 384–87

KEY CONCEPT	THEME	SKILL
3.1.III.E 3.2.II	2: Development and Interaction of Cultures.	Interpretation Contextualization Synthesis

53. Answer: A

Explanation: Orthodox Muslims emphasized the centrality of the sharia in the development of an authentic Islamic society. However, the introduction of Islam into Anatolia and its subsequent spread within the Ottoman Empire owed much to the missionary activities of Sufi practitioners, who emphasized the mystical aspects of Islam. Although an Islamic empire, the Ottoman state was influenced by local traditions. Turkish rather than Arabic was the dominant language. The more egalitarian structures of the pastoral communities of Central Asia diluted the patriarchal aspects of Islam. And shamanism, practiced among Central Asian peoples, influenced the turning dances characteristic of Sufi religious practices.

Page Reference: pp. 424, 430–32

KEY CONCEPT	THEME	SKILL
3.1.III.A 3.2.I.C	2: Development and Interaction of Cultures.	Argumentation Evidence

54. Answer: D

Explanation: The Germanic kingdoms that emerged after the collapse of the Roman Empire aspired to recreate the Roman Empire. In the eighth century, Charlemagne had the pope crown him as the new Roman emperor. In the tenth century, Otto I had himself crowned emperor by the pope.

Page Reference: pp. 477–78

KEY CONCEPT	THEME	SKILL
3.2.I.A	3: State-Building, Expansion, and Conflict.	Continuity and Change Periodization

55. Answer: D

Explanation: Most pastoral peoples lacked a written language, so a literary culture never developed. Scholars have emphasized the achievements of pastoral societies to balance or correct the negative portrayals of pastoral peoples in past scholarship. They have drawn attention to the ability of pastoral societies to adapt to their environment, their technological and political innovations, and their role in facilitating cross-cultural exchange.

Page Reference: p. 540

KEY CONCEPT	THEME	SKILL
3.1.I.E	1: Interaction Between Humans and the Environment. 3: State-Building, Expansion, and Conflict. 4: Creation, Expansion, and Interaction of Economic Systems.	Argumentation

56. Answer: C

Explanation: Neither the Igbo nor the Iroquois people had a centralized state. The Igbo people developed various means to deal with conflict, including title societies and women's associations. The Iroquois-speaking people formed a confederation through which they resolved disputes.

Page Reference: pp. 564–65

KEY CONCEPT	THEME	SKILL
3.2.I.B	3: State-Building, Expansion, and Conflict.	Comparison

57. Answer: A

Explanation: Under its emperor, Qin Shihuangdi, the Qin dynasty introduced a number of features that created a centralized administration. These included a uniform system of weights, measures, and currency as well as the standardization of the lengths of axles for carts. The written form of the Chinese language was also standardized. The Han dynasty incorporated these administrative features into their own government.

Page Reference: pp. 135–36

KEY CONCEPT	THEME	SKILL
2.2.II.A 2.2.II.C	3: State-Building, Expansion, and Conflict.	Continuity and Change

58. Answer: B

Explanation: Both Roman and Chinese rulers invoked divine will to legitimize their power. Romans worshipped deceased emperors as gods, and a religious cult developed centered on the emperor. The Chinese emperor claimed the Mandate of Heaven to justify his rule. Both empires claimed to include the entire world; Romans and Chinese referred to their empires in universalistic terms. Both the Roman and Chinese states invested in roads, bridges, aqueducts, canals, and protective walls.

Page Reference: p. 136

KEY CONCEPT	THEME	SKILL
2.2.I 2.2.II.B	3: State-Building, Expansion, and Conflict.	Comparison

59. Answer: D

Explanation: The Roman Empire extended citizenship and its attendant rights to free people within its empire. However, cultural identities remained largely intact. In contrast, the Chinese empire actively sought to assimilate newly conquered peoples. Intermarriage was encouraged.

Page Reference: p. 137

KEY CONCEPT	THEME	SKILL
2.2.I	3: State-Building, Expansion, and Conflict.	Comparison

60. Answer: A

Explanation: The political history of India and Western Europe from roughly the sixth to the eleventh centuries was characterized by a decentralized and fragmented political system dominated by local rulers. No long-lasting imperial state emerged to encompass the entire region, as in the case of China.

Page Reference: p. 143

KEY CONCEPT	THEME	SKILL
2.2.I 2.2.IV.B	3: State-Building, Expansion, and Conflict.	Comparison

61. Answer: C

    Explanation: Both the *Arthashastra* and *The Prince* shared the same pragmatic approach that emphasized how politics actually operated rather than how it ought to work. Both advised rulers to use any means available to them, including force, to achieve their goals.

    Page Reference: pp. 142, 571

KEY CONCEPT	THEME	SKILL
2.2.I	3: State-Building, Expansion, and Conflict.	Comparison

62. Answer: B

    Explanation: Historical accounts of the Greek triumph over the Persian Empire attribute the victory to Greek freedoms. According to this view, Greeks fought courageously to defend their freedoms. This led to an association of Greece with freedom and Persia with despotism. As Western Europe claimed the Greek legacy, Persia became associated with Asia and, more generally, the East.

    Page Reference: p. 126

KEY CONCEPT	THEME	SKILL
2.2.I	3: State-Building, Expansion, and Conflict.	Argumentation Interpretation

63. Answer: D

    Explanation: After the emergence of Buddhism in India, Hinduism began to evolve into a popular religion. In contrast to the philosophical abstractions characteristic of earlier forms of Hinduism, this popular form of Hinduism found more appeal among the masses. The new ideas associated with this popular Hinduism found expression in epic poems like the *Ramayana* and the *Mahabharata*.

    Page Reference: p. 179

KEY CONCEPT	THEME	SKILL
2.3.III.C 2.1.V.A	2: Development and Interaction of Cultures.	Continuity and Change Contextualization

64. Answer: A

    Explanation: The kingdom of Armenia was the first to adopt Christianity as a state religion. The emerging kingdom of Axum in what is today Eritrea and Ethiopia also adopted Christianity as the state religion around the same time. After centuries of persecution, Christianity was officially endorsed by the Roman emperor Constantine and became the state religion during the late fourth century.

    Page Reference: pp. 190–92

KEY CONCEPT	THEME	SKILL
2.1.II.D	2: Development and Interaction of Cultures.	Comparison

65.   Answer: C

Explanation: Greek thinkers emphasized logic and argumentation as a means of knowing. They valued reason over faith and encouraged people to question everything. They sought rational and secular explanations as opposed to religious and spiritual musings in their quest to understand the material world.

Page Reference: pp. 184–86

KEY CONCEPT	THEME	SKILL
2.1.II.E	2: Development and Interaction of Cultures.	Continuity and Change

66.   Answer: D

Explanation: The civil service examination system was only open to men. Although patriarchy persisted during these centuries, it was not as strict as in previous or later dynasties. The fall of the Han dynasty contributed to the decline of Confucianism, the growing popularity of Daoism, and the spread of nomadic cultures. All of these developments loosened patriarchal controls on women.

Page Reference: pp. 235–36

KEY CONCEPT	THEME	SKILL
2.1.III 2.2.III.D	5: Development and Transformation of Social Structures.	Causation

67.   Answer: B

Explanation: Beginning around 3000 B.C.E., Bantu-speaking people from what is today the southeastern part of Nigeria and the Cameroons began migrating throughout the southern half of Africa. The more than 400 languages spoken in that region all reflect linguistic origins in the Bantu language.

Page Reference: p. 282

KEY CONCEPT	THEME	SKILL
3.1II.C	1: Interaction Between Humans and the Environment.	Causation

68.   Answer: A

Explanation: The Paleolithic period is so named for the use of stone tools. During this period, humans migrated to different parts of the world. The development of a wider range of stone tools during this period reflects the adaptation to different environments.

Page Reference: pp. 4–5, 14

KEY CONCEPT	THEME	SKILL
1.1.I.B	1: Interaction Between Humans and the Environment.	Periodization

69. Answer: C

   Explanation: Agriculture developed independently in different parts of the Americas: coastal Andean region, Mesoamerica, Mississippi River valley, and perhaps the Amazon basin. The lack of animals that could be domesticated meant that agricultural societies in the Americas had to find alternative sources of protein. As a result, there was a continued reliance on hunting and fishing for sources of protein. The lack of animals also meant a lack of fertilizer. The plow and pull cart were not developed because there were no animals to pull them.

   Page Reference: pp. 32–33

KEY CONCEPT	THEME	SKILL
1.2.I.A	4: Creation, Expansion, and Interaction of Economic Systems.	Comparison Causation

70. Answer: D

   Explanation: Monotheism was not a distinctive feature in the cultural patterns of pre-Columbian America. Later civilizations like the Maya, Teotihuacán, and Hopewell reflect cultural patterns similar to those associated with the Olmecs.

   Page Reference: p. 68

KEY CONCEPT	THEME	SKILL
1.3.I	2: Development and Interaction of Cultures.	Continuity and Change

Answer Guide for Section II:
Part A

General Guidelines for Answering a Document-Based Question (DBQ):

1. Pre-Write. Create a brief outline before you start writing.
2. Write your DBQ in a multiple-paragraph structure. In your first paragraph, write an introduction that clearly states your thesis.
3. Present your arguments in body paragraphs. Body paragraphs should integrate groupings of documents, demonstrate understanding of documents, support the thesis using documents as evidence, analyze point of view, and possibly include additional relevant historical content. Present your arguments in body paragraphs that focus on a grouping of documents and that put forth a single argument centered on answering the prompt.
4. In your final paragraph, write a conclusion that includes a reworded restatement of your thesis.

AP World History DBQ essays are scored using a core scoring method with a maximum score of nine. In the basic core, you may earn the following seven points:

   ✦ one point for a thesis
   ✦ one point for addressing and understanding the documents
   ✦ up to two points for using the documents as evidence to answer the prompt
   ✦ one point for grouping the documents

> ✦ one point for analyzing Point of View (POV)
> ✦ one point for identifying and explaining the need for an additional document

If you earn ALL seven basic core points, you have the chance to earn up to two additional points in what is called expanded core. Expanded core points may be granted for the following features:

> ✦ an excellent, sophisticated, and comprehensive thesis
> ✦ insightful document analysis
> ✦ analyzing POV in all or most documents
> ✦ including extra document groupings or additional documents
> ✦ incorporating relevant historical content not found in the documents

Below is a detailed description of what you will need to do in your answer to earn each basic core point for this essay.

Thesis (1 point): To earn a point in this category, you must write a thesis that responds to the entire prompt and outlines the specific arguments you will make based on a correct usage of the documents. You will need to mention the arguments you plan on making in your answer, and you will need to avoid generalizations that do not reflect reasonable interpretations of the documents. Thesis statements will only earn a point if they appear in the first or last paragraph of the essay. Common errors in thesis writing include merely rewriting the prompt or presenting an answer to only some parts of the prompt, so make sure you address the entire prompt and briefly present the specific arguments that you will use in your answer based on the documents.

> **Prompt:** Using the following documents, analyze Chinese imperial government responses to British trade and the long-term effects of British trade on Qing dynasty China from 1750 C.E. to 1900 C.E. Identify an additional type of document and explain how it would help your analysis of Chinese government responses to and long-term effects of British trade.

Examples:

> Example Thesis: "In the period from 1750 C.E. to 1900 C.E., Qing dynasty China responded to British trade by sending formal diplomatic appeals, passing laws and regulations, and making attempts to resist the trade. In the long-term, the impacts of British trade in China led to a Chinese trade deficit draining money out of China, British invasion of China, and losses of Chinese power and lands."

> ✦ This thesis earns the point by pointing out the specific arguments based on the documents that will be used to answer the prompt. It presents BOTH Chinese responses and the long-term impacts of British trade, so it answers the entire prompt. Thesis statements can be longer than a single sentence. A multi-sentence thesis should, however, be presented in contiguous sentences.

Unacceptable Example One: "The Chinese government responded to British trade using a couple of different tactics, but British trade still impacted Qing China in the long run."

> ✦ This thesis does little other than state the obvious given the prompt.

Unacceptable Example Two: "From 1750 C.E. to 1900 C.E., Qing dynasty China was impacted negatively by British trade."

> ✦ This thesis improves upon the first example by including a characterization of the long-term impact of British trade, but it would NOT earn a thesis point because it does not answer the entire prompt.

Addressing and Understanding Documents (1 point): To earn this point, you must address ALL of the documents and demonstrate understanding of "all but one." This means that throughout your answer, you must show understanding of at least six of the seven documents.

Using Documents as Evidence (2 points): To earn two points, you must correctly incorporate at least six documents (although seven would be better) into arguments that answer the prompt. You will earn only one point if you use five of the seven documents in your arguments. If you use four or fewer documents in your essay, you will receive a zero in this category.

Grouping the Documents (1 point): Documents should be grouped in at least three ways in order to earn a point in this category. You can group documents by matching two or more documents that hold some relevant feature in common. Each example grouping below represents documents that, when used together, can make up an argument that answers the prompt.

Grouping the Documents:

Chinese Responses:

Diplomatic Interactions	Docs 1, 4, 5
Regulations on Trade	Docs 1, 2, 4
Arrogant Attitude	Docs 1, 4
Internal Debate in Gov't	Docs 2
Resistance	Docs 1, 4, 5, 6

Effects:

Chinese Trade Deficit/Brit Trade Surplus	Docs 2, 3
More Opium Trade & Loss of $ for China	Docs 2, 3, 4, 5
Disorder in China	Docs 2
Loss of Chinese Power	Docs 1, 2, 3, 4, 5, 6
Loss of Chinese Lands	Docs 2, 5, 6
Invasions of China	Docs 5, 6

Analyzing Point of View (1 Point): Many students find it challenging to earn the point in this category. The best way to earn the Point of View (POV) point is to go beyond the basic identity of the source author and the source itself, as described in the document source line. In order to write a successful POV statement, you should try to establish a better understanding of the identity of the author; you can do this by asking yourself questions about the author and the source. What is the author's gender or social class? What religion does the author follow? What is the author's profession? Does the author have an identifiable ethnicity, nationality, or other allegiance to a particular group? Is the source from a poem, essay, or novel? What was the source used for? Once you've asked these questions, go further and explain how some of these factors may have influenced the content of the source. Your complete POV statement should both identify the influences that may have shaped the author or source and explain how those particular influences have specifically affected the content of the document. Below are some examples of POV statements based on the documents from this question.

Examples of POV Statements:

Document 1: "Source: Chinese Qing dynasty Emperor Qianlong, 'Message to King George III,' a letter to the British monarch, 1793."

✦ As the Qing emperor Qianlong seeks to maintain the Mandate of Heaven, he must keep an orderly society to preserve his status as the favored son of heaven and demonstrate acceptable ruling authority over China. He sent his letter as a leader pursuing the goal of keeping power and maintaining the strength of China, which is a common concern of rulers.

Document 3: "Source: British company records, 1835–1836."

✦ British companies sought profits through trading. As profit seekers, they carefully documented the values of goods traded as a way to keep track of whether they were making money and also to allow for analysis of whether they could increase the amount of money they could make in the future. The table was created with an eye on the bottom line and excludes factors unrelated to profits, such as the social impact of sending the narcotic opium into China or the legality or illegality of this trade.

Document 6: "Source: French cartoon, 'Carving Up the Pie of China,' late 1890s."

✦ This French cartoon shows an interesting perspective. On the one hand, the cartoonist portrayed China's declining status from a European point of view. The French figure in the cartoon is removed behind those nations currently "carving up" China, so the cartoon represents a French observation of the idea that China is losing sovereignty to other nations. On the other hand, as a political cartoon, it is created by someone attempting to persuade people about the meaning of events or that some action may be advisable. In this case, the French commentary shows a symbolic figure of France not yet at the table, and it suggests that France might do well to get a slice before they are all taken by rival nations. The French cartoon shows little sympathy for the impacts of these events on China or the Chinese ruling dynasty, which is portrayed in an unsympathetic fashion.

You should write as many POV statements as you are able to produce. You can earn the POV point with as few as two correct POV statements; however, it's not uncommon to make errors in writing POV statements. For that reason, it's safer to provide more than just two in order to make up for any errors. Additionally, if you earn all of the basic core points, an extra POV statement can earn you an expanded core point.

Additional Document Statement (1 Point): A good additional document statement identifies a missing document that, if added to the provided documents, would help make a better answer to the question. You are only required to make a single additional document statement to earn a point, but you should aim to identify a minimum of three additional documents. This allows room for mistakes, and after the first correct additional document statement, any extras can earn you bonus points in the expanded core if you earn all seven points in the basic core. You should be careful to avoid the common mistake of asking for a type of document that is already provided. Additional document statements must meet three standards to be considered successful:

✦ The document suggested must be historically plausible.
✦ The statement must include an explanation as to **why** the additional document would be useful in answering the prompt.

✦ The analysis of **why** must speculate about the particulars of what the missing document might include. In other words, a successful additional document suggestion is historically possible given the time and place, includes an explanation of how the new source would help answer the prompt, and goes as far as speculating on arguments that the suggested source might support.

Document Analysis:

Document 1: "Source: Chinese Qing dynasty Emperor Qianlong, 'Message to King George III,' a letter to the British monarch, 1793." Qianlong employed a diplomatic approach to British trade in the eighteenth century. His letter shows how the Chinese tried to regulate trade and the resistance of the Chinese to unlimited or expanded British trade. The document includes an arrogant attitude of superiority, warning the British to heed China's commands. If this document is paired with other documents, it may be used to show China's declining power. Qianlong tells the British what to do, whereas later documents show the British more dominant in relations between the two nations.

Document 2: "Source: Xu Naiji, a senior official and advisor to Qing Emperor Daoguang, 'An Argument for Legalization,' 1836." This document can be used to show Chinese responses including internal debates and attempts to regulate trade with Britain. It details impacts such as a Chinese trade deficit with Britain, increased opium in China, a loss of order, and a decline in China's status when compared with Document 1.

Document 3: "Source: British company records, 1835–1836." Document 3 shows a loss of Chinese power as trade tipped in favor of Britain and China experienced a trade deficit.

Document 4: "Source: Lin Zexu, a senior official sent by Qing Emperor Daoguang to suppress the illegal opium trade, 'A Moral Appeal to Queen Victoria' 1839." Document 4 shows another diplomatic Chinese response, more attempts to regulate trade and opium, an ongoing Chinese arrogance, and resistance to British domination via trade. The impacts it shows include a loss of money and power for China.

Document 5: "Source: *The Treaty of Nanjing,* ending the First Opium War between Britain and China, 1842." Document 5 is another diplomatic response but in the form of a treaty ending a war. It shows that the Chinese fought to keep control or reestablish control of trade with Britain. Regarding long-term effects, it shows that China was invaded by Britain, lost the war, owed Britain lots of money, lost power, and also lost land while opening up to more British trade.

Document 6: "Source: French cartoon, 'Carving Up the Pie of China,' late 1890s." Document 6 shows a Chinese response of resistance in the way the caricature figure representing the ruler of China throws up his hands to indicate "stop.",China is clearly unsuccessful as the rest of the image displays a loss of Chinese power, invasions of China, and a loss of Chinese lands.

Answer Guide for Section II: Part B

2. Analyze the continuities and changes in the global process of industrial development during the period from 1750 to 1900.

What Does the Question Ask?

This question deals with the systems that organized how people worked during a period of tremendous global interactions. The question is open-ended. You can choose to write about the region or regions of the world that you know the best.

Listed below is the scoring system used to grade continuity and change-over-time essays; also included are guidelines and examples for how to earn each point for this question.

Has Acceptable Thesis (1 point)

+ The thesis needs to correctly address both continuity and change in the global process of industrial development during the period from 1750 to 1900.
+ The thesis should appear in the first paragraph (although it may also count if it is in the conclusion).
+ The thesis can be one sentence or multiple sentences.

Examples:

+ Example One: Britain remained a global leader of industrial development throughout the period from 1750 to 1900. Other countries rose in influence during this time, threatening Britain's industrial supremacy.
+ Example Two: Textiles remained an important part of industrialization from 1750 to 1900. Other products, such as steel and chemicals, changed the way that factories produced materials.
+ Example Three: From the beginning of industrialization up to 1900 and beyond, factory work has led to urbanization. A new middle class of managers and professionals emerged in the 1800s that changed the class structure.
+ Unacceptable Example: A continuity was that industrialization led to new industrial production. A change would be that China and the Pacific Rim countries became major industrial producers.
  • This is an unacceptable thesis because the continuity is self-evident and the change applies to the time period after 1900.

Addresses All Parts of the Question (2 points)

+ The essay accurately addresses both a continuity (1 point) and a change (1 point).
+ The statements of continuity and change may not appear in the thesis.

Examples:

+ Example One: Britain was the first country to go through an industrial revolution in the late eighteenth century. It continued to be dominant as an economic powerhouse throughout the nineteenth century. Japan, the United States, and Germany developed quickly. Each rose to be a strong industrial economy by 1900.
  • The first two sentences in the example above address continuity, while the next two sentences address change.

✦ Example Two: The first factories built in Europe spun thread and wove cloth. Other products, such as steel and chemicals, became more important as industrialization became more advanced. Even so, textiles continued to be a large part of industrialization.
  • The second sentence in the example above addresses change, while the third sentence addresses change.
✦ Example Three: Part of the global process of industrialization throughout modern times has been the movement of people from the countryside to the city. The factories produced wealth, and a new middle class of educated professionals arose.
  • The first statement in the example above addresses continuity, while the second statement addresses change.

Substantiates Thesis with Appropriate Historical Evidence (2 points)

✦ A piece of historical evidence is a fact that is correct and relevant to the time period.
✦ To earn the full two points in this category, an essay should have five or more pieces of evidence.
✦ To earn only one point in this category, an essay needs three or four pieces of evidence.
✦ Points for evidence can be earned even if the thesis point is not earned.

Examples:

✦ Example One: Beginning at the end of the eighteenth century, Britain's economy led the rest of the world in industrial production. Britain had the first and most sophisticated factories in all of Europe. Other countries, such as Japan, Germany, and the United States followed Britain's lead and became more industrialized. By the end of the nineteenth century, Britain was still one of the world's leading industrial countries. Other countries, however, had newer and more sophisticated factory systems that were larger and more efficient. Industrialism had become more globalized.
✦ Example Two: The first factory machines used water power for energy. Later, with the invention of the steam engine, coal-powered factories developed. Steel and chemical production created demand for new industrial goods. By 1900, the global economy revolved around providing raw materials for industrial production and finding new markets for factory-produced finished goods. Transportation systems like railroads and steamships helped to move goods that were generated from industrialization.
✦ Example Three: New industrial workers often came from rural areas and moved to factory cities. These cities, like Manchester in Britain, became densely populated and polluted. Women and children worked long hours in dangerous factories and mines. Other people became quite rich, such as the managers and investors of the factories. These educated people became an important group that changed the social and cultural aspects of modern life.

Uses Relevant Historical Context (1 point)

✦ Historical context places the issue discussed in the essay into a broader global perspective.

Examples:

✦ Example One: Industrialization spread to many countries in different parts of the world, creating a new, global trade system based on the factory system.
✦ Example Two: Industrialized countries established colonies to supply them with raw materials. Industrialization, therefore, led to imperialism.

✦ Example Three: Lower-class workers in many parts of the world were attracted to the ideas of Marxism, which explained how revolutionary change could improve their lives.

Analyzes the Process of Continuity or Change (1 point)

✦ Analysis explains why the continuity or change occurred.

Examples:

✦ Example One: Britain remained such an important industrial power throughout this time period because of its extensive colonies, which provided raw materials needed in factory production.
✦ Example Two: Railroads completely transformed the modern era because they could transport factory-made goods very cheaply across long distances. This process led to even more demand for industrialism.
✦ Example Three: Many factories preferred to hire children and women because they were paid less, were more easily intimidated, and could operate delicate machinery better than men.

Expanded Core

You must earn all seven points in the basic core before earning any points in the expanded core. Points awarded in the expanded core reflect the general excellence of the essay. Any one aspect of your essay, such as the thesis or evidence, might be particularly insightful and earn a point in the expanded core. Essays that have a high degree of analysis and historical context often earn expanded core points if they have earned all of the other basic core points. Clarity of organization, strong cause-effect analysis, and particularly insightful ideas can make your essay stand out as excellent.

Examples:

✦ Example One: A detailed description of the different phases of industrialization from 1750 to 1900 could earn points in the expanded core.
✦ Example Two: A deep analysis of the relationship between imperialism and industrialization could earn points in the expanded core.
✦ Example Three: A sophisticated essay on the different social classes that emerged as a result of industrialization could earn points in the expanded core.

Answer Guide for Section II:
Part C

3. Compare the revolutionary process in France (1789–1801) with the revolutionary process in St. Domingue/Haiti (1791–1804).

What Does the Question Ask?

This question asks you to compare two revolutionary movements at the end of the eighteenth century. You must address both of these revolutions since no choice is given in the question.

Listed below is the scoring system used to grade comparative essays; also included are guidelines and examples for how to earn each point for this question.

Has Acceptable Thesis (1 point)

+ The thesis needs to correctly address both a similarity and a difference between the revolutionary process in France (1789–1801) and the revolutionary process in St. Domingue/Haiti (1791–1804).
+ The thesis should appear in the first paragraph (although it may also count if it is in the conclusion).
+ The thesis can be one sentence or multiple sentences.

Examples:

+ Example One: Although the Haitian Revolution was primarily a slave rebellion and the French Revolution was a revolution of the middle classes, both were concerned with the expansion of rights to the lower classes.
+ Example Two: Both the Haitian and French Revolutions involved war with foreign countries. In Haiti, the foreign countries wanted to conquer the land for themselves. In the French Revolution, the foreign countries that invaded wanted to restore the French monarchy.
+ Example Three: The Haitian Revolution had a strong racial aspect, which differed from the class-based revolution in France. Both the Haitian and French revolutions were influenced by the Enlightenment.
+ Unacceptable Example: The revolutionary process in France and Haiti were similar because they were revolutionary. They also had big differences in how they were revolutionary.
  • This is an unacceptable thesis because the statements are too vague and self-evident.

Addresses All Parts of the Question (2 points)

+ The essay accurately addresses both a valid similarity (1 point) and a valid difference (1 point).
+ The statements of comparison may not appear in the thesis.

Examples:

+ Example One: In the Haitian Revolution, slaves created their own army to fight against French rule. The French Revolution also had the poor lower classes coming together at the Bastille. The goal of the slave army in Haiti was to emancipate themselves and get rid of the institution of slavery. The goal of the French Revolution, on the other hand, was to destroy the power of the nobility and the king.
  • The first statement in the example above addresses similarity, while the second statement addresses difference.

+ Example Two: Both the French revolutionaries and the Haitian slaves fought against the government of France and other European powers. The Haitians, however, formed their own separate country after the revolution. In France, however, the revolution led to a new style of French government.
  • The first statement in the example above addresses similarity, while the second statement addresses change.

+ Example Three: The revolutionaries in Haiti were African slaves fighting against white French slave owners. The revolutionaries in France were the third estate fighting against the monarchy and the noble classes. Both revolutions believed in the Enlightenment idea that all men are created equal.
  • The first statement in the example above addresses difference, while the second statement addresses similarity.

Substantiates Thesis with Appropriate Historical Evidence (2 points)

+ A piece of historical evidence is a fact that is correct and relevant to the time period.
+ To earn the full two points in this category, an essay should have five or more pieces of evidence.
+ To earn only one point in this category, an essay needs three or four pieces of evidence.
+ Points for evidence can be earned even if the thesis point is not earned.

Examples:

+ Example One: In Haiti, former slaves formed an army to fight against French slaveholders. Their leader was Toussaint, himself a former slave. In France, the revolutionaries employed universal conscription for their army so that every person in France was involved in the war effort. Mobs of lower-class people also rose up during the French Revolution and took power into their own hands. For example, a mob in Paris took over the Bastille, an ancient French prison.
+ Example Two: As the French king lost power, other countries in Europe invaded France. France later invaded other neighboring countries. The French Revolution, therefore, involved both an internal rebellion and the exportation of revolutionary values to other countries. The Haitian slave armies battled against France, Spain, and Britain in order to gain independence. When they formed their own government, it was a military dictatorship. It was the first country to be created as a result of a slave rebellion.
+ Example Three: Haiti before the revolution had an extensive plantation system worked by African slaves. These black slaves rose in a rebellion against their enslavers. A class of people who were mixed African and European ancestry also took part in the revolution. The third estate in France was formed of the peasants, poor urban people, and anyone who wasn't either clergy or nobility. The French Revolution was led by members of the third estate. Some members of the clergy and nobility also joined in supporting early revolutionary ideas.

Makes a Direct, Relevant Comparison (1 point)

+ A direct comparison is an explicit, concrete, and factually correct statement of either similarity or difference.

Examples:

+ Example One: Both the French and Haitian revolutions involved brutal wars that led to many atrocities.
+ Example Two: The French revolutionaries used the guillotine to execute enemies of the revolution. The Haitian rebels also executed members of the previous ruling class.
+ Example Three: The success of the American Revolution inspired people in Haiti and in France to fight for their freedom.

Analyzes at Least One Reason for a Similarity or Difference (1 point)

+ Analysis explains a reason for the similarity or difference.

Examples:

+ Example One: One reason for the violence of both the Haitian and French revolutions was the incredible unfairness of the previous social systems. The revolutionaries were very angry, and the elites did not surrender power easily.

✦ Example Two: Revolutions tend to become violent because radicals take over when the pace of revolutionary change is not fast enough.

✦ Example Three: The Atlantic slave trade had created a race-based labor system in the Caribbean, which caused the Haitian Revolution to have a much greater racial tone than the French Revolution.

Expanded Core

You must earn all seven points in the basic core before earning any points in the expanded core. Points awarded in the expanded core reflect the general excellence of the essay. Any one aspect of your essay, such as the thesis or evidence, might be particularly insightful and earn a point in the expanded core. Essays that have a high degree of analysis and historical context often earn expanded core points if they have all of the other basic core points. Clarity of organization, strong cause-effect analysis, and particularly insightful ideas can make your essay stand out as excellent.

Examples:

✦ Example One: Many examples of similarities and differences in the military approaches and goals of the French and Haitian revolutions could earn points in the expanded core.

✦ Example Two: An examination of the changes that occurred in each revolutionary phase could earn points in the expanded core.

✦ Example Three: Analysis of the roles of different races in the Haitian Revolution and different classes in the French Revolution could earn points in the expanded core.

PERIOD SIX
Accelerating Global Change and Realignments, c. 1900 to the Present

PART SIX
The Most Recent Century, 1914–2012

AP World History Key Concepts

6.1: **Science and the Environment**

6.2: **Global Conflicts and Their Consequences**

6.3: **New Conceptualizations of Global Economy, Society, and Culture**

The Big Picture: Since World War I: A New Period in World History?

World historians categorize events into periods (eras or ages) in an effort to make coherent the changes and continuities in that period that affect the lives of individuals, social groups, nations, civilizations—or the entire panorama of human history. The artificial beginning or ending dates are "imposed by scholars on a continuously flowing stream of events." AP World History recognizes that altering the periodization can change the historical narrative, since creating periods highlights particular events, movements, cultures, or themes, and that the context in which historians write can affect their interpretations.

The "Big Picture" question, then, for Part Six of *Ways of the World* is whether the century following 1914 constitutes a separate period in world history. There are several reasons why future historians may decide that it was not:

+ The period is very brief compared to thousands of years for other periods.
+ Because there is so much more information in recent periods, it is difficult to determine what is really significant.
+ We are too close to these events to have a historical perspective.
+ The period may have already ended, and we are now in another phase of history.

Just as all for other periods, the current one is composed of continuities that have carried over from previous eras and of changes that mark distinctive events that break from the past.

Some of the continuities include:

✦ The world wars (Chapter 20) grew out of Europe's failure to create one regional state or civilization.
✦ The wars also represent a continuation of the rivalries between European states.
✦ The Russian and Chinese revolutions (Chapter 21) were based on long-standing division within their societies, and the ideology for those revolutions came from the nineteenth century philosophy of Karl Marx.
✦ The intentions of the Russian and Chinese revolutions were similar to those of the capitalists—modernization and industrialization.
✦ The process of disintegration of great empires (Chapter 22), such as the Ottoman, Chinese, Austro-Hungarian, Russian, or European, was merely the same pattern of rise and fall of empires going back to Assyria.
✦ Other movements, such as feminism (Chapter 23), began in the West in the nineteenth century but became global phenomena in the twentieth century.
✦ Global population growth was built on past trends such as an increased food supply derived from the spread of American crops and improvements in medicine and sanitation.
✦ Global industrialization represents a continuation of processes begun with the Scientific and Industrial Revolutions.
✦ Human environmental impact in the past may have led to extinction of Paleolithic animals.
✦ Globalization is an extension of past systems such as the Silk Roads, the Indian Ocean (Sea Roads), or the trans-Saharan trading networks (Sand Roads); the spread of Buddhism, Christianity, and Islam; or the Columbian exchange.

The changes for the era beginning in the early twentieth century include the following:

✦ The two world wars of the twentieth century were new in the extent to which entire populations were mobilized and in the destructiveness they caused.
✦ Both the attempt to exterminate an entire group of people (the Holocaust) and the use of atomic weapons were unprecedented.
✦ The Russian and Chinese Communist revolutions remade their societies from top to bottom and broke with the capitalist West.
✦ The cold war presented a new global division.
✦ Not only did the great empires disintegrate, but the idea of empire became illegitimate as both the superpowers (the United States and the Soviet Union) proclaimed anticolonial ideology.
✦ More than 200 nation-states, many of them in the southern hemisphere, declared sovereignty and legal equality, resulting in a new political order for the planet.
✦ Population exploded at an unprecedented rate, quadrupling since 1900.
✦ Industrial output grew fortyfold, caused by an increasing rate of scientific and technological innovation and the wide spread of industrialization.
✦ Industrial output and population growth created environmental impacts unprecedented in scale.
✦ Globalization in the past century was unparalleled in depth and involvement of nearly the entire planet.

Tentatively, there seems to be enough new about the past century to label it as a distinct era, but what happens next will determine whether or not this will be seen as a separate era, a midpoint, or the beginning of a different age altogether.

CHAPTER TWENTY
Collapse at the Center: World War, Depression, and the Rebalancing of Global Power, 1914–1970s

AP World History Key Concepts

6.1: Science and the Environment

I. Researchers made rapid advances in science that spread throughout the world, assisted by the development of new technology.

II. As the global population expanded at an unprecedented rate, humans fundamentally changed their relationship with the environment.

III. Disease, scientific innovations, and conflict led to demographic shifts.

The revolution in science and technology, coupled with the might of the Industrial Revolution, allowed Western powers to compete in creating massive military might. Prior to World War I, Great Britain and Germany competed to create ever-stronger navies. Other military technology of World War I included poisonous gas, machine guns, barbed wire, tanks, and airplanes. The use of barbed wire and machine guns helped eliminate sweeping infantry and cavalry movements common in previous campaigns, leading to a war that quickly settled into static trench warfare.

World War II also saw an increase in the machines of destruction such as submarines, rockets, atomic bombs, and the weapons of genocide such as poisonous gas. Loss of life in both wars was immense, but different. In World War I, while 10 million lives were lost, most of them were male, creating a gender imbalance in the surviving populations. World War II blurred the lines of combatant and noncombatant in new ways, and the death toll included many more women and children, not just because of concentration camps and the Holocaust, but also because of urban bombing (including the use of nuclear weapons at Hiroshima and Nagasaki), blockades, and starvation. *See Chapter 23 for more detailed discussion of this key concept.*

6.2: Global Conflicts and Their Consequences

I. Europe dominated the global political order at the beginning of the twentieth century, but both land-based and transoceanic empires gave way to new forms of transregional political organization by the century's end.

II. Emerging ideologies of anti-imperialism contributed to the dissolution of empires and the restructuring of states.

III. Political changes were accompanied by major demographic and social consequences.

IV. Military conflicts occurred on an unprecedented global scale.

V. Although conflict dominated much of the twentieth century, many individuals and groups—including states—opposed this trend. Some individuals and groups, however, intensified the conflicts.

By 1900, people of European ancestry controlled much of the world (see Map 20.1, p. 984) through direct colonization, economic influence, and projection of political power. Germany, a state created in the 1870s, was a rapidly industrializing state that competed with France, Great Britain, and Russia both economically and militarily, and for the intangible goal of "national pride." Competition between European states led to an alliance system that prepared the way for war; on one side was the Triple Alliance— Germany, Austria-Hungary, and Italy—and on the other was the Triple Entente of Russia, Britain, and France. Sparked by the assassination of the heir to the Austrian throne by a Serbian nationalist, World War I effectively launched the twentieth century. Patriotic nationalism encouraged young men to enlist in their nation's military, only to be destroyed by the new weapons of war such as gas, tanks, and machine guns. The war led to the dissolution of large empires (such as the Ottoman, the Russian, and the Austro-Hungarian empires) and to redrawing international borders, especially in Europe and the Middle East, which led to controversies between new, competing national identities. The slaughter of Armenians by the Turks at the close of the war, although not labeled genocide (a term invented for the Holocaust), is an event that is sometimes noted as the beginning of a series of attempts to exterminate an entire ethnic group, a process that became far too common in the modern era. The involvement of colonial troops in the war also reinvigorated anticolonial movements in European overseas colonies, such as India. The war helped trigger the Russian Revolution and the beginning of a communist state (see Chapter 22).

The First World War, the Great Depression beginning in 1929, and the failure of the Treaty of Versailles that ended World War I led to disillusionment with the liberal, democratic ideals of the Enlightenment. Confronted with union strikes, street protests, and the rise of communist groups, charismatic leaders such as Mussolini and Hitler introduced fascism, which was nationalistic, militaristic, authoritarian, and anticommunist. Fascism appealed to idealized national glories of the past and promised recompense for those hurt by the war and the Depression. In Germany, propaganda focused on "the other" (Jews, Communists, weak democratic leaders, and other "traitors") as responsible for the loss of pride, economic stability, and empire that followed World War I. After rising to power, both Mussolini and Hitler took steps to remove other political parties and to assume autocratic power. Both rebuilt the military and created government projects to bring about full employment. Japan's government, too, suffered from the turmoil caused by the Great Depression, and Japanese military leaders began to assert more control in the government. Japan believed that an empire was essential for national greatness and thought that attempts by Great Britain and the United States to limit Japan's expansion were hypocritical. When Japan created a puppet state in Manchuko (Manchuria, part of China), Western powers protested, leading Japan to withdraw from the League of Nations and to begin to expand into the Pacific, where it seized territory from Western colonial empires.

German territorial expansion in Austria, Czechoslovakia, and finally Poland triggered World War II in Europe. As in the First World War, alliances quickly led to the involvement of most European countries and their colonies but with a larger Pacific theater because of Japan's involvement. Lines between combatants and civilians were blurred by total war, leading to unprecedented numbers of civilian deaths, including large numbers of women and children.

As the world recovered after the war ended in 1945, colonial possessions gained independence—sometimes peacefully through treaties and sometimes after armed conflict—and Europe's position as the political, economic, and military core of Western civilization passed across the Atlantic to the United States, marking a major change in the historical development of the West. The cold war between the United States and its allies and the Soviet Union and its allies (see Chapter 21) dominated global politics until the late twentieth century. Several regional conflicts and proxy wars broke out, but the world avoided a direct confrontation between the United States and the Soviet Union. Even during the cold war and its conflicts, some states joined a movement of nonaligned nations, attempting to remain out of the conflict between superpowers. Nongovernmental organizations such as the United Nations also were formed to help prevent a future world war. *See Chapters 21 and 22 for further discussion of this key concept.*

6.3: New Conceptualizations of Global Economy, Society, and Culture

I. States responded in a variety of ways to the economic challenges of the twentieth century.

II. States, communities, and individuals became increasingly interdependent, a process facilitated by the growth of institutions of global governance.

III. People conceptualized society and culture in new ways; some challenged old assumptions about race, class, gender, and religion, often using new technologies to spread reconfigured traditions.

IV. Popular and consumer culture became global.

World War I was a total war that allowed states to take much more control of the economy as well as other aspects of their citizens' lives, ending the Enlightenment ideal of a free economy that regulated itself without state intervention. "War socialism" meant that strikes were suspended and wages limited, the goods produced were decided by the state, and men were drafted into the military and replaced by women in the workforce.

The war inflicted great damage on the economies of Europe, which suffered even more during the Great Depression. States responded in different ways to the postwar economic challenges. The Russian Revolution had installed a communist state, which proceeded to invest in industrial and military growth. The Soviet Union, with its state-controlled economy, suffered least from the worldwide depression. Countries that exported one or two products were hardest hit as commodity prices dropped. Many of those countries began import substitution industrialization—banning certain imports and manufacturing those products for an internal market—to attempt to regain control of their economies. Democratic socialism became a popular response in some European countries, while others turned to state-sponsored capitalism and dictatorial, fascist governments. Japan's militaristic government also became more directly involved in economic policies as the Depression cut into Japanese exports. While maintaining the *zaibatsu*, the government also subsidized strategic industries and limited profits, wages, and rents. In the United States, Franklin Roosevelt adopted the economic policies of John Maynard Keynes and attempted to set up a safety net (the New Deal), but his intervention was far short of the moderate socialism of France or Britain or the more direct control of communist or fascist states.

In the aftermath of World War II, European states had to cooperate across borders in order to receive economic aid from the United States under the Marshall Plan. The European Economic Community was established in 1957, leading to the European

Union in 1994 with a common currency, the euro. Japan, under American occupation after the Second World War, was also given aid in its economic recovery. The Korean War further jump-started Japan's economic revival as the United States purchased material from Japan. The International Monetary Fund and the World Bank were also created following World War II to help emerging economies and to prevent another global depression. *See Chapters 21, 22, and 23 for further discussion of this key concept.*

Theme 1: Interaction Between Humans and the Environment

See Chapter 23 for discussion of this theme.

Theme 2: Development and Interaction of Cultures

Total war undermined Western faith in the ideals of the Enlightenment and the Scientific Revolution, ideals such as progress, toleration, and rationality. The horrors of war led Westerners to become disillusioned with their own civilization; some Westerners expressed these doubts and disillusionments in art and literature. An almost manic, pleasure-seeking era, sometimes known as the Roaring Twenties, immediately followed World War I. Popular culture, characterized by new music such as jazz and new celebrities such as movie stars, was disseminated globally by new media such as radio, records, and movies. *See Chapter 23 for additional discussion of this theme.*

Theme 3: State-Building, Expansion, and Conflict

World War I effectively launched the twentieth century. The war also transformed international political life. When the Austrian-Hungarian Empire collapsed, independent Poland, Czechoslovakia, and Yugoslavia were created based on Woodrow Wilson's principle of self-determination. These new nations, however, included other ethnic minorities within their borders, leading to further conflicts by the end of the century; these conflicts took different forms, such as the violent breakup of Yugoslavia or the peaceful separation of the Czech Republic and Slovakia. In Russia, World War I triggered the Bolshevik Revolution, which led Russia to sign a separate peace with Germany. This event also launched communism onto the world stage, where it would influence world events until the end of the twentieth century. The Treaty of Versailles, signed in 1919, set the stage for another even bloodier war twenty years in the future because of the harsh reparations that were inflicted on Germany by the victorious nations. The war also ended the Ottoman Empire and created some new countries like Turkey; other former possessions of the Ottoman Empire, such as Syria, Iraq, Jordan, and Palestine, were not considered fully autonomous but were mandates of the League of Nations under the protection of either Britain or France. Conflicting promises made during the war by the British to Arab and Jewish nationalist groups regarding Palestine set the stage for an enduring struggle. In Europe's Asian and African colonies, the war set the stage for the independence struggles that followed (see Chapter 22). World War I also brought the United States to the forefront as a global power.

The Great Depression also affected state building. As the depression wore on, states took on new roles within the economic sphere. In Italy, Germany, and other Eastern European states, the Great Depression triggered disillusionment with liberal democracy and changed the politics of these newly created countries. Italy's fascist regime suspended democracy, deported opponents, and disbanded independent labor unions and peasant groups as well as all opposition political parties. As in Italy, liberal or democratic political leaders during the 1920s faced considerable hostility in Germany. Traditional elites had withdrawn from public life in disgrace, leaving the weak Weimar Republic with the unenviable task of signing the Treaty of Versailles and enforcing it. In this setting, some began to argue that German military forces had not really lost the war but that civilian democrats, socialists, communists, and Jews had betrayed the nation. In Japan, cultural modernization and the Great Depression also triggered a conservative response. In this case, it was the military who gained power even while elections and parliament continued to function on a limited basis.

The failure of the Versailles treaty to address the problems that caused World War I led to another world war just twenty years later. This war was much more destructive and much more lethal. In the aftermath of World War II, the United Nations (UN) was created to replace the ineffective League of Nations. Although the UN has had problems in enforcing its policies, it nevertheless helped prevent the cold war between Russia and the United States from becoming a hot war between superpowers. Nonetheless, numerous regional conflicts — often proxy wars — such as the Korean War or Vietnam War, still occurred. *See Chapter 22 for more discussion of anticolonial movements in the twentieth century and Chapter 23 for global interactions.*

Theme 4: Creation, Expansion, and Interaction of Economic Systems

World War I and the Great Depression represented a fundamental change in the way capitalism was viewed. For the rich, the Great Depression meant contracting stock prices that wiped out paper fortunes almost overnight. For ordinary people, the worst feature of the Great Depression was the loss of work. Vacant factories, soup kitchens, bread lines, shantytowns, and beggars came to symbolize the human reality of this economic disaster. Just as Europe's worldwide empires had globalized the Great War, so too did economic linkages globalize the Great Depression. Cocoa prices in Ghana plunged as commodity prices dropped. Brazil destroyed an entire year's coffee crop in order to keep prices from collapsing.

In Latin America, depressed commodity prices for things such as tin and copper often led to military takeover of the state and an attempt to generate economic activity by producing goods for local markets rather than importing products. The Great Depression also sharply challenged the governments of capitalist countries and the assumption that the markets would regulate themselves and thus did not require intervention. In Britain, France, and Scandinavia, a new form of democratic socialism sought to regulate the economy and provide for a more equal wealth distribution but without total state control as in the Soviet Union or China. In Germany and Italy, fascist governments used a combination of state-sponsored tactics to provide employment; infrastructure rebuilding, control of labor unions' demands, increased production of arms and military equipment plus a violent suppression of strikes, riots, and street protests soon quieted the concerns of both the owners of industry, the middle class, and the workers. In the United States, Franklin Delano Roosevelt instituted the New Deal based on economist John Maynard Keynes's belief that government spending would ease an economic contraction. Japan was also hurt by shrinking world demand for its products during the Depression; millions of silkworm raisers were impoverished in the 1930s. Many young factory workers returned to their rural villages only to find food scarce and families forced to sell their daughters to urban brothels. Militaristic nationalism, which emphasized armament construction, helped ease the economic depression.

After World War II, international organizations such as the International Monetary Fund and the World Bank sought to ease economic burdens in developing countries. In Europe, the European Economic Community sought greater economic integration within Western Europe.

Theme 5: Development and Transformation of Social Structures

A "warrior understanding of masculinity" dominated the first half of the century, forcing women into more traditional roles as wives and mothers. During the world wars, women had temporary opportunities to join the workforce in unprecedented numbers, but at the wars' end, they returned home to traditional roles; working in factories and farms and serving as nurses on the front lines or in auxiliary roles in the military nevertheless showed both men and women how capable women were. In Russia, some 100,000 women won military honors for their fighting at the front during World War II.

It is perhaps no coincidence that women finally won the right to vote in many countries at the end of the First World War. Along with new if somewhat limited political and economic roles, women also carved out a new social role for themselves. The flapper girls in the United States and the Japanese *moga* ("modern girls") exemplified a new era where girls and boys could enjoy each other's company on equal footing and without chaperones. Communism legalized the status of women as equals, something that upset many, including fascists who pushed back on both liberalism and feminism by forcing traditional roles onto women and praising and rewarding motherhood as woman's main role in support of the state. On the other hand, women were also deliberately targeted during World War II through rapes, forced prostitution, and the economic necessities that forced some girls and women into slavery.

Strict social class distinctions also eased as a result of the massive upheaval in the first fifty years of the twentieth century. So many men died in the two world wars that social mobility was much easier for those who survived. Because of the terrible poverty that resulted from massive job losses during the Great Depression, governments began to create safety nets for people in the form of unemployment benefits, health care assistance, and minimum wage laws. These also served to equalize the social levels in Western European countries. In communist countries, de facto social equality existed.

Genocide—the deliberate extermination of a group of people, such as the Holocaust in which 6 million Jews and other groups such as Roma (gypsies) and the disabled were killed—occurred repeatedly during the twentieth century. Nazi versions of racism and anti-Semitism relied on supposedly "scientific" racial constructs of the nineteenth century and used denial of citizenship and civil rights, public beatings, and destruction of property to whip up public acceptance of the propaganda that Jews were parasites responsible for Germany's woes. Hitler's minions used Germany's industrial expertise to create his "final solution," the extermination of all Jews in Europe. This technique of dehumanization became the model for other attempted genocides in the past century. *See Chapters 21 through 23 for more discussion of social structures.*

CHAPTER TWENTY-ONE
Revolution, Socialism, and Global Conflict: The Rise and Fall of World Communism, 1917–Present

AP World History Key Concepts

6.1: Science and the Environment

II. As the global population expanded at an unprecedented rate, humans fundamentally changed their relationship with the environment.

III. Disease, scientific innovations, and conflict led to demographic shifts.

The Soviet Union under Joseph Stalin and China under Mao Zedong pushed aside all concerns except rapid industrialization. They believed that the environment and nature were something to subdue. Large collective farms, huge factories, dams, and redirected rivers for agriculture all led to massive environmental degradation. *See Chapter 23 for more discussion of this concept.*

6.2: Global Conflicts and Their Consequences

I. Europe dominated the global political order at the beginning of the twentieth century, but both land-based and transoceanic empires gave way to new forms of transregional political organization by the century's end.

II. Emerging ideologies of anti-imperialism contributed to the dissolution of empires and the restructuring of states.

III. Political changes were accompanied by major demographic and social consequences.

IV. Military conflicts occurred on an unprecedented global scale.

V. Although conflict dominated much of the twentieth century, many individuals and groups—including states—opposed this trend. Some individuals and groups, however, intensified the conflicts.

Based on the theories of Karl Marx, communist revolutionaries created a new political, social, and economic order in the twentieth century that challenged the democratic, capitalist worldview of the West. However, contrary to Marx's prediction that the proletariat (working class) revolution would spontaneously arise in an industrialized state, both the Russian and Chinese communist revolutions took place in predominantly agrarian countries. Unlike European socialists, communists did not believe in pursuing reform through the political institutions of a country; revolution seemed the only solution. In addition, while most socialist parties supported patriotic nationalism, communists believed that class solidarity transcended national borders. The Bolshevik Revolution (1917) brought Lenin and his cadre of urban workers and intelligentsia to power shortly after the abdication of Tsar Nicholas II. In China, a longer struggle between the Guomindang (the Nationalists, led by Chiang Kai-shek), the Communists (led by Mao Zedong), and the invading Japanese followed the collapse of the Qing dynasty. Not until 1949 did Mao succeed in winning the power struggle. Both revolutionary movements drew on the French Revolution. They believed that an improved society could be constructed by human actions and found their vision of an ideal society in the future rather than in a past golden age. They overthrew the old elites and disposed landowners, using peasant upheavals in rural areas led by educated leadership from the cities. They differed in that the highly organized communist party wanted economic and political equality, the abolition of private property, gender equality, and the destruction of not only the elites but the middle class as well.

Following World War II, communism spread. Stalin insisted that Eastern Europe come under Soviet control as a buffer against further invasions from Germany (or France), and he used his army of occupation to install communist governments in countries such as East Germany, Poland, Romania, Hungary, and Czechoslovakia. Yugoslavia became a communist nation but independent from control of the Soviet Union. Communism spread in Asia as well, to nations such as North Vietnam, North Korea, Laos, Afghanistan, and Cambodia. The confrontation between two worldviews—the West, led by the United States and based on capitalism and democracy, and the communist bloc led by the Soviet Union—devolved into the decades-long cold war. *See Chapters 20 and 22 for more discussion of this key concept.*

6.3: New Conceptualizations of Global Economy, Society, and Culture

I. States responded in a variety of ways to the economic challenges of the twentieth century.

III. People conceptualized society and culture in new ways; some challenged old assumptions about race, class, gender, and religion, often using new technologies to spread reconfigured traditions.

IV. Popular and consumer culture became global.

Large agrarian states such as Russia and China that had not succeeded in modernizing or industrializing in the nineteenth century were faced with huge economic and social problems. The communist movement, based on the theories of Karl Marx, seemed to offer hope to these countries to solve the problems of rural poverty and subjugation of the peasants, the lack of industrial progress or infrastructure, and sharp class divisions. By the 1970s, nearly a third of the people in the world lived under communist regimes, characterized by the following:

- state-controlled economies
- the ousting of traditional ruling elites and the middle class
- the collectivization of agriculture
- rapid industrialization (especially in heavy industry and military material) undertaken from above in a series of five-year plans
- a commitment to social and gender equality

However, these governments also repressed political parties, instituted censorship and propaganda, and controlled movements such as women's groups or youth organizations. The early promise of a classless society soon gave way to a new Community Party elite.

The state tightly controlled cultural expression in communist countries. The state used the arts as propaganda to promote its agenda. Communist governments also suppressed religion or held it up to ridicule as part of the outdated, pre-communist past.

In the West, popular consumer culture in the second half of the twentieth century was disseminated partly by the wide availability of mass media. Much of the world listened to American music (jazz, rock and roll, and later rap), watched American movies and TV shows, and desired consumer goods popularized in America. *See Chapters 20, 22, and 23 for more discussion of this key concept.*

Theme 1: Interaction Between Humans and the Environment

Rapid industrialization in both the Soviet Union and China led to massive environmental degradation. Government planners saw nature as an enemy to be conquered, so little was done to protect the environment. The construction of huge factories, mining operations, large collective farms, diverting waterways for irrigation, and dam construction all led to soil, water, and air pollution, erosion and salinization, loss of volume of seas and lakes, and contamination by pesticides and herbicides. In Russia today, 75 percent of the surface water is severely polluted and 70 million people live in cites with polluted air five times the acceptable level. A similar problem exists in China; for example, the level of air pollution in Beijing is so great that all factories were closed two weeks prior to the Olympics in 2008. In addition to these environmental disasters, poor government planning and collectivization of rural lands also led to massive starvation; in Russia, approximately 5 million people died, and in China 20 million died.

Theme 2: Development and Interaction of Cultures

Communism minimized nationalism and looked forward to a movement of the working classes that would lead to international solidarity along class lines. Communists also sought to promote cultural values of selflessness and collectivism that could support a socialist society and ensure that the arts, education, and the media conformed to approved ways of thinking. Posters, plays, operas, and movies were written to extol the values and heroes of the working class and the revolution. Censorship was strong; dissenting works were published outside of the communist bloc or were printed by hand underground and distributed in secret.

In the West, consumer culture became an important distinction from communism. In many ways, Western culture became American popular culture. American music—first jazz, then rock-and-roll, and most recently, rap—have found receptive audiences abroad, particularly among the young. American movies, McDonald's restaurants, and American brand names such as Kleenex, Coca-Cola, and Jeep became common points of reference around the world. When Mikhail Gorbachev instituted *glasnost* (openness) in the 1980s, new cultural and intellectual freedoms emerged in the Soviet Union: reporters exposed the hypocrisy of communist rule; films and the arts not only examined

Russian history, but also turned to forbidden models from the West; propaganda decreased; copies of the Bible and Quran were made available; and long-suppressed underground manuscripts saw the light of day.

Theme 3: State-Building, Expansion, and Conflict

In Russia, the social upheaval caused by the First World War and the sudden abdication of Tsar Nicholas II was so strong that the Provisional Government, composed mostly of liberal middle-class and moderate socialist leaders, could not keep up. The Provisional Government would not end the war or carry out land redistribution, both of which were called for by the people. The most effective of the radical groups that entered the vacuum created by the chaos were the Bolsheviks who seized power in October 1917, claiming they would end the war, give land to the peasants, give workers control of factories, and give non-Russians self-determination. A three-year civil war followed between the Bolsheviks and an assortment of enemies including tsarist officials, landlords, disaffected socialists, regional nationalist forces, as well as troops from the United States, Britain, France, and Japan.

Once in power, the Bolsheviks worked to cement their authority over Russia. They regimented the economy, seized grain from angry peasants, and suppressed nationalist rebellions. They integrated many lower-class men into the Red Army and into the new local governments, giving many an avenue for social mobility.

Under Stalin, the Soviet Union began to turn away from the more moderate economic policies of Lenin to a more complete command economy with all decisions made by central planners. The political system was led by a small group of Communist Party members. Peasants were forced into collectivization by Soviet officials from the cities, and those who refused to give up their farms were branded as *kulaks* (wealthy peasants) and were killed or deported to gulags (work camps) in Siberia. Severe famines followed, leaving more than 5 million dead. Stalin asked the people to make sacrifices to raise the Soviet Union to economic and military parity with its Western foes in one generation, so heavy industry and military equipment were favored over consumer goods in a series of five-year plans. Mass organizations for women, workers, and students were created under tight party control.

Stalin also moved away from traditional communist values to create a return to patriotic nationalism, traditional family ties, competition, and difference in wages. Instead of collective rule by the Soviets, authoritarian rule from the top emerged. Stalin's constant vigilance for any who might disagree with his policies led to censorship, informers, and secret police, with the arrest, death, or deportation of many intellectuals and ethnic group leaders. It is estimated that millions of Russians died from famine, warfare, and purges under Stalin's rule. Stalin determined that Soviet security required friendly governments in the region to permanently end the threat of invasion from the West. Backed by the pressure and presence of the Soviet army, communism was largely imposed on Eastern Europe from outside rather than growing out of a domestic revolution, as had happened in Russia itself. The major exception to this was Yugoslavia, where a genuinely popular communist movement had played a leading role in the struggle against Nazi occupation and came to power on its own with little Soviet help. Its leader, Tito, openly defied Soviet efforts to control Yugoslav communism.

The ideas of Karl Marx were barely known in China in the early twentieth century. A small Chinese Communist Party (CCP) was founded in 1921, aimed initially at organizing the country's minuscule urban working class. Over the next twenty-eight years, that party grew enormously, transformed its strategy, found a charismatic leader in Mao Zedong (himself the son of a peasant), engaged in an epic struggle with its opponents (the Guomindang), fought the Japanese heroically during World War II, and in 1949, emerged victorious as the rulers of China. Much of the growing support that the CCP received in the countryside came from the vigor with which it waged war against the Japanese invaders. Communist forces established themselves behind enemy lines and, despite periodic setbacks, offered a measure of security to many Chinese faced with Japanese atrocities. Furthermore, in the areas it controlled, the CCP reduced rents, taxes, and interest payments for peasants; taught literacy to adults; and mobilized women for the struggle. Once in power, the CCP addressed both of China's major problems—foreign imperialism and peasant exploitation. Mao attempted to prevent people falling back into prerevolutionary modes and launched two disastrous programs: the Great Leap Forward in the 1950s (which promoted small-scale, village industrialization) and the Cultural Revolution in the 1960s (which sent the young Red Guard out into the country to purge anti-revolutionary thoughts—often among local communist party leaders and intellectuals).

The rise of communism launched a global confrontation that restructured international life and touched the lives of almost everyone, particularly in the second half of the twentieth century. The Soviet Union and the United States had become the major political and military powers, replacing the shattered and diminished states of Western Europe. They represented sharply opposing views of history, society, politics, and international relations, leading to rival military alliances (NATO and the Warsaw Pact), a largely voluntary American sphere of influence in Western Europe, and a Soviet sphere in Eastern Europe. The Soviet military put down popular attempts to liberalize the communist governments of several countries, including Hungary and Czechoslovakia. However, even in highly volatile regions such as Berlin, no shooting war occurred between the two sides in Europe. The extension of communism into Asia—in China, Korea, and Vietnam—globalized the cold war and led to its most destructive and prolonged hot wars.

Perhaps the most iconic moment of the cold war era was the Cuban missile crisis, which brought the world close to nuclear Armageddon and gave expression to the most anxiety-ridden and dangerous dimension of the cold war—the nuclear arms race. However, the leaders of the two superpowers knew that a nuclear war would produce utter catastrophe—and perhaps the end of civilization. Still, opportunities for conflict abounded as the U.S.–Soviet rivalry spanned the globe. Using military and economic aid, educational opportunities, political pressure, and covert actions, both sides courted countries emerging from colonial rule (see Chapter 22 for further discussion).

Beginning in the 1980s, the cold war ended, "more with a whimper than a bang," with the liberalizing reforms of Mikhail Gorbachev—*glasnost* (openness), *perestroika* (restructuring), and economic and governmental reforms—which led to more calls for reform than Gorbachev had perhaps intended. Eastern European satellite states took advantage of the new reforms and broke away, most vividly symbolized by the fall of the Berlin Wall in 1989. Hard-line communists in the Soviet Union attempted a failed military coup in 1991, which ended with the dissolution of the Soviet Union into fifteen new states.

In China following the death of Mao Zedong, Deng Xiaoping opened China to capitalism but retained strict control over the political system, including using the military to put down a democratic march in Tiananmen Square in 1989. Ethnic tensions led to conflicts and dissolution of states such as Yugoslavia and Czechoslovakia. Minorities, from the Chechens in Russia to the Uighurs and Tibetans in China, demanded self-determination. Traditional communist states remain on the periphery; North Korea, Cuba, and other satellites, such as Vietnam and Laos, followed China in softening economic controls. In almost all regions (with the notable exception of North Korea), consumerism grew rapidly.

Theme 4: Creation, Expansion, and Interaction of Economic Systems

Communist regimes seized landlords' estates and redistributed that land on a much more equitable basis to the peasantry. They later sought to end private property and gain greater control over the production of food needed to support urban industrialization by collectivizing agriculture. Collectivization in China during the 1950s was a generally peaceful process, owing much to the close relationship between the CCP and the peasantry. This contrasted markedly with the earlier experience of the Soviet Union from 1928 to 1933, where peasants (who received their land under Lenin) slaughtered thousands of animals rather than surrender them to collectives under Stalin. A terrible famine ensued, with some 5 million deaths from starvation or malnutrition. Although there was less violence in China, collectivization led to administrative chaos; disruption of market networks and bad weather combined to produce a massive famine that killed 20 million people between 1959 and 1962.

Although ardently anticapitalist, both the Soviet Union and China were strong modernizers and industrializers. When industrializing, both the Soviet Union and China relied on centralized planning with successive five-year plans and state ownership of all productive capacity. Priority was given to heavy industry, massive mobilization of the nation's human and material resources, and intrusive state control over the entire process. In the Soviet Union, the cold war justified a continuing emphasis on military and defense industries after World War II and gave rise to a Soviet version of the military-industrial complex. Similarly, the need for quick and often secret decision making during the cold war gave rise in the United States to a stronger presidency and a national security state in which defense and intelligence agencies acquired great power within the government and were often unaccountable to Congress. Sustaining this immense military effort throughout much of the second half of the twentieth century was a flourishing U.S. economy and an increasingly middle-class society.

Theme 5: Development and Transformation of Social Structures

Communist parties everywhere set out to construct socialist societies once they gained power. This meant, first of all, modernizing and industrializing, attacking long-standing inequalities of class and gender, and preventing the creation of new inequalities during the process of modern development. Mass organizations for women, workers, students, and various professional groups operated under strict party control. Global industrialization fostered a conflicting set of social outcomes: rapid urbanization, exploitation of the countryside to provide resources for modern industry in the cities, and the growth of a privileged bureaucratic and technological elite intent on pursuing their own careers and passing on their new status to their children. Thus, communist efforts to permanently eliminate differences between classes and between urban and rural life largely failed.

Communist regimes also made major efforts to liberate, educate, and mobilize women. The communist states initially declared full legal and political equality for women, including the following measures:

✦ Marriage became a civil procedure among freely consenting adults.
✦ Divorce was legalized and easier to obtain.
✦ Abortion was legalized.
✦ Illegitimacy was abolished.

Women were also actively mobilized as workers in the drive for industrialization. However, in neither the Soviet Union nor China did the Communist Party undertake a direct attack on male domination within the family. Thus, most women continued to be afflicted with the double burden of housework and child care (without many of the labor-saving devices available to their capitalist sisters) as well as work outside the home—whether in factories or on rural collective farms. Moreover, women rarely achieved the top leadership positions in either country.

CHAPTER TWENTY-TWO

The End of Empire: The Global South on the Global Stage, 1914–Present

AP World History Key Concepts

6.1: Science and the Environment

See Chapter 23 for a more complete discussion of this key concept.

6.2: Global Conflicts and Their Consequences

I. Europe dominated the global political order at the beginning of the twentieth century, but both land-based and transoceanic empires gave way to new forms of transregional political organization by the century's end.

II. Emerging ideologies of anti-imperialism contributed to the dissolution of empires and the restructuring of states.

III. Political changes were accompanied by major demographic and social consequences.

IV. Military conflicts occurred on an unprecedented global scale.

V. Although conflict dominated much of the twentieth century, many individuals and groups—including states—opposed this trend. Some individuals and groups, however, intensified the conflicts.

One of the major stories of the past century is the rapid change from a world controlled by large empires, both political and economic. This process can be seen as one more example of the pattern of rise and fall of empires from the second civilizations onward; however, never before did the very idea of imperialism become anathema and never before had so many states emerged in such a short period of time (see Map 22.1, p. 1090). Chapter 22 deals with how the global south attempted to free itself from colonization and create new nation-states with stable political and economic systems. The ideas of nationalism and self-determination that sparked the decolonization movements were themselves products of European thought. Many of the early leaders of independence in Africa and Asia came from the European-educated elite, who brought home the idea of national self-government proposed by people such as Woodrow Wilson at the Versailles conference following World War I. In accounting for the rapid fall of European empires, some look to this internal conflict or "fatal flaw" in Western thought: how can a country support Enlightenment ideals for itself while subjugating another country? Additionally, the notion of conjuncture, that several factors came together at the same time, describes what precipitated the rapid loss of colonies after World War II. The world wars weakened Europe and discredited any stance of moral or cultural superiority while the new superpowers, the United States and the Soviet Union, both opposed colonialism and the United Nations provided a forum for anticolonial agitation.

The paths to decolonization and statehood differed. Some colonies managed to get their freedom with relatively little loss of blood; others only after prolonged conflict. Some movements were primarily secular; others were religious or Marxist or combined all three (such as Sukarno in Indonesia). Some (such as the Marxists movements in Vietnam and China) sought to transform society as well as gain freedom from foreign rule, while others (in most of Africa) focused on ending racial discrimination and gaining political independence without fostering new patterns of social inequality. Once independence was achieved, new nations had many issues to deal with, including exploding populations, extremely high expectations (often beyond what resources could provide), cultural diversity with little loyalty to the central state, and the creation of a new elite that tried to control the government for personal income or opportunities for personal enrichment. Political solutions included multiparty democracy (India and South Africa), Communist Party control (China, Vietnam, and Cuba), one-party democracy (Mexico, Tanzania, and Senegal), military rule (much of the time in most of Latin America, Africa, and the Middle East), dictatorship (Uganda and the Philippines). Sometimes systems followed each other in rapid succession as the current regime failed to achieve the goals of the nation.

6.3: New Conceptualizations of Global Economy, Society, and Culture

I. States responded in a variety of ways to the economic challenges of the twentieth century.

II. States, communities, and individuals became increasingly interdependent, a process facilitated by the growth of institutions of global governance.

III. People conceptualized society and culture in new ways; some challenged old assumptions about race, class, gender, and religion, often using new technologies to spread reconfigured traditions.

IV. Popular and consumer culture became global.

A major goal of the Global South was economic development—increasing production and improving distribution of wealth to raise living standards. Colonial rule had left little to build upon: low literacy rates, few people with business management experience or technological expertise, weak private economies, and transportation systems (such as railroads) built to accommodate exports instead of for national integration. In addition, these nations had little with which to bargain with transnational corporations and lacked internal investment capital. An initial concern was the degree to which state planning would help produce economic growth. Some countries followed Marxist or socialist paths, following the example of China. However, by the end of the twentieth century, confidence in these command economies had collapsed, in part due to mismanagement or corruption in many state-run enterprises, but also due to the collapse of the Soviet Union and the influence of international organizations such as the World Bank (which pushed economies in a capitalist direction).

Since many countries of the Global South were primarily exporters of cash crops or raw materials, they were vulnerable to market and commodity fluctuations. Other issues included the extent to which foreign investment and foreign aid helped or hurt in the long run. Another problem faced by emerging economies was an "urban bias"; by attempting rapid modernization and focusing on production in cities, the countryside floundered. Population growth also hurt emerging countries as well as being forced (because of limited resources and capital) to decide whether to fund large projects, such as dams or factories, or to invest in education, technical training, health care, or nutrition.

Developing countries also had to determine the extent to which modernization meant Westernization; in terms of their traditional cultures, how much of Western culture was appropriate? Feminism, consumerism, dress, music, sexual mores, religion— even democracy—became additional choices that countries and their people had to make. *See Chapter 23 for discussion of global variations in economic development.*

Theme 1: Interaction Between Humans and the Environment

See Chapter 23 for discussion of this theme.

Theme 2: Development and Interaction of Cultures

The postcolonial development of Turkey and Iran highlight different approaches to the question of the role of Islam in modern societies. Beginning in the later nineteenth century, Turkey, largely under the initial guidance of Mustafa Kemal Atatürk, turned toward becoming a modern, secular, national state after the collapse of the Ottoman Empire. Atatürk, similar to earlier reformers such as the Young Ottomans, wanted to bring European civilization to Turkey. He ended the caliphate and made Turkey into a parliamentary democracy with a secular law code and educational system. Women and men were expected to adopt Western dress. Polygamy was abolished. Women were granted more rights in inheritance, divorce, child custody; they also received the right to vote and to hold public office in 1934. The Quran was translated into Turkish, and the call to prayer was in Turkish instead of Arabic. Schools taught a Western-style alphabet that made literacy easier but also meant that much of Turkish literature prior to the twentieth century was no longer accessible. After Atatürk's death, many of his reforms were softened. In the early 2000s, a moderate Islamic party governed the country, and the military (staunch supporters of secularization) had less input.

Iran followed a different path. Shah Mohammad Reza Pahlavi, with the support of Western powers, led the oil-rich country in secular modernization in the mid-twentieth century, including granting women voting rights, investing in rural health care, education, and land reform. Industrial projects offered workers a chance to share in the profits. However, the *ulama* (Muslim religious leaders) as well as small-scale merchants felt threatened by the imposition of Western culture and education—as well as cheaper Western products. In addition, the shah's use of the secret police and military (often trained by the West) to maintain power angered many. Led by Ayatollah Ruholla Khomeini, Shi'ite religious leaders called for the shah's removal. A cultural revolution followed, one that reversed the secularization and Westernization under the shah. Iran became an Islamic republic, using Islamic law with a parliament and constitution; in practice, a group of clerics called the Council of Guardians exercised control over the constitution, elections, and legislation to ensure that all was compatible with their vision of Islam. Schools and universities were closed; when they reopened, the books, curricula, and teachers had been purified of "non-Islamic influences." Women returned to wearing hijab, sexual segregation in public was enforced, and family rights (such as the legal age for marriage) were altered to reflect sharia law. However, voting rights remained intact, and the number of women in universities increased to 60 percent. After Ayatollah Khomeini's death, his reforms were somewhat lessened, similar to what happened in Turkey following Atatürk's death.

In Iran and Turkey, both secularization and Islamicization could be measured by the effects on women's dress. In Turkey, Atatürk's aggressive Westernization led women to shed their veils and head coverings and adopt Western-style clothing. As Islamic political parties became more powerful, many women returned to more modest dress and covered their hair. The Shah of Iran, like Atatürk, encouraged women to adopt Western dress as a sign of modernity; after the Cultural Revolution and restoration of Islamic law, women once again donned the hijab.

Theme 3: State-Building, Expansion, and Conflict

Two examples of political struggles to throw off colonial domination are India and South Africa. Before the British, Indian cultural identities were local—dominated by family, caste, and village—but the British promoted a sense of Indian identity and never attempted to assimilate into Indian society, which strengthened Indians' awareness of themselves as a separate group. British colonial infrastructure, administrative and legal bureaucracy, and the use of English in the educational system and journalism all helped to link India's diverse population. This growing sense of national identity was expressed in the Indian National Congress (INC) and its leader Mohandas K. Gandhi. Like many early anticolonial movements, the INC was composed of Western-educated elites from regionally prominent, higher-caste families. At first they hoped to gain greater inclusion in the colonial government and military, not independence, but the British consistently failed to accept their demands.

After World War I, the British promised greater self-government, but following a series of repressive acts, Gandhi was able to mobilize larger segments of the population through his use of *satyagraha* (truth force), a nonviolent but confrontational approach to political action employing boycotts, strikes, and marches. He appealed to Indians to include greater rights for untouchables as well as Muslims in a secular state, which he envisioned as self-sufficient villages grounded in Indian principles of duty and morality. Not everyone in the INC shared his vision; Jawaharlal Nehru embraced modern technology and Muhammad Ali Jinnah favored separate Hindu and Muslim states. After independence, the subcontinent was divided into India (Hindu and secular) and Muslim Pakistan (see Map 22.2, p. 1097).

South Africa had achieved political independence from Britain in 1910. It was a settler colony whose 20 percent white population included both economically powerful English and politically powerful Afrikaners, Dutch settlers conquered by the British in the Boer War (1899–1902). Both British and Afrikaner groups depended for their economic success on the labor of black Africans, so any movement toward majority rule was bitterly contested. Pass laws limited the movement of Africans, and the creation of separate Bantustans (native reserves) kept Africans separated along tribal lines. Similar to the INC, the African National Congress (ANC), founded in 1912, was led by Western-educated, professional, middle-class males who at first did not want to overthrow the system but appealed to the white settlers' stated liberal, humane, and Christian values to be accept as "civilized men." They pursued peaceful strategies such as petitions and delegations sent to appeal to authorities, while denying women full membership until 1943. However, women protested the pass laws, used rural churches to organize, and joined union demands for better wages for domestic servants.

In 1948, the Afrikaner National Party came to power in South Africa on an apartheid (racial separation) platform. The ANC launched boycotts, strikes, and demonstrations against the new government, using tactics created by Gandhi during his stay in South Africa, only to be met with harsh repression, including the Sharpville massacre of unarmed demonstrators in 1960. The ANC was banned, and its leader, Nelson Mandela, was imprisoned. Nationalist groups moved underground and turned to armed struggle, as in the Soweto rebellion. Radicalization and urban violence led to a state of emergency. International pressure to end apartheid included sanctions, exclusion from sporting events, economic boycotts, and the withdrawal of foreign investment funds. This combination of external and internal pressure ultimately led to national elections in 1994, bringing the ANC to power. Similar to the INC in India, the nationalist movement was divided, but not along religious lines. Instead, division arose among the ANC, which saw itself as an alliance of everyone opposed to apartheid (even whites); the Pan Africanist Congress, which limited its membership to black Africans; and the Inkatha Freedom Party, composed of separatist-leaning Zulus. This internal division, however, did not lead to a division of the country, as had happened in India (see Map 22.3, p. 1102).

Some countries, especially in Africa and Latin America, experienced military coups. In Chile in 1972, Marxist politician Salvador Allende was elected by a slim margin. He began to move the country peacefully toward socialism by ordering wage increases and by freezing prices; by nationalizing major industries including banks, copper, coal, and steel; and by seizing large estates to redistribute land. Landowning elites, the military, the church hierarchy, wealthy businessmen, and the bureaucracy—as well as some small businessmen and middle-class people—organized a strike in 1972. The U.S. government as well as many of the affected corporations actively supported the overthrow of Allende. Headed by General Augusto Pinochet, the military overthrew Allende and instituted a repressive regime known for torture and the "disappearance" of thousands. The constitution was suspended, and political parties were outlawed. A free market economy was restored, and foreign investments were encouraged. Wealth increased, but so did rural poverty and landlessness, and wages for urban workers fell. During the 1980s, many military regimes (including Pinochet's) collapsed amid a series of global economic downturns and a movement toward the spread of democracy.

Theme 4: Creation, Expansion, and Interaction of Economic Systems

Improved economic development and quality of life were goals of all emerging nations. However, hampered by the effects of colonial rule (see Key Concept 6.3) and a world economy dominated by capitalist countries and transnational corporations and faced with sharp internal divisions along lines of class, ethnicity, gender, and religion, emerging economies struggled to fulfill the expectations that came with political independence.

Following the example of the Soviet Union, many countries expected the state to take control of their new economies, with some success in China and Cuba. In other areas, such a Turkey, India, South Korea, and much of Africa, the state provided overall planning as well as protective tariffs, licenses, loans, and subsidies but left most of the production capacity in private hands. However, as communist state-run economies collapsed (see Chapter 21), many countries have turned to market economies and privatized their state-run enterprises. Pressure from the West through international organizations such as the World Bank or International Monetary Fund pushed countries to pursue capitalist economies. This approach often led to economic growth, as in India and China, but also produced increased social inequalities. In the twenty-first century, many nations (such as China, Brazil, Russia, and Saudi Arabia) turned to state capitalism, allowing state-owned companies to buy and sell stocks on the open market, seeking a balance between market forces and state management.

In response to the Great Depression, many Latin American countries tried to shield themselves from the global economy by using their resources to make their own consumer goods and protecting their fledgling industries with tariffs, a process known as import substitution stabilization. Brazil pursued this course, leading to the rapid industrialization called the "Brazilian miracle" in the 1970s. Massive infusions of foreign capital and the accumulation of huge foreign debts, cycles of inflation, and high levels of poverty accompanied the "miracle." In the 1980s and 1990s, Brazil became more integrated into the global market by exporting automobiles, steel, aircraft, and computers. Several Asian economies (such as South Korea, Taiwan, Hong Kong, and Singapore) also chose to produce products for export, such as textiles, electronics, and automobiles.

Theme 5: Development and Transformation of Social Structures

Accompanying the rejection of empire as a political construct, nationalist movements rejected race as a basis for social or political rights. However, independence often led to new ethnic and religious rivalries and often did not overturn long-standing economic class differences, especially the poverty of rural peasants. Class conflict, rural poverty, and massive migration to urban slums led to challenges against the postcolonial educated elite who had access to high-paying jobs and privileged positions in government bureaucracies or who controlled the productive capacity of the country. In Latin America and Africa alike, these conflicts sometimes devolved into guerrilla warfare, attempted genocide, or military coups.

Nationalist movements often began with men who were part of the local elite and who had received European educations, such as Atatürk, Gandhi, Nehru, Nkrumah, Mandela, and Sukarno. Some of these leaders pursued independence as their first priority rather than embracing social reform. As in the case of Latin American independence movements in the nineteenth century, many twentieth-century independence movements at first simply removed the foreign occupiers, allowing landowners and the educated urban middle class to assume dominant roles in the new nations. Nationalist movements led by communists, such as in Vietnam and China, promised major social transformations but often led to the creation of new, party-based elites instead of a classless society. Some independence leaders such as Gandhi sought to create a society where religious, class (or caste), and ethnic divisions were diminished or eliminated. His vision was rejected by Hindus and Muslims alike.

The men who led independence movements often did not accept women into national party politics. Women, however, still contributed through strikes, boycotts, and marches. Women continued to be much affected by rural poverty, lack of education, and high birth rates in much of Africa and Latin America. However, some leaders, such as Atatürk, placed a high value on modernity, including removing educational, social, and legal inequalities for women, symbolized by their adoption of European clothing and the removal of veils. Other leaders, such as Gandhi, retained traditional gender roles at home while actively recruiting women in his *satyagraha* movement because he saw them as more naturally able to follow the discipline required of nonviolent civil disobedience. *See Chapter 23 for discussion of global feminism.*

CHAPTER TWENTY-THREE
Capitalism and Culture: A New Phase of Global Interaction, Since 1945

One of the major characteristics of the world since 1945 is globalization—not the imperial reach of the nineteenth and early twentieth centuries, but the "increasingly dense web of political relationships, economic transactions, and cultural influences." Chapter 23 explores the spread and consequences of three of these globalizations: neoliberal capitalism, liberation, and environmentalism.

AP World History Key Concepts

6.1: Science and the Environment

I. Researchers made rapid advances in science that spread throughout the world, assisted by the development of new technology.

II. As the global population expanded at an unprecedented rate, humans fundamentally changed their relationship with the environment.

III. Disease, scientific innovations, and conflict led to demographic shifts.

Science and technology led to rapid economic growth as well as population growth. In addition, because of population growth and increased consumption, humans impacted the environment in new and rapidly accelerating ways, which led to pollution, global warming, and the loss of biodiversity (see Map 23.4, p. 1165). Environmentalism began as a reaction to industrialization in England and developed into a movement to protect wilderness by creating national parks in the United States. A new wave of environmentalism began in the 1960s, first in the West as a means of protecting wild nature, and then spreading to the third world where it was seen as a means for securing food security, health, and basic survival. Developing countries came to believe that environmentalists' desires to cut back on industrial pollution and address global warming meant that the North/South industrial gap would be preserved. By the late twentieth century, environmentalism had become a global concern, stimulated by UN and other international conferences. Global environmentalism has helped to further the idea of "one world," the recognition that some issues transcend the artificial boundaries of nation-states. Environmentalism also challenged the idea of continued unconstrained growth, a foundational idea of modernity, substituting ideas of sustainability and restraint.

6.2: Global Conflicts and Their Consequences

See Chapters 20, 21, and 22 for more discussion of this key concept.

6.3: New Conceptualizations of Global Economy, Society, and Culture

I. States responded in a variety of ways to the economic challenges of the twentieth century.

II. States, communities, and individuals became increasingly interdependent, a process facilitated by the growth of institutions of global governance.

Following World War II, there was concern that the global economy might again suffer the disastrous fate that followed World War I and led to the Great Depression. In 1944 at Bretton Woods, New Hampshire, capitalist countries, led by the United States, created a number of agreements designed to promote free trade. By the 1970s, state-controlled (command) economies were struggling, and many leading capitalist countries (such as the U.S. and the United Kingdom) turned to a philosophy called neoliberalism (a reference to classical liberalism of the nineteenth century, which had advocated laissez faire capitalism) and viewed the world as a single, integrated market. Neoliberalism advocated an end to government controls on the economy, privatization of state-run enterprises, reduced tariffs, free global movement of capital, a mobile and temporary workforce, and cuts in taxation and government spending. The International Monetary Fund (IMF) and World Bank (created at the Bretton Woods conference in 1944) imposed these pro-business policies on emerging countries in need of loans.

By the late twentieth century, economic globalization led to increasingly rapid circulation of goods, capital, and people in the form of labor migration. The impact of economic globalization has led to the rapid creation of immense wealth, which has in turn led to increased life expectancies, declining infant mortality, increased literacy, and declining poverty. However, economic globalization also created instability and uneven distribution of wealth both globally and within nations. In the early years of the twenty-first century, the lack of regulation led to a global economic contraction started by the housing bubble and lending crisis in the United States.

The United States, often seen as an informal empire similar to the ones that Europeans projected onto China and the Middle East in the nineteenth century, used economic penetration, political pressure, and periodic military action to influence other countries to create societies and governments compatible with neoliberal values and interests. These policies have led to increasing global and internal opposition.

III. People conceptualized society and culture in new ways; some challenged old assumptions about race, class, gender, and religion, often using new technologies to spread reconfigured traditions.

IV. Popular and consumer culture became global.

Ideas also went global in the twentieth century, including the idea of liberation: communism promised liberation from capitalist oppression, nationalism promised liberation from imperialism, and democracy promised liberation from authoritarianism. The 1960s saw a variety of liberation and protest movements around the world. In the United States, protests covered civil rights, the counterculture, and antiwar movements; in France, students protested university conditions, to which the state responded with police brutality; the Prague Spring shook Eastern Europe and the Soviet Union, which also responded with military force. In addition, political and social activists in developing countries promoted a "third world" ideology, claiming to be creating new models of economic growth, grassroots democracy, and cultural renewal.

Another liberation movement was women's liberation, or feminism. Although feminism began in the West, in the twentieth century, women's issues went global. For example, communist governments attacked many of the aspects of traditional patriarchy in order to gain women's support. Feminism underwent a revival in the West beginning in the 1960s, and women's movements spread globally. However, the demands of Western women for sexual and occupational equality did not resonate with women in the third world for whom the more immediate issues were ending political and economic exploitation. Differences also appeared along religious and cultural lines within the women's movements. The UN declared 1975 International Women's Year.

Intellectuals since the Enlightenment had predicted the decline of religion in the face of modernity, science, communism, or globalization. The scientific community asserted that only empirical realities should be considered, those that were measurable through scientific techniques. However, major trends in the last century refute those assumptions. World religions have continued to spread and have taken on new forms; they have become a political source of community identity and conflict, while fundamentalist movements have opposed elements of secular and global modernity. *See Chapter 22 for more discussion of this key concept.*

Theme 1: Interaction Between Humans and the Environment

The twentieth century, especially after the 1960s, saw a new awareness of humanity's growth and ability to impact the environment. Future generations may well see environmental awareness as the most fundamental change of the twentieth century. The foundation of the environmental transformation rested on three factors. First was the huge growth in human population, a quadrupling in just a century, caused by advances in medical science and technology that lowered the death rate and the Green Revolution, which dramatically increased the supply of food through genetically modified seeds and fertilizers. Second was the unprecedented ability to use energy (coal in the nineteenth century and petroleum in the twentieth, but also natural gas, hydroelectricity, and nuclear power) to increase production. Third was accelerating economic growth as science and technology increased the production of goods and services.

While human activity has altered the natural world in the past, the effects have been primarily local, not on the global scale of the modern era; cropland doubled, forests and grasslands contracted, and erosion (and desertification) increased at alarming rates. Population growth has led to huge urban complexes. Shrinking natural habitats have also rapidly increased the rate of extinction of many species, while humans have remade the ecosystem to increase the plants and animals useful to them. Ninety percent of the environment today has been shaped by humans. Additionally, the global spread of industry with its use of fossil fuels has led to air pollution so bad that it is estimated that 35,000 people die from it in Mexico City every year. In the former Soviet Union, 20 percent of the population lives in regions that have been deemed "ecological disasters," and half of the rivers are severely polluted. However, global warming (caused by human activities that release "greenhouse gases" such as burning fossil fuels) is perhaps the most threatening aspect of environmental transformation. While the rate of warming is debated, consequences such as the melting of glaciers and polar ice caps, rising ocean levels, thawing permafrost, extreme storms such as hurricanes and typhoons, and increased species extinction have already been observed.

Environmentalism as a mass movement began in the 1960s with the publication of Rachel Carson's *Silent Spring* (which exposed the effects of chemical contamination on birds), the Club of Rome's publication in 1972 of a report called *Limits to Growth* (which warned of resource exhaustion and the collapse of modern, industrial-based society), and the formation in the 1980s of the Green Party in Germany, which was based on opposition to nuclear fuels. Environmentalism spread to the third world in the 1970s and 1980s, but unlike the primarily middle-class movement in the West, which called upon individuals to change their values, turn away from materialism, and appreciate the natural world, third-world environmentalism was more local and limited, more concerned with food security, health, basic survival, and social justice than with wilderness protection. For example, in India, the Chikpo (tree-hugging) movement wanted to prevent deforestation in order to preserve the livelihoods of local people; others focused on stopping construction on the Narmada River dam, which would displace many local people (in contrast, anti-dam movements in the U.S. were primarily concerned with protecting wildlife such as salmon). Many industrializing countries viewed the West's call to limit development that produced pollution and greenhouse gases as a way of perpetuating the economic divide between Global North and Global South by curtailing economic development in emerging economies. The West has argued that new industrial giants such as China and India must agree to limits on greenhouse gases if drastic climate change is to be avoided. By 2011, delegates from 194 countries to the Durban, South Africa, conference agreed to move toward a climate change treaty.

Migration has also become increasingly global. War, revolution, political repression or genocide, and the end of empires led to vast numbers of refugees.

Theme 2: Development and Interaction of Cultures

While religious belief declined sharply in countries such as the Soviet Union, France, and the Netherlands, the global expansion of Buddhism, Christianity, and Islam continued in the twentieth century. Buddhist ideas such as meditation found new expression in the West; Christianity spread to non-Muslim parts of Africa, South Korea, parts of India, and China and found 62 percent of its adherents in Asia, Africa, and Latin America; migrants from the Islamic world expanded Islam to the West.

However, religious fundamentalism (militant piety—often defensive, assertive, and exclusive) also grew. The scientific and secular focus of global modernity conflicted with the "unseen reality" that was the focus of religious belief. Traditional class, family, and gender relationships were upset by social upheavals associated with capitalism, industrialization, and modernization, often brought by Western intrusion through colonial rule, military conquest, or economic dependency. Fundamentalisms have looked to the past for models of spirituality and selectively rejected cultural aspects of global modernity but have often used the technology and sought the prosperity associated with the modern world. Education and propaganda, political mobilization, social welfare programs, and sometimes violence have been used to achieve goals. Conservative Christians emerged as a significant factor in American politics, while Hindutva (Hindu nationalism) became a major political force in India in the 1980s. The most prominent late twentieth-century religious fundamentalism took place in Islam. Earlier Islamic renewal movements, such as the Wahhabis, focused on internal problems in Muslim societies, while those of the twentieth century also reacted to Western imperialism, cultural penetration, and secularism. The UN's creation of the state of Israel in 1948 was regarded as a Western cultural outpost in the heart of Islam, which also led to the displacement of large numbers of Arab Palestinians; the Six-Day War in 1967 left the holy city of Jerusalem as well as other Arab territories under the control of Israel.

The search for Islamic alternatives to Western modernity was grounded in the belief that the Quran and sharia could provide a guide for political, economic, and spiritual life not dependent on Western ideas. Figures such as Mawlana Mawdudi in India and Sayyid Qutb in Egypt said that only a return to the "straight path of Islam" would create a revival of Muslim societies. They labeled this return to Islamic principles a *jihad* (or struggle to please God) to achieve an authentic Islamization of social and political life and to defend Islam against Western intrusions. In 1928, Hassan al-Banna created the Muslim Brotherhood in Egypt, advocating that the government act in accordance with Islamic law and principles. By the last quarter of the twentieth century, Islamic renewal was expressed in several ways. On the personal level, people became more religiously observant and participated in Sufi practices (although in some places Salafist groups rejected Sufi mysticism as non-Islamic). Many women returned to modest dress and the veil. Political leaders began to use Islamic rhetoric to maintain legitimacy. Countries such as Sudan and Pakistan adopted Islamic law. Islamic renewal movements created organizations to provide social services, took part in unions and professional organizations, and tried to use modern science and technology appropriately within Islamic culture. Some movements sought to overthrow governments, such as Iran in 1979, Afghanistan in 1996, and parts of northern Nigeria in 2000.

Hamas in Palestine and Hezbollah in Lebanon targeted Israel with uprisings, suicide bombings, and rocket attacks. The Soviet invasion of Afghanistan led to the creation of a new group, al-Qaeda ("the base" in Arabic) under Osama bin Laden. After bin Laden returned to Saudi Arabia, he became disillusioned by his country's acceptance of U.S. troops in Islam's holy land and returned to Afghanistan to plan the attack on the World Trade Center in 2001. Other al-Qaeda groups launched attacks on Western interests in East Africa, Indonesia, Spain, Great Britain, Yemen, and Saudi Arabia itself to fight "irreligious" Western modernity, American imperialism, and American-led economic globalization.

Aside from militant and revolutionary fundamentalism, there were other religious alternatives to growing disenchantment with globalization and secular modernity. Islamic political parties made strong electoral showings in the 1990s and early twenty-first century in places such as Turkey, Egypt, Jordan, Iraq, Palestine, Morocco, Tunisia, and Lebanon. Debate continued about the proper role of the state and the possibility of democracy in Islamic countries, the difference between religious law and human interpretations of it, and women's rights. In Turkey, the Gulen movement, claiming to be "faith-based but not faith limited," sought to bring Sufi mystical ideas to solve some of the problems of modern society through interfaith dialogue, multiparty democracy, nonviolence, and modern, scientifically based education for both boys and girls. Christian groups, such as the liberation theology movement in Latin America, also examined the ethical issues and growing inequality arising from globalization. In Asia, "socially engaged Buddhism" advocated social reform, educational programs, health services, and peacemaking activities. The UN designated the first week in February 2011 as World Interfaith Harmony Week.

Theme 3: State-Building, Expansion, and Conflict

See Chapters 20, 21, and 22 for more discussion of this theme.

Theme 4: Creation, Expansion, and Interaction of Economic Systems

By the late twentieth century, neoliberal economic policy and new technology that lowered transportation costs and provided almost instantaneous communication led to a "reglobalization" of the world economy that was characterized by increasingly rapid circulation of goods, capital, and people. World trade went from $57 billion in 1947 to $16 trillion in 2009, while foods and products from around the world flooded into consumer markets. Transnational corporations (TNCs), such as Mattel, Royal Dutch Shell, Sony, or General Motors, produced goods or delivered services simultaneously in many different countries. By the 1960s, some TNCs had grown so large that their assets and economic power exceeded that of many countries. Neoliberal economics allowed them to move quickly from place to place looking for the cheapest labor and lowest taxes or regulation.

Economic globalization with its reduction of controls has also created instability, such as the OPEC-generated oil crisis and stock market crash of 1973–1974 (which hurt countries in Latin America that had to choose between fuel for their new economies or repayment of their international debt) or the Asian financial crisis of the late 1990s (which caused the collapse of businesses, political turmoil, and unemployment in Indonesia and Thailand). Recently, the lack of regulation created a global economic contraction. The housing bubble in the U.S. led to foreclosures, unemployment, tightening of credit, and reduced consumer spending. Lack of global regulation transmitted this crisis to such distant places as Iceland, where the stock market dropped, three major banks failed, and its currency lost 70 percent of its value, and Africa, where the drastic demand for exports hurt countries such as Sierra Leone. China's economic slow-down has increased urban unemployment, causing a movement back to already overcrowded and poor rural regions. Unemployment in the U.S. meant that workers from Central America and the Caribbean couldn't send money back home. Contracting economies in Europe (such as in Greece, Italy, and Spain) threaten the European economic integration and the euro.

Unequal distribution of wealth is another product of economic globalization: following industrialization, the difference in income between the top and bottom 20 percent of the world was three to one in 1820; but by 1991, it was eighty-six to one, worsening the gap created by the Industrial Revolution between the Global North and the Global South (see Snapshot: Global Development and Inequality, 2011, p. 1145). The needs of the Global South are not uniform; disparities exist between the oil-rich states and agricultural producers and rapidly industrializing Asian countries (such as China, India, and South Korea) and poor African countries. Unequal distribution also occurs within nations; the offshoring of manufacturing jobs in the U.S. has forced many factory workers to move into lower-paying service-sector jobs, while other workers in high-tech industries are doing well. In Mexico, the northern part of the country has access to business and manufacturing linked to the United States, while the southern section is largely agricultural. China has a growing difference between the poorer rural areas and the cities, where income is three times higher.

Critics of neoliberal globalization, such as political activists, scholars and students, trade unions, women's rights organizations, and religious and environmental groups, have come from both rich and poor countries. They seem to agree that global free trade has favored rich countries and large corporations while it has prevented poor countries from protecting their vulnerable economies, lowered labor standards, disregarded human rights, ignored local cultures, led to environmental degradation, and increased global inequality. These critics organized protests against the World Trade Organization beginning in late 1999 and formed their own World Social Forum in 2001 to share strategies, experiences, and ideas.

From the 1980s, the U.S. has faced growing international competition, first from Europe and Japan, and later from South Korea, Taiwan, China, and India. While the U.S. share of world production was 50 percent in 1945, it had fallen to just 8.1 percent in 2008, accompanied by a growing trade imbalance. Military ventures (for example in Korea, Vietnam, Iraq, and Afghanistan) were costly and led to resistance at home. Even allies such as France resented U.S. influence and withdrew from NATO in 1967.

Intellectuals feared American "cultural imperialism." The United States refused to take part in some international organizations, such as the World Court, or to sign treaties, such as the Kyoto protocol on the environment, which led to more resistance to American cultural and economic domination.

Theme 5: Development and Transformation of Social Structures

Feminism in the West went into decline after suffrage was achieved following World War I. It revived in the turbulent 1960s with the publication of *The Second Sex* by Simone de Beauvoir and *The Feminine Mystique* by Betty Friedan. The new movement in the U.S. became known as the women's liberation movement, aligning it with other liberation movements of the time. Instead of just focusing on voting and legal rights, the liberation movement attempted to counter millennia of patriarchal attitudes and behavior, seeking equality in the workplace, freedom from the purely domestic role, and a change in traditional ideas of beauty and femininity. The advent of the birth control pill also allowed women to more freely express their sexuality. Women of color, however, did not have the same goals; most already worked outside the home and shared with men the larger issues of racism and poverty.

In the Global South, gender was also not the key issue; independence, poverty, economic development, and political oppression were more important. Women played key roles in all these movements (see p. 1100 for women's roles in South Africa), without being allowed by men to be members of the parties themselves. African feminists often saw Western feminists' goals as too individualistic, too focused on sexuality, and not concerned enough with motherhood, marriage, and poverty. They resented Western feminists' culturally charged attitudes on female genital mutilation and polygamy and perceived these attitudes as a new form of colonialism. Instead of focusing on the sexual issues that concerned Western women, women's movements in Africa focused on self-help groups attempting to meet the needs of their communities. In Muslim North Africa, women focused their attention on Family Law Codes that still defined women as minors and did not permit them to initiate divorce or obtain custody of children. In Chile, the women's movement was part of the larger movement against military oppression, torture, and "disappearance" and was a significant part of the return to democratic government in the 1990s.

By the later twentieth century, women's rights became a global focus: "women's rights are human rights" became the motto, and the UN declared 1975 as International Women's Year as well as sponsoring conferences for the next twenty years.

The international spotlight revealed several issues. First, who had the right to speak for women from patriarchal societies—those appointed by the government or more radical members of nongovernmental groups (NGOs)? Secondly, North/South divides appeared; women from the U.S. wanted to focus on political and civil rights, while others from third world or communist countries wanted to focus on economic justice, decolonization, and disarmament. Finally, Muslim women opposed equal inheritance laws because they differed from the Quran, but African women saw support of these laws as a matter of survival in countries ravaged by AIDS. Some women, such as Phyllis Schlafly, felt that the agenda of feminism undermined family life, while many in Muslim countries saw claims of gender equality and open sexuality as morally offensive, leading to a backlash that forced many women to wear veils and lead more restricted lives. In other words, "not all women share identical interests."

PRACTICE EXAM 6

WORLD HISTORY
SECTION I

Note: This exam uses the chronological designations B.C.E. (before the common era) and C.E. (common era). These labels correspond to B.C. (before Christ) and A.D. (anno Domini), which are used in some world history textbooks.

TIME — 55 Minutes
70 Questions

Directions: Each of the questions or incomplete statements below is followed by four suggested answers or completions. Select the one that is best in each case.

1. What does the French poster with the caption that reads "Day of the African Army and Colonial Troops" suggest about the role of North and West Africans in World War I?

    (A) They fought for France.
    (B) They rebelled against France.
    (C) They aided Germany.
    (D) They sided with the Central Powers.

GO ON TO THE NEXT PAGE.

2. All of the following aspects of Europe's nineteenth-century history contributed to World War I EXCEPT

(A) the emergence of Germany as a new nation-state
(B) the system created by the Triple Entente and the Triple Alliance
(C) the tolerance of Serbian terrorist acts
(D) the spread of popular nationalism

3. Which of the following reflects a response of some European countries to the Great Depression?

(A) Cultural revolution
(B) Laissez-faire capitalism
(C) Economic liberalization
(D) Democratic socialism

4. Which of the following did Japan, Italy, and Germany share in the 1930s?

(A) Widespread arrest and execution of political opponents
(B) Aggressive ambition for conquest and empire building
(C) Strong traditions of parliamentary democracy
(D) Political takeover by socialist parties

5. "By educating the young generation along the right lines, the People's State will have to see to it that a generation of mankind is formed which will be adequate to this supreme combat that will decide the destinies of the world. . . ."

Adolph Hitler, Mein Kampf, *1925–1926*

"Hence, offering our lives for the sake of the Emperor does not mean so-called self-sacrifice, but the casting aside of our little selves to live under his august grace and the enhancing of the genuine life of the people of a State. . . ."

Japanese Ministry of Education, Cardinal Principles of the National Entity of Japan, *1937*

Both passages reflect the state's control of education to prepare students for

(A) war
(B) politics
(C) sports
(D) trade

6. In what way were the origins of World War II in Asia and in Europe similar to each other?

(A) Both Japan and Germany felt they had been treated unfairly because of their defeat in World War I.
(B) Both Japan and Germany were driven by strategic and economic rivalries with the League of Nations.
(C) Both Japan and Germany fought to end racism within their own countries and in international relations.
(D) Both Japan and Germany expanded their territories through force, creating tensions with other powers.

GO ON TO THE NEXT PAGE.

7. Which of the following reflects a new pattern in Europe in the period since World War II?

   (A) The economic integration of Western European countries
   (B) The colonial exploitation of Eastern European countries
   (C) The military and cultural dominance of the United Nations
   (D) The economic and political leadership exercised by Britain

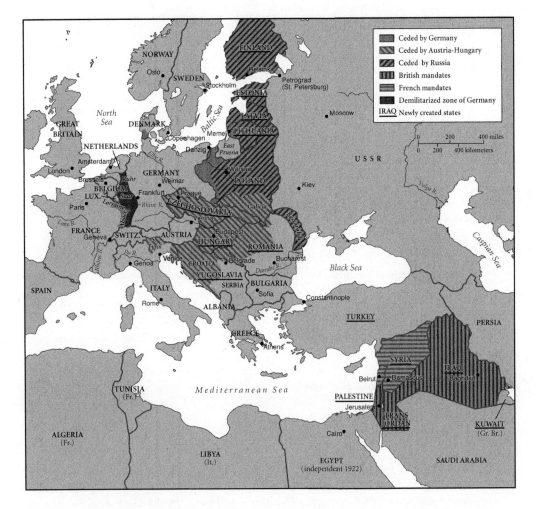

8. The map above shows Europe and the Middle East during the period

   (A) between the Renaissance and the Reformation
   (B) between the two world wars
   (C) of the New Imperialism
   (D) of the cold war

9. What did all nationalist movements in Asia and Africa in the second half of the twentieth century share in common?

   (A) The goal of political independence
   (B) The ideology of Marxist revolution
   (C) The leadership of religious figures
   (D) The use of guerrilla warfare

GO ON TO THE NEXT PAGE.

10. All of the following reflect a growing internationalism in the world after 1945 EXCEPT

    (A) the League of Nations
    (B) the United Nations
    (C) the World Bank
    (D) the International Monetary Fund

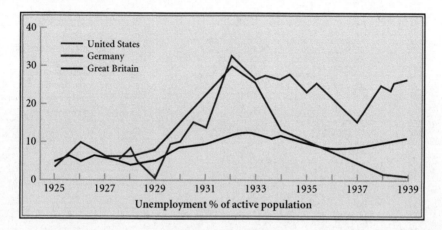

11. Which of the following conclusions is supported by the data in the chart above?

    (A) Unemployment declined in Germany as a result of the rearmament program launched by the Nazi Party.
    (B) Unemployment in Germany, Britain, and the U.S. was at its highest when the Great Depression started.
    (C) The movement of women into the labor force directly affected unemployment rates.
    (D) Republican forms of government were the most effective at confronting the root causes of unemployment.

12. "To many historians, that century [the twentieth], and a new era in the human journey, began in 1914 with the outbreak of World War I."

    ". . . this most recent century both carried on from the past and developed distinctive characteristics as well. Whether that combination of the old and new merits the designation of a separate era in world history will likely be debated. . . ."

    Robert Strayer, world historian, 2012

    In contrast to the view expressed in the first quotation, the second quotation

    (A) challenges the notion that the twentieth century represented anything new
    (B) insists that the twentieth century constituted a new period
    (C) questions the significance of World War I as an epoch-marking turning point
    (D) argues that World War I dramatically transformed the world

13. All of the following have contributed to the environmental changes of the twentieth century EXCEPT

    (A) explosive increase in the world population
    (B) new energy resources
    (C) worldwide decline in service industries
    (D) phenomenal economic growth

GO ON TO THE NEXT PAGE.

14. How have modernity, science, and globalization affected the world's religions since 1945?

    (A) Religion contributed to the scientific and secular focus of global modernity.
    (B) Religion offered a means to oppose elements of a secular and global modernity.
    (C) Religion was universally criticized for fostering superstition and ignorance.
    (D) Religions experienced sharp declines in membership and conversions.

15. Which of the following can be inferred from the information provided in the map above?

    (A) Economic development in Latin America was dependent on foreign capital and export of raw materials.
    (B) Trade with the U.S. jump-started a thorough process of industrialization across Latin America.
    (C) European indentured servants became the largest underclass in Latin America.
    (D) Bolivia was the most dependent on U.S. military intervention to maintain its economy.

GO ON TO THE NEXT PAGE.

16. All of the following were conditions that enabled Britain to be the first country to industrialize EXCEPT

   (A) a scientific culture that emphasized technology
   (B) the development of electricity
   (C) a large and mobile labor force
   (D) the abundance of coal

17. ". . . a class of laborers, who live only so long as they find work, and who find work only so long as their labor increases capital. These laborers, who must sell themselves piece-meal, are a commodity, like every other article of commerce, and are consequently exposed to all the vicissitudes of competition, to all the fluctuations of the market."

   Karl Marx and Friedrich Engels, The Communist Manifesto, *1848*

   What is the special term that Marx and Engels used to distinguish the "class of laborers" produced by industrial capitalism from workers in pre-industrial society?

   (A) Anarchists
   (B) Capitalists
   (C) Bourgeoisie
   (D) Proletariat

18. "Everyone who knows a little about aboriginal races is aware that those races which are of a low type mentally and who are at the same time weak in constitution rapidly die out when their country comes to be occupied by a different race much more rigorous, robust, and pushing than themselves."

   Reverend Bishop Hale, late 19th century

   The interpretation of human societies expressed in the above quotation reflects the influence of

   (A) Marxist ideology
   (B) Enlightenment ideals
   (C) social Darwinism
   (D) Wahhabi Islam

GO ON TO THE NEXT PAGE.

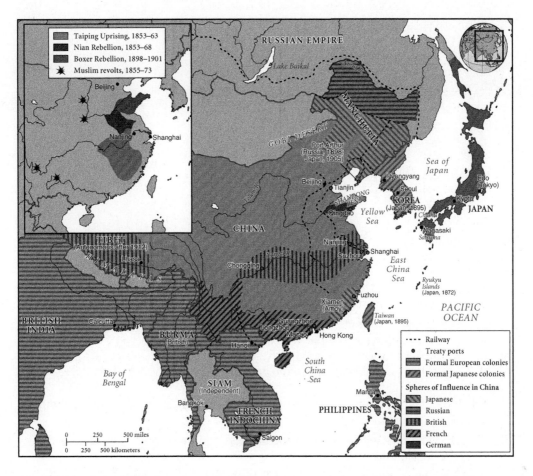

19. Which of the following was a new form of economic imperialism, shown in the map above, that was practiced in the nineteenth century?

    (A) Colony
    (B) Caliphate
    (C) Sphere of influence
    (D) Zone of autonomy

20. In 1853, the arrival in Japan of the "black ships" from which country contributed to the collapse of the Tokugawa shogunate?

    (A) Ottoman Empire
    (B) United States
    (C) Britain
    (D) China

21. All of the following countries were involved in the "scramble for Africa" EXCEPT

    (A) Germany
    (B) France
    (C) United States
    (D) Belgium

GO ON TO THE NEXT PAGE.

22. "Men are born and remain free and equal in rights."

    The quotation above from the French Declaration of the Rights of Man and Citizen reflects the influence of the
    - (A) Renaissance
    - (B) Enlightenment
    - (C) Scientific Revolution
    - (D) Protestant Reformation

23. Like the Atlantic revolutions that had happened earlier, the Spanish American revolutions challenged the absolute authority of
    - (A) nations
    - (B) republics
    - (C) monarchies
    - (D) empires

24. What common set of circumstances contributed to the abolition of slavery in the Atlantic world and the end of serfdom in Russia in the nineteenth century?
    - (A) Demands for suffrage, labor shortages, and pacifist sentiments
    - (B) Fear of rebellion, economic inefficiency, and moral concerns
    - (C) Campaigns for civil rights, Marxist ideas, and nativist feelings
    - (D) Spread of imperialism, economic protectionism, and racist ideas

25. Which of the following contributed to the contraction of the Ottoman Empire in the nineteenth century?
    - (A) Disagreement among the European states on how to divide the Ottoman Empire among themselves
    - (B) Nationalist-inspired independence movements in Greece, Serbia, Bulgaria, and Romania
    - (C) Explosive population growth in the nineteenth century
    - (D) Ottoman control of Afro-Eurasian commerce

26. Which of the following represents the influence of nationalism in the nineteenth century?
    - (A) The political unification of Germany and Italy
    - (B) The creation of the United States of Latin America
    - (C) The extension of the vote to women in New Zealand
    - (D) The end of feudalism and the abolition of slavery

27. All of the following represent new forms of forced labor in colonial economies in the nineteenth and early twentieth centuries EXCEPT
    - (A) the cultivation system in the Dutch East Indies
    - (B) statute labor in French West Africa
    - (C) coerced labor servitude in the Congo Free State
    - (D) indentured servitude in British North America

GO ON TO THE NEXT PAGE.

28. Because human activity since the late eighteenth century has fundamentally altered the earth, some scholars refer to the past several centuries as the

    (A) Enlightenment
    (B) Global Village
    (C) Columbian exchange
    (D) Anthropocene

29. "On their side is the vast wealth of their empire, unimpaired resources, experience and practice in arms, a veteran soldiery, an uninterrupted series of victories, readiness to endure hardships, union, order, discipline, thrift, and watchfulness."

    Ogier Ghiselin de Busbecq, The Turkish Letters, *1555–1562*

    Which of the following is de Busbecq describing in the quote above?

    (A) Chinese Empire
    (B) Austrian Empire
    (C) Ottoman Empire
    (D) Aztec Empire

30. Which of the following contributed to the "great dying" in the Americas?

    (A) A volcanic eruption and an earthquake that caused massive flooding
    (B) A prolonged drought that made farming impossible
    (C) The frequent warfare between the Aztec and Inca empires
    (D) Native Americans' lack of immunity to European and African diseases

31. Beginning in the sixteenth century, the global silver trade

    (A) destroyed the Spanish economy
    (B) brought about the downfall of the Chinese Empire
    (C) was important in India but had no impact on China
    (D) linked the economies of the Americas, Europe, and Asia

32. How did the Wahhabi movement respond to the religious syncretism that accompanied the spread of Islam in the eighteenth century?

    (A) It sought a return to the absolute monotheism of authentic Islam.
    (B) It encouraged the veneration of Sufi saints and their tombs.
    (C) It promoted religious tolerance by absorbing Christian practices.
    (D) It expanded the rights of women under Islamic law.

33. Which of the following represents a departure from previous thinking that all Enlightenment philosophers promoted?

    (A) The rejection of monotheism
    (B) The principle of gender equality
    (C) The belief in progress and reason
    (D) The notion of divine right of kings

GO ON TO THE NEXT PAGE.

34. From the choice of dates listed below, identify the only date that this statement by an African king could have been made: "A long time ago the great king [of England] liked plenty of trade, more than now; then many ships came, and they bought ivory, gold, and slaves; but now he will not let the ships come as before, and the people buy gold and ivory only. . . . Why does the king do so?"

   (A) 1520
   (B) 1620
   (C) 1720
   (D) 1820

35. Which of the following resulted from the Columbian exchange?

   (A) The emergence of Western Europeans on the world stage
   (B) The introduction of corn and potatoes into the Afro-Eurasian diet
   (C) The rivalry between Catholic Spain and Protestant England
   (D) The interaction between the Mesoamerican and Andean civilizations

36. All of the following resulted from the creation of European empires in the Americas EXCEPT

   (A) the transfer of plants, animals, and diseases between the "old" and "new" worlds
   (B) the emergence of an Atlantic world connecting the Americas to Afro-Eurasia
   (C) the widespread cultivation of American food crops in Europe, Asia, and Africa
   (D) the demographic collapse of pastoral and agrarian societies in Europe and Asia

37. Which of the following was an incentive for the Portuguese to find a direct sea route to Asia?

   (A) To circumvent the Muslim and Venetian monopolies on Indian Ocean trade
   (B) To establish colonies for their growing population and create markets for their goods
   (C) To challenge Chinese and Arab control of the Indian Ocean trading networks
   (D) To establish a base on the eastern end of the Silk Road

38. All of the following religious movements blended elements from different spiritual traditions EXCEPT

   (A) Sikhism
   (B) Sufism
   (C) the bhakti movement
   (D) the Wahhabi movement

39. In what respect was the Thirty Years' War in Europe similar to the conflict between the Ottoman and Safavid empires in the Middle East?

   (A) Both began as a succession dispute that resulted in the collapse of the Holy Roman Empire.
   (B) Both erupted from a dispute over who held the rightful claim to the papacy and the caliphate.
   (C) Both involved political rivalries for territory and doctrinal differences over a shared religion.
   (D) Both began as civil wars and resulted in a stalemate that still stands today.

GO ON TO THE NEXT PAGE.

40. Which of the following did the Scientific Revolution in Europe and the kaozheng movement in China both emphasize?

    (A) Introspection
    (B) Virtue
    (C) Empiricism
    (D) Salvation

41. Which of the following would be the most useful source of evidence for research about the effect of the Atlantic slave trade on African society in the early modern period?

    (A) Published speeches by white abolitionists
    (B) Sales records of European slave traders
    (C) Slave codes from the Caribbean
    (D) Political treatises by Enlightenment thinkers

42. All of the following are conventionally identified as early signs of the modern world that first emerged in the centuries from 1450 to 1750 EXCEPT the

    (A) emergence of Islam as the dominant faith in Africa and Asia
    (B) processes of globalization initiated by European expansion
    (C) elements of modernity expressed in the Scientific Revolution
    (D) dominance of Europeans in the Americas and the seas

43. All of the following reflect how Buddhism changed from the original teachings of the historical Buddha as a consequence of its spread along the Silk Roads EXCEPT

    (A) Buddhist monks led ascetic lifestyles and withdrew from society
    (B) Buddhist monasteries in oasis towns engaged in secular activities
    (C) the Buddha was worshipped as a deity
    (D) local gods were incorporated as bodhisattvas

44. During the seventh and eighth centuries, trade along the Silk Roads was facilitated by the security measures provided by all of the following states EXCEPT

    (A) Abbasid dynasty
    (B) Mughal dynasty
    (C) Tang dynasty
    (D) Byzantine Empire

45. Which of the following contributed to the growth of Swahili civilization between 1000 and 1500?

    (A) The shift of global trade from the Mediterranean to the Atlantic
    (B) The destruction of the Silk Roads in the wake of the Mongol conquest
    (C) The spread of the Black Death from Asia to Europe
    (D) The expansion of Indian Ocean commerce following the rise of Islam

46. The spread of the Black Death from China to Europe in the fourteenth century occurred during an era of increased contact following the

    (A) spread of Islam
    (B) spread of Buddhism
    (C) Manchu conquest
    (D) Mongol conquest

GO ON TO THE NEXT PAGE.

47. Which of the following contributed to what some scholars describe as China's "economic revolution" during the Song dynasty?

    (A) The launching of maritime expeditions in the Indian Ocean basin
    (B) The adoption of a fast-ripening and drought-resistant strain of rice from Vietnam
    (C) The establishment of tributary relations with pastoral peoples in inner Eurasia
    (D) The importation of food crops from Central Asia, North Africa, and Eastern Europe

48. All of the following can be used as evidence for researching how Chinese women's lives changed from the Tang to the Song dynasty EXCEPT

    (A) paintings and statues of women
    (B) accounts by Ibn Battuta
    (C) writings by Confucian scholars
    (D) laws governing property and dowries

49. Which of the following represents China's ideal model for managing relations with the pastoral peoples of the northern steppes and other non-Chinese peoples since the Han dynasty?

    (A) The encomienda system
    (B) The hacienda system
    (C) The emperor system
    (D) The tribute system

50. All of the following features of pre-Islamic Arabia influenced the beliefs and practices of Islam EXCEPT the

    (A) mass printing of translations of the Bible in vernacular languages
    (B) growing identification among Arabs as "children of Abraham"
    (C) monotheistic ideas of Jews, Christians, and Zoroastrians living in Arabia
    (D) wide acceptance of Allah as the leader in the Arab pantheon of gods

51. Which of the following played an important role in transmitting ancient Greek learning to Western Europe and the Islamic world after the fall of the Roman Empire?

    (A) Ottoman Empire
    (B) Byzantine Empire
    (C) Mughal Empire
    (D) Songhay Empire

52. Between 1000 and 1500, the rise of the Swahili and Italian city-states illustrates the relationship between

    (A) religion and military conquest
    (B) science and cultural diffusion
    (C) politics and artistic styles
    (D) commerce and state building

GO ON TO THE NEXT PAGE.

53. Historians point to all of the following to argue that the High Middle Ages represented a new phase of European civilization EXCEPT the

    (A) increase in agricultural productivity that stimulated long-distance trade
    (B) gradual consolidation of political authority under national monarchies
    (C) doubling of the population of Europe from the tenth to the fourteenth century
    (D) unification of Europe under the papal authority of the Catholic Church

54. All of the following reflect long-term effects of the Black Death EXCEPT the

    (A) contraction of the Ottoman Empire
    (B) decline of serfdom in Europe
    (C) collapse of the Mongol Empire
    (D) closure of the Silk Roads

55. What did the Xiongnu, Turks, and Mongols have in common?

    (A) They made Buddhism the official religion of the state.
    (B) They independently developed agriculture at the same time.
    (C) They were all pastoral peoples who established empires.
    (D) They were all tribute states of Ming dynasty China.

56. All of the following motivated Europeans to launch maritime expeditions beginning in the fifteenth century EXCEPT

    (A) a desire for direct access to the markets of Asia and Africa
    (B) the rivalries among competing European states
    (C) an interest in foreign cultures and languages
    (D) a missionary zeal to spread Christianity

57. The Persian Empire and the Mauryan Empire both used which of the following to keep informed about developments throughout the empire?

    (A) Palace memorials
    (B) Public notices
    (C) Traveling merchants
    (D) Imperial spies

58. How did the infiltration of Germanic tribes into the Roman Empire beginning in the fourth century affect Western European civilization?

    (A) The Germanic tribes introduced Christianity to Western Europe.
    (B) The nomadic culture of the Germanic people defined Western civilization.
    (C) German replaced Latin as the official language of the Catholic Church.
    (D) Germanic and Roman culture were synthesized, creating a hybrid civilization.

59. Which of the following facilitated the spread of Greek culture during the Hellenistic era?

    (A) Rivers
    (B) Cities
    (C) Laws
    (D) Maps

GO ON TO THE NEXT PAGE.

60. Which of the following is a feature common to both Buddhism and Hinduism?
    - (A) The notion of rebirth
    - (B) The worship of Allah
    - (C) The focus on the material world
    - (D) The commitment to social equality

61. All of the following reflect the influence of Confucianism on Chinese civilization EXCEPT the
    - (A) civil service examination system
    - (B) value attached to education
    - (C) veneration of the natural world
    - (D) view of the state in familial terms

62. How did views of the Buddha and Jesus change as the religions they founded spread?
    - (A) Both were transformed by their followers into gods.
    - (B) Both were regarded as the ancestor of their followers.
    - (C) Both were depicted symbolically as bodhisattvas.
    - (D) Both were seen as martyrs who died resisting religious persecution.

63. All of the following have been proposed by scholars as factors that led to the practice of slavery within the First Civilizations EXCEPT the
    - (A) concept of private property
    - (B) influence of patriarchy
    - (C) early domestication of animals
    - (D) notions of racial difference

64. Which of the following civilizations during the second-wave era had the most rigidly defined social structure?
    - (A) China
    - (B) Persia
    - (C) Axum
    - (D) India

65. Peasant rebellions in China were often inspired by popular versions of
    - (A) Hinduism
    - (B) Confucianism
    - (C) Daoism
    - (D) Legalism

66. Which of the following has been identified as a factor contributing to the collapse of the Moche, Maya, and Chaco cultures?
    - (A) Foreign invasion
    - (B) A century of devastating flooding
    - (C) A long-term drought
    - (D) Massive rebellions that overthrew the Maya emperor

GO ON TO THE NEXT PAGE.

67. In contrast to cities in other civilizations of the time, cities in the Niger Valley civilization

    (A) had their own centralized political structure headed by a monarch
    (B) were run by complex bureaucracies staffed by priests
    (C) were constantly engaged in warfare with one another
    (D) operated without the coercive authority of a state

68. Which of the following is evidence suggesting that Paleolithic people altered their environment by deliberately setting fires to encourage the growth of particular plants?

    (A) The proliferation of fire-resistant eucalyptus trees in Australia
    (B) The absence of weeds throughout Africa and the Middle East
    (C) The domestication of wild grains and seeds in Mesopotamia
    (D) The centrality of fire in rituals associated with agriculture

69. How did the north/south orientation of the Americas and the east/west axis of North Africa and Eurasia affect how the Agricultural Revolution unfolded within each region?

    (A) Crops only spread in those regions near the equator, which explains why the Americas never experienced an Agricultural Revolution.
    (B) Differences in climatic and vegetation zones in the Americas slowed down the spread of crops, while similar environments within the Afro-Eurasian region facilitated the spread of crops.
    (C) The direction of monsoon winds enabled agricultural knowledge to spread throughout the Americas much faster than in the Afro-Eurasian region.
    (D) The proximity of the Americas to the Pacific Ocean enabled it to complete its Agricultural Revolution centuries before similar processes began in the Afro-Eurasian region.

70. Recent scholarship has pointed to all of the following to explain the emergence of patriarchy in the First Civilizations EXCEPT the

    (A) development of animal-drawn, plow-based agriculture
    (B) association of women with nature as opposed to culture
    (C) inherent nature of inequalities between men and women
    (D) emergence of large-scale warfare with professionally led armies

STOP

END OF SECTION I

WORLD HISTORY
SECTION II

Part A
(Suggested writing time—40 minutes)
Percent of Section II score—33 1/3

Directions: The following question is based on the accompanying Documents 1–7. (The documents have been edited for the purpose of this exercise.)

This question is designed to test your ability to work with and understand historical documents.

Write an essay that:

+ Has a relevant thesis and supports that thesis with evidence from the documents.
+ Uses all of the documents.
+ Analyzes the documents by grouping them in as many appropriate ways as possible. Does not simply summarize the documents individually.
+ Takes into account the sources of the documents and analyzes the authors' points of view.
+ Identifies and explains the need for at least one additional type of document.

You may refer to relevant historical information not mentioned in the documents.

1. Using the following documents, analyze nineteenth- and twentieth-century women's movements for continuities to and changes from the women's rights advocated in the era of the Enlightenment and French Revolution by Mary Wollstonecraft (Document 1). Identify an additional type of document and explain how it would help your analysis of the continuities and changes in women's rights movements.

GO ON TO THE NEXT PAGE.

Document 1

Source: Mary Wollstonecraft, female writer and philosopher, *A Vindication of the Rights of Woman*, 1792.

Contending for the rights of woman, my main argument is built on this simple principle, that if she be not prepared by education to become the companion of man, she will stop the progress of knowledge and virtue . . . but the education and situation of woman at present shuts her out from such investigations . . .

Consider, sir, dispassionately these observations, for a glimpse of this truth seemed to open before you when you observed, "that to see one-half of the human race excluded by the other from all participation of government was a political phenomenon that, according to abstract principles, it was impossible to explain."

Consider — I address you as a legislator — whether, when men contend for their freedom, and to be allowed to judge for themselves respecting their own happiness, it be not inconsistent and unjust to subjugate women, even though you firmly believe that you are acting in the manner best calculated to promote their happiness? Who made man the exclusive judge, if woman partake with him of the gift of reason?

In this style argue tyrants of every denomination, from the weak king to the weak father of a family; they are all eager to crush reason, yet always assert that they usurp its throne only to be useful. Do you not act a similar part when you force all women, by denying them civil and political rights, to remain immured in their families groping in the dark? . . . They may be convenient slaves, but slavery will have its constant effect, degrading the master and the abject dependent . . .

Let there be then no coercion established in society, and the common law of gravity prevailing, the sexes will fall into their proper places. And now that more equitable laws are forming your citizens, marriage may become more sacred; your young men may choose wives from motives of affection, and your maidens allow love to root out vanity.

[I]f women are not permitted to enjoy legitimate rights, they will render both men and themselves vicious to obtain illicit privileges.

I wish, sir, to set some investigations of this kind afloat in France; and should they lead to a confirmation of my principles when your constitution is revised, the Rights of Woman may be respected, if it be fully proved that reason calls for this respect, and loudly demands JUSTICE for one-half of the human race.

GO ON TO THE NEXT PAGE.

Document 2

Source: Elizabeth Cady Stanton, American activist for women's suffrage, "The Solitude of Self," 1892.

The point I wish plainly to bring before you on this occasion is the individuality of each human soul. . . . In discussing the rights of woman, we are to consider, first, what belongs to her as an individual, in a world of her own. . . .

The strongest reason for giving woman all the opportunities for higher education, for the full development of her faculties . . . for giving her the most enlarged freedom of thought and action; a complete emancipation from all forms of bondage, of custom, dependence, superstition; from all the crippling influences of fear, is the solitude and personal responsibility of her own individual life. The strongest reason why we ask for woman a voice in the government under which she lives; in the religion she is asked to believe; equality in social life, where she is the chief factor; a place in the trades and professions, where she may earn her bread, is because of her birthright to self-sovereignty; because, as an individual, she must rely on herself. No matter how much women prefer to lean, to be protected and supported, nor how much men desire to have them do so, they must make the voyage of life alone. . . . It matters not whether the solitary voyager is man or woman. . . . Alike amid the greatest triumphs and darkest tragedies of life we walk alone. . . .

GO ON TO THE NEXT PAGE.

Document 3

Source: Raden Adjeng Kartini, Muslim Indonesian feminist's letter to a friend, 1899.

I do not belong to the Indian world, but to that of my pale sisters who are struggling forward in the distant West.

If the laws of my land permitted it, there is nothing that I had rather do than give myself wholly to the working and striving of the new woman in Europe; but age-long traditions that cannot be broken hold us fast cloistered in their unyielding arms . . . All our institutions are directly opposed to the progress for which I so long for the sake of our people. Day and night I wonder by what means our ancient traditions could be overcome.

Even in my childhood, the word "emancipation" enchanted my ears; it had a significance that nothing else had, a meaning that was far beyond my comprehension, and awakened in me an evergrowing longing for freedom and independence—a longing to stand alone . . .

I am the eldest of the three unmarried daughters of the Regent of Japara . . . My grandfather . . . was a great leader in the progressive movement of his day, and the first regent of middle Java to unlatch his door to that guest from over the sea—Western civilization. All of his children had European educations. . . . It was a great crime against the customs of our land that we [girls] should be taught at all, and especially that we should leave the house every day to go to school. For the customs of our country forbade girls in the strongest manner ever to go outside of the house.

When I reached the age of twelve, I was kept at home—I must go into the "box." I was locked up, and cut off from all communication with the outside world, toward which I might never turn again save at the side of a bridegroom, a stranger, an unknown man whom my parents would choose for me, and to whom I should be betrothed without my own knowledge. . . . I went into my prison. Four long years I spent between thick walls, without once seeing the outside world.

At last in my sixteenth year, I saw the outside world again. Thank God! Thank God! I could leave my prison as a free human being and not chained to an unwelcome bridegroom . . .

I do not desire to go out to feasts, and little frivolous amusements. That has never been the cause of my longing for freedom. I long to be free, to be able to stand alone, to study, not to be subject to any one, and, above all, never, never to be obliged to marry.

But we must marry, must, must. Not to marry is the greatest sin which the [Muslim] woman can commit; it is the greatest disgrace which a native girl can bring to her family.

And marriage among us—Miserable is too feeble an expression for it. How can it be otherwise, when the laws have made everything for the man and nothing for the woman? When law and convention both are for the man; when everything is allowed to him?

GO ON TO THE NEXT PAGE.

Document 4

Source: Alexandra Kollontai, female government official and ambassador of the Soviet Union, "Communism and the Family," 1920.

Will the family continue to exist under communism? . . . [One] fact that invites attention is that divorce has been made easier in Soviet Russia. . . . A working woman will not have to petition for months or even for years to secure the right to live separately from a husband who beats her and makes her life a misery with his drunkenness and uncouth behaviour. Divorce by mutual agreement now takes no more than a week or two to obtain. . . .

[T]he old family in which the man was everything and the woman nothing . . . is changing before our very eyes. . . . It is the universal spread of female labour that has contributed most of all to the radical change in family life. . . . Capitalism has placed a crushing burden on woman's shoulders: it has made her a wage-worker without having reduced her cares as housekeeper or mother. Woman staggers beneath the weight of this triple load. . . .

The circumstances that held the family together no longer exist. The family is ceasing *to be necessary either to its members or to the nation as a whole.* . . .

All that was formerly produced in the bosom of the family is now being manufactured on a mass scale in workshops and factories. . . . The family no longer produces; it only consumes. . . . The individual household is dying. It is giving way in our society to collective housekeeping. . . .

In place of the old relationship between men and women, a new one is developing: a union of affection and comradeship, a union of two equal members of communist society, both of them free, both of them independent, and both of them workers. No more domestic bondage for women. No more inequality within the family. No need for women to fear being left without support and with children to bring up. The woman in communist society no longer depends upon her husband but on her work. . . . She need have no anxiety about her children. The workers' state will assume responsibility for them. Marriage will lose all the elements of material calculation which cripple family life. Marriage will be a union of two persons who love and trust each other. . . .

In place of the individual and egoistic family, a great universal family of workers will develop, in which all the workers, men and women, will above all be comrades. This is what relations between men and women in the communist society will be like. These new relations will ensure for humanity all the joys of a love unknown in the commercial society, of a love that is free and based on the true social equality of the partners.

GO ON TO THE NEXT PAGE.

Document 5

Source: Combahee River Collective, a women's organization centered in Boston, Massachusetts, "A Black Feminist Statement," 1977.

We are a collective of Black feminists who have been meeting together since 1974. . . . [W]e are actively committed to struggling against racial, sexual, heterosexual, and class oppression . . . based upon the fact that the major systems of oppression are interlocking. . . .

[W]e find our origins in the historical reality of Afro-American women's continuous life-and-death struggle for survival and liberation. . . . Black women have always embodied an adversary stance to white male rule. . . . Black feminist politics also have an obvious connection to movements for Black liberation, particularly those of the 1960s and 1970s. . . . It was our experience and disillusionment within these liberation movements, as well as experience on the periphery of the white male left, that led to the need to develop a politics that was anti-racist, unlike those of white women, and anti-sexist, unlike those of Black and white men. . . . [A]s we developed politically we [also] addressed ourselves to heterosexism and economic oppression under capitalism. . . .

Although we are feminists and Lesbians, we feel solidarity with progressive Black men . . . We struggle together with Black men against racism, while we also struggle with Black men about sexism. . . . We are socialists because we believe that work must be organized for the collective benefit of those who do the work and create the products, and not for the profit of the bosses. . . . We need to articulate the real class situation of persons . . . for whom racial and sexual oppression are significant determinants in their working/economic lives. . . . No one before has ever examined the multi-layered texture of Black women's lives. . . .

The inclusiveness of our politics makes us concerned with any situation that impinges upon the lives of women, Third World and working people. . . . One issue that is of major concern to us and that we have begun to publicly address is racism in the white women's movement. . . . Eliminating racism in the white women's movement is by definition work for white women to do, but we will continue to speak to and demand accountability on this issue. . . .

GO ON TO THE NEXT PAGE.

Document 6

Source: Benazir Bhutto, Muslim female politician and later Prime Minister of Pakistan, "Politics and the Muslim Woman," 1985.

[O]ne of the first things that we must appreciate about the religion of Islam is that there is no one interpretation to it. . . .

I would describe Islam in two main categories: reactionary Islam and progressive Islam. We can have a reactionary interpretation of Islam which tries to uphold the status quo, or we can have a progressive interpretation of Islam which tries to move with a changing world, which believes in human dignity, which believes in consensus, and which believes in giving women their due right. . . .

The references [in the Quran] are to men and women. . . . The attributes are the same. Both are the creatures of God. Both have certain rights. Both have certain duties. . . . [T]hey have to give alms to the needy, they have to help orphans—the behavior is applicable to both men and women. It is not religion which makes the difference. The difference comes from man-made law. It comes from the fact that soon after the Prophet died, it was not the Islam of the Prophet that remained. What took place was the emergence or the reassertiveness of the patriarchal society, and religion was taken over to justify the norms of the tribal society. . . .

[W]hy is it that today in Muslim countries, one does not see that much of women? . . . Why is it that women are secluded? Why is it that women are subject to social control? Why is it that women are not given their due share of property? . . . It has got nothing to do with the religion, but it has got very much to do with material or man-made considerations. . . . It is not Islam which is averse to women rulers, I think—it is men.

GO ON TO THE NEXT PAGE.

Document 7

Source: Zapatista Army of National Liberation, Chiapas, Mexico, *The Women's Revolutionary Law*, 1994.

[T]aking into account the situation of the woman worker in Mexico, the revolution supports their just demands for equality and justice in the following Women's Revolutionary Law.

First: Women, regardless of their race, creed, color or political affiliation, have the right to participate in the revolutionary struggle in a way determined by their desire and capacity.

Second: Women have the right to work and receive a just salary.

Third: Women have the right to decide the number of children they will have and care for.

Fourth: Women have the right to participate in the affairs of the community and hold positions of authority if they are freely and democratically elected.

Fifth: Women and their children have the right to primary attention in matters of health and nutrition.

Sixth: Women have the right to an education.

Seventh: Women have the right to choose their partner, and are not to be forced into marriage.

Eighth: Women shall not be beaten or physically mistreated by their family members or by strangers. Rape and attempted rape will be severely punished.

Ninth: Women will be able to occupy positions of leadership in the organization and hold military ranks in the revolutionary armed forces.

END OF PART A

WORLD HISTORY
SECTION II

Part B
(Suggested planning and writing time—40 minutes)
Percent of Section II score—33 1/3

Directions: You are to answer the following question. You should spend 5 minutes organizing or outlining your essay.

Write an essay that:

+ Has a relevant thesis and supports that thesis with appropriate historical evidence.
+ Addresses all parts of the question.
+ Uses world historical context to show continuities and changes over time.
+ Analyzes the process of continuity and change over time.

2. Analyze the continuities and changes in human interaction with the environment since 1900.

END OF PART B

WORLD HISTORY
SECTION II

Part C
(Suggested planning and writing time—40 minutes)
Percent of Section II score—33 1/3

Directions: You are to answer the following question. You should spend 5 minutes organizing or outlining your essay.

Write an essay that:

+ Has a relevant thesis and supports that thesis with appropriate historical evidence.
+ Addresses all parts of the question.
+ Makes direct, relevant comparisons.
+ Analyzes relevant reasons for similarities and differences.

3. Compare the economic transformations of China and Russia during the twentieth century.

STOP

END OF EXAM

Answer Key for Practice Exam 6

Answers for Section I:
Multiple-Choice Questions

1. A	19. C	37. A	55. C
2. C	20. B	38. D	56. C
3. D	21. C	39. C	57. D
4. B	22. B	40. C	58. D
5. A	23. C	41. B	59. B
6. D	24. B	42. A	60. A
7. A	25. B	43. A	61. C
8. B	26. A	44. B	62. A
9. A	27. D	45. D	63. D
10. A	28. D	46. D	64. D
11. A	29. C	47. B	65. C
12. C	30. D	48. B	66. C
13. C	31. D	49. D	67. D
14. B	32. A	50. A	68. A
15. A	33. C	51. B	69. B
16. B	34. D	52. D	70. C
17. D	35. B	53. D	
18. C	36. D	54. A	

Scoring the Multiple-Choice Section

Use the following formula to calculate your raw score on the multiple-choice section of the exam:

$$\underline{\hspace{4cm}} \times 0.8571 = \underline{\hspace{4cm}}$$

Number correct   Weighted Section I score
(out of 70)   (do not round)

The highest possible score for the multiple-choice section is seventy correct answers, for a score of 60.

Rationales:

1. Answer: A

 Explanation: Both sides in WWI recruited soldiers from their colonies. Since North and West Africa during WWI was part of the French empire, the African soldier portrayed in the poster was fighting for France. The poster honors the wartime contributions of the African soldiers, as suggested by the caption.

 Page Reference: pp. 985, 1028

KEY CONCEPT	THEME	SKILL
6.2.IV.A	3: State-Building, Expansion, and Conflict.	Evidence Interpretation

2. Answer: C

Explanation: The immediate cause of WWI was the assassination of the heir to the Austro-Hungarian throne, the Archduke Francis Ferdinand, by a Serbian subject involved in the terrorist group Union or Death (aka the Black Hand). The hard-line position assumed by Austria-Hungary, as indicated by its ultimatum to Serbia, attests to a lack of tolerance of Serbian terrorism.

Page Reference: pp. 982–83

KEY CONCEPT	THEME	SKILL
6.2.II.B 6.2.IV.B	3: State-Building, Expansion, and Conflict.	Causation

3. Answer: D

Explanation: In response to the global effects of the Great Depression, governments in Britain, France, and Scandinavia in particular began to regulate the economy more. Electoral politics also played a more important role as governments sought to alleviate poverty and redistribute wealth peacefully through reform.

Page Reference: p. 993

KEY CONCEPT	THEME	SKILL
6.3.I.B	4: Creation, Expansion, and Interaction of Economic Systems.	Causation

4. Answer: B

Explanation: In 1931, Japan invaded Manchuria. In 1935, Italy invaded Ethiopia. In the latter half of the 1930s, Germany annexed Austria and invaded the Sudetenland.

Page Reference: p. 1003

KEY CONCEPT	THEME	SKILL
6.2.IV.B	3: State-Building, Expansion, and Conflict.	Comparison

5. Answer: A

Explanation: In the 1930s, both Germany and Japan were preparing for war. Immediately upon assuming control of the state, Hitler turned his ideas into policies, using the state's control of the schools and media to glorify martial values. The Japanese state, controlled by the military in the 1930s, sought to create obedient subjects as Japan embarked on what would evolve into WWII.

Page Reference: pp. 998, 1002

KEY CONCEPT	THEME	SKILL
6.2.IV.A	2: Development and Interaction of Cultures. 3 : State-Building, Expansion, and Conflict.	Evidence Comparison Interpretation

6. Answer: D

Explanation: Japan's invasion of China in 1937 launched the war in Asia, with the attack on Pearl Harbor in 1941 leading to the merging of the two wars. Britain and France finally responded with force to German military aggression after the invasion of Poland.

Page Reference: p. 1003

KEY CONCEPT	THEME	SKILL
6.2.IV.B	3: State-Building, Expansion, and Conflict.	Comparison Causation

7. Answer: A

Explanation: For centuries, European countries had fought with one another, as exemplified by the two world wars. After WWII, Western European countries joined together in a number of organizations that increasingly integrated their economies, paving the way for the European Union. The Marshall Plan also encouraged economic cooperation.

Page Reference: pp. 1012–13

KEY CONCEPT	THEME	SKILL
6.3.II.D	4: Creation, Expansion, and Interaction of Economic Systems.	Continuity and Change Periodization

8. Answer: B

Explanation: After WWI, the Austro-Hungarian and Ottoman empires collapsed, and the German Empire contracted. From that territory, new states were created, and existing states expanded. In the case of the former lands of the Ottoman Empire, the fledgling states that emerged were placed under the supervision of the League of Nations.

Page Reference: pp. 987–89

KEY CONCEPT	THEME	SKILL
6.2.I.A	3: State-Building, Expansion, and Conflict.	Periodization Continuity and Change

9. Answer: A

Explanation: Although ideologies, perspectives, and tactics varied, the goal of the nationalist movements that spread throughout Asia and Africa after WWII was to end colonial rule and gain political independence. Some movements attached the struggle for independence to programs for socioeconomic transformations, while others focused exclusively on ending foreign rule.

Page Reference: p. 1093

KEY CONCEPT	THEME	SKILL
6.2.II.B	3: State-Building, Expansion, and Conflict.	Comparison

10. Answer: A

    Explanation: The League of Nations was dissolved after WWII, replaced by the United Nations. The UN offered an international forum for member nations to peacefully work out their differences, and the World Bank and IMF sought to regulate the global economy.

    Page Reference: p. 1012

KEY CONCEPT	THEME	SKILL
6.3.II.A 6.3.II.B	4: Creation, Expansion, and Interaction of Economic Systems.	Periodization

11. Answer: A

    Explanation: After assuming power in 1934, the Nazi Party began rearming Germany in preparation for war. Men joined the armed forces, and job opportunities expanded with the creation of a new military.

    Page Reference: pp. 998, 1006

KEY CONCEPT	THEME	SKILL
6.2.IV.B	3: State-Building, Expansion, and Conflict. 4: Creation, Expansion, and Interaction of Economic Systems.	Synthesis

12. Answer: C

    Explanation: The second quotation expresses uncertainty about whether the twentieth century constitutes a distinctive enough era as to deserve to be categorized as a new historical period. In contrast, the first quotation presents the argument made by some historians that WWI represented a sharp enough break from the past to warrant the designation of the twentieth century as a separate period.

    Page Reference: p. 973

KEY CONCEPT	THEME	SKILL
6.2.IV.B	3: State-Building, Expansion, and Conflict.	Interpretation Periodization

13. Answer: C

    Explanation: In the twentieth century, three factors combined that amplified the impact of human activity on the environment. The world population increased fourfold in the twentieth century. New sources of energy like hydroelectricity, natural gas, and nuclear power were developed. The production and circulation of goods and services accelerated economic growth.

    Page Reference: p. 1164

KEY CONCEPT	THEME	SKILL
6.1.II.A	1: Interaction Between Humans and the Environment.	Causation

14. Answer: B

    Explanation: The resurgence of religious fundamentalism worldwide reflected an effort to define an alternative modernity that embraced rather than rejected the centrality of religion. Although fundamentalist movements opposed the secularism of modernity, their rejection of global modernity was selective rather than wholesale. Some fundamentalist groups entered politics, as reflected in the emergence of the "religious right" in the United States.

    Page Reference: pp. 1155–57

KEY CONCEPT	THEME	SKILL
6.3.III.C	2: Development and Interaction of Cultures.	Causation

15. Answer: A

    Explanation: Latin America's place in the global economy was to supply raw materials and agricultural products to the industrialized world. This is illustrated in the legend, which shows that all the major exports from Latin America were food products and raw materials. Foreign investment, principally from Britain but also from the U.S. and other European countries, financed economic development in Latin America.

    Page Reference: pp. 854–55

KEY CONCEPT	THEME	SKILL
5.1.II.A	4: Creation, Expansion, and Interaction of Economic Systems.	Interpretation

16. Answer: B

    Explanation: Agricultural innovations increased yields, which contributed to population growth. The enclosure movement, by pushing small farmers from the land, created a supply of labor able to move where new job opportunities emerged. Coal and iron ore were plentiful and easy to access. The Scientific Revolution in Britain encouraged technological innovation with its emphasis on observation, experimentation, precision in measurements, mechanical devices, and practical commercial applications.

    Page Reference: pp. 834–35

KEY CONCEPT	THEME	SKILL
5.1.I.A	4: Creation, Expansion, and Interaction of Economic Systems.	Causation

17. Answer: D

    Explanation: Marx predicted that industrial capitalist society would eventually be sharply divided between a small bourgeoisie that controlled the state and a huge proletariat that comprised those exploited by the capitalist system. To highlight the distinctive stage of history ushered in by industrial capitalism, Marx used the term *proletariat* to refer to the workers produced by industrial capitalism.

    Page Reference: pp. 843, 869

KEY CONCEPT	THEME	SKILL
5.1.V.A	4: Creation, Expansion, and Interaction of Economic Systems.	Continuity and Change

18. Answer: C

Explanation: In the nineteenth century, racial stereotypes were given scientific validity by Europeans who believed that race and civilization were inextricably linked. In social Darwinism, Charles Darwin's theory of evolution was used to distinguish between the "strong" and "weak" states and to rank human societies along racially defined lines.

Page Reference: p. 884

KEY CONCEPT	THEME	SKILL
5.2.III	2: Development and Interaction of Cultures.	Interpretation

19. Answer: C

Explanation: By the end of the nineteenth century, China was divided into spheres of influence amongst Britain, France, Germany, Russia, and Japan. Although China was not formally colonized, the concessions it made to foreign powers undermined its sovereignty. Each country was able to establish military bases, build railroads, and avail itself of the natural resources in its respective sphere of influence.

Page Reference: pp. 937–38

KEY CONCEPT	THEME	SKILL
5.2.I.E	3: State-Building, Expansion, and Conflict.	Contextualization

20. Answer: B

Explanation: In 1853, the United States sent a fleet commanded by Commodore Matthew Perry to "open" Japan to global commerce, sanctioning the use of force if necessary. Japanese people referred to the American ships as "black ships."

Page Reference: pp. 949, 967

KEY CONCEPT	THEME	SKILL
5.2.II.A	3: State-Building, Expansion, and Conflict.	Causation Contextualization

21. Answer: C

Explanation: The "scramble for Africa" refers to the partitioning of Africa in the last quarter of the nineteenth century. Only European countries were involved. France controlled northwest Africa, Germany had colonies in the southern half of the continent, and Belgium held the Congo. The United States did not establish colonies in Africa.

Page Reference: p. 885

KEY CONCEPT	THEME	SKILL
5.2.I.C	3: State-Building, Expansion, and Conflict.	Contextualization

22. Answer: B

Explanation: The National Assembly responsible for writing the French Declaration drew from the ideas of Enlightenment thinkers. This quotation reflects John Locke's notion of the state of nature as a state of freedom and equality where every person possesses natural rights. The French revolutionaries were inspired by such Enlightenment ideas to resist the absolutist monarchy of France in 1789.

Page Reference: pp. 745–46, 788

KEY CONCEPT	THEME	SKILL
5.3.I.C 5.3.I.D 5.3.III.B	2: Development and Interaction of Cultures.	Interpretation Causation

23. Answer: C

Explanation: Revolutionaries in France, the United States, and Latin America all opposed the absolute authority of the monarchy, particularly the power to arbitrarily impose taxes on them. They were all inspired by Enlightenment ideals of popular sovereignty and republican forms of government based on a social contract.

Page Reference: p. 795

KEY CONCEPT	THEME	SKILL
5.3.III.B	3: State-Building, Expansion, and Conflict.	Comparison

24. Answer: B

Explanation: In the nineteenth century, economies based on free labor proved more successful than those dependent on labor servitude such as slavery and serfdom. Europeans felt more keenly the contradiction between Christian and Enlightenment ideals with the existence of slavery and serfdom. The frequency of rebellions also increased European anxiety. Together, these factors contributed to the abolition of slavery and serfdom.

Page Reference: p. 799

KEY CONCEPT	THEME	SKILL
5.3.I.E	5: Development and Transformation of Social Structures.	Comparison Contextualization

25. Answer: B

Explanation: The spread of nationalism in the nineteenth century inspired movements for independence throughout the colonized world. Within the Ottoman Empire, Greece, Serbia, Bulgaria, and Romania successfully broke away and established their own nation-states. The Ottoman Empire was too weak to crush the movements, particularly in the face of British and Russian support of many of the independence movements in the Balkans.

Page Reference: pp. 942–43

KEY CONCEPT	THEME	SKILL
5.2.II.C	3: State-Building, Expansion, and Conflict.	Causation Contextualization

26.   Answer: A

Explanation: The spread of nationalism, especially in the nineteenth century, led to political unification in Germany and Italy. By the early 1870s, both emerged for the first time as sovereign nation-states.

Page Reference: p. 802

KEY CONCEPT	THEME	SKILL
5.3.II	3: State-Building, Expansion, and Conflict.	Causation Contextualization

27.   Answer: D

Explanation: Statute labor was prevalent in West Africa until 1946. Colonial regimes required locals to provide ten to twelve days of uncompensated labor a year to work on public projects. In the cultivation system in the Dutch East Indies in the nineteenth century, local farmers were required to devote 20 percent or more of their farmland to the cultivation of select cash crops and sell them to the colonial state at arbitrarily low prices to meet their tax obligations. In the Congo Free State in the early twentieth century, the Belgian government authorized private companies to force the local population to collect rubber.

Page Reference: pp. 893–94

KEY CONCEPT	THEME	SKILL
5.4.II.B	4: Creation, Expansion, and Interaction of Economic Systems.	Continuity and Change Comparison

28.   Answer: D

Explanation: The Industrial Revolution transformed humanity's relationship to the earth. The technological breakthroughs that followed enabled humans to control and exploit nature in unprecedented ways that irrevocably altered the environment. Hence, scholars characterize the past few centuries as Anthropocene, or the Age of Man.

Page Reference: pp. 773–74

KEY CONCEPT	THEME	SKILL
6.1.II.A	1: Interaction Between Humans and the Environment.	Periodization

29. Answer: C

Explanation: The Ottoman Empire reached its peak in the sixteenth century. The Austrian Empire, on the western fringe of the Ottoman Empire, felt threatened by Ottoman expansion, particularly after the Ottoman siege of Vienna in 1529. As a diplomat for the Austrian Empire visiting the court of Suleiman I, ruler of the Ottoman Empire from 1520 to 1566, Busbecq was remarking on those features of the Ottoman Empire that made it militarily powerful.

Page Reference: pp. 646, 655–57

KEY CONCEPT	THEME	SKILL
4.3.II.B	3: State-Building, Expansion, and Conflict.	Interpretation Contextualization

30. Answer: D

Explanation: The "great dying" refers to the steep decline in the indigenous population of the Americas after the arrival of the Europeans. The long isolation of the Americas from the Afro-Eurasian world, combined with the absence of domesticated animals in the Americas, meant that Old World diseases (smallpox, measles, typhus, influenza, malaria, yellow fever) were unknown in the New World. The European arrival brought these diseases to the Americas, and the indigenous people, having never been exposed to such diseases, had no immunity against them.

Page Reference: pp. 622–23

KEY CONCEPT	THEME	SKILL
4.1.V.A	1: Interaction Between Humans and the Environment.	Causation

31. Answer: D

Explanation: Rich silver deposits in South America and Japan fueled and linked the global economy during the early modern period. Europeans used the silver from the Americas to purchase goods in Asia. Spain played a vital role in the global flow of silver, shipping the silver from its mines in Bolivia to Acapulco in Mexico and then across the Pacific to the Philippines.

Page Reference: pp. 679–80

KEY CONCEPT	THEME	SKILL
4.1.IV.B	4: Creation, Expansion, and Interaction of Economic Systems.	Contextualization Periodization

32. Answer: A

Explanation: Muhammad ibn Abd al-Wahhab, from whom the movement gets its name, represented the perspective of orthodox Muslims who condemned any deviation from the original teachings of Islam as heresy. Followers of the Wahhabi movement saw local adaptations of Islamic principles and practices as a dilution of Islam. They called for a renewal of Islam that would return to the absolute monotheism of what they considered authentic Islam.

Page Reference: pp. 735–37

KEY CONCEPT	THEME	SKILL
4.1.VI.A	2: Development and Interaction of Cultures.	Causation Contextualization Continuity and Change

33.   Answer: C

Explanation: Continuing intellectual trends introduced in the Scientific Revolution, Enlightenment thinkers emphasized progress and reason in their writings. The emphasis on progress encouraged people to view the future with optimism rather than look back on the past with nostalgia. The emphasis on reason promoted a new approach to knowledge based on empirical evidence rather than blind faith.

Page Reference: pp. 745, 748

KEY CONCEPT	THEME	SKILL
5.3.I.B	2: Development and Interaction of Cultures.	Continuity and Change

34.   Answer: D

Explanation: African kingdoms like Dahomey, Asante, and, to a lesser extent, Benin regulated the slave trade and relied on the revenues it generated. However, Britain abolished the slave trade within its territories in 1807. The statement by the king of Asante in the quotation expresses his consternation at this sudden change in attitude toward the slave trade on the part of the British government, which had, in the previous century, played a leading role in the international slave trade.

Page Reference: pp. 695, 708

KEY CONCEPT	THEME	SKILL
4.2.I.C 5.3.I.E	4: Creation, Expansion, and Interaction of Economic Systems.	Contextualization

35.   Answer: B

Explanation: New World crops like corn, potatoes, and cassava spread quickly to the Old World and soon became staples in many European, African, and Asian diets. As relatively cheap sources of food, such crops contributed to population growth.

Page Reference: p. 624

KEY CONCEPT	THEME	SKILL
4.1.V.D	4: Creation, Expansion, and Interaction of Economic Systems.	Causation

36.   Answer: D

Explanation: The European arrival and subsequent settlement of the Americas initiated a period of intensive interaction referred to as the Columbian exchange. This involved the transfer of plants and germs between the Western and Eastern hemispheres and the introduction of domesticated animals into the Americas. It created a new global economy that connected the entire world in an unprecedented way.

Page Reference: pp. 624–25, 629

KEY CONCEPT	THEME	SKILL
4.1.IV.D 4.1.V.A 4.1.V.B-C	3: State-Building, Expansion, and Conflict.	Causation

37. Answer: A

Explanation: At the beginning of the early modern period, Europe was on the margins of the global economy. The trade in goods from Asia along the land routes was controlled by Muslim traders in the Middle East. The distribution of these goods throughout Europe was monopolized by Italian merchants, especially those in Venice. From its position on the Atlantic coast, Portugal saw an opportunity to circumvent the Muslim and Italian monopolies by finding a water route around Africa to reach Asia.

Page Reference: p. 671

KEY CONCEPT	THEME	SKILL
4.1.III.B	3: State-Building, Expansion, and Conflict.	Causation

38. Answer: D

Explanation: In South Asia, Sikhism and the bhakti movement both combined elements from Hinduism and Islam. Sufi Islam incorporated elements from shamanism. All three religions illustrate the creation of syncretic religions.

Page Reference: pp. 361, 738–39

KEY CONCEPT	THEME	SKILL
4.1.VI.A 4.1.VI.D	2: Development and Interaction of Cultures.	Comparison

39. Answer: C

Explanation: The Thirty Years' War was a conflict between Protestants and Catholics that erupted in the Holy Roman Empire but soon involved most of Europe. The periodic warfare between the Ottoman and Safavid empires stemmed from the religious divide between those who followed a Shia version of Islam and those who followed the Sunni version. The wars were as much about religious uniformity as about territorial expansion and political control.

Page Reference: pp. 578, 723

KEY CONCEPT	THEME	SKILL
4.3.III 4.1.VI.A	2: Development and Interaction of Cultures. 3: State-Building, Expansion, and Conflict.	Comparison

40. Answer: C

    Explanation: Variously translated as "seek truth from facts" and "research based on evidence," the kaozheng movement in China emphasized methods of inquiry that emphasized verification, precision, accuracy, and rigorous analysis in all fields of inquiry. The Scientific Revolution emphasized observation, deduction, experimentation, and mathematical reasoning. In this respect, both emphasized empiricism.

    Page Reference: pp. 738, 744

KEY CONCEPT	THEME	SKILL
5.3.I.A	2: Development and Interaction of Cultures.	Comparison

41. Answer: B

    Explanation: Sales records of European slave traders not only show the number of slaves purchased, but also the gender breakdown. These records can be used to make inferences about the demographic changes that resulted from the Atlantic slave trade. They would reveal not only a decline in numbers, but also a skewed sex ratio since most enslaved Africans in the Atlantic system were male.

    Page Reference: p. 694

KEY CONCEPT	THEME	SKILL
4.2.II.C	5: Development and Transformation of Social Structures.	Evidence Causation

42. Answer: A

    Explanation: Scholars have identified three distinctive features of the modern world: globalization, modernity, and European hegemony. The European arrival in the Americas initiated the Columbian exchange and created truly global networks of exchange. The new approach to knowledge based on reason introduced in the Scientific Revolution, along with the concomitant embrace of progress and secularism, are seen as harbingers of modernity. Finally, European colonization of the Americas and European control of the sea routes indicate the ascendancy of Europe.

    Page Reference: p. 611

KEY CONCEPT	THEME	SKILL
4.1.III.B-D	2: Development and Interaction of Cultures. 3: State-Building, Expansion, and Conflict.	Periodization

43. Answer: A

    Explanation: The spread of Buddhism from India to the rest of Asia owed much to the merchants who traveled the Silk Roads. Many of the Buddhist monasteries established in the oasis towns that dotted the Silk Roads acquired great wealth; their artwork featured scenes of entertainment. The worship of Buddha and the proliferation of bodhisattvas came to define the Mahayana form of Buddhism.

Page Reference: p. 323

KEY CONCEPT	THEME	SKILL
3.1.III.D	2: Development and Interaction of Cultures.	Continuity and Change Causation

44. Answer: B

Explanation: Trade along the Silk Roads prospered during periods when strong states ensured the safety and security of merchants and travelers. During the seventh and eighth centuries, the Byzantine Empire, Abbasid dynasty, and Tang dynasty stretched across Eurasia. The presence of these powerful states created optimal conditions for long-distance trade along the Silk Roads that stretched across Eurasia.

Page Reference: pp. 318–19

KEY CONCEPT	THEME	SKILL
3.1.I.D	4: Creation, Expansion, and Interaction of Economic Systems.	Contextualization Causation

45. Answer: D

Explanation: The Swahili city-states emerged during this time as thriving centers of trade on the western edge of Indian Ocean commercial networks. In each city-state, goods from the interior of Africa were exchanged for products from China, Persia, India, and other distant civilizations. Indian Ocean commerce expanded following the rise of Islam as Muslim merchants and sailors established communities of traders from East Africa to the south China coast.

Page Reference: pp. 332–33

KEY CONCEPT	THEME	SKILL
3.1.I.A	3: State-Building, Expansion, and Conflict. 4: Creation, Expansion, and Interaction of Economic Systems.	Causation Contextualization

46. Answer: D

Explanation: At its height, the Mongol Empire stretched across much of Eurasia. The most likely source of the Black Death has been traced to China. From there, the plague spread westward along the trade routes that crisscrossed the Mongol Empire, eventually reaching Europe.

Page Reference: pp. 537–39

KEY CONCEPT	THEME	SKILL
3.1.IV.B	1: Interaction Between Humans and the Environment.	Causation Contextualization

47. Answer: B

Explanation: The introduction of a more resilient and productive strain of rice from Vietnam increased the food supply. This resulted in a doubling of the Chinese population, from 50–60 million in the Tang to 120 million by the Song. Increased rice production not only made China the most populous country in the world at the time but also the most prosperous.

Page Reference: pp. 369, 387

KEY CONCEPT	THEME	SKILL
3.1.IV.A	4: Creation, Expansion, and Interaction of Economic Systems.	Causation

48. Answer: B

Explanation: Artwork from the Tang depicted robust women engaging in physical activities like horseback riding. Artwork from the Song depicted women as delicate, fragile, and thin. Historians have interpreted these changes in artistic depictions of women as an indication of the greater restrictions placed upon women in the Song. Song writers like Sima Guang, reflecting Neo-Confucian ideas, also commented on proper relations between men and women, which echoed earlier views from the Han dynasty of women as submissive, docile, and passive. Under Song law, women benefitted from the expansion of property rights and gained greater control over their dowries.

Page Reference: pp. 371–72

KEY CONCEPT	THEME	SKILL
3.2.I.A 3.3.III.B	5: Development and Transformation of Social Structures.	Evidence Continuity and Change

49. Answer: D

Explanation: The tribute system was based on the Chinese belief that China was the "Middle Kingdom" and all other societies were barbarians. Foreigners wishing to gain access to the markets of China had to perform rituals that acknowledged the superiority of China and accept their subordinate status in their relationship with China. In return, the Chinese emperor bestowed gifts and titles. Dynasties since the Han used the tribute system to manage foreign relations with northern nomads, countries in Asia, and the European countries that arrived in the sixteenth century.

Page Reference: pp. 373–76

KEY CONCEPT	THEME	SKILL
3.1.I.E	4: Creation, Expansion, and Interaction of Economic Systems.	Contextualization Continuity and Change

50. Answer: A

Explanation: The monotheism of Islam reflects the influence of the Jewish, Christian, and Zoroastrian communities in Arabia. Reflecting the influence of Judaism,

Arabs began to identify themselves as "children of Abraham." Allah, the Islamic name for God, was the main god worshipped by local Arabs.

Page Reference: p. 414

KEY CONCEPT	THEME	SKILL
3.1.III.A	2: Development and Interaction of Cultures.	Causation Continuity and Change

51. Answer: B

Explanation: After the fall of the Roman Empire, the Byzantine Empire preserved much of ancient Greek learning. Its strategic position as a major intersection of long-distance trade routes enabled it to pass along that cultural tradition to Western Europe and the Arab world.

Page Reference: pp. 474–75

KEY CONCEPT	THEME	SKILL
3.1.III.D	2: Development and Interaction of Cultures.	Continuity and Change Contextualization

52. Answer: D

Explanation: The increased activity in the Indian Ocean basin contributed to the growth of the Swahili city-states in East Africa. Each city-state was ruled by its own king and competed with the others in the Indian Ocean trade. In the Italian peninsula, Venice, Genoa, Pisa, and Milan emerged as virtually independent city-states due in large part to their monopoly of the trade routes in the Mediterranean. Wealthy merchants and bankers exercised political power; they could issue and enforce laws as well as appoint officials.

Page Reference: pp. 332–33, 493

KEY CONCEPT	THEME	SKILL
3.2.I.B 3.1.I.A	3: State-Building, Expansion, and Conflict.	Comparison Causation

53. Answer: D

Explanation: The years 1000 to 1300 are conventionally referred to as the High Middle Ages. This period was marked by expansion and growth. New lands were opened up for cultivation, resulting in higher agricultural yields, which in turn contributed to population growth and revived long-distance trade routes that had closed after the collapse of the Roman Empire. Monarchs also began to consolidate their power, and the prototypes of European states such as France and England began to take shape.

Page Reference: pp. 480, 482

KEY CONCEPT	THEME	SKILL
3.2.I.B	3: State-Building, Expansion, and Conflict.	Argumentation Periodization Continuity and Change

54. Answer: A

Explanation: In Europe, the death toll from the Black Death created a severe labor shortage that benefitted workers who could now demand better wages and conditions. In the countryside, numerous peasant rebellions weakened serfdom. Since the Black Death traveled along the trade routes that connected the different parts of the Mongol Empire, the disease spread quickly, hastening the end of the Mongol Empire and the closure of the Silk Roads.

Page Reference: pp. 538–39

KEY CONCEPT	THEME	SKILL
3.1.IV.B	1: Interaction Between Humans and the Environment.	Causation

55. Answer: C

Explanation: The Xiongnu, Turks, and Mongols were all pastoral societies that started out as loose alliances under the leadership of a central leader. The Xiongnu Confederation was the dominant force in the northern steppes of Central Asia during the classical era. The Mongols ruled over much of Eurasia in the thirteenth century. The Turks ruled over the Ottoman Empire.

Page Reference: pp. 135, 519, 522

KEY CONCEPT	THEME	SKILL
3.2.I.B	3: State-Building, Expansion, and Conflict.	Comparison

56. Answer: C

Explanation: Europe's place on the margins of the global economy, combined with the Ottoman Empire's control of the land routes across Eurasia motivated Portugal and Spain in the fifteenth century to sponsor maritime voyages. They hoped to find a direct water route to Asia and Africa where most of the highly sought-after goods were located. The competitive nature of the European state system also motivated states to expand. Europeans also hoped to find Christian converts and allies in the struggle against Islam.

Page Reference: p. 575

KEY CONCEPT	THEME	SKILL
4.1.III.B-C	3: State-Building, Expansion, and Conflict.	Causation

57. Answer: D

Explanation: Mauryan and Persian rulers relied on a large contingent of spies to keep tabs on the local population, particularly those living in the remote regions of the empire. In the Persian Empire, imperial spies were referred to as the "eyes and ears of the King."

Page Reference: pp. 121, 142

KEY CONCEPT	THEME	SKILL
2.2.II.A	3: State-Building, Expansion, and Conflict.	Comparison

58. Answer: D

Explanation: The Germanic kingdoms that emerged in Western Europe in the twilight years of the Roman Empire began to identify themselves as Visigoths, Franks, Anglo-Saxons, and other ethnicities. At the same time, they were influenced by the culture of the Roman Empire. Many embraced Christianity and Roman law. After the fall of the Roman Empire, a distinctive culture began to emerge that combined Latin and Germanic elements.

Page Reference: pp. 139–40

KEY CONCEPT	THEME	SKILL
2.3.III.C 2.2.IV.B	2: Development and Interaction of Cultures.	Causation

59. Answer: B

Explanation: The Hellenistic era (323–30 B.C.E.) refers to the period initiated by the conquests of Alexander the Great. The many cities within the empire that Alexander founded functioned as conduits for culture, transmitting Greek culture throughout much of the classical world. Alexandria in Egypt was perhaps the most famous city at the time.

Page Reference: p. 128

KEY CONCEPT	THEME	SKILL
2.2.III.A	2: Development and Interaction of Cultures.	Periodization

60. Answer: A

Explanation: Buddhism incorporated many elements from Hinduism, including the notion of rebirth. Other Hindu ideas that were incorporated into Buddhism were the concept of karma, the practice of meditation, and the ultimate goal of breaking free from the cycle of rebirth.

Page Reference: pp. 175, 177

KEY CONCEPT	THEME	SKILL
2.1.I.B 2.1.II.A	2: Development and Interaction of Cultures.	Comparison

61. Answer: C

Explanation: The civil service examination system was based on the Confucian classics. Confucianism emphasized education as the means to moral cultivation and self-improvement. According to Confucianism, the state was the family writ large; just as children were expected to be filial to their parents, so too were subjects to be loyal to the emperor.

Page Reference: pp. 169–72

KEY CONCEPT	THEME	SKILL
2.1.II.B 2.1.III	2: Development and Interaction of Cultures.	Causation

62. Answer: A

Explanation: According to many scholars, neither the Buddha nor Jesus claimed divine status during their lifetimes. However, as Buddhism and Christianity spread, the Buddha and Jesus were elevated to divine status. In Mahayana Buddhism, the Buddha became a supernatural being worshipped by followers. In the early years of Christianity, followers like Saint Paul and Saint John began referring to Jesus as the Son of God.

Page Reference: p. 188

KEY CONCEPT	THEME	SKILL
2.3.III.C	2: Development and Interaction of Cultures.	Comparison Continuity and Change

63. Answer: D

Explanation: Although there is no consensus on the exact origins of slavery in history, scholars have highlighted certain aspects of the First Civilizations that most contributed to the emergence of slavery as a widespread practice. Some argue that the early domestication of animals offered a model for the enslavement of people. Others have emphasized the role of war, patriarchy, and the notion of private property.

Page Reference: p. 229

KEY CONCEPT	THEME	SKILL
2.2.III.D 3.3.III.C	3: State-Building, Expansion, and Conflict. 5: Development and Transformation of Social Structures.	Causation Argumentation

64. Answer: D

Explanation: Although India's caste system was more fluid in practice, it was still the most rigidly defined social structure among the First Civilizations. The notion of caste was associated with ritual purity and based on the assumption of inherent inequality and permanent difference. This limited social mobility during a person's lifetime.

Page Reference: pp. 225–28

KEY CONCEPT	THEME	SKILL
2.2.III.B 3.3.III.B	5: Development and Transformation of Social Structures.	Comparison Periodization

65. Answer: C

Explanation: Popular forms of Daoism highlighted supernatural healings, collective trances, and public confessions of sin. They often offered disaffected peasants a unifying set of ideas about rebelling against the state. One such Daoist-inspired peasant rebellion was the Yellow Turban Rebellion that contributed to the fall of the Han dynasty.

Page Reference: p. 223

KEY CONCEPT	THEME	SKILL
2.1.II.C 3.3.III.C	2: Development and Interaction of Cultures. 5: Development and Transformation of Social Structures.	Causation

66. Answer: C

Explanation: Evidence suggests that extended periods of drought contributed to the decline and eventual collapse of these civilizations in the Americas. Beginning in the sixth century, a combination of factors, including frequent droughts, undermined the Moche civilization, which finally fell in the late eighth century. A drought that began in 840 led to the end of the Maya civilization by the end of that century. In the latter half of the twelfth century, a prolonged drought closed the Chaco center.

Page Reference: pp. 275, 281, 287

KEY CONCEPT	THEME	SKILL
2.2.IV.A 3.3.II.A	1: Interaction Between Humans and the Environment.	Comparison Causation

67. Answer: D

Explanation: Most cities of the time were controlled by imperial centers. The cities of the Niger Valley showed a notable absence of a centralized political structure. Although they were complex urban centers, the archaeological evidence suggests that they functioned without the coercive authority of a state.

Page Reference: p. 271

KEY CONCEPT	THEME	SKILL
2.2.III.A	3: State-Building, Expansion, and Conflict.	Comparison

68. Answer: A

Explanation: Evidence suggests that Paleolithic people deliberately set fires in order to encourage the growth of particular plants

Page Reference: p. 22

KEY CONCEPT	THEME	SKILL
1.1.I.A	1: Interaction Between Humans and the Environment.	Causation Evidence

69. Answer: B

Explanation: Because of the geographic positioning of North and South America on opposite sides of the equator, climatic differences were greater than within Eurasia and North Africa, which were positioned north of the equator. Consequently, crops that developed in one region of the Afro-Eurasian world easily took root in other parts. In contrast, the spread of crops between the Americas was very slow because they had to adapt to different environments.

Page Reference: p. 34

KEY CONCEPT	THEME	SKILL
1.2.I.A 1.2.I.C	1: Interaction Between Humans and the Environment.	Comparison Causation Synthesis

70. Answer: C

Explanation: Evidence suggests that Paleolithic societies were egalitarian, without the sharp divisions between men and women characteristic of later civilizations. Scholars argue that patriarchy emerged with the rise of the First Civilizations as a consequence of plow-based agriculture, which was dominated by men; the identification of women with nature and men with culture; and the spread of warfare. All these developments contributed to a private/public distinction that was gendered feminine/masculine.

Page Reference: pp. 73–74

KEY CONCEPT	THEME	SKILL
1.2.II.D	5: Development and Transformation of Social Structures.	Causation Comparison Argumentation

Answer Guide for Section II:
Part A

General Guidelines for Answering a Document-Based Question (DBQ):

1. Pre-Write. Create a brief outline before you start writing.
2. Write your DBQ in a multiple-paragraph structure. In your first paragraph, write an introduction that clearly states your thesis.
3. Present your arguments in body paragraphs. Body paragraphs should integrate groupings of documents, demonstrate understanding of documents, support the thesis using documents as evidence, analyze point of view, and possibly include additional relevant historical content. Present your arguments in body paragraphs that focus on a grouping of documents and that put forth a single argument centered on answering the prompt.
4. In your final paragraph, write a conclusion that includes a reworded restatement of your thesis.

AP World History DBQ essays are scored using a core scoring method with a maximum score of nine. In the basic core, you may earn the following seven points:

*   one point for a thesis
*   one point for addressing and understanding the documents
*   up to two points for using the documents as evidence to answer the prompt
*   one point for grouping the documents
*   one point for analyzing Point of View (POV)
*   one point for identifying and explaining the need for an additional document

If you earn ALL seven basic core points, you have the chance to earn up to two additional points in what is called expanded core. Expanded core points may be granted for the following features:

✦ an excellent, sophisticated, and comprehensive thesis
✦ insightful document analysis
✦ analyzing POV in all or most documents
✦ including extra document groupings or additional documents
✦ incorporating relevant historical content not found in the documents

Below is a detailed description of what you will need to do in your answer to earn each basic core point for this essay.

Thesis (1 point): To earn a point in this category, you must write a thesis that responds to the entire prompt and outlines the specific arguments you will make based on a correct usage of the documents. You will need to mention the arguments you plan on making in your answer, and you will need to avoid generalizations that do not reflect reasonable interpretations of the documents. Thesis statements will only earn a point if they appear in the first or last paragraph of the essay. Common errors in thesis writing include merely rewriting the prompt or presenting an answer to only some parts of the prompt, so make sure you address the entire prompt and briefly present the specific arguments that you will use in your answer based on the documents.

> **Prompt:** Using the following documents, analyze nineteenth- and twentieth-century women's movements for continuities to and changes from the women's rights advocated in the era of the Enlightenment and French Revolution by Mary Wollstonecraft (Document 1). Identify an additional type of document and explain how it would help your analysis of the continuities and changes in women's rights movements.

Examples:

> Example Thesis: "Later nineteenth- and twentieth-century women's rights advocates continued to pursue the goals expressed by Wollstonecraft in appeals for political rights, equality, and education, but their goals differed from hers in their appeal for the rights to avoid marriage, greater emphasis on rights to work, and a new focus on addressing racism."

> ✦ This thesis earns the point by identifying the specific continuities and changes based on the documents that will be used to answer the prompt. It presents BOTH continuities and changes, so it answers the entire prompt. Thesis statements can be longer than a single sentence. A multi-sentence thesis should, however, be presented in contiguous sentences.

> Unacceptable Example One: "There were changes and continuities in women's movements from the time of Mary Wollstonecraft to those of later nineteenth- and twentieth-century feminists."

> ✦ This thesis does little other than state the obvious given the prompt.

> Unacceptable Example Two: "Later feminists showed very different views from those expressed by Mary Wollstonecraft in the era of the French Revolution. They placed more emphasis on their right to work and on problems related to racism."

> ✦ This thesis improves upon the first example by including some specific changes, but it would NOT earn a thesis point because it does not answer the entire prompt.

Addressing and Understanding Documents (1 point): To earn this point, you must address ALL of the documents and demonstrate understanding of "all but one." This means that throughout your answer, you must show understanding of at least six of the seven documents.

Using Documents as Evidence (2 points): To earn two points, you must correctly incorporate at least six documents (although seven would be better) into arguments that answer the prompt. You will earn only one point if you use five of the seven documents in your arguments. If you use four or fewer documents in your essay, you will receive a zero in this category.

Grouping the Documents (1 point): Documents should be grouped in at least three ways in order to earn a point in this category. You can group documents by matching two or more documents that hold some relevant feature in common. Each example grouping below represents documents that, when used together, can make up an argument that answers the prompt.

Continuities:

Men Making Laws	Docs 1, 2, 3, 6
Appeals for Political Rights	Docs 1, 2, 5, 6, 7
Appeals for Equality	Docs 1, 4, 7, (implied in 6)
Calls for Education	Docs 1, 2, 3, 7
Against Tradition	Docs 4, 5, 6, 7, (implied in 1, 2, 3)
Appeals for Liberation/ Emancipation/Freedom	Docs 1, 2, 3, 5

Changes:

Racism as Issue	Absent in Doc 1; present in Doc 5
Women's Right to Work	Absent in Doc 1; present in Docs 2, 4, 5, 7
Movement as Group Effort	Absent in Doc 1; present in Docs 4, 5, 7
Rights within Marriage	Docs 1, 4
Right Not to Marry	Absent in Doc 1; present in Docs 2, 3, 5, 7

Analyzing Point of View (1 Point): Many students find it challenging to earn the point in this category. The best way to earn the Point of View (POV) point is to go beyond the basic identity of the source author and the source itself, as described in the document source line. In order to write a successful POV statement, you should try to establish a better understanding of the identity of the author; you can do this by asking yourself questions about the author and the source. What is the author's gender or social class? What religion does the author follow? What is the author's profession? Does the author have an identifiable ethnicity, nationality, or other allegiance to a particular group? Is the source from a poem, essay, or novel? What was the source used for? Once you've asked these questions, go further and explain how some of these factors may have influenced the content of the source. Your complete POV statement should both identify the influences that may have shaped the author or source and explain how those particular influences have specifically affected the content of the document. Below are some examples of POV statements based on the documents from this question.

Examples of POV Statements:

Document 1: "Source: Mary Wollstonecraft, female writer and philosopher, *A Vindication of the Rights of Woman*, 1792."

✦ As an author and philosopher, Mary Wollstonecraft created and presented arguments and ideas to a reading audience. As a woman philosopher pursuing a nontraditional role during the late eighteenth century, Wollstonecraft made arguments that if accepted would have led to greater acceptance of educated women. Her arguments may have been motivated and influenced by a desire to achieve greater societal acceptance for her own work and for people like herself.

Document 4: "Source: Alexandra Kollontai, female government official and ambassador of the Soviet Union, 'Communism and the Family,' 1920."

✦ As a government official holding a position of power in a communist society, Alexandra Kollontai expressed opinions supporting communist government as a positive good. As a government official with an interest in promoting the benefits of the government that gave her a position of authority, she would have been unlikely to express negative opinions about communism, which would have undermined the government and possibly led to the loss of her position. And further, as a communist woman in government, her views about capitalism would be negative since communism was a system of government aiming to solve the problems of capitalism. It would have been surprising if she had said anything positive about capitalism.

Document 7: "Source: Zapatista Army of National Liberation, Chiapas, Mexico, *The Women's Revolutionary Law*, 1994."

✦ *The Women's Revolutionary Law* was a public statement made by a group of rebels seeking to overthrow the established political order in Mexico and to gain support from people who might help them. The statement proposes laws that would meet women's needs in society and draw women into supporting the revolutionary movement. The document is best understood as an attempt to sell the benefits of the revolution to people who might be unhappy with the current political order. As a sales pitch, it focuses on positive promises and does not include criticisms of the tactics used by the revolutionaries.

You should write as many POV statements as you are able to produce. You can earn the POV point with as few as two correct POV statements; however, it's not uncommon to make errors in writing POV statements. For that reason, it's safer to provide more than just two in order to make up for any errors. Additionally, if you earn all of the basic core points, an extra POV statement can earn you an expanded core point.

Additional Document Statement (1 Point): A good additional document statement identifies a missing document that, if added to the provided documents, would help make a better answer to the question. You are only required to make a single additional document statement to earn a point, but you should aim to identify a minimum of three additional documents. This allows room for mistakes, and after the first correct additional document statement, any extras can earn you bonus points in the expanded core if you earn all seven points in the basic core. You should be careful to avoid the common mistake of asking for a type of document that is already provided. Additional document statements must meet three standards to be considered successful:

✦ The document suggested must be historically plausible.
✦ The statement must include an explanation of **why** the additional document would be useful in answering the prompt.
✦ The analysis of **why** must speculate about the particulars of what the missing document might include. In other words, a successful additional document suggestion is historically possible given the time and place, includes an explanation of how the new source would help answer the prompt, and goes as far as speculating on arguments that the suggested source might support.

Document Analysis:

Document 1: "Source: Mary Wollstonecraft, female writer and philosopher, *A Vindication of the Rights of Woman*, 1792." Wollstonecraft included a number of principles in her appeals for women's rights including calls for education, appeals for political participation and equality, and a reference to justice. Notable quotable sections include: on education—"if she be not prepared by education to become the companion of man, she will stop the progress of knowledge and virtue . . ."; on justice and equality—"Who made man the exclusive judge, if woman partake with him of the gift of reason?" and ". . . truth seemed to open before you when you observed, 'that to see one-half of the human race excluded by the other from all participation of government was a political phenomenon that, according to abstract principles, it was impossible to explain'" and "Consider—I address you as a legislator—whether, when men contend for their freedom, and to be allowed to judge for themselves respecting their own happiness, it be not inconsistent and unjust to subjugate women, even though you firmly believe that you are acting in the manner best calculated to promote their happiness?"

Document 2: "Source: Elizabeth Cady Stanton, American activist for women's suffrage, 'The Solitude of Self,' 1892." Similar to Wollstonecraft's views, Stanton calls for education, "a voice in government," and, ultimately, equality. Stanton differs in appealing for women's right to work, "a place in the trades and professions, where she may earn her bread" and, by implication, a call for women to have the right not to marry "because of her birthright to self-sovereignty; because, as an individual, she must rely on herself. No matter how much women prefer to lean, to be protected and supported, nor how much men desire to have them do so, they must make the voyage of life alone."

Document 3: "Source: Raden Adjeng Kartini, Muslim Indonesian feminist's letter to a friend, 1899." Kartini might be used to make arguments that women's rights sought to overturn traditions, faced difficulties because men made the laws, and called for women's education and emancipation. It expresses a difference in a longing to avoid marriage as seen in, "I long to be free, to be able to stand alone, to study, not to be subject to any one, and, above all, never, never to be obliged to marry."

Document 4: "Source: Alexandra Kollontai, female government official and ambassador of the Soviet Union, 'Communism and the Family,' 1920." Kollontai makes explicit calls for women's rights to equality, a movement against traditions, and a sense that women need rights in marriage, which echo themes of Wollstonecraft in Document 1. Kollantai differs from Wollstonecraft in including the explicit right of women to work and in advocating a group effort to achieve women's rights.

Document 5: "Source: Combahee River Collective, a women's organization centered in Boston, Massachusetts, 'A Black Feminist Statement,' 1977." Like Wollstonecraft, the Combahee River Collective sought political rights, equality, the overturning of traditions, and emancipation or freedom. Differences in their appeal, as compared to Wollstonecraft's in Document 1 include a concern about racism, inclusion of women's right to work, the idea of the movement as a collective effort, and an explicit desire to be able to choose not to marry.

Document 6: "Source: Benazir Bhutto, Muslim female politician and later Prime Minister of Pakistan, 'Politics and the Muslim Woman,' 1985." Similar to Wollstoncraft, Bhutto notes that men make the laws, appeals for political rights, seeks equality, and rails against traditional culture. Students may note a difference in Bhutto's appeal for women's rights in the geographic and cultural origins of that appeal outside of Western nations, such as France, England, and the United States.

Document 7: "Source: Zapatista Army of National Liberation, Chiapas, Mexico, *The Women's Revolutionary Law*, 1994." Document 7 shows similarities to Wollstonecraft in advocating for women's political rights, equality, and education and for an end to tradition. It differs from Wollstonecraft in calling for women's right to work, representing a group effort, and supporting a woman's right to avoid marriage.

Answer Guide for Section II: Part B

2. Analyze the continuities and changes in since 1900.

What Does the Question Ask?

This question deals with broad issues relating to a big theme of world history. You can answer this question in a variety of ways as long as your essay addresses how people have interacted with the environment. Much like almost every AP World History Exam question, different students can take very different approaches to this question and still do very well.

Listed below is the scoring system used to grade continuity and change-over-time essays; also included are guidelines and examples for how to earn each point for this question.

Has Acceptable Thesis (1 point)

+ The thesis needs to correctly address both continuity and change in human interaction with the environment since 1900.
+ The thesis should appear in the first paragraph (although it may also count if it is in the conclusion).
+ The thesis can be one sentence or multiple sentences.

Examples:

+ Example One: Human population rose dramatically during the twentieth century. Large numbers of people continued to move to large urban areas throughout this time period.
+ Example Two: Negative effects of industrialization have continued to harm the environment from 1900 to the present. New dangers associated with nuclear energy, however, have changed the threats to the global environment.
+ Example Three: New environmental political movements have changed governmental policies relating to the environment. The exploitation of natural resources for economic gain has remained a constant factor since 1900.
+ Unacceptable Example: Humans interacted with the environment throughout the twentieth century. Some aspects of this interaction have remained the same and some have changed.
  • This is an unacceptable thesis because it merely repeats aspects of the question without adding any specifics.

Addresses All Parts of the Question (2 points)

+ The essay accurately addresses both a continuity (1 point) and a change (1 point).
+ The statements of continuity and change may not appear in the thesis.

Examples:

- ✦ Example One: A population explosion in the past several decades transformed how humans related to the environment. As more and more people live on the planet, cities continue to be the places with the greatest growth.
  - • The first statement in the example above addresses change, while the second statement addresses continuity.

- ✦ Example Two: Air and water pollution were present in 1900, and they remain a serious issue today. More recently, nuclear power plants added a new type of radioactive pollution to the environment.
  - • The first statement in the example above addresses continuity, while the second statement addresses change.

- ✦ Example Three: Green and other environmental movements have become more popular since the late twentieth century. Despite their influence, nations around the world since 1900 have continued cutting down forests, mining, using up water, and otherwise exploiting the environment.
  - • The first statement in the example above addresses change, while the second statement addresses continuity.

Substantiates Thesis with Appropriate Historical Evidence (2 points)

- ✦ A piece of historical evidence is a fact that is correct and relevant to the time period.
- ✦ To earn the full two points in this category, an essay should have five or more pieces of evidence.
- ✦ To earn only one point in this category, an essay needs three or four pieces of evidence.
- ✦ Points for evidence can be earned even if the thesis point is not earned.

Examples:

- ✦ Example One: Global population has been increasing dramatically, especially in less developed countries in Asia and Africa. This population boom has led to environmental problems, particularly water shortage. Most of the growth has been in urban areas, like Mexico City and New Delhi. In these cities, slums have developed with horrible living conditions. The population explosion has also created more stress on global food supplies.
- ✦ Example Two: Pollution in the twentieth century comes in a variety of forms. Water supplies have been polluted by industrial and human waste. Air pollution from industrial smokestacks remains a problem. Deforestation has occurred in tropical rain forests and across the world. Many animal and plant species have become extinct in the past hundred years. Nuclear radiation leaks in Japan have poisoned the environment.
- ✦ Example Three: Environmentalism as a political movement has gained momentum in the past several years. These green movements have protested the use of nuclear energy around the world. Recycling has become much more popular in industrial countries, cutting down on the need to exploit new resources. Even so, many countries have increased their reach into the environment for natural resources. The use of deep-sea oil rigs and exploration for rare timber resources have led people to parts of the globe that were previously untouched by humans.

Uses Relevant Historical Context (1 point)

- ✦ Historical context places the issue discussed in the essay into a broader global perspective.

Examples:

- ✦ Example One: As populations have increased in certain areas, people have migrated to other parts of the world for better opportunities.
- ✦ Example Two: Increasing industrialization around the world has led to new threats to the global environment.
- ✦ Example Three: The environmental movement in some parts of the developing world has been linked to the drive for more rights for poor people who live in rural areas.

Analyzes the Process of Continuity or Change (1 point)

- ✦ Analysis explains why the continuity or change occurred.

Examples:

- ✦ Example One: Improvements in medicine, hygiene, and food supplies led to the great population explosion of the twentieth century.
- ✦ Example Two: The loss of large amounts of natural habitat has led to a sharp decline in the number and variety of animal species.
- ✦ Example Three: A greater awareness of the dangers of environmental problems has led to more people supporting environmentalism.

Expanded Core

You must earn all seven points in the basic core before earning any points in the expanded core. Points awarded in the expanded core reflect the general excellence of the essay. Any one aspect of your essay, such as the thesis or evidence, might be particularly insightful and earn a point in the expanded core. Essays that have a high degree of analysis and historical context often earn expanded core points if they have earned all of the other basic core points. Clarity of organization, strong cause-effect analysis, and particularly insightful ideas can make your essay stand out as excellent.

Examples:

- ✦ Example One: Analysis of the variety of factors contributing to population growth and settlements could earn points in the expanded core.
- ✦ Example Two: An essay that describes a large number of environmental issues within the context of change and continuity could earn points in the expanded core.
- ✦ Example Three: Linking environmentalism to relevant political and social developments that have emerged since 1900 could earn points in the expanded core.

Answer Guide for Section II:
Part C

3. Compare the economic transformations of China and Russia during the twentieth century.

What Does the Question Ask?

This question covers a span of 100 years, so the economic comparison of China and Russia could focus on several different time periods. Each country transformed its economic system multiple times in the twentieth century. A discussion of labor systems can count as relating to economics.

Listed below is the scoring system used to grade comparative essays; also included are guidelines and examples for how to earn each point for this question.

Has Acceptable Thesis (1 point)

+ The thesis needs to correctly address both a similarity and a difference in cultural developments for two of the three civilizations.
+ The thesis should appear in the first paragraph (although it may also count if it is in the conclusion).
+ The thesis can be one sentence or multiple sentences.

Examples:

+ Example One: The economic systems of China and Russia were inspired by communism for most of the twentieth century. The Soviet Russian system focused on the working class, while the Chinese system focused on the peasants.
+ Example Two: Both China and the Soviet Union forced the rapid industrialization of their economies. The Chinese started from scratch, but the Soviets already had some factories before rapid industrialization.
+ Example Three: In the later part of the twentieth century, both China and Russia became open to free market economics. The Chinese, unlike the Russians, still kept many aspects of their communist system.
+ Unacceptable Example: Both the Russians and the Chinese had revolutions during this period. These revolutions differed because the Chinese fought against the Nationalist Party while the Russian revolutionaries fought against the Tsar.
  • This is an unacceptable thesis because it compares the revolutions rather than the economic systems of the countries.

Addresses All Parts of the Question (2 points)

+ The essay accurately addresses both a valid similarity (1 point) and a valid difference (1 point).
+ The statements of comparison may not appear in the thesis.

Examples:

+ Example One: Lenin believed that the revolutionary class consisted of factory laborers. Mao thought that the change should come from the huge mass of the peasantry. In both systems, the communist leaders geared economic transformation to the lower classes.
  • The first statement in the example above addresses difference, while the second statement addresses similarity.

+ Example Two: The industrializations of China and the Soviet Union were structured by central planning from their governments. The industrialization of the Soviet Union occurred much earlier and involved much larger industrial projects than China's.
  • The first statement in the example above addresses similarity, while the second statement addresses difference.

+ Example Three: With the fall of the Soviet Union, Russia abandoned the communist model and adopted capitalism. The Chinese, however, followed a blended approach of capitalism and communism at the same time. In the latter half of the twentieth century, both countries restructured and modernized their economies.
  • The first two sentences in the example above address difference, while the third sentence addresses similarity.

Substantiates Thesis with Appropriate Historical Evidence (2 points)

- ✦ A piece of historical evidence is a fact that is correct and relevant to the time period.
- ✦ To earn the full two points in this category, an essay should have five or more pieces of evidence.
- ✦ To earn only one point in this category, an essay needs three or four pieces of evidence.
- ✦ Points for evidence can be earned even if the thesis point is not earned.

Examples:

- ✦ Example One: Mao's *Little Red Book* contained a number of slogans about the value of farmers to the economy of China. The communist victory in the Chinese Civil War meant that the economy focused much less on landlords and business owners. The communists formed large communes for agricultural production. The Soviet Union saw the working proletariat at the center of their economic system. Lenin created committees of workers that he called soviets to organize factory production.
- ✦ Example Two: Stalin started the first five-year plan to reorganize industrialization in the Soviet Union. New factories and infrastructure projects sprang up to produce equipment like tractors and trucks. A great deal of the production went to military uses. Mao's industrial policy was known as the Great Leap Forward. He wanted smaller-scale manufacturing in villages and rural towns.
- ✦ Example Three: The Soviet Union fell apart in the 1990s, ending the period of communist economic policies. Russia opened up its economy to the free market system of the West and found that it couldn't compete. The Chinese system was a blend of capitalism within a communist government. Chinese companies built enormous factories using cheap labor to produce export goods; this approach has helped the Chinese economy become one of the strongest economies in the world.

Makes a Direct, Relevant Comparison (1 point)

- ✦ A direct comparison is an explicit, concrete, and factually correct statement of either similarity or difference.

Examples:

- ✦ Example One: Mao and Lenin structured their economic plans around Marxist ideology.
- ✦ Example Two: The industrial policies of both communist China and the Soviet Union did not focus on the production of consumer items for the masses.
- ✦ Example Three: Both China and Russia opened up to global trade as part of their transition to free market reforms.

Analyzes at Least One Reason for a Similarity or Difference (1 point)

- ✦ Analysis explains a reason for the similarity or difference.

Examples:

- ✦ Example One: Since both China and Russia underwent communist revolutions in the twentieth century, both countries stressed the idea of equality in how they ran their economic systems.
- ✦ Example Two: The centrally planned economies of the Soviet Union and communist China led to corruption and inefficiency that eventually slowed economic growth.

✦ Example Three: Both Russia and China made the transition to a free market because of the economic problems that existed in both systems as a result of communist central planning.

Expanded Core

You must earn all seven points in the basic core before earning any points in the expanded core. Points awarded in the expanded core reflect the general excellence of the essay. Any one aspect of your essay, such as the thesis or evidence, might be particularly insightful and earn a point in the expanded core. Essays that have a high degree of analysis and historical context often earn expanded core points if they have all of the other basic core points. Clarity of organization, strong cause-effect analysis, and particularly insightful ideas can make your essay stand out as excellent.

Examples:

✦ Example One: An essay with sophisticated comparisons between the Soviet and Chinese forms of communism could earn points in the expanded core.
✦ Example Two: A sophisticated discussion comparing the details of Stalin's Five Year Plan to Mao's Great Leap Forward could earn points in the expanded core.
✦ Example Three: The analysis of several aspects of both economic systems in the past few decades could earn points in the expanded core.

Text Credits

DBQ Part One, Document 1 N.K. Sanders. Excerpts from *The Epic of Gilgamesh*, translated with an introduction by N. K. Sandars. (Penguin Classics 1960, Third Edition 1972).) Copyright © N. K. Sandars, 1960, 1964, 1972. Reproduced by permission of Penguin Books, Ltd.

DBQ Part One, Document 2 Pritchard, James B. (ed.); *Ancient Near Eastern Texts Relating to the Old Testament — Third Edition with Supplement.* © 1950, 1955, 1969, renewed 1978 by Princeton University Press. Reprinted by permission of Princeton University Press.

DBQ Part One, Document 3 Translated by Samuel Kramer in *The Sumerians, University of Chicago Press, 1963. Copyright ©* University of Chicago Press, 1963.

DBQ Part One, Document 4 L.W. King. Law and Justice in Ancient Mesopotamia. Excerpts from The Law Code of Hammurabi, translated by L.W. King, 1915.

DBQ Part One, Document 5 Miriam Lichtheim. "The Occupations of Old Egypt: Be a Scribe," from Ancient Egyptian literature : a book of readings / by Miriam Lichtheim. Copyright © 1975 by University of California Press. Used by permission.

DBQ Part One, Document 6 Adolf Erman, The Literature of the Ancient Egyptians, translated by Aylward M. Blackman (London: Methuen, 1927), 136–37.

DBQ Part One, Document 7 Henri Frankfort, *Ancient Egyptian Religion: An Interpretation,* translated by Aylward M. Blackman. Copyright © 2000 by Dover Publications. Reprinted by permission of Dover Publications.

DBQ Part Two, Document 1 William Stearns Davis, *Readings in Ancient History: Illustrative Extracts from the Sources, Vol 2: Greece and the East.* Allyn and Bacon, 1912.

DBQ Part Two, Document 2 Benjamin Jowett. In Praise of Athenian Democracy: Pericles, Funeral Oration. Excerpt from Thucydides, translated into English, to which is prefixed an essay on inscriptions and a note on the geography of Thucydides, by Benjamin Jowett. Second edition, Oxford, Clarendon Press, 1900. Book II, para. 37–41.

DBQ Part Two, Document 3 Han Fei. "Governing a Chinese Empire: The Writings of Master Han Fei, Third Century B.C.E." Adapted from *The Complete Works of Han Fei*, Vol. I, translated by W.I. Liano, copyright © 1939. Used by permission of Arthur Probsthain — Oriental & African Bookshop, London, UK.

DBQ Part Two, Document 4 King Asoka, "Rock Edicts," from *The Edicts of King Asoka: An English Rendering,* translated by Ven . S. Dhammika. Copyright © 1993 by Ven. S. Dhammika. Reprinted by permission of the Buddhist Publication Society.

DBQ Part Two, Document 5 Sima Qian, "Emperor Shihuangdi inscription on Mount Langya" from *Records of the Grand Historian: Qin Dynasty,* translated by Yang Hsien-Yi and Gladys Yang. Copyright © 1979 by the Foreign Language Press. Reprinted by permission of Columbia University Press.